Rehabilitating the Old City of Beijing

Urbanization in Asia

This series focuses on the massive social, economic, cultural, and political transformation taking place as southern Asian countries develop vast urban centres. The future of this highly populated region is an urban one, and the majority of its people will inhabit cities by 2020.

T.G. McGee, professor in the Department of Geography at the University of British Columbia, is the general editor.

T.G. McGee and Ira M. Robinson, editors, *The Mega-Urban Regions of Southeast Asia*

George C.S. Lin, *Red Capitalism in South China: Growth and Development of the Pearl River Delta*

Wu Liangyong, *Rehabilitating the Old City of Beijing: A Project in the Ju'er Hutong Neighbourhood*

Wu Liangyong

Rehabilitating the Old City of Beijing: A Project in the Ju'er Hutong Neighbourhood

UBCPress / Vancouver

© UBC Press 1999

All rights reserved. No part of this publication may be reproduced, stored in a retrieval system, or transmitted, in any form or by any means, without prior written permission of the publisher, or, in Canada, in the case of photocopying or other reprographic copying, a licence from CANCOPY (Canadian Copyright Licensing Agency), 900 - 6 Adelaide Street East, Toronto, ON M5C 1H6.

Printed in Canada on acid-free paper ∞

Originally published in Chinese by China Architecture and Building Press.

ISBN 0-7748-0726-1

Canadian Cataloguing in Publication Data

Liangyong, Wu.
  Rehabilitating the old city of Beijing

  (Urbanization in Asia, ISSN 1196-8583; 3)
  Includes bibliographical references and index.
  ISBN 0-7748-0726-1

  1. Urban renewal – China – Peking. 2. City planning – China – Peking. 3. Ju'er Hutong (Peking, China). I. Title. II. Series.

  HT178.C552P453   307.3'416'0951156   C99-910426-8

UBC Press gratefully acknowledges the ongoing support to its publishing program from the Canada Council for the Arts, the British Columbia Arts Council, and the Department of Canadian Heritage of the Government of Canada.

UBC Press
University of British Columbia
6344 Memorial Road
Vancouver, BC V6T 1Z2
(604) 822-5959
Fax: 1-800-668-0821
E-mail: info@ubcpress.ubc.ca
www.ubcpress.ubc.ca

Contents

Foreword
Peter G. Rowe / vii

Preface
Aprodicio A. Laquian / xi

Acknowledgments / xiv

Introduction / xvii

1 The City of Beijing in Historical Perspective / 3

2 Planning and Development in Beijing since 1949 / 16

3 Residential Development and the Renewal of Derelict Houses / 44

4 Organic Renewal in Historic Cities / 56

5 Traditional Courtyard Houses and a New Prototype / 66

6 Planning and Design of the Ju'er Hutong Project / 104

7 Post-Occupancy Evaluation and Lessons from the Planning and Design Experience / 163

8 The Continuing Debate over Redevelopment / 182

9 Future Prospects / 188

10 Conclusion / 196

Appendices / 213

Notes / 223

Glossary of Chinese Terms / 230

Bibliography / 232

Index / 237

Foreword

Contemporary attempts, the world over, to modernize and rehabilitate inner cities immediately confront several important issues. First, the adequate provision of dwellings for urban inhabitants is no longer simply a matter of housing but, rather, of the much more complicated task of community development and, ultimately, of building coherent, useful, and pleasant pieces of a city in which to live, work, and play. This shift of focus, in turn, immediately raises the question as to whether a community can, in fact, be constructed through building, to which the answer is probably that it cannot. Communities, at root, are social constructs that, for sure, can be either enhanced or impeded to a certain extent by what is built but that are not, in any final analysis, directly tied to building itself. Nevertheless, the adequacy of space standards in housing and in related outdoor areas remains a very important consideration – all the more so in times and locations of scarce resources. Moreover, displacement of residential populations, either through a conversion of the existing land use or through processes like gentrification, also remains an important social issue, precisely because it involves the uprooting of both individuals and communities. Furthermore, often the central cause of such community displacement is bound up with the economics of building and of property development, pushing many inner-city urban areas to construct at higher and higher densities.

A second issue of importance is the manner in which older parts of well-established cities are to be regarded as being either more or less useful in their present state. This topic is usually the subject of considerable debate and, globally, of different attitudes at different times. Throughout much of the post-Second World War era, for instance, urban renewal and the wholesale replacement of old dilapidated city precincts with entirely new and different types of structures was quite acceptable. Today, by contrast, in most parts of the world, it is clear that traditional urban patterns of settlement are to be valued not only for their strict historical significance, but also for their aura. Such an attitude, in turn, immediately elicits a confrontation between advocates of modernization and advocates of tradition. In the urban-architectural realm of cities, concerns about appropriate expression must inevitably acknowledge this tension between "old" and "new" and, in many cases, strike an appropriate balance. Unfortunately, this can result in historic preservation and conservation practices that, if not thoughtfully considered and applied, can result in either gentrification and social displacement or the sustained underdevelopment of an area due to there being no possibility for any new building.

Finally, there is the issue of what types of urban strategy to employ within a broad rehabilitation project. Master plans have often helped rationalize and guide the allocation of necessary resources, although too strong a belief in the perfectibility of a city, especially from on high, has also failed miserably to provide humane and liveable environments. A trust in economic forces and in indirect incentives and disincentives has also been well placed, although, again, the belief that markets always serve everybody well clearly has its limits. Recently, the idea of "projects and not plans" emerged in urban planning, with considerable success in Europe and elsewhere, embodying the idea that many different well made and locally determined building projects, with some coordination, was a better alternative than grand schemes and master plans. Now, all three strategies can be seen at work in urban revitalization and rehabilitation, but when to select one rather than another is nowhere near as obvious as it might once have been.

Today, government officials, practising professionals, and interested academics in many parts of China (and certainly in Beijing) confront many, if not all, of these issues. Urban housing is woefully inadequate and in short supply. In order to relieve chronic overcrowding – the national urban average is no more than six square metres per person – inner-city areas are being redeveloped with far better space standards, and yet often at much higher densities, in order to accommodate the rising price of urban property. One result is usually displacement of inner-city residential populations to the periphery of cities, where housing estates can be constructed for them more easily and economically. Another result is that the historic residential lane and "lane culture" of bigger cities, like Beijing and its *hutong*, or Shanghai and its *lilong*, are rapidly disappearing to make way for large modern commercial complexes. Everywhere in urban China – or so it seems – the expressive tension and the search for an urban-architectural identity between traditional and modern, internationally available, ways of making and shaping buildings is plainly manifest, unfortunately often falling into kitsch.

Indeed, at a broad cultural level this bivalence has persisted in China from well before the beginning of this century, first in the conceptual linguistic distinctions of *ti* (essence) and *yong* (function) and then later in Mao Zedong's distinctions between *jinghua* (quintessence) and *zaopo* (sediment), first espoused in his cultural canon of 1940, *On New Democracy*. Strategic thinking and questions about the actual efficacy of master plans have also emerged in contemporary urban China, as many municipalities struggle to rid themselves of wasteful state-owned enterprises and to more firmly establish functioning property markets. Moreover, the need, within this planning milieu, to develop exemplary models and to experiment with specific projects has been well recognized. Nevertheless, the idea that these urban conditions, these debates, and these different urban development strategies always existed (even in relatively contemporary China), or that modernization is somehow an inevitable progressive force, denies the fact that China is modernizing very rapidly and that human agency is involved in this process. Specific people have made and continue to make decisions about China's and Beijing's urban realm, and consequently arguments over what to do and how to do it are shared by these participants, who bring with them their own various backgrounds and beliefs.

From the outset in post-war modern China, Professor Wu Liangyong has been one of the central figures in these discussions and debates, and he has grown in both stature and influence as he has had the opportunity to become more involved in China's urban development and revitalization. A graduate in architecture from the National Central University in Nanjing, during the early 1940s Wu studied under Yang Tingbao, one of the architectural and academic luminaries of the time and, indeed, in modern Chinese architecture. Wu then quickly went to work with another luminary – Liang Sicheng – more or less as he founded Tsinghua University's present School of Architecture in Beijing. Liang was strongly committed to the preservation, perpetuation, and extension of traditional architectural and urban principles, having been a co-founder of the Institute for Research in Chinese Architecture in the 1930s and having done so much for the cause of Chinese architecture, often under extremely arduous conditions. No sooner had he taken up his post in Beijing, when Wu, at Liang's urging, enrolled in the urban design program at the Cranbrook Academy of Art under Eliel Saarinen, returning to China and Beijing in 1951. After the privations of the Cultural Revolution he then went on to succeed Liang – who tragically died during the revolution – as head of the school at Tsinghua. More than that, however, Wu Liangyong clearly took on the mantle of his former mentors – Yang and Liang – as, arguably, the senior statesman and worrier in that great tradition within which Chinese intellectuals seem constantly to feel anxious about the fate of their nation. Furthermore, Wu has remained true to Yang, Liang, and Saarinen in believing that tradition does matter but that society must also move ahead and acknowledge its contemporary circumstances.

The Ju'er Hutong – one of the primary foci of this book – is one of Wu Liangyong's most recent building projects. He, like other academics in China, enjoys the opportunity to put things into practice under the state-sponsored architectural institute system in which universities like Tsinghua actively participate. The project, which began in earnest in 1979, is significant in so far as it addresses all of the issues raised earlier and stands as one of the few models in present-day Beijing truly worthy of emulation. Regarding the matter of community, it is certainly community-based, involving input and participation by potential users, but it does not tightly define one particular kind of community. In the face of pressures to gentrify, Ju'er Hutong has remained, for the most part, in the hands of its indigenous population, even if they often live elsewhere and use the units as needed sources of income. The density of the project, from the perspective of some government officials, is, no doubt, probably too low for the underlying property values. Nevertheless, it is well within acceptable margins, including levels set by the successful six-storey walk-up apartments that have recently been infused into most Chinese inner-city areas.

As a matter of strategic planning interest, the Ju'er Hutong is certainly not about master plans, although, as Wu Liangyong describes in this volume, the project does derive fairly directly from well founded planning principles for Beijing, dating well back into the modern era. It is certainly an example, in this regard, of how one might redevelop the extraordinary lane – *hutong* – structure of the Chinese capital. And, with regard to architectural language, the Ju'er Hutong project is neither traditional nor entirely modern but, rather, an attempt to merge both. Although clearly based upon a traditional courtyard design, it is not simply an adaptation of this type of residential environment; rather, it is a scheme in which the underlying spatial principles of the courtyard house are maintained, to the extent possible these days, resulting in a prototype that demonstrates the efficacy of low-rise, relatively high-density housing and mixed-use environments for both preserving and, more important, resuscitating Beijing's inner-city life during this modern era. Consequently, the book itself, while focusing on the rehabilitation of Beijing and a specific project, is more general. It is about a coherent and well thought out approach towards inner-city redevelopment, and the experience gained and the lessons learned from this city and this project have a much wider appeal. In addition, the book is of inestimable historical value (and unconsciously so, at that). It is the measured work, unfortunately very rare, of one of China's major modern architects, urban designers, and academics.

Peter G. Rowe
Raymond Garbe Professor of Architecture and Urban Design
Dean, Faculty of Design, Harvard University

Preface

> Here, where Heaven and Earth are in perfect accord,
> where the four seasons come together,
> where the winds and the rains gather,
> where the forces of yin and yang are harmonized,
> one builds a royal capital.
>
> —Zhou Li

Scholars of Chinese urban history may debate whether the quotation cited above can be attributed to the Duke of Chou, whom Confucius so admired, or whether it is a much later addition to the *Zhou Li* text annotated by Han dynasty scholars. However, there is no doubt that it perfectly fits the planning of the city of Beijing. It is an acknowledgment of the continuity of the importance of cities in China's development that, to this day, we continue to be absorbed by the problems posed by a city like Beijing. This book, by Professor Wu Liangyong, brings to contemporary city planning the issue of what to do with a great capital city in this age of globalization.

There is no doubt that Beijing is one of the greatest capital cities in the world. This book by Professor Wu, *Rehabilitating the Old City of Beijing*, puts before us the dilemma of how to plan and govern such a city in modern-day terms. As mentioned by Professor Wu, there are several options one may take in attempting to bring Beijing up to date. One could meticulously preserve its historical artifacts and transform it into a "museum city," in much the same way that its historic centre, the Forbidden City, has been preserved as the *Gugong* (the Palace Museum). Or one could heed the injunction to transform Beijing from a "consumptive" into a "productive" city, raze all the remnants of its feudalistic past, and turn it into a modern city of skyscrapers, shopping malls, fast food courts, and entertainment centres. Or one can just leave it as it is. This book, however, maps out a middle way between these extreme forms of action and inaction.

The Beijing of the Yuan, Ming, and Qing dynasties is still seen in the physical survival of its palace complexes, courtyard houses, and street patterns. Since 1949, however, the inner city has been home to many urban poor families who are crowded into what Professor Wu calls "courtyard houses without courtyards." Surveys have shown the sorry state of basic urban services in the city core (water shortage, inadequate sanitation, poor solid waste collection and disposal). Reports on "old and dilapidated housing" in Beijing point to the problems created by intense overcrowding and the social and even physical dangers arising from living in such ancient quarters.

There is a view, however, that this high-density living is what gives the centre of Beijing its present-day vitality. Unlike many Western cities that have socially deteriorating cores, Beijing maintains the community cohesion and vitality that makes it such a liveable habitat. The strong sense of community among the *hutong* (narrow lane) dwellers, the lively and colourful street markets, the efficient work of street and neighbourhood committees, and the obvious pride shown by residents in the greenery and beautification of their cramped homes and communities indicate the essence of what civilized city life is all about.

At the same time, one hears the argument of economists that the land values in Beijing's core are not being fully exploited by current land uses. Beijing's historic cityscape is famously low-density; virtually all buildings built prior to this century are only one-storey high. Now, there are pressures from developers and urban planners to achieve higher floor space ratios in order to take advantage of land values. Urban designers clamour for a modern central business district (CBD) with awe-inspiring architecture and memorable edifices and complexes.

As China pursues a market-oriented policy, albeit one with Chinese characteristics, the pressures to redevelop Beijing so as to turn it into a global city worthy of being the capital of the most populous country in the world will continue. Already, considerable controversies rage over the setting up of fast food outlets and high-rise hotels in the historic city centre. There is also much debate about the proliferation of housing projects, high technology zones, and manufacturing and industrial sites on the urban periphery, as the traffic problem is said to be exacerbated by these sprawling developments. There are very real concerns about Beijing's traffic, the worsening air pollution, what to do with the mounting piles of solid waste, and the critical shortage of water. Planners relevantly ask: does Beijing really need a steel mill within its boundaries? Is it really necessary to pave over rich agricultural land on the urban periphery to construct more high-rise dwellings and build more roads?

The planners and urban authorities of Beijing have much to be concerned about. The master plan of the capital city provides a vision and development goals, but it does not, and cannot, anticipate all the details that a rapidly changing world imposes on the capital city. International trends in city planning offer very few lessons for Beijing, as the sorry state of megacities all over the world contrasts most sharply with Beijing's architectural, aesthetic, and cultural vitality.

The Ju'er Hutong experiment that Professor Wu depicts in this book is one approach to city planning that attempts to grapple with the many contradictions faced by inner-city redevelopment in Beijing. The project tries to capture the social, economic, and cultural aspects of high-density urban life that makes the city centre of Beijing such a liveable human community. One can even say that the Ju'er Hutong experiment tries to come up with an urban design that will make possible the intense human interactions of the Chinese courtyard on several high-rise floors. To the extent that the design of the physical structures can anticipate and influence patterns of human interactions, the Ju'er Hutong project attempts to provide the spatial setting for the pursuit of desirable life ways.

The beauty of the Ju'er Hutong project is that it provides an observable urban laboratory within which the longitudinal effects and impact of the experiment can be studied. It thus fit most logically into the Asian Urban Research Network (AURN) project that the Canadian International Development Agency (CIDA) supported from 1990 to 1998, under the leadership of the Centre for Human Settlements, University of British Columbia. As a sub-component of this project, which included research teams in Beijing, Shanghai, Guangzhou, Bandung, and Ho Chi Minh City, the Ju'er Hutong experiment contributed immensely to the comparative study of how rapidly expanding mega-cities cope with problems of deteriorating urban cores.

This book has much to teach city planners and urban authorities dealing with inner-city problems. Although the Beijing situation may appear unique (how many cities can claim to have been the continuously occupied capital of a country for so many years?), the principles that influence the planning of Beijing (and the design of the Ju'er Hutong experiment) remain universally relevant. The planning community, therefore, owes a great deal to Professor Wu for writing this book and for documenting the philosophical, social, cultural, and aesthetic considerations that went into the redevelopment plans for the inner city of Beijing and the design of the Ju'er Hutong experiment.

Aprodicio A. Laquian
Centre for Human Settlements
University of British Columbia

Acknowledgments

What was achieved in Ju'er Hutong was due to a collective effort. The project had to overcome so many obstacles that many times I tried, unsuccessfully, to offer the job to others. Architecture is, after all, a practical discipline, and our project team eventually persevered through both the design and construction stages. During the first phase, observing ideas being turned into physical reality within a space of some 2,000 square metres was very exciting. The project also brought unexpected joy when it won awards in China, Asia, and the United Nations.

Acknowledgment is due not only to the present team, but also to those who worked on related projects in the past. In particular, I would like to thank the following: Wang Diemin, Huang Hanmin, and Hu Zhengfan for the Shichahai Planning and Design Project in 1979; Zhang Shouyi, Li Deyao, and Yang Xiaohui for the Fahuasi Derelict Housing Survey in 1983; Liu Yan for the study of Integrated Conservation in the Old City of Beijing in 1986; Lu Qiu for the International Symposium on Housing Studies in West Germany in 1987; Liu Xiaoshi, advisor to the Ju'er Hutong Rehabilitation Project; Liu Yan and He Hongyu for the Survey of Number 41 Ju'er Hutong in 1987; Yin Zhi and Liu Wenjie for the Preliminary Rehabilitation Proposal for Ju'er Hutong in 1988; Lu Liansheng, Liu Wenjie, and Guo Gengrui for Phase 1 of the Ju'er Hutong Rehabilitation in 1989; Chen Gang and Yang Jinsong for the Survey of the 8.2-hectare street block around Ju'er Hutong in 1990; Xu Yingguang and Liu Wenjie for the First Survey of the 84-hectare rehabilitation area in 1991; Lu Liansheng, Liu Wenjie, Guo Gengrui, and Lian Zheng for Phase 2 of the Ju'er Hutong Rehabilitation in 1991; Yang Jinsong, Hu Shaoxue, and Xu Yingguang for the Plan for Phase 3 of the Ju'er Hutong Rehabilitation in 1992; Gao Xiaolu and Chen Sui for the Plan for Phase 4 of the Ju'er Hutong Rehabilitation in 1993-4; and Fang Ke and Zhang Hong for the Design of No. 1 Ju'er Hutong in 1997.

Credit should also be given to those who have been involved in assembling the original Chinese version of this book, especially Liu Wenjie for compiling the first draft and for his post-occupancy assessment report of Phase 1; Zhang Jie for writing about the Old City of Beijing; Liu Yan for her survey report for Number 41 Ju'er Hutong; Zuo Chuan and Deng Qing for their survey of the relocated households in Phase 1; Yang Jinsong, Gao Xiaolu, and Liu Wenjie for their studies of the new courtyard type house; Gao Xiaolu for planning studies for Phase 4; Lou Qingxi and Yao Lixin for providing the photos and diagrams; Yao Tongzhen for compiling and editing the manuscript; and Lin Zhiqun, Zeng Shaofen, Liu Xiaoshi, Mao Qizhi, and Zhang Jie for their valuable comments on the draft.

Architecture requires input from the authorities, clients, and the community. The Ju'er Hutong project received guidance and support from the Beijing Municipal Government, Tsinghua University, the Capital Planning Commission, the Capital Construction Commission, the Housing Reform Office of the City Planning Bureau, the East City District Government, the East City District Housing Development Corporation, and the residents of the Ju'er Hutong neighbourhood. Individuals and groups of planners and architects from other countries also rendered their encouragement and support, among whom Mr. Peter Elderfield and Ms. Diane Dicon, the directors of the British Building and Social Housing Foundation, are notable for their organization of the International Study Visit of Housing in Beijing in 1994 and their kind recommendation of the Ju'er Hutong project for the 1992 United Nations World Habitat Award.

The early stages of the project were carried out with little financial help; the design fees in the later stages barely covered the cost of making design models. The motivated team members from the Institute of Architectural and Urban Studies kept working in spite of the difficulties. As the second phase was about to be completed, the project received funding from a Canadian International Development Agency (CIDA) program and the Asian Urban Research Network (AURN), which has also underwritten the publication of this English edition of *Rehabilitating the Old City of Beijing* by UBC Press. This is acknowledged with gratitude.

Last, but not least, I must also acknowledge others who are concerned with the publication of the English version of this book, among them especially Dr. Aprodicio Laquian, Professor at the UBC Centre for Human Settlements (CHS) and the Director of AURN, for promoting the book's publication and for writing a preface to it; Professor Peter Rowe, the Dean of the Graduate School of Design at Harvard University, for his generous and ebullient foreword to this book; Professor Brahm Wiesman, former Director of CHS, for his consistent encouragement of the Ju'er Hutong project and his careful revision of the first draft of the English version of this book; Dr. Daniel

Abramson, Dr. Zhang Jie, Dr. Jin Ying, and Liu Jian for translating the original Chinese version into English; and Fang Ke for helping to write the last chapter of this book.

Wu Liangyong

Permission notes
The Publisher is grateful for permission to reprint material currently held in copyright. An honest attempt has been made to secure permission for all material used, and if there are any errors or omissions, these are wholly unintentional and the Publisher will be grateful to learn of them.

Introduction

Origin of the Ju'er Hutong Project

Since I began teaching at Tsinghua University in 1946, I have witnessed myriad changes in and around the City of Beijing. As a planner and an architect, I have been involved in studies, plans, and projects in this city: but each time, the work was focused on a particular issue and lacked a general overview. Although I was often aware of the need to consider the entirety of Beijing's development, my workload prevented me from sorting out the underlying principles of this larger problem.

An opportunity arose when I began to write about the Ju'er Hutong pilot project. As I was documenting the planning and implementation of the project, I found myself dealing with a great variety of issues that have long been subjects of debate concerning the regeneration of the Old City of Beijing. In the early 1950s, when, in addition to my teaching duties, I was involved in the city planning of Beijing as one of the advisors to the Municipal Government of Beijing, there was a broad debate about how to preserve Beijing as a great historic and cultural city (*lishi wenhua mingcheng*). The debate particularly focused on the practical problems of reconciling preservation with urban development. This involved such questions as whether to conserve historic buildings that might block transportation. With regard to the development of the traditional neighbourhoods and courtyard houses in the Old City, views diverged considerably, although not as much as they do today.

It was at this time that I first considered researching the preservation of the traditional neighbourhoods and courtyard houses of Beijing. In 1951, based on a case study survey of the courtyard houses in Huashi ("the Flower Market") outside Chongwenmen, I made a report to the Committee of Urban Planning of Beijing concerning this issue. However, no systematic study was undertaken until 1978, after the end of the Cultural Revolution. Although at that time the preservation of historic and cultural monuments such as palaces and temples began to receive considerable attention, the preservation of traditional neighbourhoods and courtyard houses did not.

Moreover, the serious long-standing shortage of housing aggravated the conflict between the demand for new housing construction and the preservation of traditional neighbourhoods. The residential quarters are poorly maintained, overcrowded, and lack amenities. The courtyard houses, which once had been the sanctuary of family life, had been deformed into unsightly shelters shared by several households. Some even crumbled, while others were replaced by apartment blocks.

Under these circumstances, I, together with some of my colleagues at Tsinghua University, initiated a systematic study of the preservation of Beijing's traditional neighbourhoods and courtyard houses. We began with a review of the Master Plan of Beijing and a planning proposal for the Shichahai Area, in which the concept of "organic renewal" and new courtyard house design prototypes were first proposed; from then on, a long and continuous series of studies has been carried out under my direction.

In 1987, Beijing launched a practical experiment in rehabilitating the derelict houses in the Old City. As our earlier studies had well prepared us for this task, we were given charge of the planning and design of a project in the Ju'er Hutong neighbourhood, which was approved as the first phase of one of four initial experimental projects scattered throughout the Old City. Our work began in the courtyard at Number 41 Ju'er Hutong, where the dwellings were in especially bad condition. The first phase was finished in 1991, with a construction area of only 2,760 square metres. Later, as the second phase of this project was successfully completed, the experiment received favourable comments from all over the country and even caught considerable attention from abroad. It was honoured with six domestic awards in the field of architecture, including the Architectural Creation Award (representing the highest level of architectural design in China) and some international awards, including the ARCASIA 1992 Gold Medal Award for Architectural Excellence and the 1992 World Habitat Award. This is the only time in the past decades of Beijing's urban development that one single project has received so many honours and awards. With all these honours as great encouragement, we continued into the third and fourth phases of the project.

This short history provides some background for understanding how this manuscript began in 1993. This book is neither about the history of Beijing's planning, a topic with which I have dealt in "A Brief History of Ancient Chinese City Planning"(*Urbs et Regio* 38, 1986), nor is it a monograph about the preservation of Beijing's Old City, an issue that I have discussed in a series of treatises since the end of the 1970s (see, for example, Wu, 1992); rather, it provides a specific discussion of the preservation of the traditional neighbourhoods in the Old City of Beijing, with particular emphasis on the theory and methodology of architectural design. As far as I know, no one has done this before.

The Significance of the Ju'er Hutong Experience

Fundamental Principles for the Rehabilitation of Old Cities

Since 1950, whenever we talk about the development of old cities, we have been apt to use the Chinese term *"jiucheng gaizao,"* which implies complete rebuilding. However, this seems inappropriate to a great historic and cultural city like Beijing, which is both a piece of cultural heritage and a city living in the present. From this point of view, the Old City of Beijing is an organism that has some features that are not suited to the demands of contemporary life and that need to be carefully adapted; its rehabilitation should be a process involving metabolic change rather than total clearance and rebuilding. This is what I mean by the theory of organic renewal, which is the fundamental principle behind the Ju'er Hutong experimental project. To some extent, it is a concept hitherto unknown in Beijing's urban development. Although similar principles of urban development had been put forward in past decades, none of them has been taken seriously. The Ju'er Hutong experiment provided an opportunity to put this theory into practice, and its success has attested to the theory's feasibility.

Preservation and Development of Courtyard Houses

As early as the 1950s, a negative attitude towards the architectural form of the courtyard house became popular among both administrators and professionals in China. Courtyard houses, they argued, were the product of feudalism, and they were obsolete because they could not adequately house multiple families. However, my own long-term research and practice brings me to a completely different conclusion.

In the specific case of the Old City of Beijing, on the one hand, it is impossible to preserve all the courtyard houses without touching anything, and, on the other hand, it is unwise to keep them merely as an ossified form of architecture. It is my intention to avoid this path. As is evident from the long history of Chinese cities, the prototype of the courtyard house has been transformed into a specific system that characterizes the urban fabric of most historic cities of China. It is so undeniably rational that it should not be casually negated. In fact, the negative attitude mentioned above was not based upon conscientious studies. Rather than leading to the use of creative proposals for the preservation of traditional courtyard houses, this attitude led, year after year, to their replacement with the most mundane caricatures of high-rise towers and slab apartment buildings. There was no substantial progress in solving either the housing problem or the question of how to preserve the Old City. By comparison, through looking at courtyard houses as bundles of cultural heritage that are still functional, I have tried to find a practical methodology that will enable the preservation of the historical and cultural value of the Old City as well as promote sustainable development and provide a solution to the housing shortage. So far, we have achieved in the first phase of the Ju'er Hutong project the integration of social, economic, environmental, and cultural benefits.

The principle of organic renewal is drawn from long-term speculation and thorough study. Though formulated in the light of the specific conditions of Beijing's Old City, it is applicable to most of China's historic and cultural cities, all of which are concerned with the preservation of both urban fabric and traditional neighbourhoods. However, the Ju'er Hutong project is not the only answer to this problem, nor is the courtyard house prototype the only alternative architectural form. It is necessary to continue improving the principle of organic renewal in accordance with the specific conditions of different cases in order to arrive at valid approaches and valid architectural forms. Creative solutions to the practical problems of urban development can only be achieved through reflective design.

In this sense, the Ju'er Hutong pilot project is a theoretical and methodological exercise that, when fully reviewed, may not only serve as a platform for academic debate and as a basis for planning further ventures but, perhaps more significantly, may also illustrate how an academic concept can be put into practice through research and development. This project has demonstrated such potential and promise.

Current Status of the Ju'er Hutong Project and Rehabilitation of Beijing's Old City

Since this manuscript was first published in Chinese in 1993, the planning for the rehabilitation of the Ju'er Hutong neighbourhood has continued and has expanded to include not only Phases 3 and 4 but also a plan for the entire block of *hutong* in which Ju'er Hutong is located – the Nan Luogu Xiang area. The realization of the first two phases of the Ju'er Hutong project as well as progress in planning the preservation of Nan Luogu Xiang have both demonstrated the appropriateness of organic renewal as an approach to rehabilitating the Old City of Beijing. That the developer in charge of the construction has acknowledged the project's considerable profitability is further proof of the feasibility of this approach. However, despite all the achievements, there have been significant delays in the implementation of the latter two phases of the project, and this requires some explanation. The main reasons for this circumstance are as follows:

- Frequent changes of personnel in the administrative departments concerned and in the development corporation have made day-to-day operations increasingly difficult and have inevitably deferred the realization of the latter phases.
- From 1993 to 1996, Beijing, due to special political conditions, suffered from an over-heated boom in real estate development. Market prices for

real estate rose dramatically and remain unreasonable even now. The situation was most severe within the Old City proper, where, immune to local government control, large-scale commercial real estate development brought enormous profits. In comparison, small-scale residential projects like Ju'er Hutong were at a disadvantage.
- Despite receiving so many domestic and international awards, not to mention uniformly positive comments, the Ju'er Hutong project seems not to be successful enough to persuade many government officials and professional figures to give up their deep-rooted preferences for bulldozing, completely rebuilding, putting in rows of high-rise apartments, and so on – all of which are actions that have proved wrong-headed in the history of urban development.

At present, the Beijing Municipal Government's policy is to allocate the lots designated for rehabilitation within the city proper to different development corporations in the hope of renewing the Old City by means of large-scale real estate development. In fact, the rehabilitation of a historic city must not be driven entirely by profit, and such an approach is ultimately fruitless. I insist that, instead of being rehabilitated through large-scale clearance and rebuilding, the Old City should be rehabilitated through small-scale improvements that are carried out with great care.

Although Phases 3 and 4 of the Ju'er Hutong project have been postponed, I, together with my research team, am still researching potential theories and methodologies. These include experiments in small-scale improvement planning for the Guozijian (Imperial College) and the Baita Si (White Pagoda Temple) neighbourhoods.

At this moment, Beijing is at a crossroads in its development and is confronted with an enormous challenge: to review the experiences and lessons of past urban development and to tread a path for the future. A rational theory needs to be tested, modified, and substantiated through practice; this is certainly true for the theory of organic renewal, which was born of the Ju'er Hutong experiment. Recently, it has been applied in the renewal of the historic centres of Suzhou, Xi'an, and Jinan, and it has been further improved in the process.

Reasons for Publishing This Book Now
Today, the process of urban renewal is proceeding at an accelerating pace in the Old City of Beijing. More and more large-scale office buildings and department stores are springing up under the stimulation of profit, while more and more traditional courtyard houses are being destroyed. I am usually full of bitter pain when I see the consequences of rebuilding in utter disregard of the values of history and culture. Fortunately, this situation is slowly changing. The public is beginning to follow with interest the rehabilitation

of the Old City, which is increasingly the subject of many newly published works.

Under these circumstances, I have begun to consider this manuscript's international significance and the need to publish it in English. The following points are my chief thoughts:

- Based upon an analysis of the values of Beijing's Old City, we have recognized the significance of its traditional neighbourhoods and courtyard houses and the importance of their preservation. Thus, though a considerable number of courtyard houses have been destroyed, we unflinchingly continue to support their preservation. We scrupulously adhere to the creed that it is "never too late" for preservation.
- Practice in China demonstrates that the principle of organic renewal is appropriate not only to the Old City of Beijing, but also to other historic and cultural cities, such as Suzhou, Xi'an, and Shaoxing, which are as important to the world's urban heritage as is Beijing. Moreover, this practice promises to become an integral part of international experience in small-scale rehabilitation. It is necessary, in the light of this principle, to further carry on the study of urban fabric and the courtyard house prototype.
- It is understandable that architects are concerned with forms and styles of architecture. But it cannot be emphasized strongly enough that any form and style of architecture is a creation that has come about in accordance to the city's or region's specific historical, geographical, and cultural conditions as well as to its specific ways of building. This was so in the past and it will be so in the future – in all countries of the world.

In light of the above analysis, I believe that, from the point of view of urban renewal, the theoretical value of the Ju'er Hutong project goes beyond the Old City of Beijing and is relevant to an international discussion on theoretical and practical approaches to the rehabilitation of old neighbourhoods. It is only natural that so many foreign scholars are interested in this project and have paid so much attention to it. However, it is only a starting point. This book does not aim to introduce the entirety of the project itself but, rather, a specific approach to architectural design: holistic design thinking. Moreover, it brings to international readers our experiences in the Ju'er Hutong project. It is hoped that these experiences will be helpful to them in their search for new approaches to urban renewal.

Organization

This book consists roughly of two parts: Chapters 1 through 5 provide an overview of urban development and planning in the Old City of Beijing, and Chapters 6 through 10 are concerned with housing rehabilitation in the Old City, with particular reference to the Ju'er Hutong experiment.

The development of the City of Beijing is reviewed in Chapter 1 through a discussion of its historical significance and urban morphology. Chapter 2 analyzes, in retrospect, planning and construction in Beijing since 1949. It centres upon the contradiction between preservation and development, and surveys the theoretical propositions and practices regarding this contradiction. Chapter 3 further analyzes housing development by recounting the origin and background of the derelict and hazardous housing in the Old City, and it then reviews remedies for the situation. It also introduces the concept of "rehabilitation through organic renewal" as well as "the new courtyard complex." Chapter 4 develops the concept of rehabilitation through organic renewal by outlining how the intrinsic structures and principles of a city need to be respected in the process of renewal. An organic renewal leads to an organic order in the physical forms of the city. Chapter 5 investigates the origin and evolution of the gridiron cities in China and the development and perfection of the courtyard-based neighbourhood structure, which gives rise to the Old City's unique urban fabric. It also discusses the desirability and feasibility of a design approach that aims to recover and to redevelop Beijing's inherent urban fabric.

The development of planning and design ideas are reviewed in Chapter 6, particularly those concerning the urban fabric and housing types that led to the Ju'er Hutong experiment. The planning and design process and proposals for future phases are also examined. Chapter 7 summarizes the lessons from the experiment and proposes further development of the new courtyard house system. A comprehensive evaluation of the experiment is provided, based on the findings of three surveys on living conditions before renewal, the new neighbourhood, and the families relocated to nearby areas. These surveys reveal that after the renewal living conditions improved. Chapter 8 moves on to more general issues related to housing renewal in the historic city areas, such as the complex issues surrounding renewal of derelict housing. These issues are still undergoing vigorous debate and require further methodological development. An overview of the experiment is provided in Chapter 9, along with an attempt to sketch the future tasks that were already on the horizon when the initial manuscript of this book was completed in Chinese in 1994. Finally, Chapter 10, the conclusion of this English edition, brings the project and its related issues up to date.

Wu Liangyong
Tsinghua University, Beijing

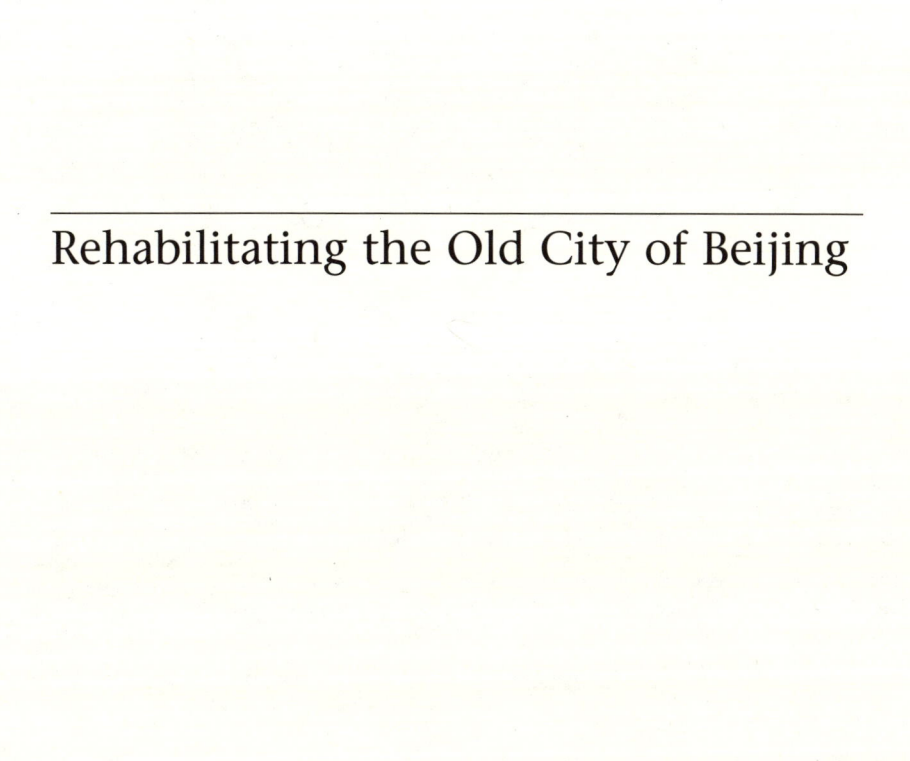

Rehabilitating the Old City of Beijing

1
The City of Beijing in Historical Perspective

This book begins with the historical planning of the Old City of Beijing, particularly as it evolved within the ancient tradition of Chinese capital city planning. Instead of describing this tradition from the beginning to the end – a story that is told in a great many other works[1] – this chapter will highlight Beijing's particular importance within it. I will propose that Beijing's traditional importance as an urban form continues to hold value for the city today.

From the view of history, Beijing has survived as the ideal Chinese capital city through successive dynasties; from the view of design, it is a unique masterpiece of worldwide importance with regard to urban planning, urban design, landscape design, and architectural design. As this historic cultural city plays a unique role in the history of urban construction throughout the world, it should be preserved, and any kind of new urban development should build on the traditional principles of urban design that, to some extent, have decided the past failure or success of Beijing's urban development.

The Ultimate Imperial Capital in China

The Old City of Beijing is considered to be one of the treasures of urban history. It is the last in a long line of imperial capitals in China (see Figure 1.1 and Appendix 1). Unlike most of its predecessors, which perished at the end of the dynasties in which they were created, Beijing evolved through the last three dynasties of the Yuan, Ming, and Qing. It has become the ultimate example of ancient Chinese city planning.

Surrounded by mountains on three sides, Beijing was built on a strategic site at the northern end of the North China Plain. This is an area where ancient roads converged from the Central China Plain to the south, the Mongolian Plateau to the northwest, and the Song-Liao Plain to the northeast. The first known human settlement in the region, that of Peking Man, dates back some 230,000 to 700,000 years. Remains of the earliest walled cities of the early dynasties of Shang (sixteenth to eleventh century BC) and Zhou (eleventh century to 771 BC) were unearthed near Liulihe in the southwestern suburbs of present-day Beijing. While there is more to be explored by archaeologists, there is sufficient evidence that the site was an important military town as well as a commercial centre for trade and cultural exchange between peoples from the northern plateau and southern plains.

The city became Nanjing, or South Capital, of the Qidan (Khitan) people's Liao dynasty in AD 938. The Nüzhen (Jurchen) people's Jin dynasty chose the site to be their Zhongdu, or Middle Capital, in AD 1153. Expanded on the foundations of Liao Nanjing, Zhongdu was modelled on Kaifeng, the capital of Northern Song, the dynasty that was defeated by the Jin army. Jin craftsmen were sent to Kaifeng to conduct an intensive survey of the city and its buildings. Some of the garden rockery in Kaifeng was even brought back to Zhongdu, where it can still be seen today in certain parts of the Imperial Gardens known collectively as Sanhai, or the "Three Seas."

It was not until the Yuan dynasty (AD 1271-1368), however, that Beijing became the capital of a unified empire. A new city, Dadu, or Grand Capital, was constructed to the northeast of Zhongdu. Ingeniously adapting to the topography of the site, the planners of Dadu laid out a rectangular walled city measuring 6.6 kilometres by 7.4 kilometres. It was here that the ideal Wangcheng (Royal City) prototype, as described in the ancient treatise *Kaogongji*, was first applied in an elaborate fashion to the planning and construction of an imperial capital in China.

The plans of major capital cities in Chinese history are outlined in Figure 1.1. By assembling the different town plans into chronological order, some observations may be made about the evolution of urban morphology. It is instructive to follow this series of transformations in terms of the physical forms of the capital cities, from those of the Warring States Period (475-221 BC) to Chang'an of the Han dynasty, Yecheng of Cao Cao's Wei, Chang'an of the Tang dynasty, Luoyang of the Northern Wei, and Kaifeng of the Northern Song right up to the various incarnations of Beijing in the Yuan, Ming (AD 1368-1644), and Qing (AD 1644-1911) dynasties. The planning ideas for Beijing may be traced back not only through its development in the last three dynasties, but also through the development of contemporaneous cities (such as Nanjing of the Ming dynasty) and of cities that existed in earlier periods. The City of Beijing may thus be regarded as the ultimate crystallization of the planning and design of Chinese imperial capitals.[2] It has been suggested that Beijing was the largest city in the world in the period between AD 1450 and 1899 in terms of population size (except during the period between AD 1650 and 1700, when Constantinople overtook it by a small margin).[3]

Today, no other Chinese city has as many registered cultural relics and historic buildings as does Beijing; it is a history book written in brick, wood,

The City of Beijing in Historical Perspective 5

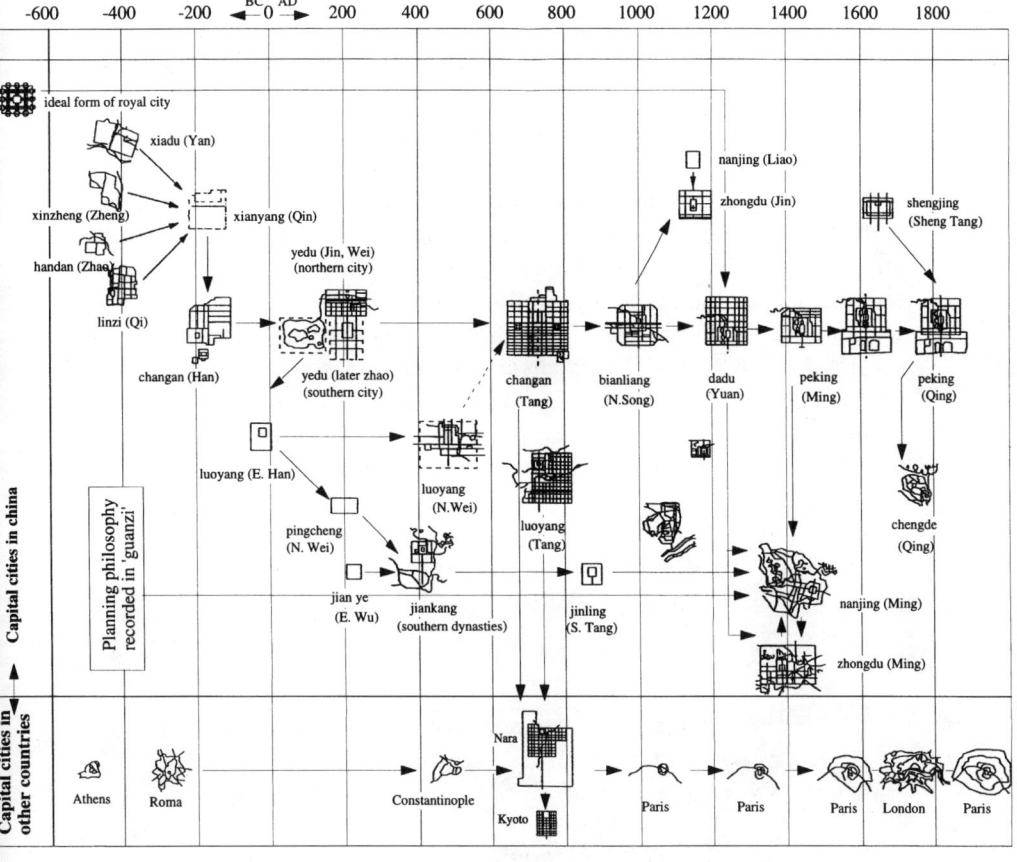

Figure 1.1 Evolution of Chinese capital cities (all city plans are drawn to the same scale)
Source: Wu 1986, 89-90.

stone, and other building materials. It inherited the best achievements of Chinese city planning from the premodern period. The ancient cities of Chang'an, Luoyang, Kaifeng, and others no longer exist, but through this great "book" of Beijing, we can form a mental picture of the scope and forms of city planning in the past. For example, apart from its overall layout, which reflects the ideal Royal City described in *Kaogongji*, the Qianbulang (the Thousand-Step Corridor in front of the Gate of Tiananmen, destroyed in the 1950s to make way for present-day Tiananmen Square) resembled the design of the central square in Cao Cao's Yecheng and Song Kaifeng. From the Gate of Wumen, we can obtain an image of the ancient watchtowers. From the palatial complexes of the Forbidden City, we can discover the evolution of the architectural complexes of imperial palaces and halls from the Tang and Song dynasties onwards. The prosperous business section outside Zhengyangmen reminds us of the Yongqiaoshi market in Luoyang during the Northern Wei or the streets and markets in Kaifeng during the Northern Song periods. The gardens in the western suburbs of Beijing are reflective of the gardens and retreats in Xianyang during the Qin dynasty, and those of Chang'an during the Han dynasty. The artificial hill Jingshan (originally named *Wansuishan*) was raised behind the Forbidden City by the Ming in an explicit attempt to recreate the relation between the natural hill Zijinshan and the Ming Palace in Nanjing, which was the first Ming capital. Indeed, the full Chinese name of the Forbidden City, *Zijincheng*, was taken from the name of the hill in Nanjing. Both Jingshan and the artificial hill in Beijing's Beihai Park are also reminiscent of earlier imperial gardens, including the Hualinyuan and Xiyouyuan in Luoyang during the Northern Wei, the Xineiyuan in Tang Chang'an, and the Genyue in Kaifeng during the Northern Wei. Clearly, many of the historic sites of Beijing exemplify achievements of city planning under different dynasties in China (Figures 1.2 to 1.4).

An Unparalleled Masterpiece of City Planning

Professor Liang Sicheng's remark that "Beijing is an unparalleled masterpiece

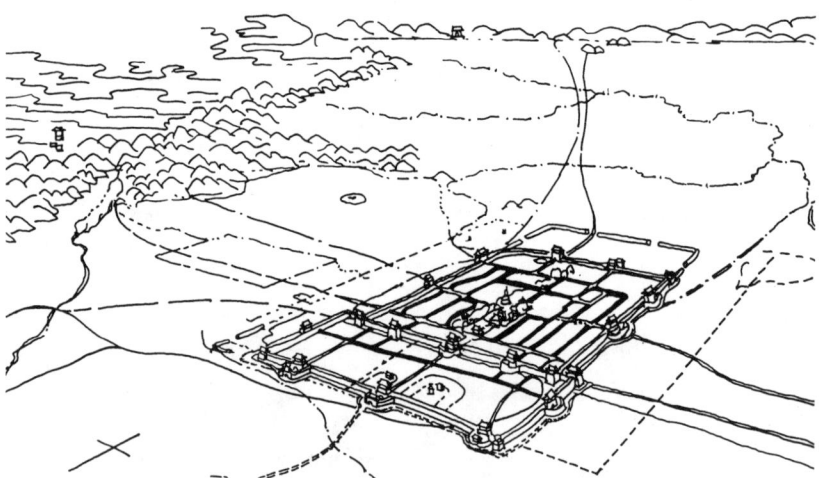

Figure 1.2 **The physical form and urban structure of Beijing.** "Beijing is a planned entity ... Therefore we must first of all realize the value of the wonderful structure which gives the city its intrinsic character. The system of architecture in Beijing as a whole could be the most intact, the most extraordinary, and most precious piece of art that still retains its vitality in the tradition [of planning classical Chinese capital cities]. This would be the point of departure in any attempt to understand the city."
Source: Liang 1986, 55.

of city planning" is no exaggeration.[4] This, in fact, summarizes the admiration by historians, architects, and planners from around the world who, approaching this unique piece of planning and design in their own ways, employed it to establish their views of the culture and art it exhibited. From the designer's point of view, it was an extraordinary monument and the ultimate achievement of a civilization.[5] The city was described as "possibly the greatest single work of man on the face of the earth."[6] It was compared to ancient bronze art for its astonishing order and wonderful composition.[7]

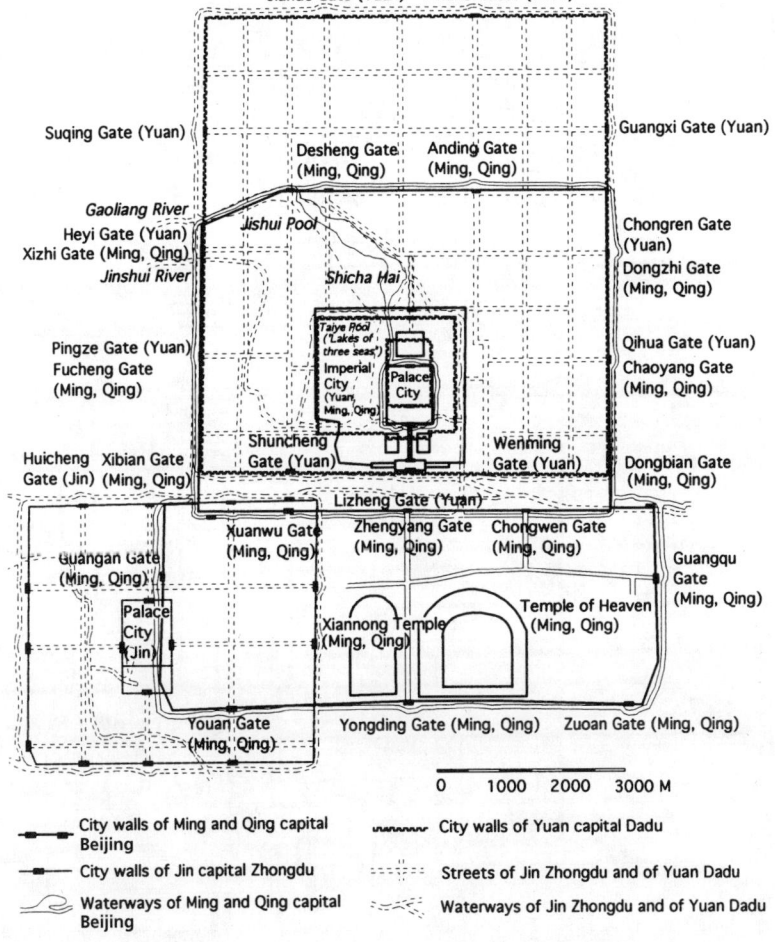

Figure 1.3 Evolution of Beijing's site since the twelfth century: Zhongdu in the Jin dynasty, Dadu in the Yuan dynasty, and Beijing in the Ming and Qing dynasties
Source: Wu 1986, 67.

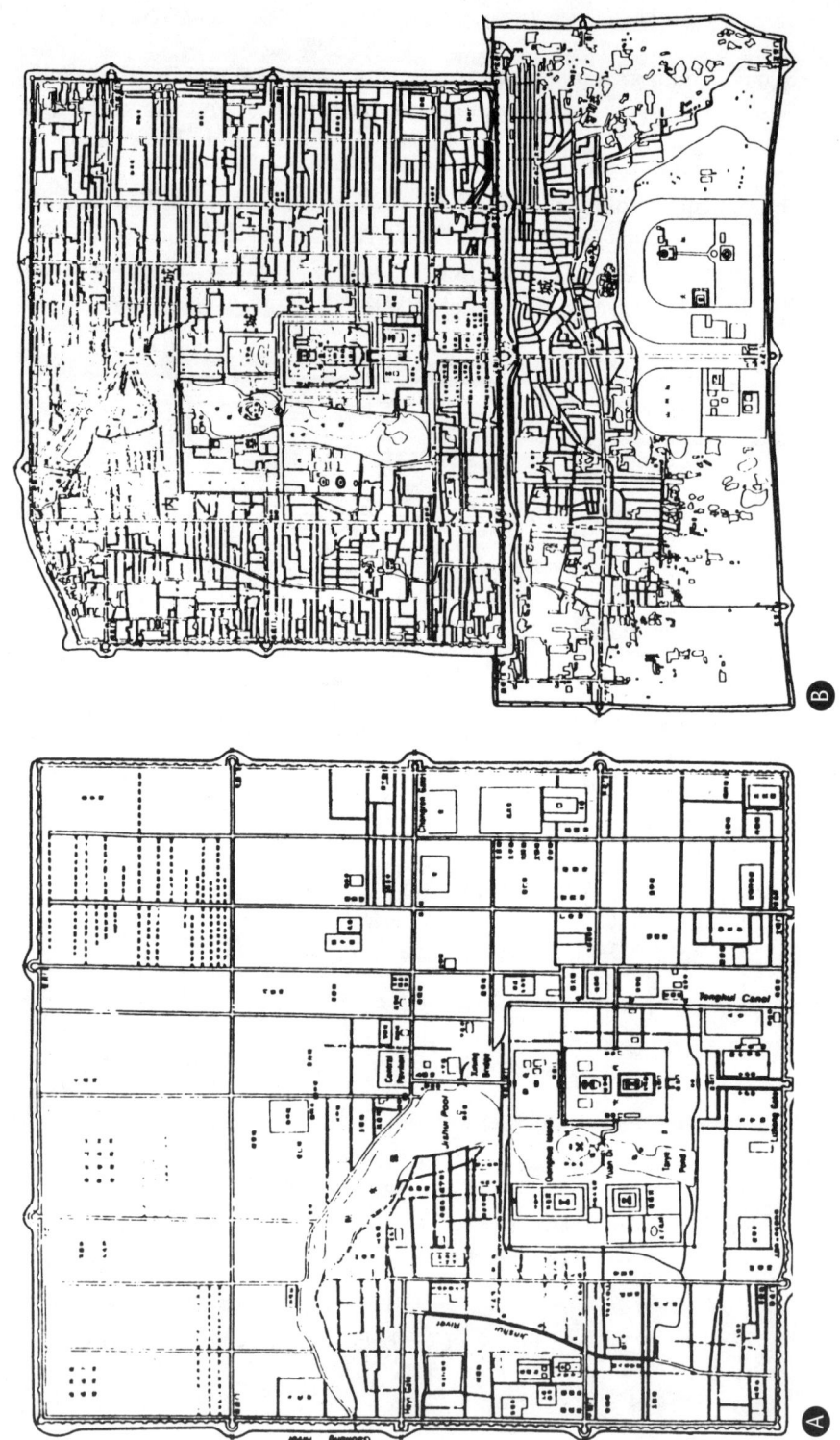

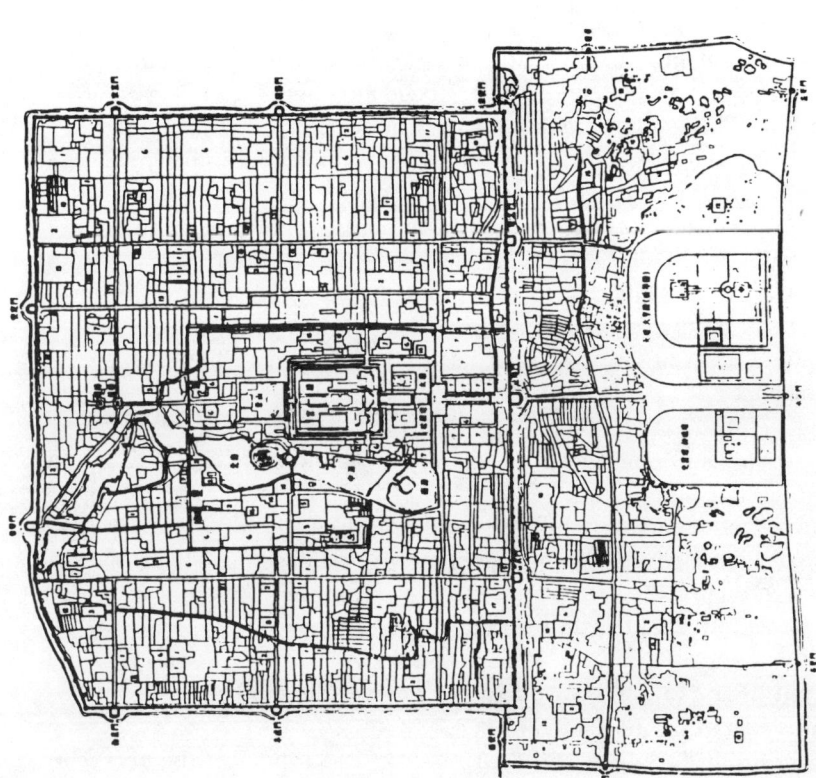

Figure 1.4 **The plans of Yuan Dadu and of Ming and Qing Beijing.** Ⓐ Dadu, capital of the Yuan dynasty. Ⓑ Beijing, capital of the Ming dynasty. Ⓒ Beijing, capital of the Qing dynasty. Since the early tenth century, Beijing gradually evolved into the political centre of the nation. First, the Liao dynasty established its sub-capital, Nanjing, there in AD 938. The Jin dynasty had its capital, Zhongdu, established on the same site in 1153. Ever since then, the Yuan, Ming, and Qing dynasties have all had their capitals set up here. Although the exact location of the city changed from dynasty to dynasty, a physical continuity still exists.

Source: Hou 1988, 27-8, 31-2, 41-2.

The clear and symmetrical city plan of Beijing is one of the great spectacles of the world.[8] It was regarded as a three-dimensional design in which the soaring palaces, pagodas, and gateways were laid down amidst low-lying houses to achieve special effects.[9] The wards in the city were enveloped by the main thoroughfares so that the neighbourhoods became enclaves free of traffic. At the same time, infinite variations of form and colour were created within a simple gridiron framework.[10] The gateways, together with the surrounding landscape and streets, composed unique picturesque scenes.[11] All in all, "the city is deeply enmeshed in ritualistic formulae and religious concepts which do not concern us now," but which provide "a rich storehouse of ideas for the city of today."[12] Beijing, as the most precious piece of Chinese architectural and planning heritage, should continue to provide us with inspirations in planning and design.

Almost half a century ago, Liang Sicheng argued that:

> Beijing is a planned entity ... Therefore we must first of all realize the value of the wonderful structure which gives the city its intrinsic character. Beijing's architecture as an entire system is the most intact anywhere in the world, and as a most extraordinary and precious work of art, it still retains its vitality and maintains its tradition. This should be the point of departure for any attempt to understand the city. The majority of monuments in fact are not free-standing buildings; rather they are often architectural complexes, each of which consists of quite a few buildings interrelated in a particular manner. This feature in itself is the city's most valuable contribution to art and architecture. The Forbidden City is one of the most notable examples of this kind. Preservation therefore should not be confined to a single hall, or a single temple, or a single pagoda; great care needs to be given to the surrounding buildings which are part of the entire complex, and to the overall setting of the complex. We can no longer afford or tolerate monuments or groups of monuments being destroyed either directly or indirectly, trapped in awful surroundings, or divided up in a way which was never intended.[13]

Indeed, the entire built form of Beijing was not only characterized by the magnificence and powerful expression of its architecture, but also by its sequence of endlessly changing spaces, all of which are organized by or related to the city's 7.9-kilometre-long north-south central axis (Figure 1.5). It was through the presentation, transition, and interrelation of space that the visual forms achieved their purpose and effect.

Layout of the Imperial City and the Palace City, and the Development of the Central Axis

Within the first months of occupying Yuan Dadu in 1368, the new Ming

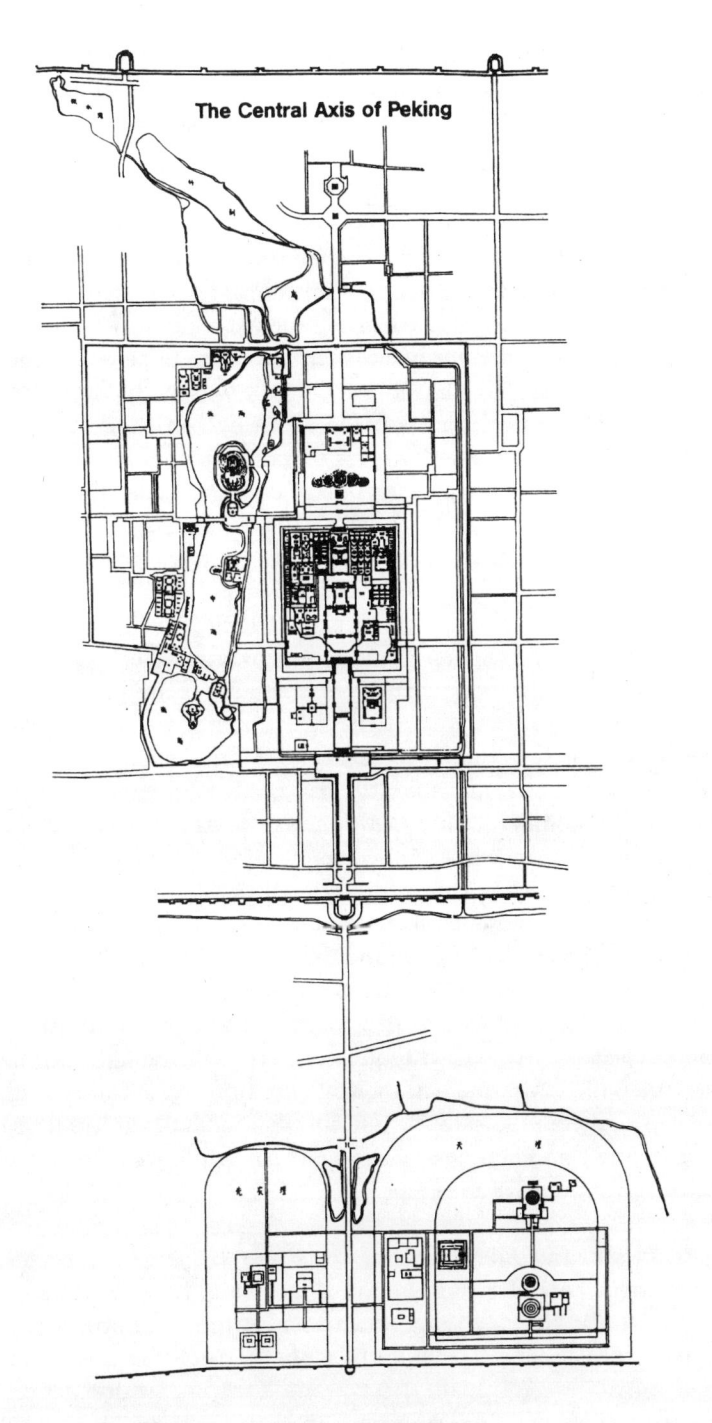

Figure 1.5 **The central axis of Beijing**
Source: Wu 1986, 71.

administration moved the city's northern wall south 2.9 kilometres. In 1419, the southern wall was moved south about one kilometre, creating the Inner City of 6,650 metres by 5,350 metres that remains today. Then, in 1553, a new wall was built to enclose the city's southern suburbs, creating the Outer City of 7,950 metres by 3,100 metres. The total area within the Inner and Outer city walls is sixty-two square kilometres. The Imperial City, which is square in shape (2,500 metres by 2,700 metres), is in the centre of the Inner City. It has four gates on each side, with the Gate of Tiananmen (Gate of Heavenly Peace) on the south side being the main entrance. Inside the Imperial City is the Forbidden City (or Palace City); the Imperial Gardens; and the residences of the princes, noblemen, and artisans serving them. The Palace City (960 metres from north to south by 760 metres from east to west) functioned as both the centre for government administration and the formal imperial residence. Construction of both the Imperial City and Forbidden City took fourteen years (1407-21) to complete.

Through all these changes in the shape of the city since the Yuan dynasty, the original central axis of Dadu was conserved and used to relate each new element in the city's plan. In the course of building the Outer City, the Drum Tower, and the Bell Tower, the central axis was extended to 7.9 kilometres and became the most magnificent urban axis of the premodern world. It endowed Beijing with a unique character and a sense of order. Both the distributions of architectural complexes and the alignment of a sequence of space make this central axis the city's backbone. Starting at Yongdingmen (the Gate of Tranquility) in the south, the axis passes through nine gates to reach the main audience hall, Taihedian (the Hall of Supreme Peace) in the Palace and finishes at the Drum Tower and Bell Tower. The main buildings on this central axis present silhouettes of various heights and forms. The courtyards and squares in front of the halls, gateways, and other important edifices vary in length and breadth to provide a sense of rhythm and climax. Between the Daqingmen (the Palace Gate) and Kunninggong (the Empress's Palace), there are eight squares and courtyards on the central axis. In particular, the sixth square in the sequence from Taihedian measures 2.5 hectares. The sheer physical scale is impressive enough, but it is the sophistication of the commanding architectural space that overwhelms the visitor to the great house of the emperor.

Streets, Lanes, and Alleyways
Beijing's street system during the Ming and Qing dynasties inherited the traditions of the Yuan dynasty, which divided the city into many blocks with main streets that ran from north to south, parallel to the central axis. Each of the north-south main streets was like a spine, with lanes on both sides that ran mostly from east to west. The trunk and branches are distinct and well ordered; the layout of buildings was clear and definite. Along most

of the broad and busy main streets there were buildings for commerce and handicrafts, while residential buildings were laid out in rows along the narrow and quiet lanes. The planning of such residential blocks was in accordance with the design of *siheyuan* house itself, a basic courtyard house of quadrangular shape.

Another salient point in the layout is the artistic treatment of architectural complexes: improvements to the scenery are common in the design. Decorative structures, such as archways over the streets (*pailou*), entrance gates (*menlou*), entrance arches (*juanmen*), side gates of government offices (*yuanmen*), and screen walls (*yingbi*) were erected to break up the long, monotonous stretches of the street. At the same time, main buildings were located at certain points on the streets or set at appropriate angles in order to create splendid vistas.

Unity and Variety in Form and Colour

As the capital of a feudal society, Beijing based its morphology on a patriarchal caste-like social system and expressed a strong sense of hierarchy, which extended from the grandest to the humblest buildings. Despite its feudal origins, however, even today we can appreciate Beijing's resulting aesthetic. One of its manifestations is unity and variety in the composition of architectural groupings. Analyzing the architectural complex of the whole City of Beijing, one finds that palaces, temples, and houses are all composed of buildings of rather simple forms and limited height. The rhythmic spatial composition of different complexes of similar buildings created a regularity in silhouette, owing to the use of only a few basic types of roofs and timber-based structural systems.[14] Masonry-bearing wall construction was limited largely to city walls, watchtowers, and pagodas. Multi storey wood construction was limited to two-storey shophouses in a few dense commercial areas and to two-storey pavilions within palace compounds.

Under such limitations, the planning of the City of Beijing still brought into full play the spatial techniques of classical architecture. The tall palaces, towers on the city walls, pagodas, and the human-made Jingshan Hill were all located at sites that accentuated their prominence, and each controlled a visual space within a certain area. Loftiness was achieved by building up the ground beneath the buildings' foundations, by enlarging the structural members and the size of the structural bays, and by increasing the number of *dougong* (brackets) supporting the roof. The limited height of housing for ordinary residents provides a striking contrast to these edifices, giving the latter an even more dominant position on the skyline.

The unity and variety of colour also strengthens the artistic effect of the architectural complex. The palaces, temples, and other ceremonial buildings have bright primary colours: red walls, white pedestals, crimson columns, and green eaves. Contrasting with them are the plain, simple grey-coloured houses of common people, who were not allowed to decorate as they pleased. But, like green leaves behind bright flowers, they made the architectural arrangement of the whole city more colourful and splendid. Under the typically clear and sunny skies of pre-industrial Beijing, the buildings became brighter and more beautiful in the sunshine. The roofscape of the city was also special: it was composed of soaring roofs of yellow, green, and blue and a vast number of small, grey housetops, which were all unified in their graceful curvature, like so many waves upon the sea. In short, the ordering of the architectural complexes not only exhibited the achievement of architecture in China, it also contributed to the world's compendium of inspiring examples of urban design.

Natural Landscape in a Formal Plan
The integration of the natural landscape into the geometrical layout was another important achievement in the planning of the city. Lakes, islands, and wooded areas, with their highly irregular shapes, were skilfully introduced into a plan primarily composed of squares and rectangles. The result was a fine contrast and complementarity that enhanced the solemnity of the general layout and added natural beauty to the architectural complexes. The planting of trees in Beijing also followed a unique pattern: trees were grown throughout the city, but planting was most dense surrounding the main architectural complexes. Within the complexes, the squares in front of the central halls and the main courtyards of the palaces were paved with stone or brick but were bare of plants, which highlighted the prominence of the buildings. The large-scale planting of trees also beautified the city and created a great deal of recreational space, although the fine landscaping and gardens were only designed for the enjoyment of a few noblemen in certain districts.

Garden-making in Beijing can be traced back to the early period of the Liao and Jin dynasties. Many of the gardens built during this period were expanded in the Ming dynasty, such as those in the imperial summer resorts and the hunting grounds in Fragrance Hill and Jade Spring Hill, which sprawled into the north of Haidian district in the northwestern suburbs. Moreover, the Ming rulers opened a new garden, Nanyuan, in the southern suburbs. In the Qing dynasty, beginning from the reign of the Emperor Kangxi, keen attention was paid to the building of imperial gardens of unprecedented number and scale in the northwestern suburbs and more distant locales. Among the so-called "three hills and five gardens" in the Beijing region, *Bishu Shanzhuang* (Mountain Resort to Flee the Summer Heat) in Chengde and *Jingji Shanzhuang* (Mountain Resort of Tranquil Living) in Panshan are the best. However, there was so much focus placed on these gardens that the construction of Beijing proper was neglected. The Qing emperors and their retinues spent as much as eight months of every year in these rural retreats, which rivalled Beijing as important centres of political affairs. Today, nearly a century after the collapse of the last dynasty, Beijing's neglect at the hands of the Qing still forms the background of the debate over the Old City's conservation and development.

Summary
The planning and design ideas manifested in the City of Beijing during the Ming and Qing dynasties reveal the culture and aspirations of the time. Today, although the old values and lifestyles have become less relevant, the physical space still imposes upon us a sense of timeless order, dignity, and magnificence and is open to new understandings and interpretations. We should treasure and preserve the great heritage and design philosophy embodied in the architecture and gardens. In Professor Liang's words, "the crucial issue is that the different types of buildings and complexes match each other perfectly; they have achieved a perfect relationship with the plan of Beijing as a whole. It was with the overall command [of physical space] that the City of Beijing represented at its best the characteristic style of design, and the wisdom and vision of city planning in the Chinese culture."[15]

Sad to say, the importance of this historic city does not seem to have received the recognition it deserves in international urban history, despite the great efforts made by pioneers such as Liang Sicheng and Hou Renzhi. Although preservation of the city's monuments has made great strides during the past two decades, the conservation of Beijing as a whole has not been given sufficient consideration. It is against this background that issues of conservation and development are examined in this book.

2
Planning and Development in Beijing since 1949

As there are many monographs concerning the urban planning and development of Beijing since the foundation of the People's Republic of China, this chapter will mainly deal with the key issues of the city's historic preservation: that is, the preservation of the Old City of Beijing and its cultural heritage and natural scenery. The urban development of Beijing entered a new era in 1949, and, ever since, the contradiction between preservation and development has become more and more serious. The argument about the alternatives of "centring new development in the Old City of Beijing" and "setting up a new administrative centre in the west suburbs of Beijing" was the crucial point of urban development at that time. Although the latter choice might have been more practical, the former was adopted by the policy makers of the time. This resulted in a great deal of new construction in the Old City and, ultimately, compromised the traditional features of the city's structure and landscape.

Unfortunately, the gravity of this consequence has not been adequately appreciated. At present, the struggle between preservation and development still rages on, with the focus shifting from the location of the administrative centre to the location of the central business district. Based on long-term research on this issue, I offer a series of principled suggestions for Beijing's urban development. Fundamentally, these are, at the macro-level, integrated regional development, multi-centred development, and comprehensive conservation of the Old City, and, at the micro-level, urban design and architectural design that respect Beijing's historic context.

First Plans for the New Capital

Debate on the Choice of Site

When the People's Republic of China was founded in October 1949, one major task for the new government was to establish a capital appropriate to a nation that had an ancient and continuous civilization and that was also experiencing a rebirth, a nation that had long been the world's most populous and yet was only now being run by the people.[1] The decision to locate the capital in Beijing presented great opportunities and challenges for political leaders, planners, and architects. Immediately, the plan for the capital became embroiled in controversy. Some people proposed that government offices should be centred in the Old City, while others preferred a brand new centre west of that site. This controversy touched on the fundamental issue of a master plan for Beijing.

The location debate was broadly represented by two proposals: (1) the old centre plan of Zhu Zhaoxue and Zhao Dongri and (2) the west suburb plan of Liang Sicheng and Chen Zhanxiang. Those in favour of expanding in the Old City argued that because it was the historic capital, and because the founding ceremony of the People's Republic was held in Tiananmen Square in the centre of the Old City, it seemed natural that it should be the seat of the new government. However, there was no detailed design accompanying this proposal (except a diagram showing the placement of office buildings along Chang'an Boulevard to the east and west of Tiananmen Square). There was little mention of the significance of the Old City or the historic architecture it contained. The idea underpinning this proposal was that making way for a new world required destroying the old.

The west suburb proposal, on the contrary, put forward a series of overall planning strategies and designs based on planning theories. Its authors thought that "building offices in a piecemeal fashion is no solution." In their words:

> modern administrative structures will require an area larger than the Old City, and it would be impossible to find sites of appropriate location and sufficient size within the city walls. [If the Old City were to be expanded] it would cause problems for the whole city. [To house the increasing population] more than 130,000 houses would need to be demolished. This would be a massive amount. Introducing modern high-rise buildings to the central heritage area would alter the street patterns and damage townscape, which would be contradictory to our principles concerning the protection of cultural relics. Infilling new buildings along the main thoroughfares would immediately increase the volume and complexity of traffic flows, [and] serious problems would then occur due to the long distance ... between government institutions. [To establish a new city, on the other hand, would] observe the principles of location, establish a reasonable relationship with the residential quarters, [and] achieve a balanced development for the whole city. [New government buildings] would not have to be sandwiched in an inappropriate setting, [and] it would become easier to protect the heritage buildings.[2]

However, Liang only presented a few sketches and diagrams; the hurried discussion did not allow time for a grand urban design that would capture the imagination (Figures 2.1 and 2.2). Moreover, the scheme was handicapped by the west suburban area's distasteful public image. First, during their occupation of Beijing during the Second World War, the Japanese had already planned to develop a new city there. Although only a very small area was actually built, this memory was enough to discredit Liang's scheme to a certain degree. Then, during the civil war in the late 1940s, this area was the seat of the General Command for the Suppression of Communists before it was taken over by the People's Liberation Army. It would have been difficult to find any political appeal in an out-of-the-way place like the west suburbs at that time; in contrast, the magnificent Old City appeared far more attractive. The Gate of Tiananmen had by then been confirmed as the symbol of the Neodemocratic Revolution, and its image was placed at the centre of the national emblem. The political significance could not have been more clear.

Compared to planning for the design of the national colours and emblem, planning for the capital was a far more complex issue; and sufficient time should have been allotted for research and discussion. Unfortunately, a hasty decision was reached in favour of expansion within the old centre. Such hastiness was later manifested most dramatically when the walls and gates of the Old City were demolished; today, citizens at all levels of society regret this loss.

The ideology of the time, the experience of Moscow, and the ideas of many Soviet planning specialists all had a bearing on the choice of the site of New China's capital. Once the Old City expansion plan was chosen, there was little chance for any alternative. Consequently, the implications of the proposal were not studied in any detail. Discussion of the choice was suffocated not only by politics, but also by a lack of modern planning theories. There was also a pragmatic reason for there being so little discussion: with few resources available, the opportunity for large-scale work seemed very remote. Once the government offices were settled in existing buildings, a kind of inertia set in and there was little incentive to move. Year by year, the Old City centre was redeveloped to adapt to the needs of growth, and radial and ring roads were built. The more growth there was, the more expansion was needed. It is not unreasonable to say that most of Beijing's conservation and traffic management problems stem from the choice of this site.

To a certain extent, the argument that the Liang-Chen plan had no economic basis in the early 1950s was true. At that time, China was in a devastated state after years of war. In its first three years, the People's Republic had to make the best use of existing building stock while reconstructing the economy. The situation was worsened by the Korean War; any major construction at that time was simply out of the question. That the Liang and

Chen proposal did not come in a publicly understandable visual form was also a death blow. Even some additional sketches might have helped.

The Liang-Chen plan also lacked the grandeur expected at the time. The idea that the new republic should aspire to project an impressive image was repeatedly stated by politicians at all levels.[3] At that point, only Tiananmen possessed the desired grandeur. There was no alternative vision, even though the Liang-Chen plan implied the laying of a new north-south axis through the new centre in the west suburbs. If this axis had been made longer and more explicit, starting from Fuhai Lake in the old Summer Palace in the north and ending at the railway station in Fengtai in the south, it might have given the new city a grander look than the Old City. At the same time, as the east-west Chang'an Boulevard was extended west to the industrial areas in Shijingshan, the two new axes would have naturally declared the "green heart" in the Yuyuantan-Gongzhufen area the perfect place for a new administrative centre. In hindsight, more time should have been devoted to the discussion of the proposed site (Figure 2.3).[4]

The short-sightedness of the decision to rebuild Beijing's old centre, however, should not obscure the many great achievements of Beijing's planning and construction over the last forty years. Given the stultifying effect of so many periodic political and economic upheavals, construction in Beijing has proceeded at an amazing pace. The new building stock is now many times larger than the original. The tragedy is that so much of the new construction took place where there had once been valuable historic buildings and open space. The increasing number and severity of problems that stem from the planning decision made in the 1950s demonstrates the validity of the Liang-Chen plan, which wanted to separate the new areas from the old in order to meet different functional needs. Even in the very early 1950s, it was not difficult to predict the great pressure that would be placed on the Old City should a new centre not be set up outside. The Old City simply could not cope with massive new development, and the destruction of many of its historic sites was inevitable. Despite his position as the deputy director of the City Planning Committee of Beijing, Professor Liang, a conservation-minded planner and architect, still felt powerless to save many historic buildings from demolition. Occasional victories, such as the case of the Tuancheng in Beihai, were few and far between.[5]

The plan for Beijing in the early years of the People's Republic was strongly influenced by the Soviet approach to planning. Soviet policies for city and building reuse, conservation, and renewal can be summarized as follows.[6] First, as described above, the Old City centre was adopted as the capital. This was believed to be more economical than building a new centre in the west suburb. Second, the Old City was to be rebuilt as quickly as possible. It was concluded that over 80 percent of the city was comprised of single-storey buildings, most of which were very old. As hundreds or even thousands of

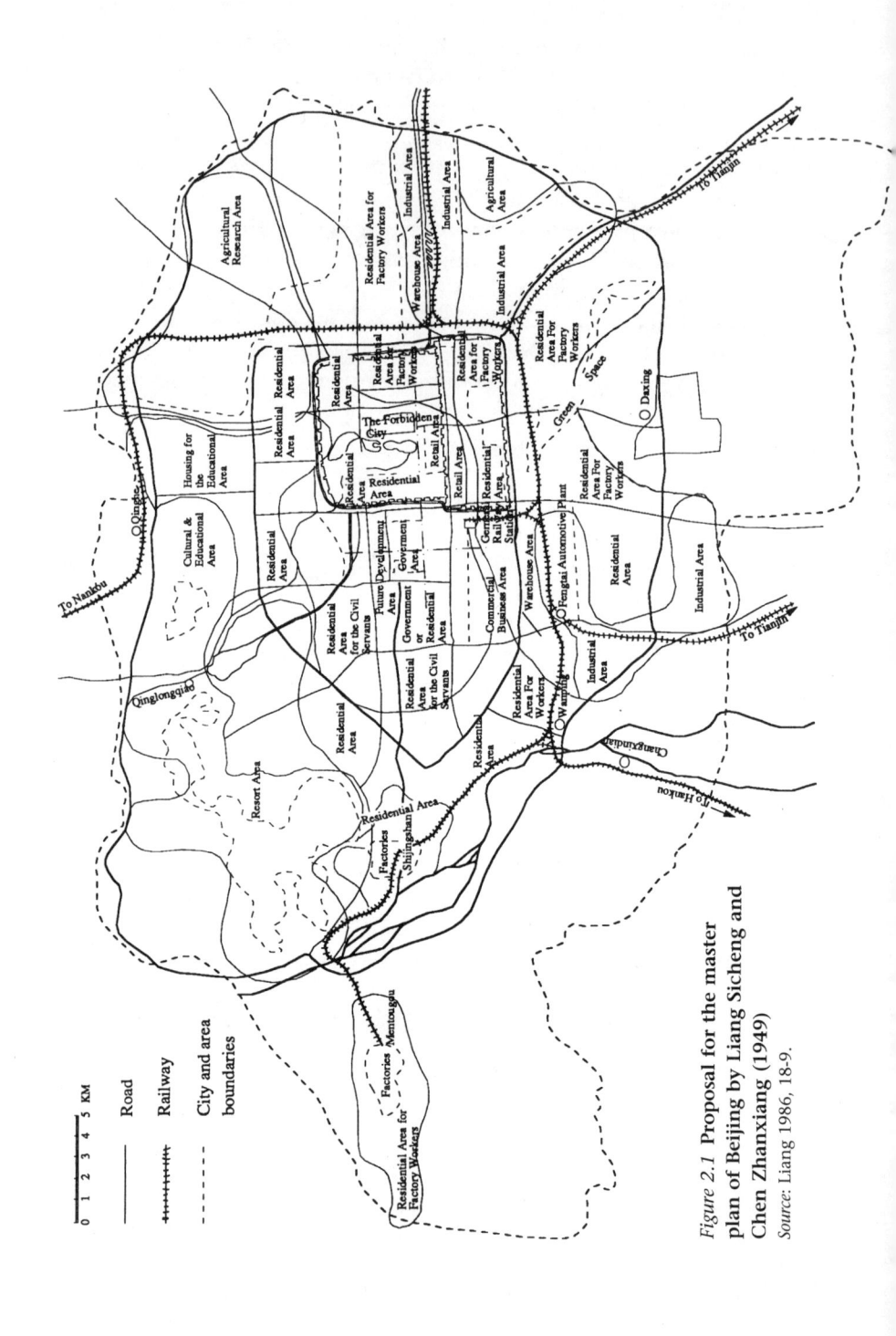

Figure 2.1 Proposal for the master plan of Beijing by Liang Sicheng and Chen Zhanxiang (1949)
Source: Liang 1986, 18-9.

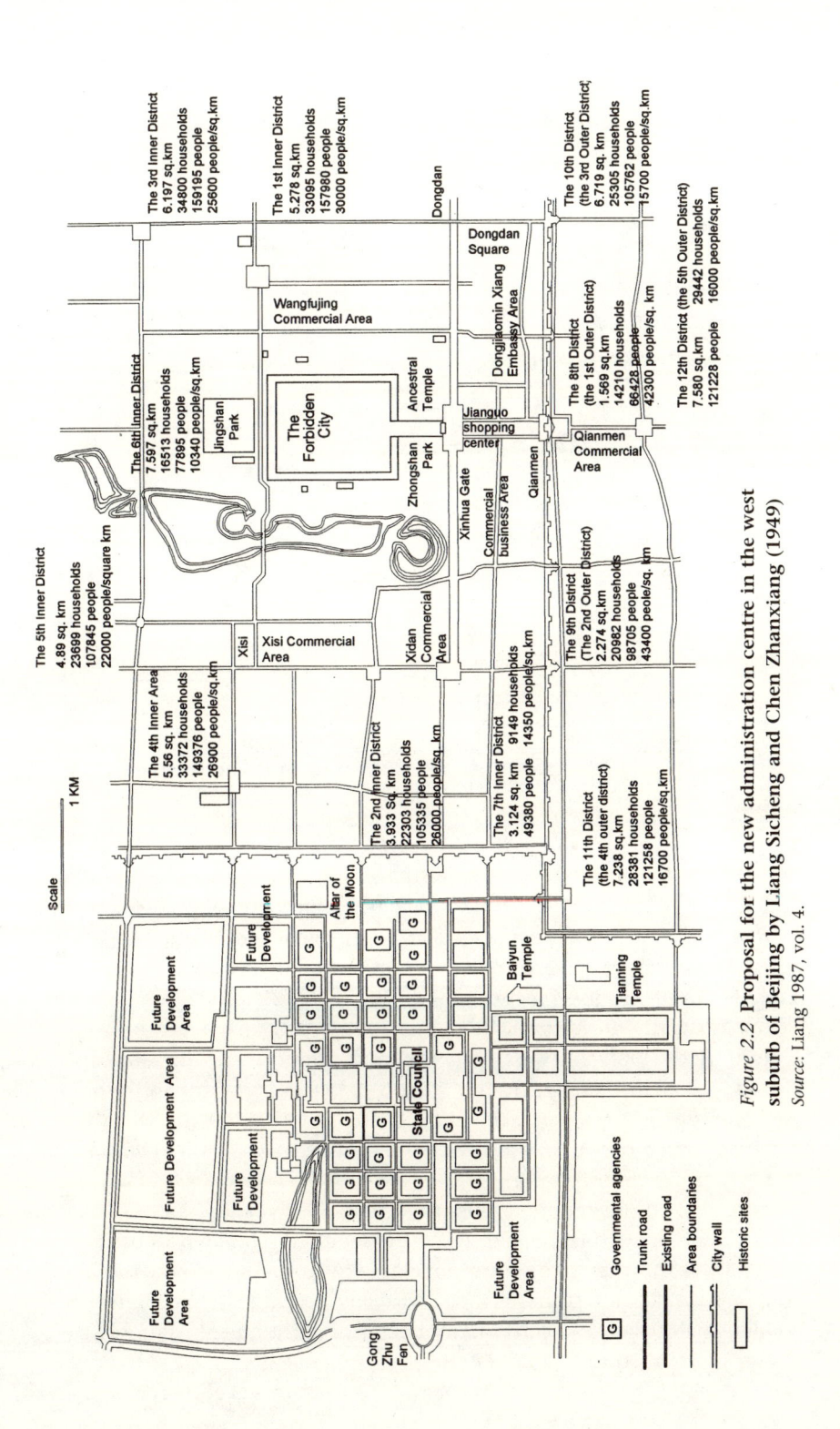

Figure 2.2 Proposal for the new administration centre in the west suburb of Beijing by Liang Sicheng and Chen Zhanxiang (1949)
Source: Liang 1987, vol. 4.

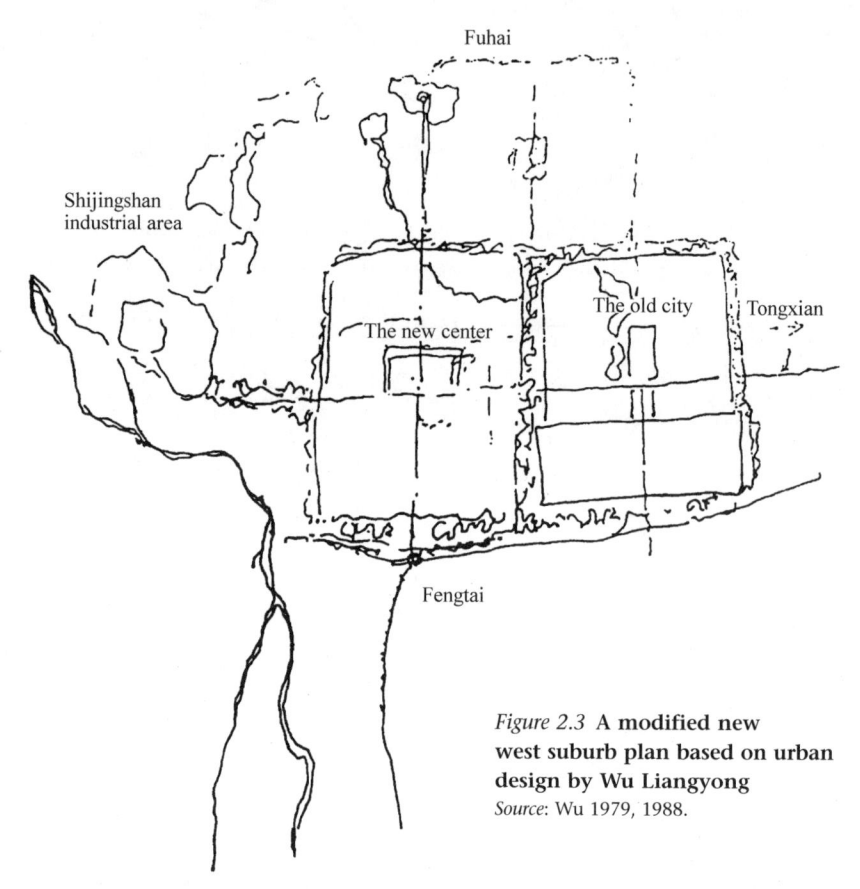

Figure 2.3 **A modified new west suburb plan based on urban design by Wu Liangyong**
Source: Wu 1979, 1988.

houses were collapsing every year, it would be much easier to rebuild Beijing than to rebuild more modern cities such as Shanghai and Tianjin. A grand renewal plan was set up to redevelop the entire Old City within ten years, at a rate of 1 million square metres of demolition and 20 million square metres of construction each year.

Third, redevelopment was emphasized and conservation ultimately neglected, although initially the two were to proceed hand in hand. Ironically, the decision made in the early 1950s to redevelop the Old City destroyed much of the best of the city, including many grand mansions, and yet left much of the worst unchanged for forty years. Even today, renewal is still considered more important than conservation, and existing buildings are poorly maintained. The over-ambitious renewal plan has precluded even short-term conservation; since it was presumed that the old buildings would soon be redeveloped, virtually no funds were allocated to building maintenance. Regulations for building refurbishment required that houses be repaired only according to their original size, usage, structure, and materials. As a result, up to the eve of the Cultural Revolution in 1966, the number of dilapidated houses in Beijing more than doubled, and this became an acute problem.

Proposal for the Beijing Master Plan of 1951
In 1951, after the choice of site was settled, a further proposal for the Beijing master plan was put forward for consideration by the Urban and Rural Planning Group at the Department of Architecture at Tsinghua University.[7] This was essentially an attempt to find a compromise that would accommodate, as much as possible, the ideas in the Liang-Chen plan, although it was accepted that the Old City would be the centre of the new capital. The main ideas were:

1. To develop Tiananmen Square as a symbolic public centre, with some limited government administrative buildings on both the east and west sides.
2. To build most of the government institutions in the west suburbs in order to reduce development pressure in the Old City centre.
3. To focus certain administrative functions in the Old City and to encourage cultural and leisure activities and tourism. (This is not the same as proposing a "museum city" – an idea that has often been criticized and has been incorrectly attributed to Liang.)
4. To plan diplomatic activities and industries in the east suburbs.
5. To designate the northwest suburbs as a cultural and academic district based on the universities already there (e.g., Tsinghua and Yenching), new universities, and the planned Academia Sinica.
6. To create separate ring and radial road systems for the old and new areas (not to be confused with the concentric ring roads actually implemented later).

Although this proposal was based on the limited information available at the time, it was supported by the municipal authorities, including the City Planning Commission. A model of the master plan was displayed at the May 1951 Anniversary of Tsinghua University, to which Liang Sicheng invited Xue Zizheng, the Secretary General of the Municipal Government of Beijing. Xue expressed approval of the plan, and it was understood that it should be developed further. Unfortunately, in the general upheaval brought about by successive political movements during the following two decades, the proposal was not implemented until after the Cultural Revolution.

In retrospect, the 1951 proposal was very practical. It was a sketch upon which much of the later master plan was based. In certain areas, particularly in the west suburbs, its ideas were adopted in part. Most new construction for government ministries has indeed taken place to the west of the Old City. Regretfully, however, no strict urban plan has remained in force over the past forty years. The massive construction and modern development scattered randomly throughout the city have not achieved the unity and harmony that were so much a tradition in the buildings and building complexes of old Beijing.

Explorations in Conservation and Development
Over the last forty years, many professionals from all over the country, and especially from the city's planning institutions, have been involved in the urban development of Beijing. Among these are professionals from the School of Architecture (formerly the Department of Architecture) of Tsinghua University. The following is an outline of the concepts and work developed by my team (within the School of Architecture) concerning the coordination of conservation and development.

Issues Concerning Regional Integration
With its great size, Beijing embraces and facilitates many kinds of activities and functions – perhaps too many. The problems that arise from this can have no real solution unless an integrated regional development policy is established. At the super-regional level, it refers to the mega-metropolitan area consisting of Beijing, Tianjin, and Tangshan; at the sub-regional level, it refers to Greater Beijing (Figures 2.4 and 2.5).[8]

Besides Beijing, there are a number of important cities and towns on the North China Plain. Because they are geographically very close to one another, there are practical advantages to each specializing in different economic activities and land use. Tianjin is by most counts China's third largest metropolis,[9] and it is less than 150 kilometres from Beijing. Its new seaport at Tanggu also serves Beijing. Tangshan provides the bulk of coal for the region, and Beidaihe and Chengde are important national resort towns. As all these urban centres have a strong link with Beijing in one way or another, Beijing's future should be planned within a wide regional context of industry, tourism, transport, water resources, forestry, and energy development.[10]

Beijing is the focal point of the regional road network, and each of the five major roads that connect the city with its region creates potential for development in that direction. In the near future, however, development is likely to take place between Beijing and Tianjin due to the increasing link between these two cities. There is no doubt that once the express motorway is expanded, the link will be further strengthened. As a result, Lanfang – a city midway between Beijing and Tianjin – will have more development opportunities. Similarly, cities like Tangshan, Fengrun, and Qinhuangdao will have high growth potentials. The small- and medium-size towns in the Beijing-Tianjin-Tangshan region will also have an increasing role to play in the region's urbanization process.

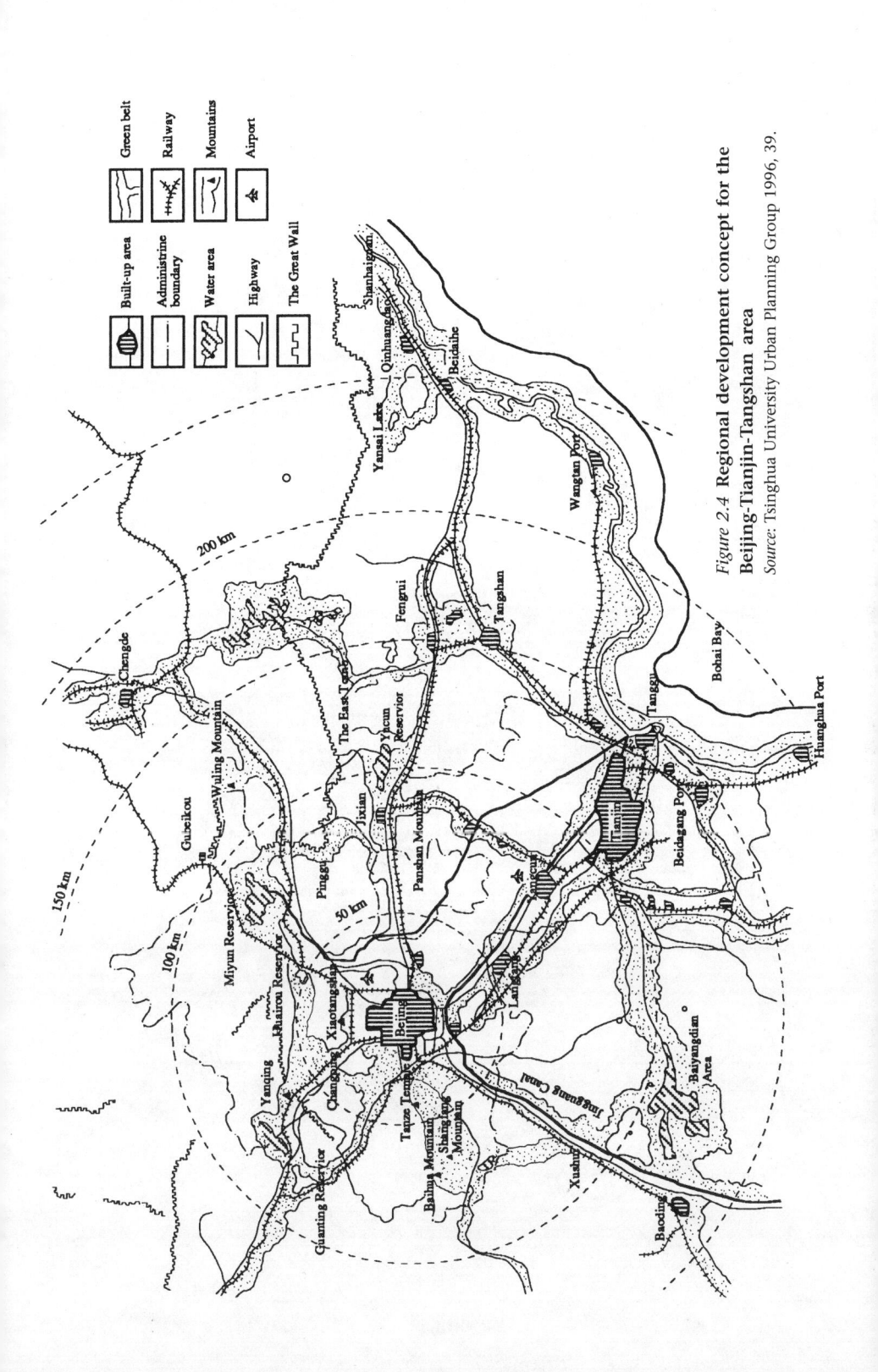

Figure 2.4 Regional development concept for the Beijing-Tianjin-Tangshan area
Source: Tsinghua University Urban Planning Group 1996, 39.

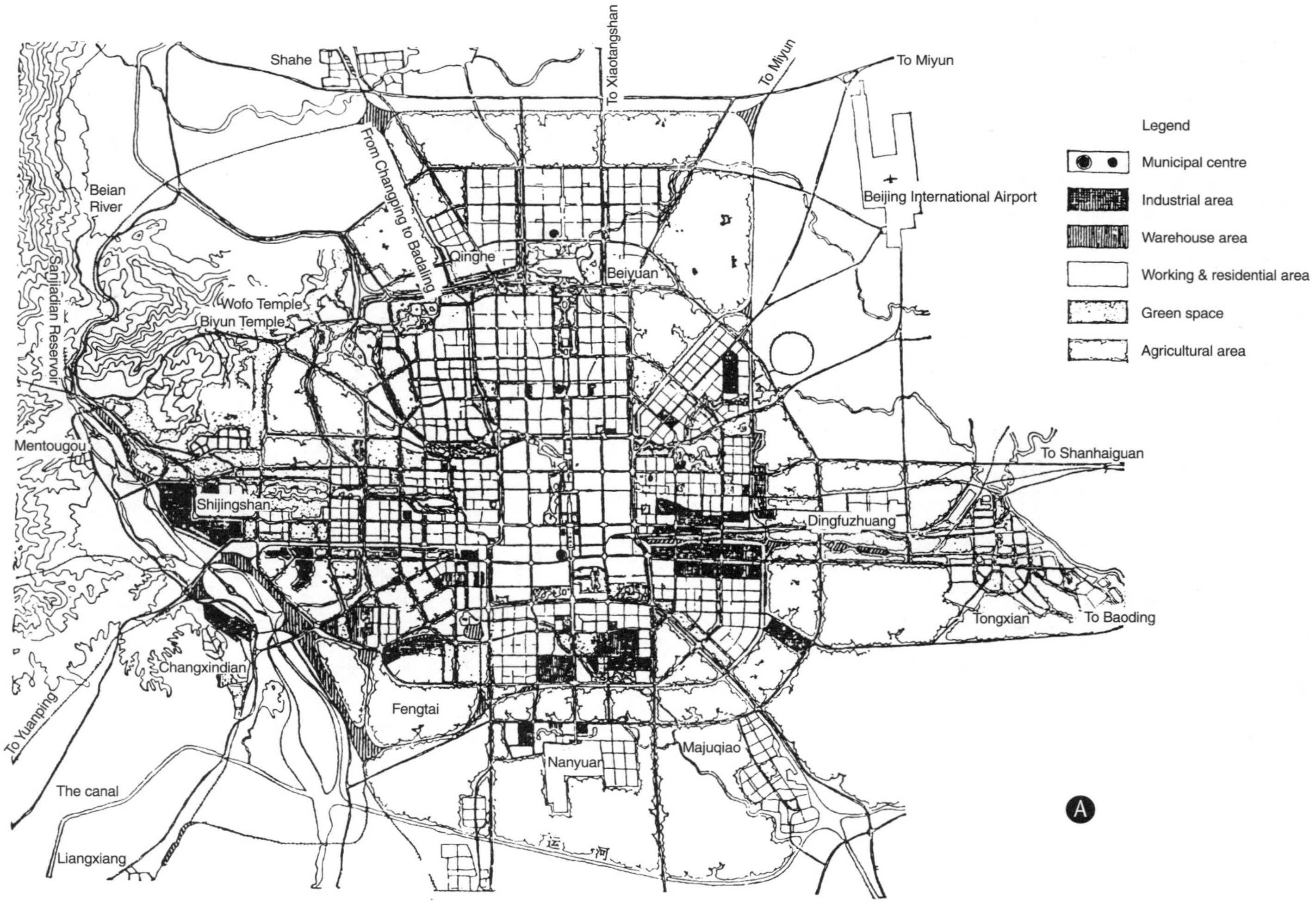
Legend
Municipal centre
Industrial area
Warehouse area
Working & residential area
Green space
Agricultural area
Shahe
To Xiaotangshan
To Miyun
To Miyun
Beijing International Airport
Beian River
From Changping to Badaling
Qinghe
Beiyuan
Wofo Temple
Biyun Temple
Sanjiadian Reservoir
Mentougou
To Shanhaiguan
Shijingshan
Dingfuzhuang
Tongxian
To Baoding
Changxindian
To Yuanping
Fengtai
Nanyuan
Majuqiao
The canal
Liangxiang
运 河
A

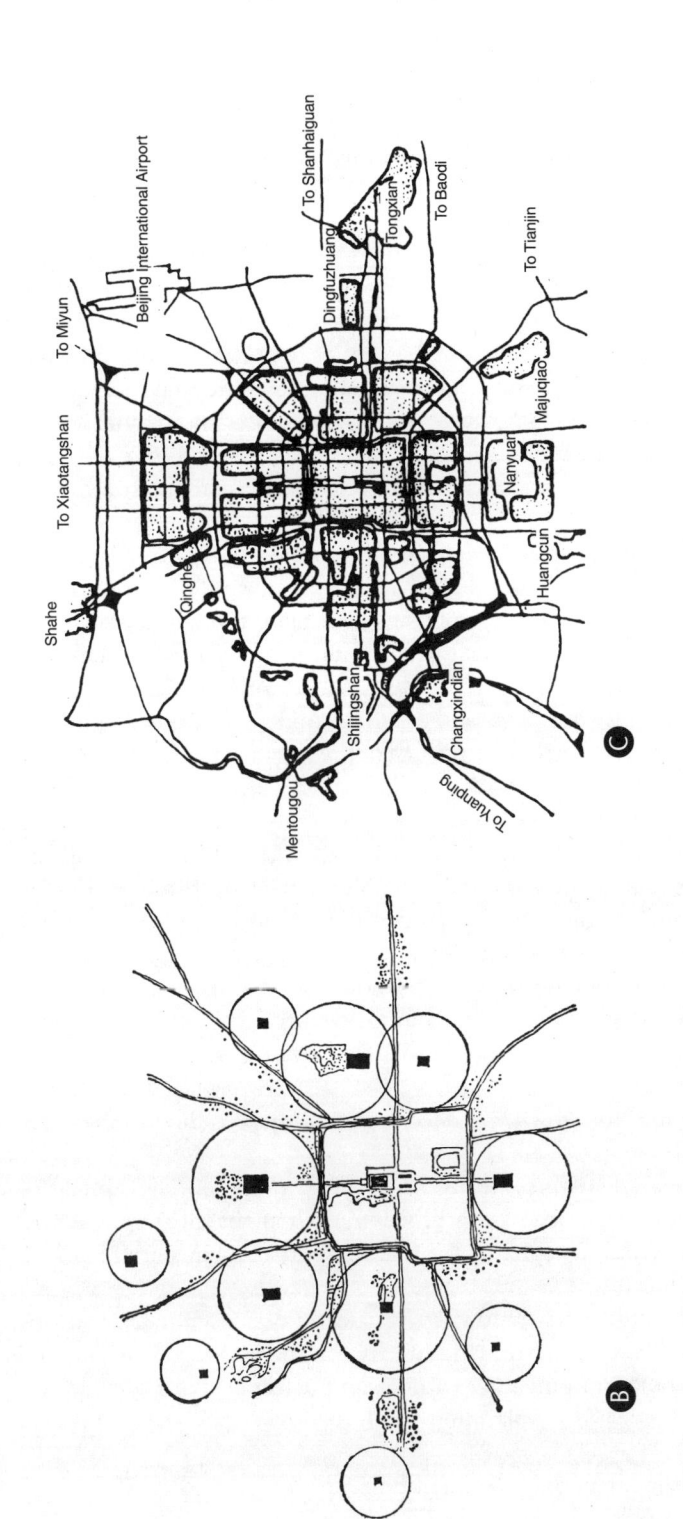

Figure 2.5 Multi-centre cluster development strategy for Beijing.
Ⓐ Proposal for Beijing's master plan. Ⓑ Structural analysis of master plan. Ⓒ Locational analysis of master plan.
Source: Tsinghua University Urban Planning Group 1996, 40.

The development of Greater Beijing cannot be isolated from this super-region. An integrated regional approach has the benefit of solving some current problems, such as water shortage and urban sprawl, and bringing prosperity to the whole region. The concept of regional integration put forward long ago by Mumford may still give inspiration to the modern planners of this region.[11] As early as the 1950s, a large metropolitan region of 16,800 square kilometres was demarcated for Beijing. Today, the built-up area is about 1,370 square kilometres, or 8 percent of the total. The rest provides the city with a vast hinterland. The surrounding counties have developed considerably modernized agriculture, forestry, manufacturing, and service sectors, including some high-tech industries. This has helped to relieve the city proper from further pressure caused by accelerated urbanization.

Decentralized Poly-Nuclear Development
Before 1949, Beijing was predominantly a concentric city, with the Forbidden City at its centre. In 1950 the Liang-Chen plan, though not adopted, proposed an embryonic poly-nuclear urban form. Since 1958, when a revised master plan came into effect, a cluster development strategy was introduced, which also reserved some agricultural land around the city. Although the idea was inspiring, the area of preserved agricultural land was too limited and the clusters of development too scattered to support any self-contained community centres.

In 1979, the Urban Planning Group at Tsinghua University revisited this concept and recommended to the Beijing Municipal Government a decentralized poly-nuclear development policy that would transform the existing mono-centric pattern, which was already under great strain. This policy would create relatively self-contained communities that had their own centres and would allow flexible growth in different directions.[12] Specifically, the Urban Planning Group proposed that the government:

1. Restructure the city, which was developed mainly according to the 1953 master plan.
2. Reduce development pressure by controlling inappropriate functions and activities and, at the same time, strengthen the city's role as the political and cultural centre of the country and encourage tourism and conservation.
3. Develop self-sufficient new towns with clearly defined functions at the periphery, and preserve farm land in between the built-up areas in order to prevent them from merging with urban nuclear areas.
4. Increase traffic speed by planning trunk roads on open space between city districts.
5. Provide development axes for the future.

This poly-nuclear development policy aimed to resolve the problems caused by expansion of the city proper and the increasing pressure for growth by building new suburban towns, decentralizing the city centre, establishing new suburban satellite towns, and developing sub-centres. This new thinking was partly due to recognizing that the far-suburb satellite towns in Beijing were developing very slowly and had proved ineffective in relieving development pressure in the city proper. In view of this, the team proposed that it would be more effective to build near-suburb towns whose connection with the city would resemble the garden suburbs of London. Planning proposals from the team at Tsinghua were accepted, to a varied extent, by the municipal authorities. Those proposals that were approved included the plan for Haidian District in the northwest suburbs and its district centre, plans for extending the north axis, site planning for the Asian Games, and plans for the new science and technology park in the northwestern suburbs.

Issues Concerning Open Space

The historic City of Beijing is highly integrated with the natural environment. Its character owes a great deal to natural landscape features in and around the city – particularly the large lakes in the central area and the dense groves of trees in the city's architectural space. There is a need for the city's green space to be improved and increased not only because it would serve as more desirable recreational space, but, more important, because it would help to improve the general quality of the environment and would provide hazard-relief from such disasters as earthquakes.

Accessibility to some form of natural open space has been one of the most fundamental and yet difficult goals of modern urban planning, from the incorporation of parks and boulevards in the plans of nineteenth-century industrializing metropolises like London, Paris, Vienna, and New York, to the "urban wilds" movements of contemporary "post-industrial" cities. In the historic city centre of Beijing, the large area occupied by the Forbidden City, water surfaces, and imperial parks is an asset that is rare in other large international cities. The unique lakes and open spaces within the city should be carefully preserved not only by prohibiting encroachment, but also by controlling building heights.

Faced with a serious land shortage for residential and office uses in Beijing, planners tend to increase building density without recognizing the consequences. Green spaces are the most vulnerable parts of the city because they easily fall victim to development. It will be too late when the city is developed and little open space is left; it is preferable to legislate now with regard to preservation and enlargement of the open space and water surface at the centre of the city.

Issues concerning Transport Networks

The traditional street system in Beijing is in a chess-board pattern. The streets are lined with trees that endow the city with a sense of regularity, grandeur, and comfort. Although this tradition is continued in new street designs, the most recent Master Plan of Beijing, dominated by traffic planning, treats road systems, landscaping, and building forms separately. In the future, more careful thought should be given to the following issues:[13]

1. Integration of road systems with green spaces and water surfaces.
2. Separation of main roads from the major shopping streets and precincts.
3. Separation of cars, bicycles, and pedestrian traffic.
4. Integration of new designs with the existing spatial system in the city, including existing streets, squares, and *hutong* (alleyways).
5. Efficient connection between above- and below-ground traffic.
6. Consideration for architecture and landscaping as well as for traffic in road design.
7. Mixed use around traffic junctions both above and below ground.

Among the many problems pertaining to Beijing's road system and traffic management, the Second Ring Road is a clear example of insufficient planning leading to missed opportunities for improvement.[14] If the city wall had not been demolished, then the Second Ring Road could have been built outside it. It would have formed tree-lined avenues more beautiful than those along the city walls in Xi'an. Even after the demolition of the city wall, there was still an opportunity to turn the site into nice linear parks like those in Hefei. The site of the Second Ring Road could have been planned as tree-lined avenues and plazas, with link roads for local traffic, similar to suggestions made for Vienna's Ringstrasse in the late nineteenth century (Figure 2.6). It could also have been built for through traffic by opening a parallel road to serve the buildings alongside it. Even now, careful urban design could improve the image of the Second Ring Road. For instance, large building complexes could restore its image at the edge of the city, and new landmarks could be created near the site of the old city gates. Other parts of the urban network could also be improved with similar designs.

Integrated Conservation of the Old City

There are two fundamental questions that need to be answered before one can deal with any technical issues concerning conservation in Beijing. The first is whether conservation is really necessary; the second is what the tasks of conservation are and how they can be implemented. Although planners, architects, and critics commonly share the idea that Beijing is a significant

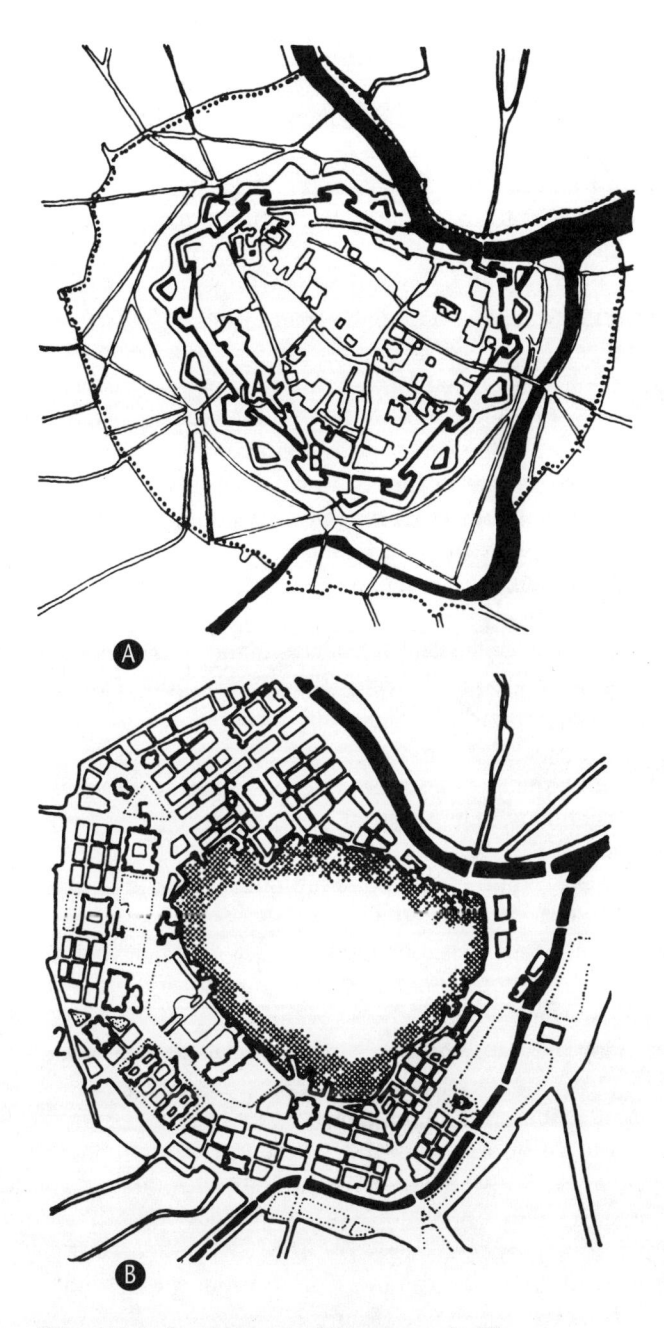

Planning and Development in Beijing since 1949 31

Figure 2.6 **Redevelopment of Ringstrasse in Vienna.**
Ⓐ Vienna in 1857, before the development of the Ring.
Ⓑ The Ringstrasse plan.
Source: Morris 1979, 191.

historic city that is a masterpiece of city planning and design, many of them also believe that some historic artifacts, such as city walls, must disappear as a natural process of development. This argument is easily rebutted by the successful examples of Rome and Xi'an, where the preserved city walls help to create space that is appreciated by the public. Others argue that since most of historic Beijing has been destroyed, it appears to be too late to conserve the rest. If there is a need for any conservation at all, then it will be enough only to conserve the fragmented remains of individual historic artifacts. I, however, believe that, by definition, conservation never comes too late.

I have frequently argued for an integrated urban conservation policy for Beijing, but this should not be misinterpreted as a policy to freeze the whole city as it is.[15] One compelling reason for a comprehensive, integrated conservation policy is that Beijing is no common historic city: it is a unique example of capital-city design in China. It is the largest imperial capital in Chinese urban history, and it crystallizes the evolution of traditional urban Chinese capitals during different imperial periods, as was discussed in Chapter 1. Another reason for an integrated conservation policy is that Beijing possesses a clear and rigorous spatial layout and an ordered urban form that endows it with a unique character, the conservation of which necessitates treating the city as a whole. This will include:

1. Designating the most important historic areas, in which strict measures of protection are to be enforced.
2. Preserving the Forbidden City as a key area.
3. Preserving a certain number of traditional courtyard houses that are still in reasonably good condition.
4. Issuing a more detailed zoning plan for building height and bulk control.
5. Preserving traditional shop precincts, theatres, and other buildings with local character.
6. Preserving important historic sites of special value.

The architectural space in the Old City combines the geometric (the dominant feature) with the natural (the subordinate feature). These two features complement each other. For this reason, both the buildings and their environs are objects of conservation. Although redevelopment is inevitable in the city, the integrity of the design of historic Beijing needs to be protected. This is the definition of integrated conservation, which should be the basis of any further redevelopment (Figure 2.7).

Preserving the Horizontal Skyline
From the perspective of spatial configuration, historic Beijing is characterized by its horizontal skyline and may be called a "horizontal city." The Old

City was dominated by the centrally located Jingshan Hill and the White Pagoda in Beihai. The city was also controlled by ten magnificent gate towers on the city wall. Within the city, numerous grand mansions punctuated the rhythm and order of the landscape.[16] Apart from its human landscape,

Population density proposal (persons/ha)

Floor area ratio proposal

Building density control proposal

Building height control proposal (m)

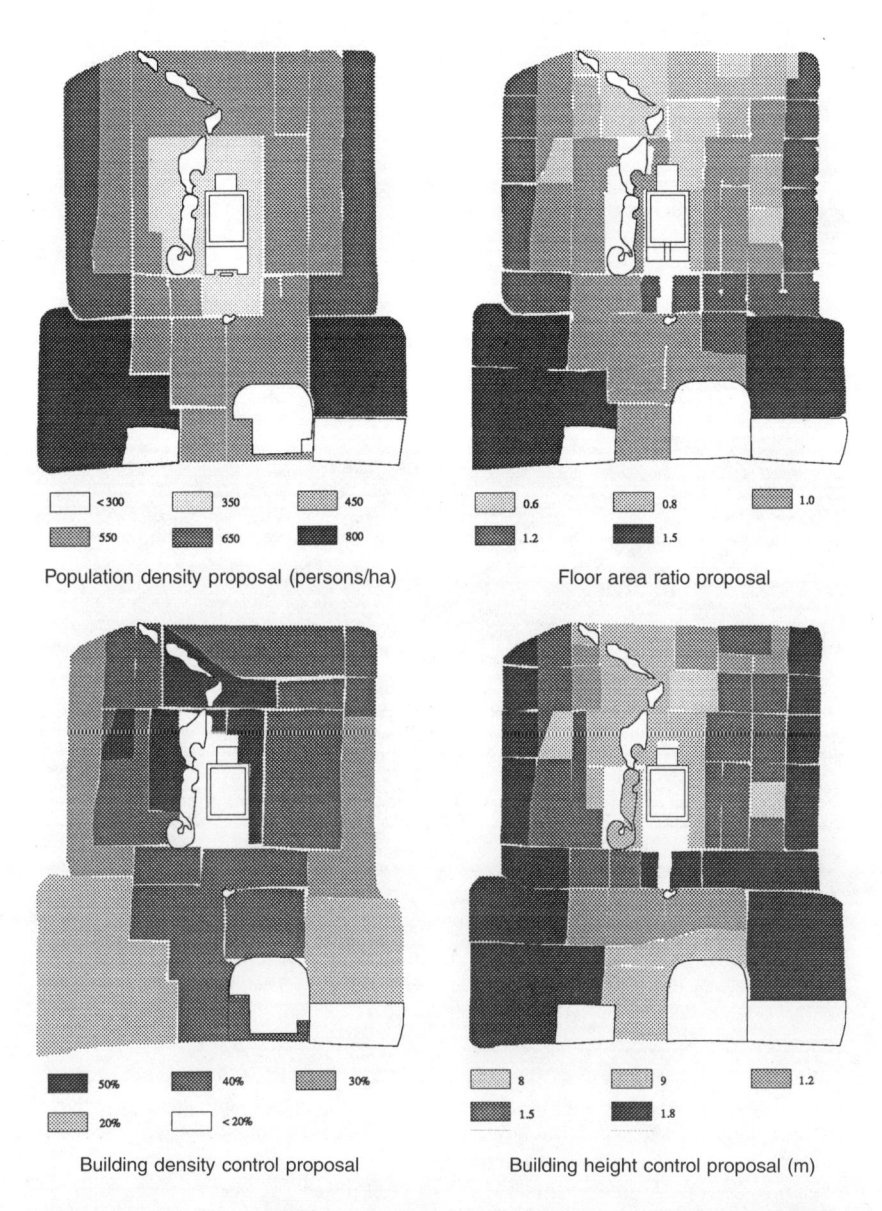

Figure 2.7 **Proposals for the integrated conservation of the Old City of Beijing (1986)**
Source: Liu 1987, Figs. 3-7, 3-8, 3-9, 3-10.

34 *Planning and Development in Beijing since 1949*

Figure 2.8 **Scenarios of building height control in Beijing.**
Ⓐ Historically, there was a strictly proportional relationship in building height in the Old City. Ⓑ If high-rise buildings were to be located at will, then the original physical order would be totally lost. Ⓒ If the proposed building height control is adopted with most of the high-rise buildings located outside the Old City, then the horizontal outline will be preserved. Ⓓ Beijing is a city with a three-dimensional design. Lack of control in building height will result in serious damage to the magnificent skyline. In the past, the Drum and Bell Towers stood above the courtyard houses and trees. Now, multi-storey buildings have sprung up here and there. I remain to be convinced that this is the destiny of history; rather, it may be simply lack of imagination on the part of planners and designers.
Source: Wu 1979.

Beijing's plan introduced nature by way of large areas of water (such as Beihai) and wooded hills (such as Jingshan). The view of the distant Western Hills can be appreciated from many points in the city. All these make building height zoning necessary. The proliferation of modern buildings of varying height, bulk, and layout can easily spoil the form of the historic city if there is no sensible overall planning.

The low profile of the rooftops of houses was also punctuated by carefully arranged grand buildings that were spaced so as to create an inspiring cityscape. It is necessary to control the development of this "horizontal city" in terms of building form and colour as well as in terms of height and mass. Traditionally, horizontal Beijing was covered with trees that towered over gold and grey curvingly pitched roofs. With the increase of tall buildings, the roofscape was altered; the new monotonous flat roofs have detracted from the city's traditional beauty (Figure 2.8).

For some time, many planners and architects have been pushing the municipal authorities to issue building height regulations. A Building Height Zoning Act was finally passed by the municipal government in 1987 (Figure 2.9), and this was followed by the High-Rise Building Act, 1989, which controlled high-rise blocks in the city. The design and location of tall buildings has been monitored ever since, but the mistakes that had already been made are most regrettable.

Conservation and Development along the Central Axis

Beijing's 7.9-kilometre central axis was one of the most magnificent to be found in premodern cities; it creates order and grandeur on an enormous scale. Along this axis there are a series of important buildings that form the city's dominant parts. This central axis, strengthened by the expansion of Tiananmen Square in the late 1950s, is the backbone of the city and should not be destroyed. The height and volume of new buildings around the dominant points of this axis should, therefore, be controlled. The extension of the central axis should also be well planned and designed in order to form a sensible ending or transition that will preserve its integrity.

Continuity of the Street Pattern

The traditional road system in Chinese cities has a long history. Even Le Corbusier, whose Plan Voisin proposed the obliteration of Paris's central Right Bank blocks and streets, appreciated the continuing value of Beijing's street system in his book *City of Tomorrow*. Among Beijing's planners and architects, however, there is little agreement on how the existing city structure should be treated when redevelopment takes place. Redevelopment that aims only to solve vehicular traffic problems risks destroying the traditional cityscape.

Any new development in the important Old City areas should be put under strict planning control. This includes Dongdan and Dongsi in the east; Xidan and Xisi in the west; Dashalan, Liulichang, and Xianyukou in the south; and the Drum Tower shopping areas in the north. Some of these areas may be pedestrianized, especially where traffic pressure is intense (e.g., at Dongdan and Xidan, where redevelopment should be closely supervised).[17]

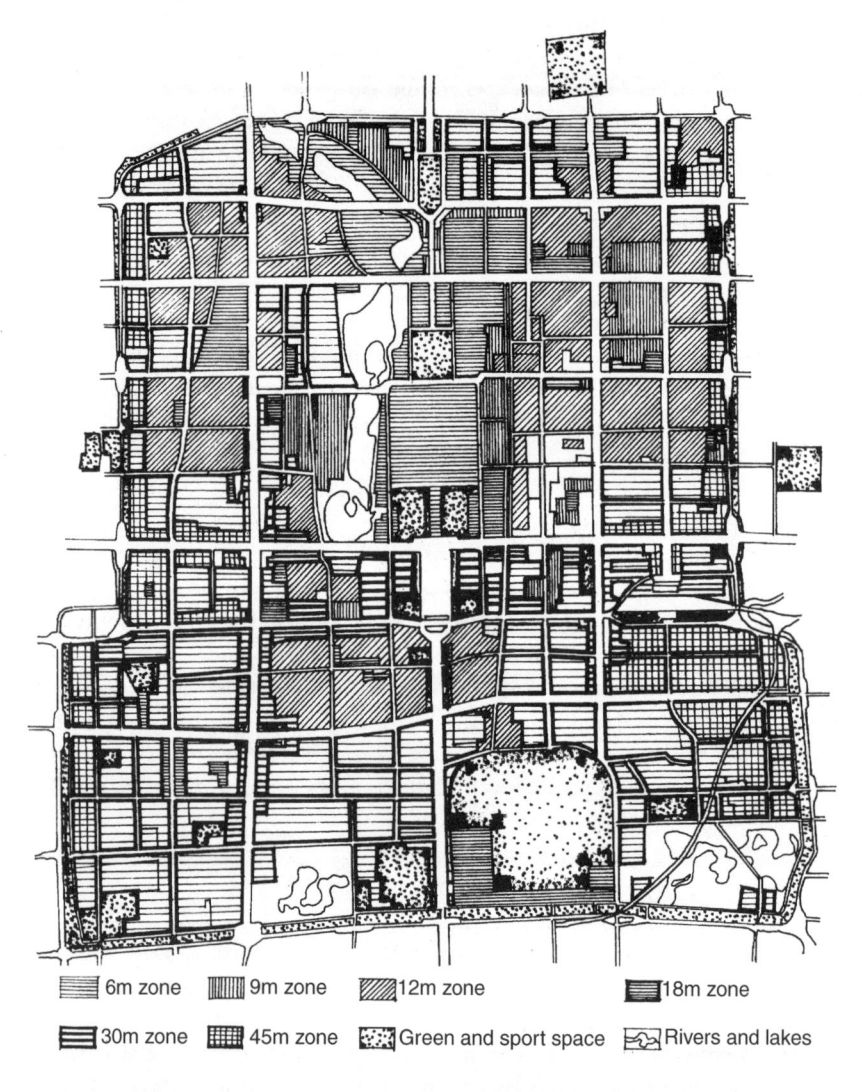

Figure 2.9 **Building height control for the Old City of Beijing (officially issued in 1987).** The official issuance of building height control regulations is worth celebrating. However, there are still many pitfalls in its implementation.
Source: Beijing Municipal Institute of Urban Planning and Design, June 1990.

Some streets in the Old City are still characterized by important landmarks on either side (e.g., Chao-Fu Dajie, which crosses the city from Chaoyangmen in the east to Fuchengmen in the west, passing the princely mansion of Fujunwang Fu, the traditional commercial intersection in the east at Dongsi, the Forbidden City, Jingshan, Beihai, the traditional commercial intersection in the west at Xisi, and the temples of Guangji Si and Baita Si).[18] My experience in several urban design projects since 1981 (e.g., in Dashalan, Liulichang, and the Drum Tower areas, and in the Yonghegong-Guozijian area) has convinced me that as long as the problems in the old areas are well understood, feasible solutions that are agreeable to the needs of modern living may be found.

Continuity and Development of the Traditional Courtyard Houses
In 1951, I conducted one of the earliest studies of traditional courtyard houses in Beijing. It examined the east- and west-oriented housing within the courtyards of the Huashi neighbourhood outside Chongwengmen. In 1981, having observed the massive featureless housing blocks going up in the Old City, I felt the need to find some alternative forms. Low-rise, high-density housing incorporating the courtyard layout was one consideration. At the same time, an appeal was made to refurbish and renovate the old traditional courtyard houses that were still in reasonably good condition, especially in the vicinity of the central axis and the Imperial City. The scheme implemented at the Shichahai area near the Drum Tower demonstrated this idea in embryonic form.[19] In the Imperial City, preserving the existing courtyard houses should be the basic policy. New buildings there should be confined to two- or three-storey quasi-courtyard houses; old buildings should be installed with modern facilities. Beyond the Imperial City, a differential zoning policy is needed. The Ju'er Hutong project, a further development of such an idea, has proved to be practical. The housing prototype created in the Ju'er Hutong experiment may be applied to other Old City areas where two- to four-storey buildings are preferred. This, of course, need not preclude other sensible alternatives.

Colour Control and Urban Conservation
Historically, Beijing's colouring was an integral part of its visual character. Colour design and control are important aspects of modern urban design theories, as they preserve and enhance a sense of place; they can improve the general quality of a city's image and soften the impact of unappealing buildings. The Japanese city of Yokohama, in enhancing its environmental quality, has successfully implemented colour control policy as a key urban design strategy in its dock area. Similar cases exist in Chinese cities: recently, in Shanghai, some of the main streets were washed and painted according to the original design of the old buildings. In Suzhou, the characteristic

"white wall and black tiles" image has been reinforced by the local planning authority. In Beijing, therefore, traditional colouring can also be maintained by adopting control policies, especially in the important historic areas.

The dominant central axis, the geometric urban layout and architectural composition, the harmonious composition of colour, the emphasis on important buildings, the rhythm and variation of the city skyline, and the integration of the city with nature are all important aspects of urban conservation in Beijing. They combine to give a sense of wholeness to the city and should, consequently, be considered in an integrated way. Any conservation policy that treats these aspects in isolation is unlikely to succeed. Moreover, integrated conservation also demands subtle differences in regulations with regard to the characteristics of different areas in the city; thus, a grading system for conservation areas is needed in order to distinguish objectives and to suggest measures for obtaining them.[20] The 62-square-kilometre Old City has undergone diverse development experiences and varying qualities of traditional building stock. Conservation in the Old City should focus primarily on the central axis, the Forbidden City, the Three Seas, the Temple of Heaven, and their surroundings. Secondary priority should be given to the other demarcated historic sites and buildings, while tertiary priority should be given to other important historic areas. When the underlying principles of forms in the city are clearly understood, then, accordingly, urban design policies can be established for building height, form, density, and land use in different areas.

Urban and Architectural Design of the Old City

Reinforcing the Intrinsic Order of the Old City

Urban design is critical to Beijing's urban conservation. As the most important historic Chinese city, Beijing demands the best urban design; however, the current conservation regulations are too simplistic to cope with the city's real problems. There is an urgent need for urban design guidelines that provide a comprehensive directive for the city's land use, building height, building mass, colour schemes, building form, transport, landscaping, and infrastructure. This approach would establish an intermediate stage of control between structural urban design (i.e., determination of the road network, location of other infrastructure, and levels of building density) and architectural design. At this stage, the object area, or "urban tissue," is studied in detail, and guidelines are established for its integration with the historic structure and form of the city. At the same time, the guidelines leave ample flexibility and freedom for architectural design. This comprehensive policy should be instituted in the form of law or building codes.[21]

The foremost consideration in formulating design guidelines is to take into account the traditional physical order of the Old City and to make reference to those traditional city planning and architectural design principles that still have validity today. Preservation and improvement are especially required for the historic sites surrounding the Forbidden City, the Temple of Heaven, the Qianmen-Liulichang shopping area, Chengxian Jie (Guozijian and the Confucius Temple), and Shichahai. New development in these areas should be designed in such a way that local character is enhanced rather than weakened. Priority should also be given to historic areas with architectural importance that form unique views within the city. In addition, some key historic buildings that have been neglected in the past should also be restored properly (Figure 2.10). In the intermediate zone outside of the core conservation areas, new buildings should be designed carefully to provide a harmonious setting for the important historic areas (Figure 2.11).[22]

Apart from the listed historic residential areas, there are still many old courtyard houses that will be redeveloped; for the complexes in modest condition, renovation and refurbishment would be the most appropriate action. Even though the derelict houses may be demolished, the existing courtyard patterns, street layout, and trees are worth preserving. Without a suitable background of residential buildings, the palaces and temples will not retain their original glory.

Improving Design Quality
In conservation, mere protection of the old is not enough; there is also a need for well designed new structures. In Beijing, the number of important historic sites and buildings listed are only a tiny proportion of the total building stock. The scale of new development has been overwhelming, and the amount of new buildings has exceeded that of the old. Years of redevelopment have tipped the balance between the traditional and the modern building stock. In the early 1950s, there were some 17 million square metres of buildings within the city walls, mostly single-storey courtyard houses. Today, out of a total stock of 33 million square metres, old buildings make up 11 million square metres. Within the 11 million square metres of old buildings, only 2.1 million square metres are palaces, mansions, and traditional courtyard houses.[23] In the 8.2-hectare Ju'er Hutong neighbourhood, however, only 2 percent of the stock is Grade 1 (worth preserving); 16 percent is Grade 2 (adaptable); and 82 percent is Grade 3 or worse (derelict and to be demolished).[24] Indeed, the less important traditional buildings should also be carefully re-examined so that they can avoid unnecessary demolition and be protected under effective policies.

However, the reality is quite depressing because a thorough understanding of the importance of preservation and conservation is lacking. Past condemnation of any attempt to preserve ancient buildings as architectural classicism caused much confusion – confusion that continues even

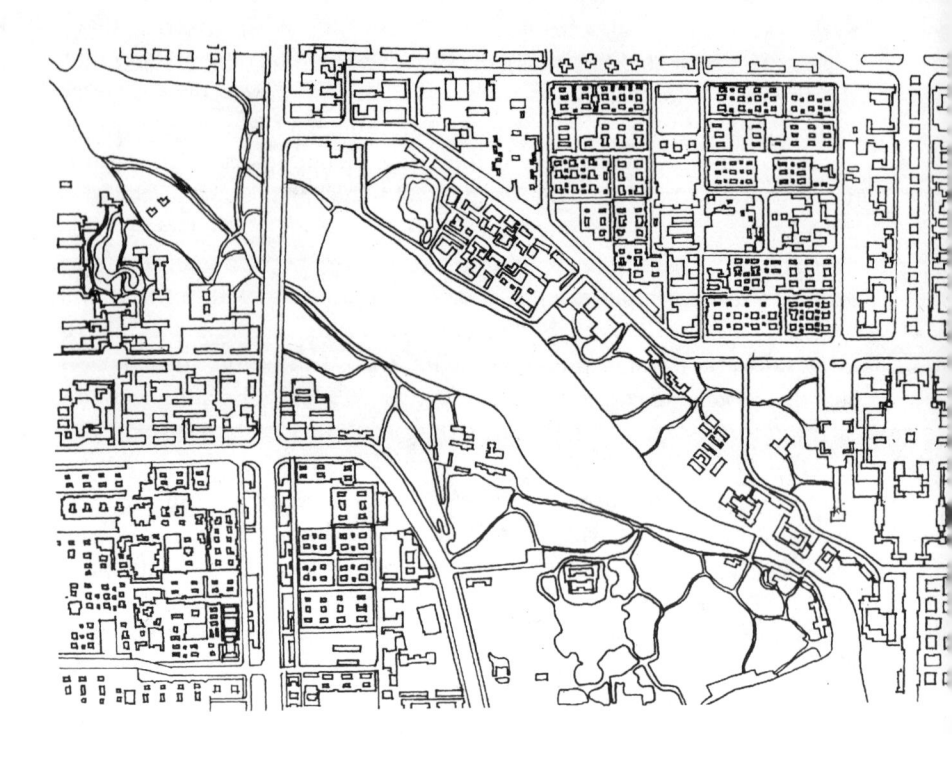

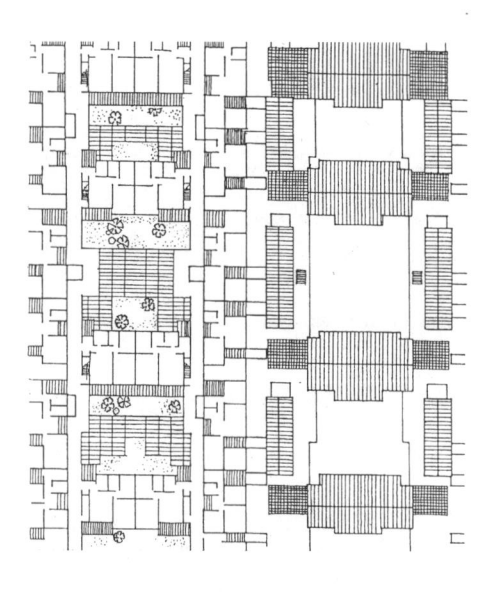

Figure 2.10 **Early studies: Planning studies for the Shichahai area, 1979.** The ideas of organic renewal and quasi-courtyard houses were applied to the Shichahai plan. In particular, the following three things were clarified: protection of historic sites and view corridors; principles of organic renewal; and the concept of new courtyard house types.
Source: School of Architecture, Tsinghua University.

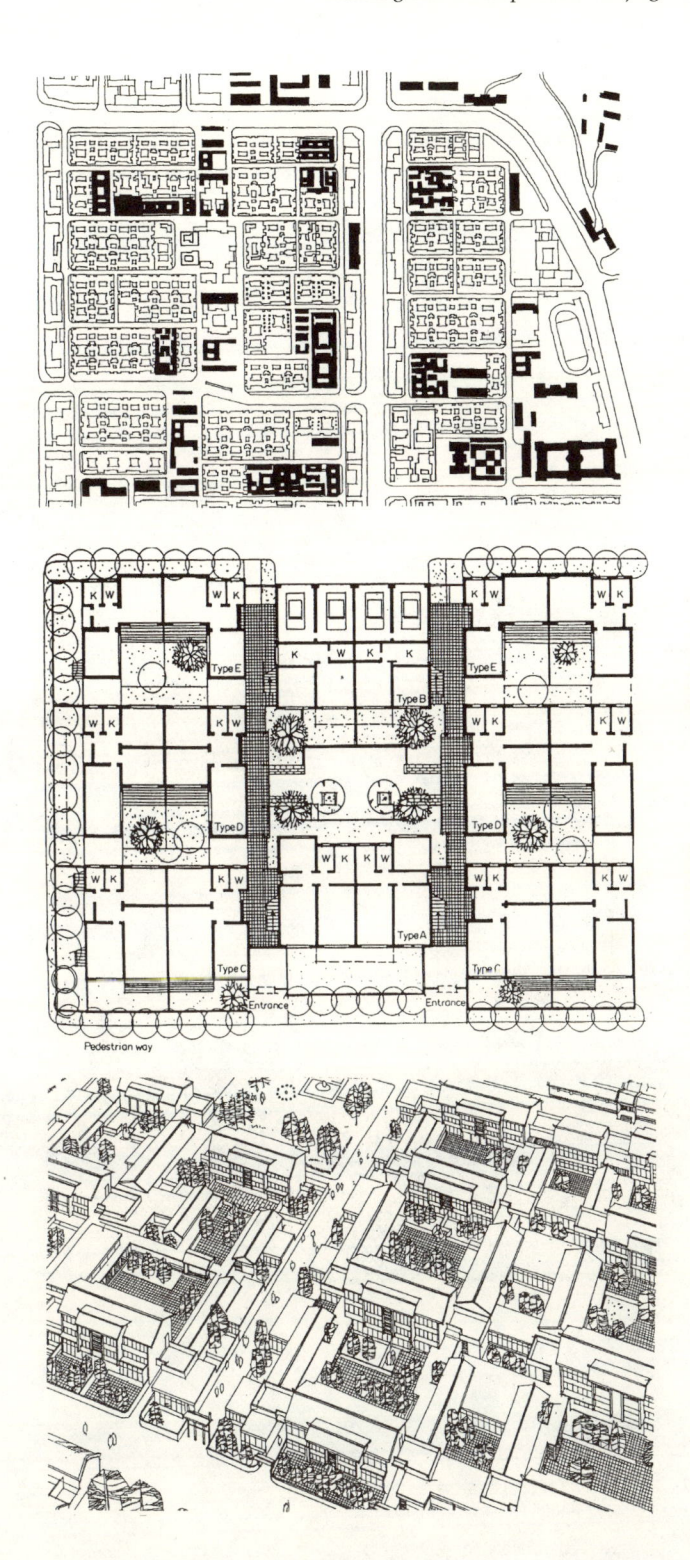

Planning and Development in Beijing since 1949 41

today. For many, the best that can be done to "respect tradition" is to use fragmented traditional motifs as decoration on essentially modernist urban designs. Beijing should demand a higher architectural design standard than this. As the national capital, it is an example for the rest of the

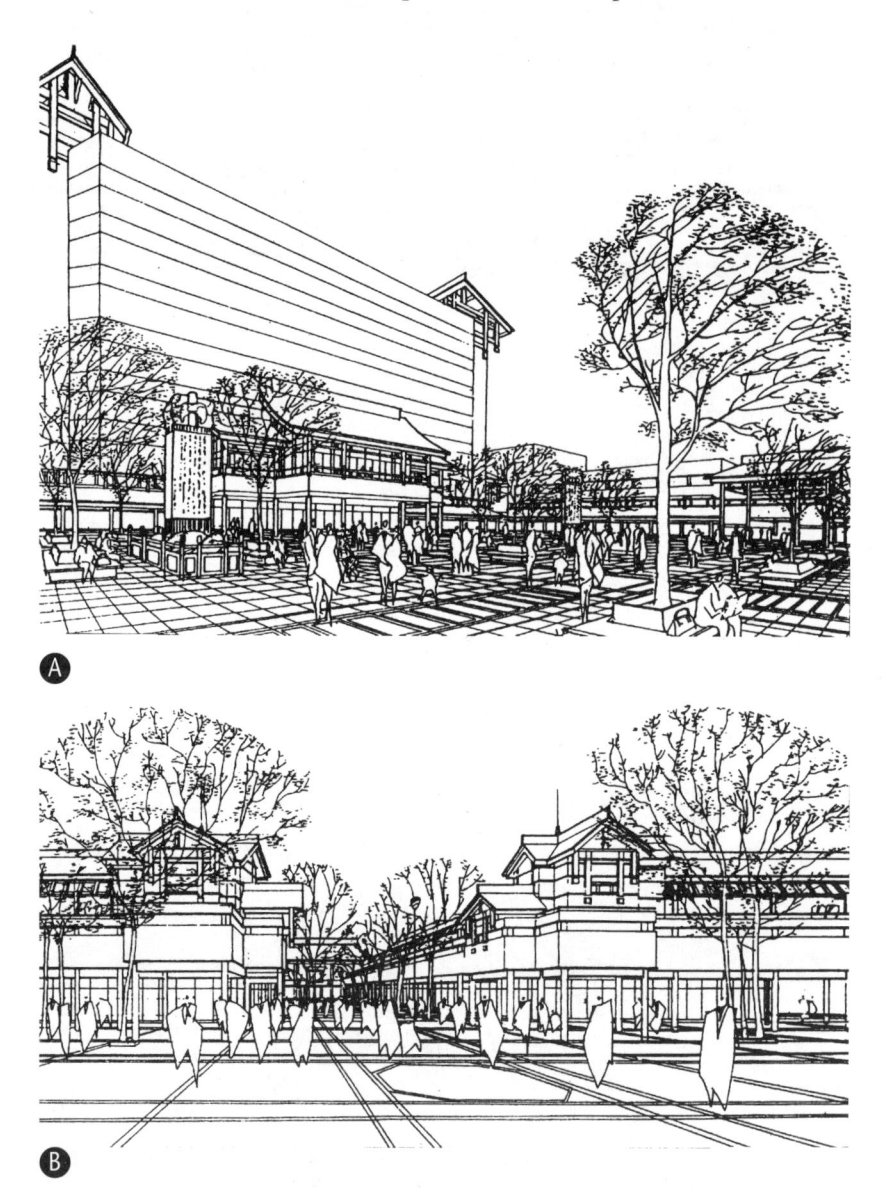

Figure 2.11 **Conceptual design for the Longfusi Market.**
Ⓐ Longfusi Plaza, with the two steles from a Ming dynasty temple.
Ⓑ Longfu Xijie viewed from the plaza.
Source: School of Architecture, Tsinghua University.

country. And requiring a higher architectural design standard implies not only solid buildings, but also designs that respect the physical order of the city. The 1983 revision of the Master Plan of Beijing emphasized both this point and the importance of the city's design in "reflecting modern spirit, traditional culture and local characteristics." At the local level, building designs should aim to enforce or create the spirit of the place. Because architecture is always set in a certain context of time, space, and social conditions, it is crucial for architects and designers to understand the characteristics of the city, including urban form, scale, architectural tradition, culture, and so on. It is also necessary to distinguish development in the Old City areas from development in the new areas. Failure to do this will produce a design that is both too general and abstract, yet also quite specifically destructive.

New design in Beijing should be closely supervised and guided by a committee of experts endowed with real power. As cities in China are undergoing great social and economic transformation, their planning and development urgently require rational policy making, legislation, modern management, and scientific programming. More attention is particularly needed in planning research to improve the urban environment. Urban design should be employed as a scientific framework for planning and statutory guidelines. Project programming, environmental impact evaluation, and effective design policies for construction in the historic environment are also essential in continuing the existing urban culture.

In short, over the last forty years (and especially over the last decade) the main research work conducted by myself and my colleagues at Tsinghua concerning Beijing focused on:

1. Regional planning, urban planning, urban development, and architectural design in which theory is combined with practice.
2. Conservation and development that recognizes cultural value, including its historic, aesthetic, and ecological aspects. This includes a focus on the practical value of the existing cityscape (in functional, economic, and social terms) and attempts to incorporate it into each project while at the same time coordinating protection, reuse, and renovation.[25]
3. Creative urban conservation and development. Different countries, regions, and cities have their own traditions and physical orders; therefore, it is crucial to understand their respective problems before recommending solutions.
4. Research and deliberation on changing lifestyles and technological developments that have had tremendous influence on urban conservation and development. Short-term redevelopment has been especially damaging: difficult problems benefit from time spent on research and deliberation.

3
Residential Development and the Renewal of Derelict Houses

As Beijing's urban development progressed, there gradually emerged an awareness of the need to preserve the larger-scale historic buildings. Much less attention has been paid to the preservation of traditional residential areas. Since the beginning of the 1950s to the end of the 1970s, in spite of great achievements in new housing construction, the traditional residential quarters of Beijing's Old City suffered from haphazard rebuilding as their occupants struggled to meet the immediate demands of daily life; little importance was attached to the urban fabric of the Old City or to the fine points of urban and architectural design. In the late 1980s, the renewal of the Old City's derelict houses became an explicit goal of municipal policy. Although many of the specific measures adopted were imperfect, the overall goal was laudable, as many houses in the Old City were in such bad condition that there was no real alternative to rebuilding them. Unfortunately, the program has over-reached itself. Only a small proportion of the Old City's neighbourhoods have been designated for preservation; the great majority are to be demolished and rebuilt on a large scale. Even after most of the derelict houses in the Old City have been renewed, the pace of rebuilding has not stopped and the bulldozers continue to roll over courtyard houses regardless of their quality and condition. We must all wake up to this alarming situation.

Housing Development since 1949
Among the variety of contradictions between development and conservation in Beijing, the issue of housing raises the most intense discord. Since 1949, Beijing has experienced unprecedented housing development in order to meet the demand of a rapidly expanding urban population. By the end of 1991 (Figures 3.1 and 3.2), the total housing stock was 10.5 million square metres, 9 million square metres of which were constructed after 1949. In other words, there is six times as much new stock as old. As a result, the average living space per person increased from 4.7 square metres in 1949 to

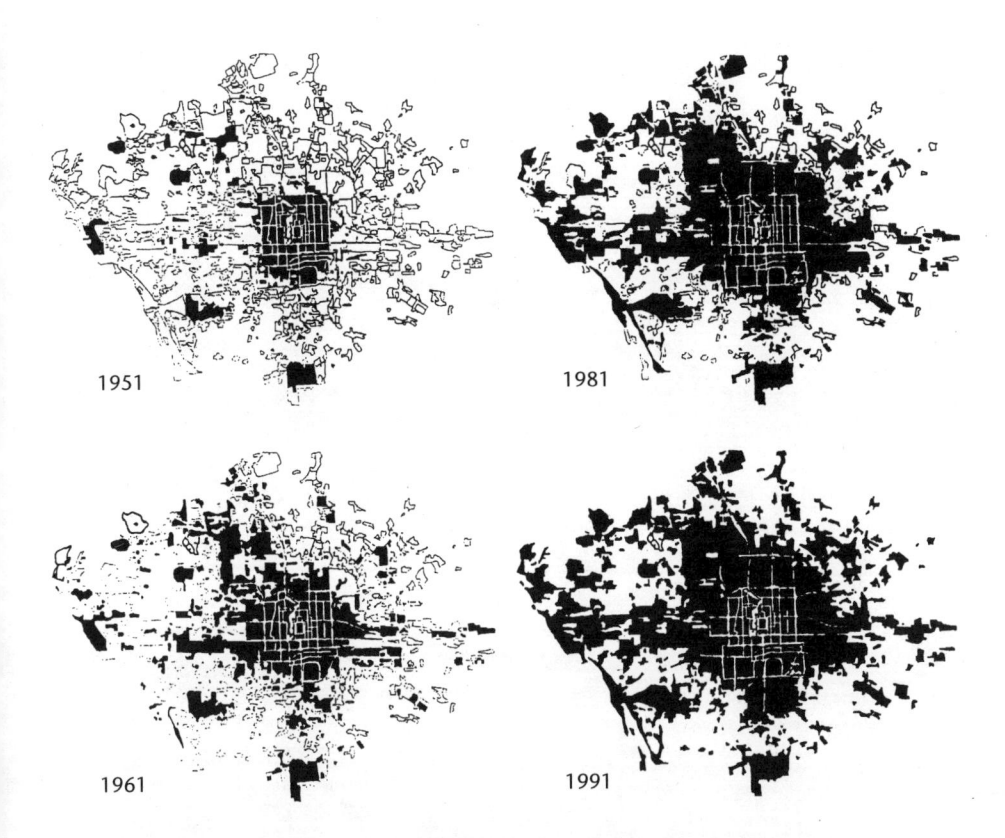

Figure 3.1 **Urban growth in Beijing: Expansion of the urban built-up area (1951-91)**
Source: Unpublished statistics from the Beijing Municipal Institute of Urban Planning and Design 1991.

8.0 square metres in 1991. During the period between 1981 and 1992, between 4 and 5 million square metres of new housing was built each year, which greatly improved the housing conditions in Beijing.[1]

Problems in New Housing Development

In the early 1950s, housing development primarily took place in small neighbourhoods consisting of simple apartment buildings that were three to four storeys tall. The neighbourhoods became larger and the buildings taller, until during the 1960s apartment buildings were generally five to six storeys. In the 1970s, high-rise blocks of ten to sixteen storeys began to appear, and since the 1980s, twenty-storey and higher tower blocks have been built. Residential density in the new housing areas has also increased from 500 to 1,000 persons per hectare. In recent years, most apartment buildings have been built with standardized prefabricated systems. Major components,

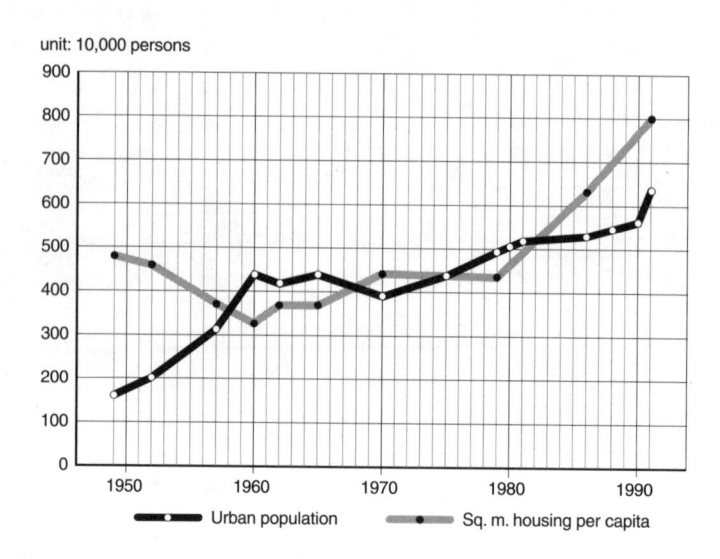

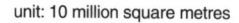

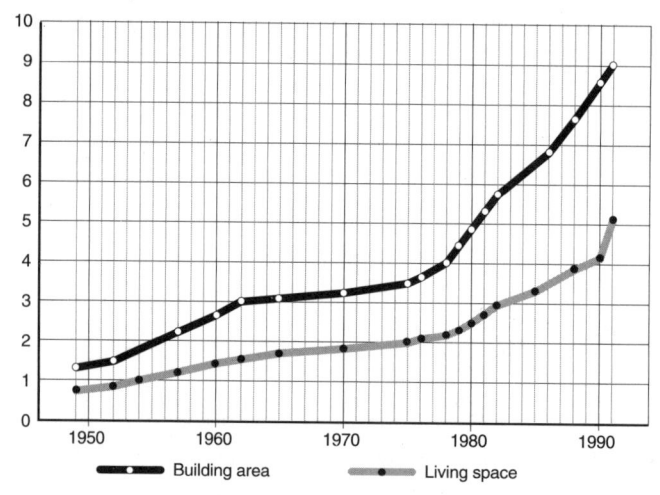

46 *Residential Development and the Renewal of Derelict Houses*

Figure 3.2 **Urban growth in Beijing:**
Increase of population and housing floorspace (1950-90)
Source: Diagrams by Professor Zhao Bingshi, Tsinghua University Department of Urban Planning and Design, c.1991.

including floors, walls, ceilings, windows, doors, balconies, and staircases, are manufactured products. Prefabrication, which minimizes the amount of on-site construction work and allows centralized quality control, does reduce costs; however, it does not improve the visual form or social function of the buildings.

Since 1949, most housing construction has taken place in the newly developed areas outside the Old City and in the industrial satellite towns in the suburbs. Housing renewal in the Old City proceeded in ad hoc infill fashion. To meet the pressing demand for housing within the Old City, many traditional courtyard houses had to be demolished to make way for multi-storey apartments. Conservation has become a difficult problem in the traditional areas. On the one hand, good quality courtyard houses are likely to be occupied with wealthier or more powerful work units, which tend to have resources to redevelop them; on the other hand, old houses in very poor condition are often neglected and continue to deteriorate because they are usually owned by weak work units or the local government property management bureau, whose resources are inadequate even for basic maintenance. Consequently, the appearance of many historic areas in the Old City has been radically altered, both from above and from below.

Statistical surveys during 1990 and 1991 provide some sense of the extent of Beijing's poor housing conditions. In 1990, a detailed six-month survey to identify the derelict housing areas in all eight of the central urban and near-suburban districts of Beijing revealed that there was a total of over 21 million square metres of single-storey houses in the Old City – 44 percent of the total one-storey housing area in all eight districts.[2] According to the grading system used by the Municipal Property Management Bureau, any housing that is of Grade 3, 4, or 5 quality was considered "old and dilapidated," or derelict, and most of this was single-storey housing.[3] Areas with high concentrations of derelict houses were designated as renewal areas. Nearly three-quarters of all derelict housing was located in the Old City in 128 renewal areas, which amounted to 6.3 million square metres of residential floor area. Another 3.9 million square metres of derelict housing area were scattered in other areas.

According to Ministry of Construction building standards, another estimate in 1991 for seven of the eight central urban and near-suburban districts concluded that there were 16 million square metres of derelict housing. Some 10.5 million square metres of this was concentrated in 221 parcels that occupied 21 square kilometres in total. Within the Old City, there were an estimated 8 million square metres of derelict housing, occupying 16 square kilometres, in which approximately 800,000 people lived.[4] In all the surveys that have been made of Beijing's derelict housing areas, most are located along the site of the former city walls and city gates, where the Second Ring Road passes, and outside the walls of the Temple of Heaven (Figure 3.3). Historically, these areas were slums, and although public housing schemes were implemented after 1949, not all of the poor housing was eliminated.

The general conditions of the infrastructure and services in and around the housing renewal areas are inadequate, and most of the houses have no

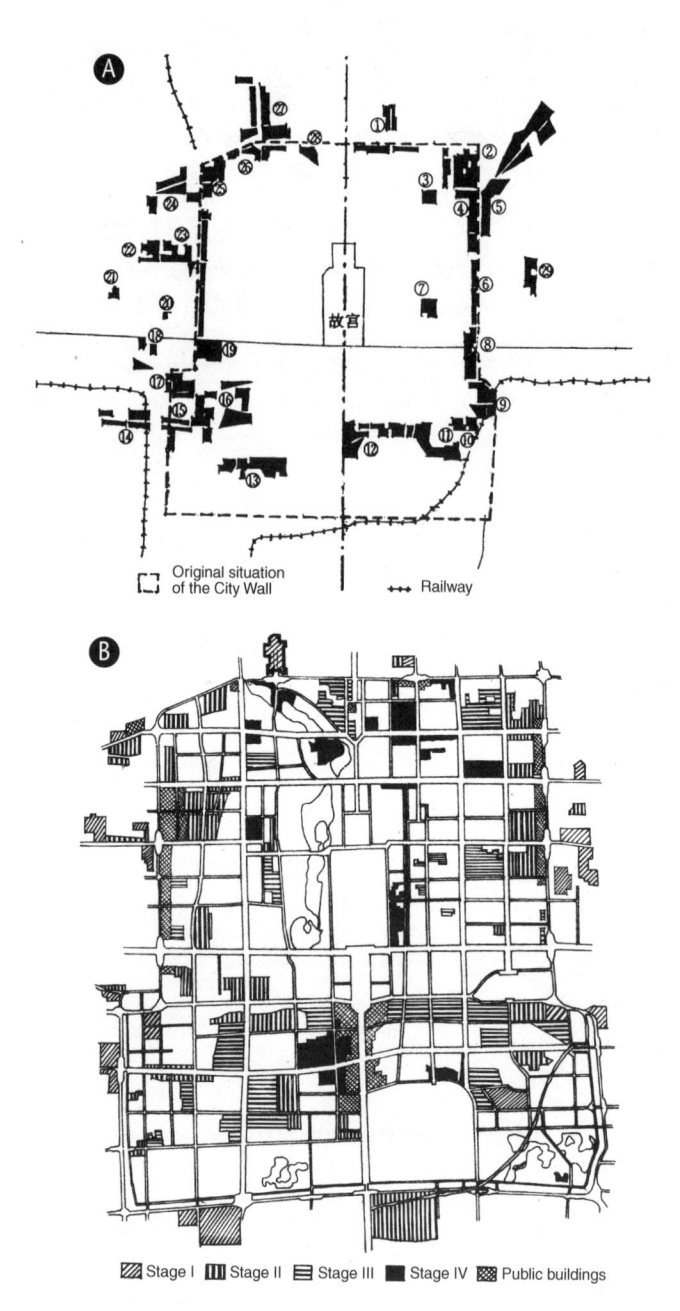

48 Residential Development and the Renewal of Derelict Houses

Figure 3.3 **Distribution of derelict housing in Beijing.**
(A) Twenty-nine areas of derelict housing. (B) Phasing Plan for the Old and Dilapidated Housing Renewal Program.
Source: (A) Zhang and Li 1996, 153; (B) Tsinghua University Urban Planning Group 1996, 196.

direct water supply, sewerage, proper kitchens, or other basic facilities of modern life. The road conditions in some of these areas remain extremely poor. The areas lack open space, and the high population density results in serious overcrowding. In many families, three generations have to share one room. Countless young married people have no choice but to live separately from their spouses due to the lack of accommodation. A survey by the West City District Government in 1991 reported that 8.8 percent of the families have a per capita floor space of less than two square metres. Seventeen percent of the families were identified as having housing difficulties, and another 12.4 percent were experiencing some form of inconvenience.[5]

Several economic and social factors have caused the difficulties in the derelict housing areas. First, the residents are usually employed by district-owned work units which, in the past forty years, had little or no resources to improve housing provisions. Second, some of the residents are immigrants who have been unable to find suitable accommodation. Some returned to Beijing from the army or were reassigned to work there; others returned after having been forced to leave during the Cultural Revolution. The overall scarcity of housing meant that these newly established residents were placed at the very end of a long waiting list for better housing. Third, in recent years the divorce rate has risen remarkably in the city, and increasing rates of family break-up have aggravated the problem. Fourth, as no further accommodation has become available to the expanding families of retired workers from the district-owned units, overcrowding has resulted.[6]

Three Stages of Housing Renewal in the Old City

First Stage: 1950s

Housing problems in Beijing's Old City are partly inherited from pre-1949 slums and are partly due to inappropriate policies applied over the last forty years. Prior to 1949, there were 17 million square metres of building stock in the walled city, more than 11 million square metres of which was housing. The area of derelict buildings accounted for 0.8 million square metres, or 5 percent of the total, among which 0.6 to 0.7 million square metres was housing. Traditionally, housing forms in Beijing were mostly single-storey courtyard houses. Each courtyard complex was either owned by one rich family or shared by many poor families. Housing conditions were the poorest immediately outside the city gates, where people with very low incomes lived; many of these houses were badly constructed and maintained.

Since the early 1950s, the city government has made a great effort to improve housing conditions. Between 1949 and 1956, when China underwent "Three Years of Economic Recovery" and the "First Five-Year Plan," Beijing saw the beginning of housing development. However, owing to the economic conditions at that time, housing had a much lower priority than did industrial and agricultural development. The scale of new housing construction was small and the building standards low. In terms of existing housing, the policy was to fully reuse the building stock. Rent collected from existing housing was used first to meet the needs of building maintenance and to improve infrastructure. Some slum areas were redeveloped, too (e.g., Longxugou in the south of the city).

Second Stage: 1960s and 1970s

Under the influence of leftist policy from the late 1950s to the late 1970s, housing was regarded only as social welfare and was classified as a non-productive sector. Rent was reduced three times since 1958, when investment in infrastructure, also classified as non-productive, began to shrink as well. The lowest rent, 0.12 *yuan* per square metre per month, was equal to the price of a pack of cheap cigarettes. The low rent collected could not pay for repairing the existing housing stock, and there was no fund for new housing construction. In the meantime, the residential population in the Old City grew rapidly.

During the Cultural Revolution, normal economic and physical planning was abandoned. Urban development in Beijing was also left in a state of stagnation and chaos. While some unplanned, poor-quality development took place without sufficient investment in infrastructure, severe neglect ensured that the number of derelict houses increased considerably. Between 1966 and 1974, the Old City saw a total construction of 2 million square metres, about half of which was housing. Most housing projects were carried out with no overall plan. At first, the simple two- to three-storey housing blocks built earlier were renovated to accommodate more families, but the low construction standards later caused endless maintenance problems for the district housing authorities. Then, traditional houses began to be demolished to make way for five- to six-storey apartment blocks, which could provide almost three times as much living space as could the old stock. Two-thirds of the new stock was to be allocated to the original residents and one-third was used to accommodate families from elsewhere. Although construction standards were substantially raised, the higher residential density of the new buildings caused further strain on infrastructure, including water, gas, heating, electricity, and sewerage, all of which saw little expansion. These apartment blocks were also damaging to the physical order of the city and will continue to be obstacles to the restoration of the Old City's visual quality.

Third Stage: 1970s and 1980s

Since the mid-1970s attention has been paid to the housing crisis in Beijing. Between 1973 and 1976, some residential development took place, including high-rise housing along Qiansanmen Street. After the Cultural

Revolution, comprehensive housing development policies came into force; however, three of these were harmful to the city. First, since 1974, development control was relaxed and work units were allowed to develop housing on their own premises. Second, after the Tangshan earthquake, extensions were encouraged within the existing courtyards in order to ease the housing shortage. It was estimated that temporary shelters covering 2 million square metres were erected in this way. As a result, only one-fifth of the courtyard houses remain in reasonable shape now. Third, for some time, high-rise buildings, which severely damaged the visual quality of the Old City, were favoured.

Between 1974 and 1986, the Old City saw the construction of about 7 million square metres of new housing, which represented 70 percent of the city's total new housing development since 1949. Development on such a scale within this limited area had a serious impact on the Old City's overall structure, land-use pattern, and historic sights. Many princely mansions and good courtyard houses were destroyed or altered completely, and the city's environmental quality deteriorated considerably. In some areas, housing development was not accompanied by the necessary service provision; existing municipal utilities and schools were overloaded. The uncontrolled infill development, especially with high-rise blocks, destroyed the traditional vistas and blocked visual corridors. "The horizontal and open spaces of the Old City and their leafy environment are disappearing amidst the apartment blocks."[7]

The high-rise developments in particular have most altered the visual cityscape. By 1989, 1,000 high-rise blocks were completed and 800 were under construction throughout Beijing proper. High-rise buildings cost more, occupy more space during construction, take longer to build, and are expensive to operate and maintain. During the 1980s, it became clear that high density may be achieved without high-rise buildings. At the end of 1989, the Beijing Municipal Government declared that no more high-rise development was to take place within the Old City, which was defined as the area inside the Second Ring Road.

Renewal of Derelict Housing in Housing Reform

Renewal of Derelict Housing and Development of New Residential Areas

The Old City occupies a mere 62 square kilometres, and yet, in the past forty years, too many industries, government offices, and commercial enterprises have concentrated there, causing heavy congestion and deterioration of environmental quality. To a certain extent, new construction in the near suburbs has helped to ease the pressure on the city core. The suburbs have attracted both people and employment away from the Old City, and population density has begun to drop. Since the 1980s, the Beijing Municipal Government has built thirty-five new residential clusters, or estates, of over 30,000 square metres each according to the principles of "comprehensive development."[8] In the near suburbs, more residential development is on the way; such new construction will further decentralize the population and help with the renewal of derelict housing in the Old City.

At the end of April 1990, the Beijing Municipal Government selected the first group of thirty-seven areas of derelict housing for renewal (twenty-two were within the Old City, eleven were in the near suburbs, and four were in the far suburbs). The total area covered 340 hectares, in which there were 1.6 million square metres of derelict housing occupied by 50,000 families. By autumn 1991, work was begun in twenty-seven areas: seventeen in the Old City, six in the near suburbs, and four in the far suburbs.

Renewal and Housing Economics
Generally speaking, housing development in Beijing was slow, mainly because low rent and welfare policies retarded the growth of a healthy market. Today, the chief obstacle to renewal is still lack of funds. It is estimated that there are about fifteen to twenty square kilometres in the Old City that need to be redeveloped or renovated and that this requires a total of 42 to 60 billion *yuan*. It seems that only with housing reform and commercialization will this be possible. Housing reform was initiated as early as 1978, when the central government encouraged local governments, work units, and individuals to invest in housing provisions together with the state. This contrasted with the previous sole dependence on state funding, which fell far short of needs. The new system provides incentives to investment from non-state sources. In 1987, the Beijing Municipal Government initiated some experimental projects to test the technical feasibility of various renewal approaches. These projects included Ju'er Hutong, Xiaohoucang, Dongnanyuan, and Debao. Several more approaches to financing have emerged since then. Outlined below are the measures that were first introduced in the pilot projects of the late 1980s and that have since remained the basis of most housing renewal projects in the Old City of Beijing.

First, the low-rent welfare housing provision was replaced by private ownership. Original residents were encouraged to buy their own redeveloped apartments at a preferential price that only covered the basic cost. They could pay in one lump sum and enjoy a 20 percent discount or pay in instalments over a period not exceeding ten years. Low-interest loans were made available at approved banks. At the same time, some residents could buy or rent their new housing units in the original neighbourhood through their employers. In such cases, the employers could either pay for the housing or provide a substantial subsidy. Those families who wished to move back but were too poor to purchase their new units could rent the new flats.

The rent was usually kept low, but they or their employers were required to pay a lease deposit of fifty to eighty *yuan* per square metre. The deposit was used to supplement development capital, and the interest on the deposit was retained by the owner as a supplement to the rent. The deposit would be refunded when the tenants left. For a long time, rent only covered one-fifth of maintenance costs, which led to poorly managed housing stock. Funding to sustain the existing stock continues to fall short, as does financing for expansion. A continued increase in home ownership by residents of the Old City should help to improve funding for both maintenance and development. By the end of August 1991, for example, the West City District had raised more than 10 million *yuan* through sales and leasing to original residents, of which 3.8 million *yuan* was in sales receipts and 4.5 million *yuan* was in lease deposits.[9]

A second component of the program was to offer favourable terms to those who were willing to move to suburban areas. Because of the rent differential in the city core and the suburbs, the housing units given up by the original residents could be leased or sold at a price higher than the payment for their resettlement, which increased capital for development. In the housing renewal areas, some families could be rehoused in the original neighbourhood after redevelopment, as described above, while others, who could not afford the new units in the redeveloped neighbourhood even at the preferential price, were given the option of paying less for larger units in suburban areas. These suburban units are usually developed or brokered by the developer of the renewal project. For households that could not afford to remain in the redeveloped neighbourhood and did not wish to move to the suburbs, a third option was to exchange their right to a unit in the redeveloped neighbourhood directly with another household in the Old City.

A third component was the developer's ability to sell or lease the units not taken by the original residents as commodity housing on the property market. The sale and leasing of commodity housing and office space became another effective way of obtaining financial resources for renewal. For example, 63 percent of the total investment in Xiaohoucang and 85 percent of the total investment in Debao was recovered through the sale of commercial space and commodity housing on their redeveloped sites. In another renewal project in the Wanmingsi neighbourhood, commodity housing alone recovered 86 percent of the total investment. Due to emerging differences in land value, housing prices can change dramatically from place to place. By 1993, commodity housing in the Old City was renting at 3,500 *yuan* per square metre or more, while in the near suburbs it was renting at about 2,500 *yuan*. By 1997, the lower-end commodity housing rents had increased by almost three times. However, those new apartments in redeveloped inner-city neighbourhoods sold to the original residents must still be offered at preferential prices of as little as 600 *yuan* per square metre. There is an incentive, therefore, from both the developer's and the government's point of view, to limit the number of original residents who may return: the more units sold as commodity housing, the more funds can be raised for profit and further redevelopment.

Finally, the government offers certain preferential policies to the developer in order to reduce the cost of redevelopment. As redevelopment in the Old City involves many problems, the role of the government is significant. Efficient management and a legal framework are crucial, especially in large-scale relocation work. The government's preferential policies could include interest-free loans for the preliminary work, tax incentives for property development, and reduction of infrastructure charges. All of the residents' employers are also required to contribute financially to the redevelopment; the amount of the contribution depends upon how the residents are to be resettled afterwards. Moreover, housing cooperatives are emerging as a new form of Old City neighbourhood redevelopment. In the first phase of the Ju'er Hutong project, a housing cooperative was set up with an initiative from the East City District government. Its membership was limited to the residents in the designated renewal areas who joined by paying a deposit every month as a share. They were given priority with regard to purchasing housing according to an index that took into account their financial contribution, length of membership, length of employment, age, living conditions, and so on. The municipal government has also issued special preferential policies for housing cooperatives.

Problems and Future Development

Main Problems

While Beijing has made remarkable progress in renewing dilapidated housing in the Old City in recent years, many problems have also emerged. The lack of state funding is one of the most serious concerns. The central government has given Beijing 200 million *yuan* to finance its various Old City redevelopment projects, but, in the end, each project has a very limited fund. The current housing reform program creates excessively high prices – prices that, even taking into consideration preferential rates, are too high to enable most residents to buy the redeveloped housing units. Many residents tend to apply for a lease instead. To balance accounts, the developers have to build as much floor area as is permitted and to encourage original residents to move out so that more units may be sold at market prices. As a result, most of the projects have a high building density and a poor environment. In addition, unclear lines of responsibility between the various levels of government and the development agencies, and the speed with which most projects are implemented, has kept infrastructure improvement chronically lagging behind housing development. The lack of funds further diminishes any hope for upgrading services in the neighbourhoods. Even new suburban development lacks proper infrastructure facilities, services, and schools, and this exacerbates residents' reluctance to move out, despite the incentives offered by municipal authorities and developers.[10]

Recommendations for Future Development
Current inner-city neighbourhood redevelopment is mainly managed by the district governments; there is poor coordination at the municipal level. Stronger coordination among different redevelopment programs can provide a better financial base for the large-scale improvement of existing infrastructure and services. The central government is also expected to provide more loans to the programs and to take more responsibility for infrastructure work. Another area in need of improvement is the infrastructure facilities in the old areas; this should be planned differently from the new areas in order to make the best use of existing facilities. Property management is a new problem arising from current housing reform. Mixed property ownership has emerged in the newly redeveloped neighbourhoods, and this requires a new management approach to facilitate further development and maintenance of infrastructure. Finally, the improvement of old housing stock not yet developed should not be overlooked. The renewal program, because of its huge scale, will require ten years or more to complete, even if it continues at optimal speed. This suggests that many houses have to be maintained in the meantime. Effective financial and technical measures are also required for this end.

4
Organic Renewal in Historic Cities

Regarding the rehabilitation of the Old City of Beijing, there are two different attitudes that naturally lead to two different approaches. The first approach insists that, in spite of the historic value of the Old City, it cannot meet the demands of today's life and, therefore, it must be rebuilt completely. The second approach, that of "organic renewal," recognizes that certain aspects of the Old City's urban structure have lasting value, and it seeks to preserve them by adapting them to modern life. This approach seeks to establish a new organic order based on adaptation rather than on complete replacement.

Housing is a critical component of the fabric and texture of a city. The Italian scholar Alvise Caruaro pointed out four centuries ago that the magnificence of Venice was not only composed of grand monuments, but also of numerous simple and modest houses and dwellings (Figure 4.1).[1] Similarly, the City of Amsterdam has a unique urban style of great diversity, despite the very simple housing floor plans and regular layout of the residential quarters (Figure 4.2). Beijing is no exception. While the colourful appearance of Venice and Amsterdam derives from the richness in the detailing of their house facades, it is the infinitely variable and yet clearly identifiable spatial arrangements of courtyards and pavilions that provides the richness and splendour of Beijing's urban space. Even the plain and simple appearance of the humbler buildings plays a part by throwing into sharp relief the brilliance of the monumental edifices. This design heritage should not be overlooked.

Rethinking Urban Redevelopment Policies in Beijing

Neglect of Traditional Residential Areas
In many industrialized cities, large-scale development has led to serious environmental deterioration. Beijing is facing a similar situation. In the past forty years, many historic gardens and buildings have been destroyed, and new construction, especially of high-rise buildings, has threatened many

Figure 4.1 **Houses in Venice.** The basic floor plans of houses in Venice are limited in type, but there are rich variations in facade and articulation.
Source: Trincanato 1980.

important historic sites. In recognition of the need to preserve it, the State Council listed Beijing as an important historic city in 1982. The municipal government has also declared a development policy that aims both to protect the character of the historic capital and to achieve the goal of modernization that is stipulated in the master plan. However, according to the plan, half of the 40 square kilometres of built area in the Old City is to be renewed. The care taken in implementing this renewal is critical to the conservation of the Old City.

However, among the more than 200 buildings and sites listed for conservation, the protection of old imperial palaces, government offices, temples, gardens, and other major historic building complexes has received most of the attention, while the conservation of traditional residential areas has hardly been seen as an issue.[2] In particular, conservation of courtyard houses

Figure 4.2 **Houses in Amsterdam.** The houses along the canals have similar floor plans and yet rich variations in the design of gables.

has always been controversial because even those who advocated protection could not produce any practical solutions. Although the Master Plan of Beijing designates some quarters as "courtyard house conservation areas" (such as the Nan Luogu Xiang block in which Ju'er Hutong is located), their total floor space takes up a mere 300,000 square metres out of a total of 10 million square metres of old courtyard houses throughout the Old City.[3] The traditional housing outside the designated areas seems to have been totally abandoned to potential demolition. In fact, if no adequate measures are worked out, it will not be possible to preserve even the protected areas; for even as the development agencies are kept at bay, desperately overcrowded residents continue to fill in the courtyards and to rebuild the pavilions (Figure 4.3).

Designs for the redevelopment of old residential areas in Beijing mainly adopt the *xiao qu*, or housing estate model, which has been used widely in suburban development since the 1950s. In the great majority of cases, no design effort has been made to continue the order and structure of the traditional housing. The integrity of the historic areas is broken due to the ad hoc infill of multi-storey and high-rise buildings.

Large-Scale Demolition and Redevelopment

It has been generally expected for many years that when the day came, redevelopment would take the form of large-scale demolition and rebuilding. However, plan after plan was never realized because of the difficulty in raising sufficient funds. When a plan actually succeeded in breaking ground,

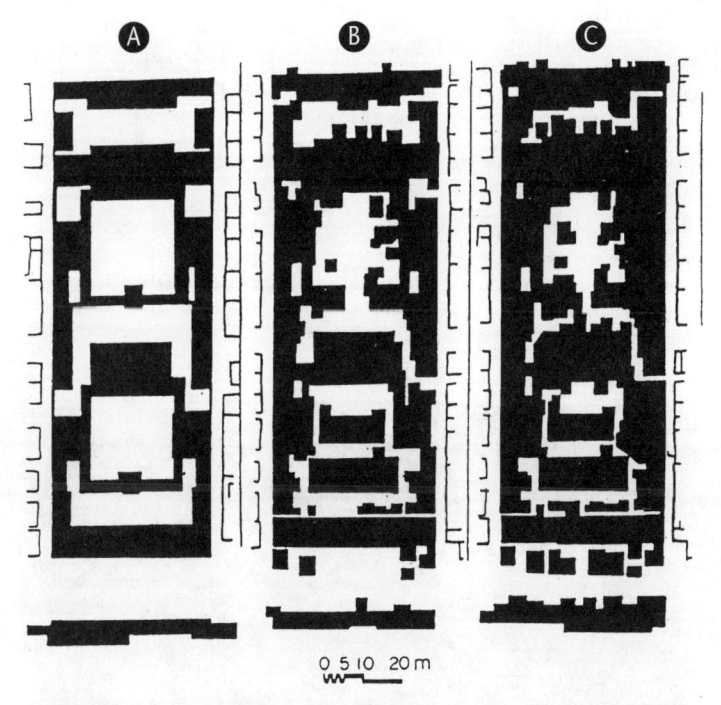

Figure 4.3 **Transformation of a courtyard house complex in Beijing.**
Ⓐ Early 1950s: floor space 2,440.5 m^2. A courtyard complex. Ⓑ Late 1970s: floor space 3,196.5 m^2, 131 percent of what it was in the early 1950s. Ⓒ 1987: floor space 3,786.5 m^2, 155 percent of what it was in the early 1950s. A courtyardless compound.
Source: Zhu and Fu 1988.

60 Organic Renewal in Historic Cities

invariably it was only partially implemented and left truncated – a few high-rise buildings looming chaotically over a jumble of old one-storey houses, reminding them, as it were, of their doom. In the Guanyuan neighbourhood, for example, a new estate was planned (as is shown in Figure 4.4), but only the tall slab buildings along its northernmost edge were ever built.

The high costs and unattractive results of this approach have made many rethink the large-scale redevelopment strategy, but unfortunately it remains the favoured approach of planning and construction authorities, who believe it is the fastest, cheapest, and most controllable way of achieving the required floor space. These same agencies, however, have failed to address the fact that ad hoc redevelopment is not only due to lack of adequate funds, it is also due to the power of particular central government agencies that, since the 1950s, have occupied the former princely residences and the

Figure 4.4 **Guanyuan xiao qu, located in the northwest corner of the Old City of Beijing.** Neither the uniform dwellings nor their layout in barracks-like rows in any way reflect their urban context. Unfortunately, this is a strong trend taking place all over the country.

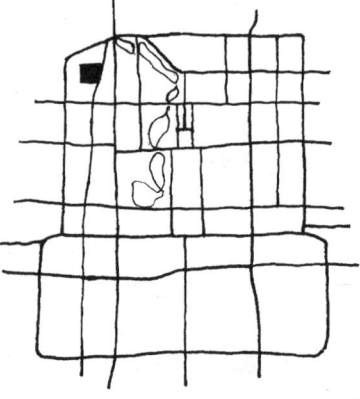

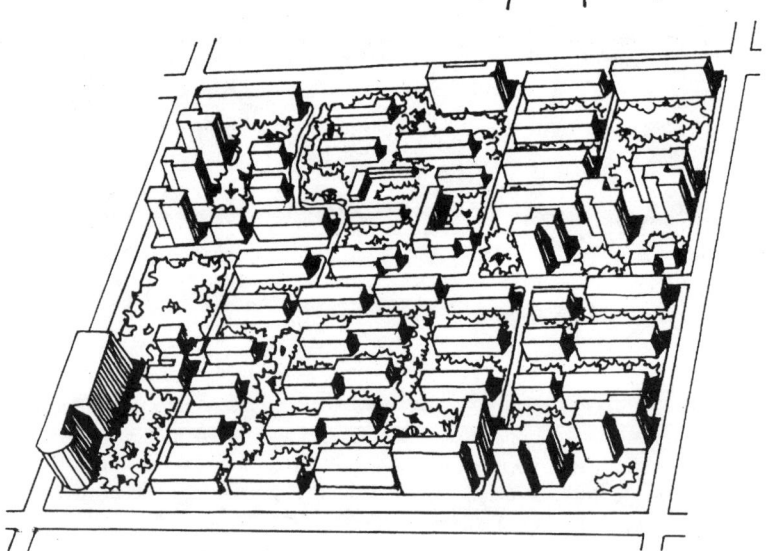

best and largest of the courtyard houses. Driven by their own requirements for expansion, these institutions have freely redeveloped the compounds under their control. The open spaces in the complexes fell victim to this process, and most of the old buildings were also demolished. Under these circumstances, neither the interests of conservation nor those of large-scale, planned redevelopment have been able to prevail.

For all the research and discussion that has been carried out concerning the problems of the former irrational housing and real estate management system, which is supposed to be reformed as part of the overall socio-economic restructuring, actual housing reform has only very recently begun to be implemented. Yet, no renewal methodology has been capable of integrating housing reform into the rehabilitation of historic housing areas. The time has come for a new strategy to be worked out – a strategy based on more profound theoretical thinking.

Theoretical Premises for Organic Renewal

Organic Renewal of the Physical Environment

Metaphorically speaking, the city is a living organism. Its components and tissues are always undergoing a metabolic process. The regeneration of urban tissues evolves with the survival of those elements that continue to be useful and relevant, and the elimination of those that are no longer suitable. Planned development should gradually and efficiently substitute, in a conscious way, the unsuitable with the suitable without seriously impairing the overall functioning of the city.

Over the past forty years, such an organic process has not been the norm in developing Beijing. A salient example is the deterioration of the old courtyard houses. In terms of building quality and historic value, the Old City can be classified into five types of environment: the first is areas where the most important historic buildings are located; the second is areas in which the traditional buildings are still in reasonably good condition; the third is areas of mixed building quality; the fourth is areas consisting mostly of run-down buildings; and the fifth is areas already redeveloped with multi-storey and high-rise buildings. The residential land area in types two, three, and four accounts for more than 65 percent of the total residential land in the Old City.[4] If solutions are worked out separately for each of these types, then a highly complex problem may be broken down into simpler parts, each of which can adopt a suitable strategy. With each type, rehabilitation may start from a small area proportional to the funds available, and the scale of work may be expanded until it is self-sustainable. This is the practical meaning of organic renewal (Figure 4.5).

Research into building and environmental quality in the Old City has helped to estimate the potential tasks, financial requirements, and the time

62 *Organic Renewal in Historic Cities*

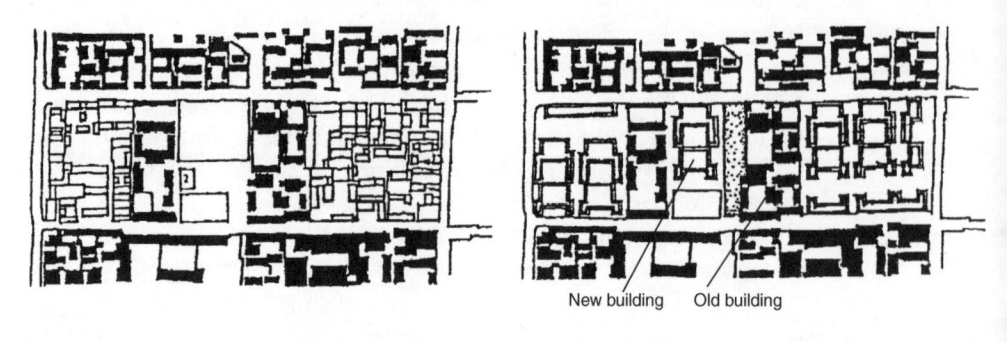

Existing neighbourhood ■ Retained old buildings

New building   Old building

Rehabilitation proposal

Ⓐ

Ⓑ

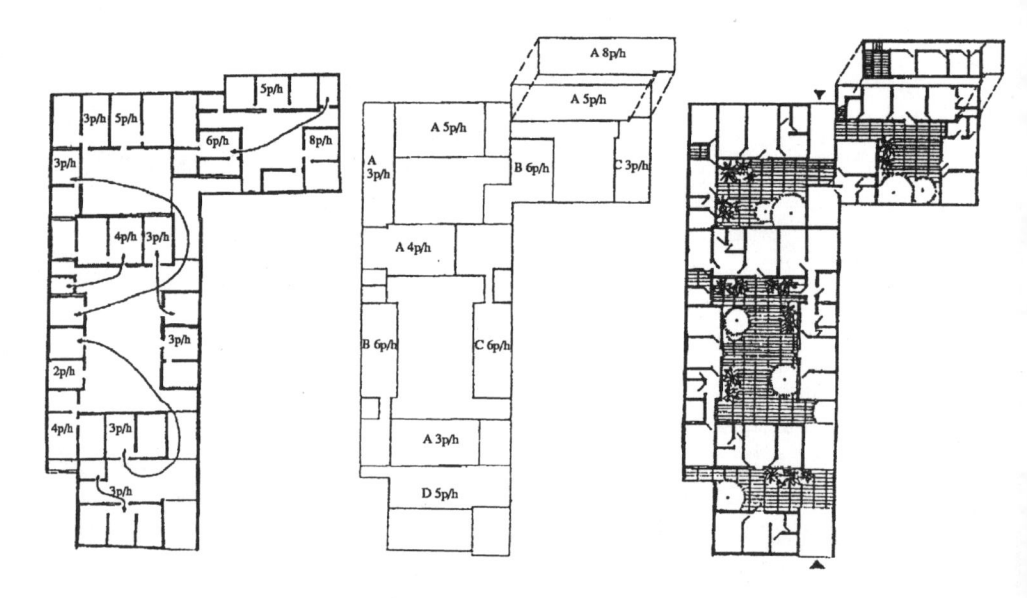

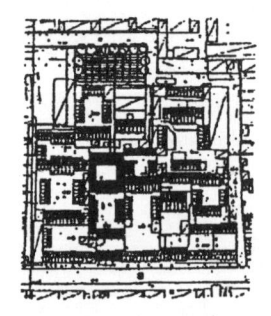

Figure 4.5 **Organic renewal in the Old City.**
The courtyard complexes of good building quality are retained and those of bad quality are replaced with new courtyard-type houses. **Ⓐ** Within one retained courtyard complex: old dilapidated buildings are to be replaced by groups of new courtyard-type houses. **Ⓑ** Further rationalization to improve living space for each household.

horizon needed for the renewal program. These tasks fall into three categories. First, the historically important buildings and local landmarks, including old trees, although already a small part of the historic areas, would require regular maintenance and, in certain cases, restoration. Second, buildings in very poor condition need to be demolished; their number is increasing year by year. Third, the rest of the stock, which falls into a grey area, needs to be treated differently from case to case. These three tasks require different renewal policies, according to the proportion of the buildings involved. There should be careful treatment, particularly for the third task, because many areas fall into this category.

As housing renewal in Beijing is a massive program that will last for more than ten years, many housing areas that are in need of redevelopment have to wait for a considerable period of time; thus, adequate maintenance can prolong their use. The residents of these areas are interested in self-help housing in order to improve their living conditions. In many run-down housing areas, about half of the residents have already extended their houses themselves. This kind of self-help may not be permissible under planning regulation, but it exists and plays an important role in the daily life of millions of ordinary residents. The municipal government should consider an effective policy to support it both financially and technically. The maintenance of existing houses not only helps to stop the derelict housing problems from becoming worse, but also contributes to the general improvement of the city environment.

In 1987, a survey of housing conditions in three courtyard house complexes in the Guozijian neighbourhood showed that the cost of rehabilitation was only one-fifth that of redevelopment. Although the rehabilitation proposed in the survey was not implemented, a similar approach to rehabilitation succeeded in Suzhou and proved to be practical.[5] Good-quality buildings, like good-quality clothes, should be used and reused. As the traditional Chinese saying has it: "Wear it new three years, wear it old three years, mend it and wear it for yet another three years." This is just as true of an entire urban structure, which is constantly being used and inhabited, as it is of clothes.

Therefore, besides applying to traditional housing areas, the principles outlined above could also be applied to the maintenance and rehabilitation of historic areas as a whole. This includes tourist areas, urban regions where land use is undergoing great transition, areas affected by new and large-scale development, and areas suffering from blight and dereliction. Similar attention, moreover, should be given not only to buildings, but also to public space and infrastructure; for example, in some parts of Beijing the drainage system built during the Ming dynasty is still in use.

Organic Renewal of the Socio-Economic Structure

The reader may have noted by this point that the concept of organic renewal owes much to the work of Jane Jacobs following the drastic slum clearance and urban renewal programs implemented in American cities in the middle of this century.[6] It is important to point out, however, that the concept of "urban blight," and its associated causes and problems (which so concerned Jacobs), is less clearly understood in the Chinese context. Jacobs's writings highlight the relationship between the deteriorating physical environment in blighted areas and the consequent loss of tax revenues, the increase in government subsidies, and the worsening of crime and social delinquency. In offering a solution to these problems, she suggests that a program that avoids "cataclysmic" investment in urban renewal can help to regenerate the local economy at a grassroots level and raise the general standard of living.

In today's Beijing, we are seeing precisely the scale and mode of renewal that Jacobs condemned. However, the consequences of this approach for Beijing's revenues, neighbourhood economies, and crime rates are even more difficult to ascertain than were its consequences for New York's. This is because Beijing and China are undergoing a social and economic transformation that is even more profound than that being experienced by American cities. But it is precisely this uncertainty that dictates a cautious, experimental, and reflective approach to Beijing's renewal. The city's development is closely related to its political, economic, social, and cultural activities. In the midst of a great transformation, the cultural and aesthetic value of Beijing's historic environment is one of the surest and most constant factors to consider. We can be certain that the radical political, economic, and social changes being experienced in Beijing will affect the city's physical environment in a dramatic manner. These changes need to be understood in our pursuit for the city's successful renewal.

An Organic Order through Continuous Organic Renewal

A Sustainable Development Strategy

In the context of rapid change, the concept of sustainability is particularly useful as a guide to urban development. The term, formally put forward by Madame Brundtland of the United Nations in 1987, is widely accepted with regard to the conservation of the natural environment.[7] It may be applied equally with regard to the conservation and development of the built environment. Sustainable development, in this context, means that the built environment achieves harmony with nature, that people's living standards are improving gradually but continuously, that urban infrastructure and land use are regulated according to the local ecological context, and that solutions to current problems do not create greater future problems.

Organic renewal is part of the sustainable development strategy. It recommends a suitable scale of development, humane design, and coordination of present and future needs. Although the ideas of organic renewal and conservation have been developed through a series of studies and projects in Beijing since the 1950s, past urban policies tended to favour large-scale development and rapid results. In fact, housing renewal is such a complex matter that many aspects need to be studied further, including planning and design, revenue raising, construction, maintenance, and evaluation of outcomes.

Towards a New Organic Order
Conservation of the physical order does not imply a negative attitude towards development in the present. On the contrary, successful conservation may only be achieved through well planned development. Even from the aesthetic point of view, it would be undesirable to maintain the Old City in some "pristine" historic state, even if this were possible; rather, new construction need only respect certain basic rules and structures that allow some sense of order to continue into the future. There are, therefore, two points to bear in mind when considering the preservation of Beijing's beauty. First, the monumental buildings, such as those in the Forbidden City, Temple of Heaven, Jingshan Hill, and the Three Seas, have been protected and will not be directly affected by neighbourhood redevelopment. Second, these monuments cannot retain their full glory without an overall sense of spatial order across the Old City. Similar aesthetic principles should, therefore, be followed in both redevelopment and rehabilitation. The design of individual new buildings should attempt a high level of expressiveness and be worthy of the historic tradition and the spirit of the place. New buildings should also, on the other hand, harmonize with the historic context so as to enhance, rather than weaken, the physical order already in existence. Such principles were summarized in classical Chinese aesthetics as "harmony with diversity, and contrast without chaos."[8]

Of course, the Old City was functionally much simpler in the past. Its former building technology, infrastructure requirements, and land-use needs cannot compare to what is needed today. The variation and diversity of physical forms currently surrounding us reflect the heterogeneity of modern urban life; they present us with a trying problem, while simultaneously providing us with many opportunities for solving it. Perhaps this is what most deeply challenges planners today.[9] The following chapter outlines the basic rules and structures within which new neighbourhood planning and housing design should be attempted if the Old City of Beijing is to become both harmonious and diverse.

5
Traditional Courtyard Houses and a New Prototype

While the promotion of organic renewal is one of my chief urban planning goals, the creation of a new courtyard house prototype is one of my chief architectural goals. The courtyard house is a popular form of architecture that can be found in many countries besides China – from India, across Asia, to the Mediterranean, and even in Latin America. Among the features that distinguish the Chinese courtyard house is its evolution: it has had a particularly close relationship with the planned layout of irrigation channels, settlements, markets, and street grids. This is especially true of the Beijing courtyard house – the *siheyuan*. The formation of the residential neighbourhoods of Beijing generally follow a hierarchical fish-bone-shaped structure of access, from major street to small lane (*hutong*) to courtyard house, that extends in a systematic way from the most public spaces to the most private. This urban layout, combined with the characteristic low, undulating, and tree-dominated roofscape, is what most distinguishes Beijing from the cities of the West. These features, therefore, are what need to be respected and maintained in any new development within the Old City if Beijing is to preserve its unique character.

The Grid System in Historic Chinese Cities
As is the case for Beijing's overall urban form, Beijing's neighbourhood layout can be traced back deep into Chinese urban history. In historic Chinese cities, the prevalence of a grid system is perhaps related to the *jingtian*, or "well and field," system used in ancient times.[1] Despite the lack of agreement among historians about the definition and significance of the *jingtian* system, some hypotheses may be put forward for discussion.

Land Division
Land development requires construction of roads, ditches, and bridges, which in flat areas would be most easily accomplished in a grid pattern. Such a chess-board pattern is reflected in the ancient oracle bone (*jiaguwen*)

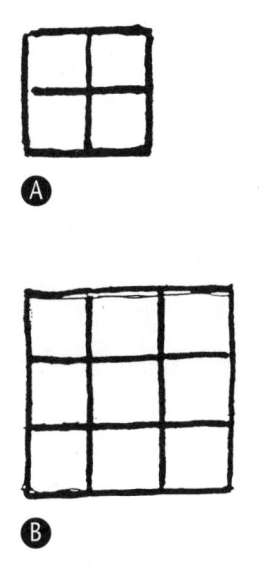

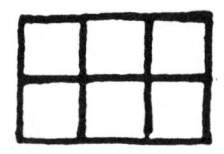

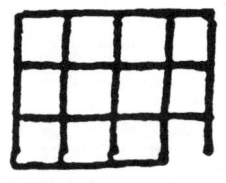

Figure 5.1 **Gridiron patterns derived from division of farmland.** **A** Various forms of ancient Chinese inscriptions for the character *tian*, or field. **B** The nine-square division, which could have been used as the basic division in Chinese cities of antiquity. **C** The remaining patterns of Roman land division (*centuriato*) can still be clearly identified in the north suburb of Imola, Italy. The remains of *centuriato* can be seen on plains throughout the Roman Empire. Much of the gridiron division was kept long after the ancient farming system ceased to exist and can still be detected along the boundaries of estates and the alignment of roads and canals.
Source: (C) Benevolo 1980, 215.

inscriptions for "field" (*tian*) (Figure 5.1).² Such geometric patterns were also employed by many other ancient civilizations outside China.³

Unit of Cultivation

In *Tianxia Junguo Libishu*, Gu Yanwu noted that even up to the mid-Ming dynasty (fifteenth to sixteenth century) in Fengyang, Anhui Province, the ancient organization of cultivation was still in use.⁴ "Every five households share one well; each household has five people, and is granted fifty *mu* of land."⁵ Five households thus had two hundred and fifty *mu* of their own land to cultivate. There were also fifty *mu* of public land, which the five households cooperatively cultivated.⁶ Thus land division was related to the organization of agriculture (Figure 5.2).

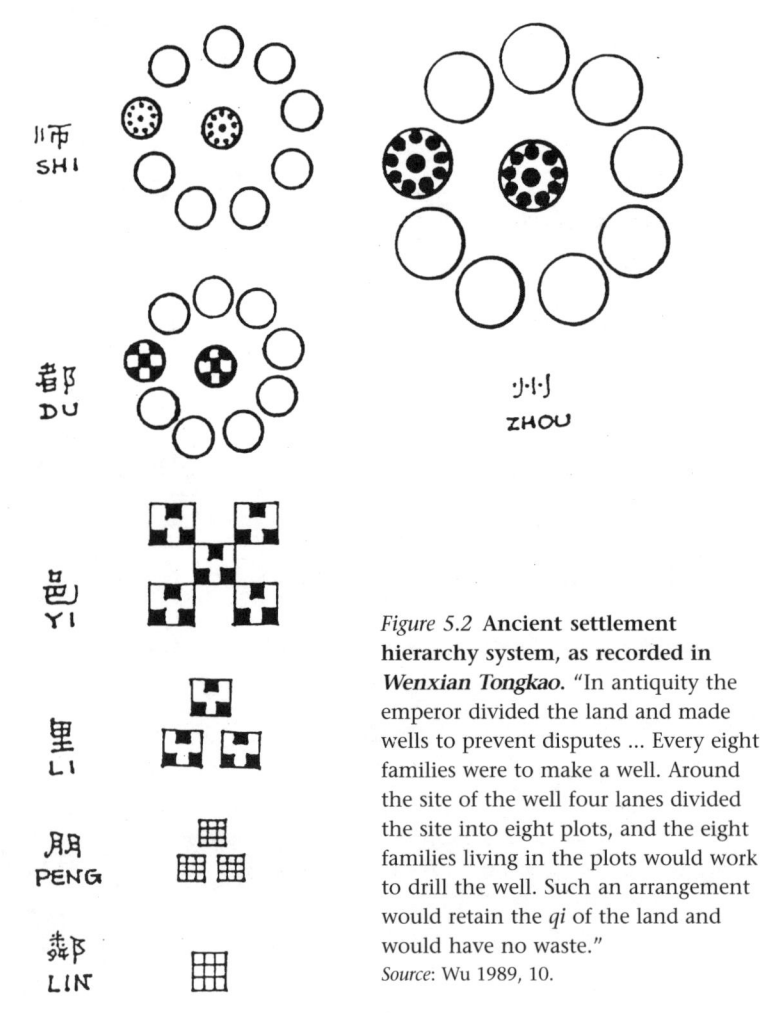

Figure 5.2 **Ancient settlement hierarchy system, as recorded in *Wenxian Tongkao*.** "In antiquity the emperor divided the land and made wells to prevent disputes … Every eight families were to make a well. Around the site of the well four lanes divided the site into eight plots, and the eight families living in the plots would work to drill the well. Such an arrangement would retain the *qi* of the land and would have no waste."
Source: Wu 1989, 10.

Unit of Settlement

It would be natural to assume that the pattern of land division in the fields was adopted in the layout of early settlements, but the evidence that can be gathered today is primarily philological. The excavation of ancient city sites has also confirmed the widespread use of the grid form in cities of that time. The Royal City (*Wangcheng*) schema, as recorded in *Kaogongji* – in particular its nine-square pattern – bears formal resemblance to the *jingtian* pattern.[7]

Jingshi: The Place of Trade and Exchange

It is no accident that *jing*, meaning "well," forms part of the word *jingtian*. The well provides water, which is essential to human life. It is not uncommon to find a neighbourhood centred around a well. Some historians suggest that the word *hutong*, for "lane," was derived from the word "well" in the Mongolian language during the Yuan dynasty.[8] Before 1949, the built urban area of Beijing contained over 3,000 streets, alleys, and *hutong*, of which 87 had the word "well" (*jing*) in their names.[9] The significance of the well in a neighbourhood unit also lies in the fact that it was one of the most natural places for people to gather; this, in turn, led to trade and exchange. This role can be seen in many different cultures (Figure 5.3).[10]

It is perhaps fair to say that the "nine-square" pattern is a very important source of Chinese settlement form, however complicated the connections and evolutionary processes have been. The traditional prototypes of buildings and building complexes have evolved for hundreds, and even thousands, of years based on such perceptions of rectangular forms. Knowledge of these forms is an essential prerequisite to the understanding of built forms in the historic neighbourhoods and the buildings contained in them.

From Wards to Neighbourhoods

The Transformation of Residential Quarters

The long history of the courtyard house prototype is illustrated by the remains of a courtyard house excavated in Zhouyuan, Shaanxi Province (Figure 5.4). It was developed over thousands of years in the grid settlement structure and has long been the basic element in the traditional neighbourhood.[11] In ancient China, the residential quarters in the city were called *lüli*; a *li* refers to a group of courtyard houses aligned in some form. The residential quarters from the Han dynasty (206 BC-AD 220) to the Tang dynasty (AD 618-907) took the form of wards, which were large walled street blocks. Gates of a ward would open to the streets during daytime and close at night. Only the ruling elite was entitled to have direct access to the street. Within the ward there were lanes of alleyways providing access to individual houses. Such wards, called *fangli*, were the basic units of the residential quarters in

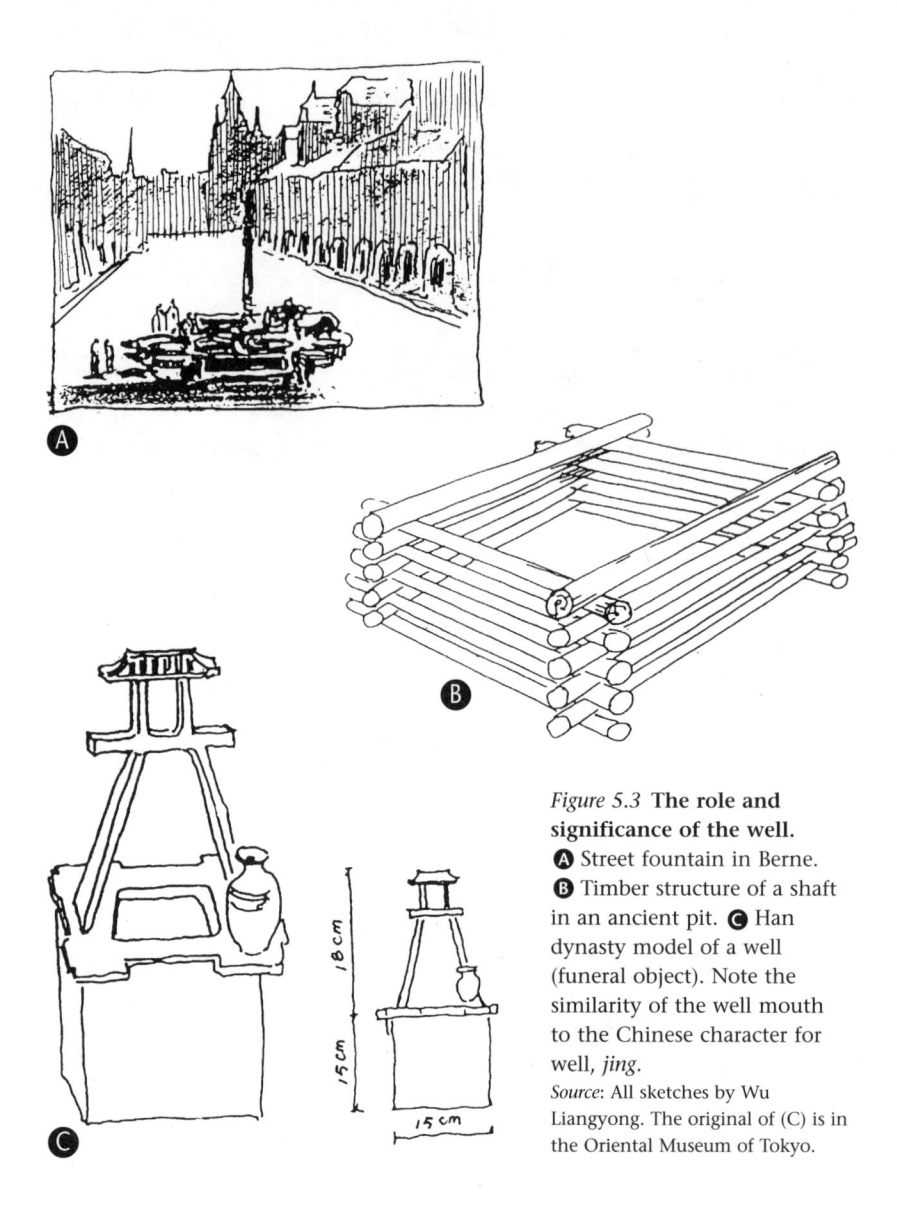

Figure 5.3 **The role and significance of the well.**
Ⓐ Street fountain in Berne.
Ⓑ Timber structure of a shaft in an ancient pit. **Ⓒ** Han dynasty model of a well (funeral object). Note the similarity of the well mouth to the Chinese character for well, *jing*.
Source: All sketches by Wu Liangyong. The original of (C) is in the Oriental Museum of Tokyo.

the city. For example, Luoyang in the Northern Wei dynasty had 320 *fangli*, and Chang'an in the Tang dynasty had 108 *fangli*. As a result of the city being laid out in wards, its inhabitants were put under effective control.

From the late Tang dynasty, however, the ward system was no longer strictly applied. In the early period of the following Song dynasty, the development of trade and commerce in the cities started to transform the *fangli* system. While the administrative structure of the wards remained,

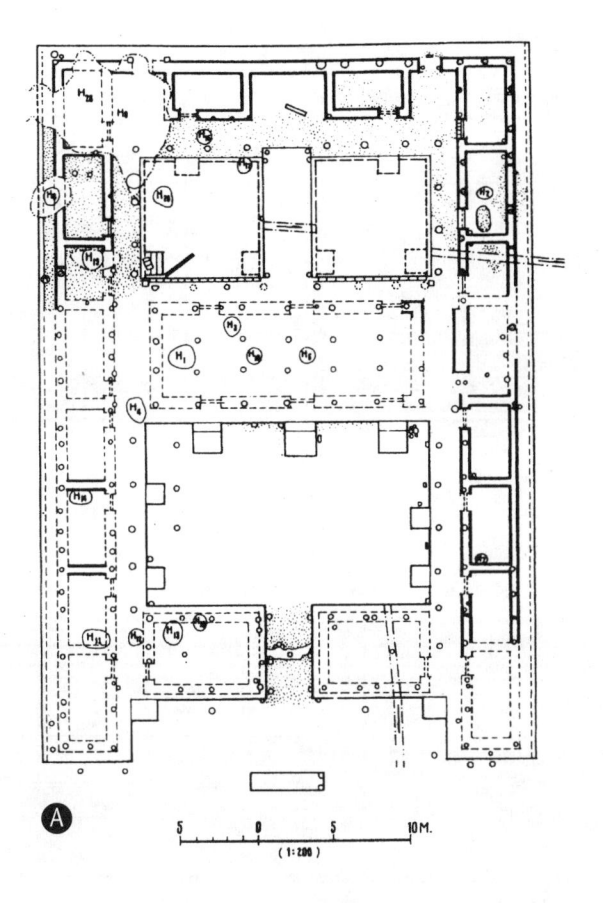

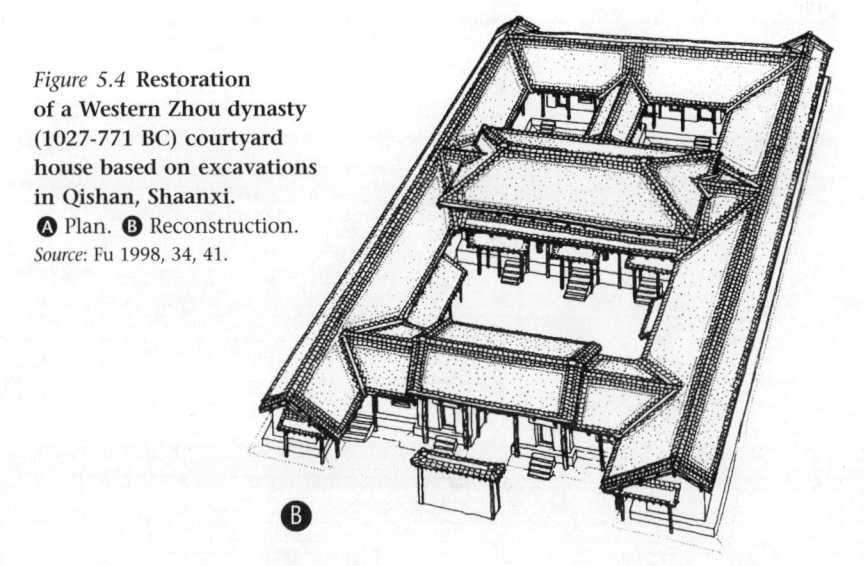

Traditional Courtyard Houses and a New Prototype 71

Figure 5.4 **Restoration of a Western Zhou dynasty (1027-771 BC) courtyard house based on excavations in Qishan, Shaanxi.**
Ⓐ Plan. Ⓑ Reconstruction.
Source: Fu 1998, 34, 41.

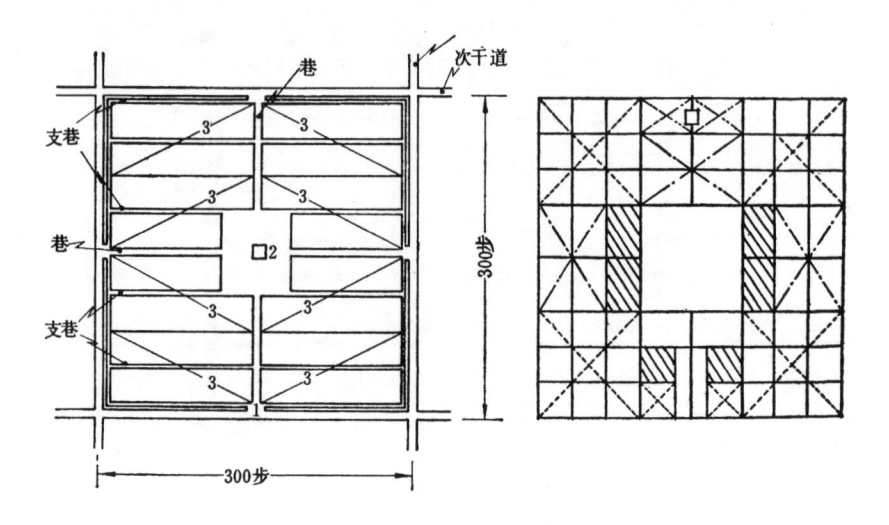

72 Traditional Courtyard Houses and a New Prototype

Figure 5.5 **Possible arrangements of neighbourhoods in an ideal royal city.**
The neighbourhoods were first called *li*, or *lüli*, and later *fang*. The organization of these basic residential units had a profound influence on the planning structure of a city. Above and at right are a few conjectural diagrams by He Yejü, showing the possible arrangements of the neighbourhoods. Measurements shown are in paces.
Source: He 1985, 120-1, 123.

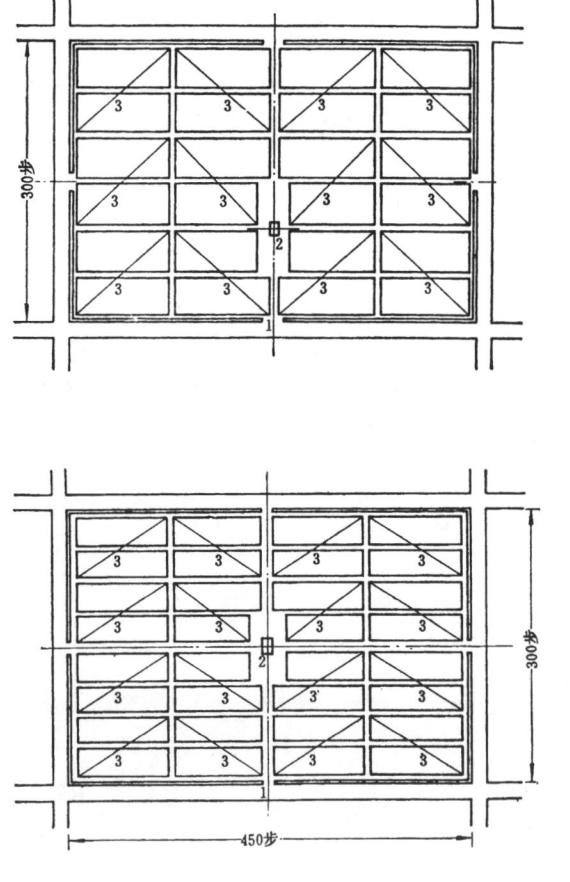

the walls and gates disappeared and the neighbourhoods began to have direct access to the street. This was a turning point in Chinese urban history and marked an important change in the morphology of the cities (Figure 5.5). The boundaries of the wards were no longer clear; rather, the residential quarters became a continuous precinct integrated by a fish-bone-like street-lane-alleyway system. Such a pattern can be seen in *Pingjiangfutu*, the historic plan of Suzhou (Figure 5.6). In some cities, the boundaries and gateway access of the old *fangli* remained, symbolically, in the form of gate towers, memorial archways (*pailou*), and so on. The word *fang* is also retained in certain place names, as in certain neighbourhoods in the city of Kaifeng and in the Sanfang Qixiang (Three Wards and Seven Lanes) section of Fuzhou. In Suzhou, Fuzhou, and Beijing, some *fangli* structures were still being built at the beginning of this century and are still standing. The famous *lilong* neighbourhoods of Shanghai are a modern adaptation of this ancient urban form.

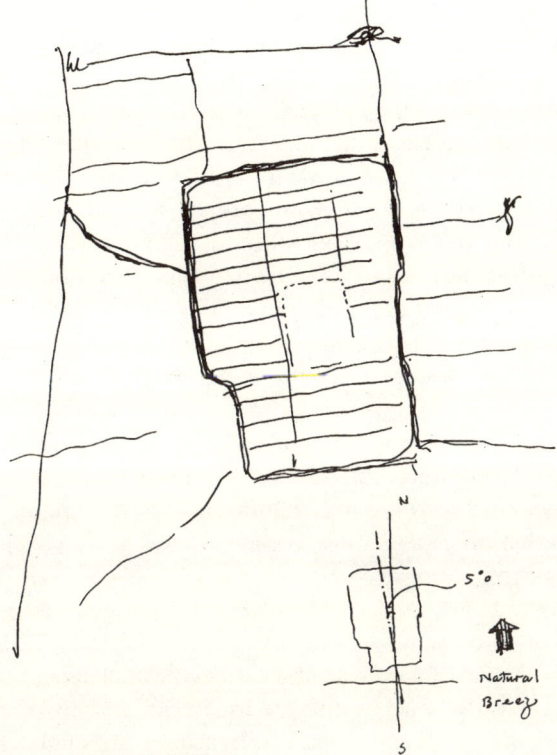

Figure 5.6 **The street layout in Suzhou.**
The north-south streets are at an angle of 3°54', as is shown in the inserted diagram, which gives the best natural ventilation in the city. The fish-bone-like grid gives buildings a good orientation for sunlight, good natural ventilation in the summer and protection from cold wind in the winter, and the shortest street facade for each individual house so that land use is at its most efficient.

The plan of Dadu in the Yuan dynasty reflected the transformed layout of residential quarters. The street-lane-alleyway system has its clear parentage in the plan of Kaifeng. Much of the layout of these residential quarters remained through the Ming and Qing dynasties and can still be seen in Beijing today. It would appear that the City of Beijing consciously adopted the *Wangcheng* schema of *Kaogongji* and the design of the residential quarters of Kaifeng. Thus, although certain elements of the *fangli* system remain in Beijing, this last of China's imperial capitals possessed a subtler urban structure, in which there was slightly more integration of the urban fabric at the scales of the city, the block, the neighbourhood, and the lane.

Urban Fabric and Hierarchy of Access at Different Scales
The historic city of Beijing is ordered at many different scales, from the largest (the entire city) to the smallest (the rooms within the house) (Figures 5.7 and 5.8). This order is summarized as follows:

1. *The City.* A north-south central axis dominates the physical form of the whole city; on either side of it are two north-south running thoroughfares that together form the backbone of the city.
2. *The Street Block.* At this scale, such as in the Zhaohui-Jinggong Fang (described in greater detail below), the fish-bone-like structure is repeated. Lanes and alleyways are used to connect the neighbourhoods, which themselves are made up of one or more smaller blocks.
3. *The Neighbourhood.* The fish-bone-like transportation network is also present, especially in large neighbourhoods, where a series of major *hutong* (usually running east-west) are either joined by smaller transverse *hutong* or lead to even smaller dead-end *hutong* that occasionally run between housing plots. It is important to note, though, that the fish-bone or tree-like structure is not absolute; that is, the great majority of *hutong* intersect with larger streets at *each end*. The hierarchy, therefore, is created partly by branching but, more significantly, by varying the width of the lanes so that, in general, they become narrower as they become shorter and closer to the houses.
4. *The Hutong.* At this level, the circulation system extends to the tip of the border between the hierarchical circulation system and the hierarchical courtyard system. But even this border has a spatial dimension in the form of gatehouses that open both onto the *hutong* and into the compound.
5. *The Courtyard Compound.* A gradual transition from public spaces to private living areas takes place here. The many areas in between provide opportunities for people from different households to meet (if they are sharing one compound, as most do in the old neighbourhoods today) and to engage in a range of activities that may not be appropriate in modern apartments.

6. *The Building.* The degree of privacy within the apartments may be understood in a similar hierarchical way. Buildings almost universally have an odd number of bays and are entered through the central bay, which contains the most public room, leading to more private rooms on the sides. The best buildings lie on the central axis of the compound, preferably facing south.
7. *The Room.* Even individual rooms have traditionally been furnished according to the hierarchy established at the higher scales. Invariably, only one side of the room is fenestrated – almost entirely so – and the back wall opposite the window is the place to put family altars (symmetrically

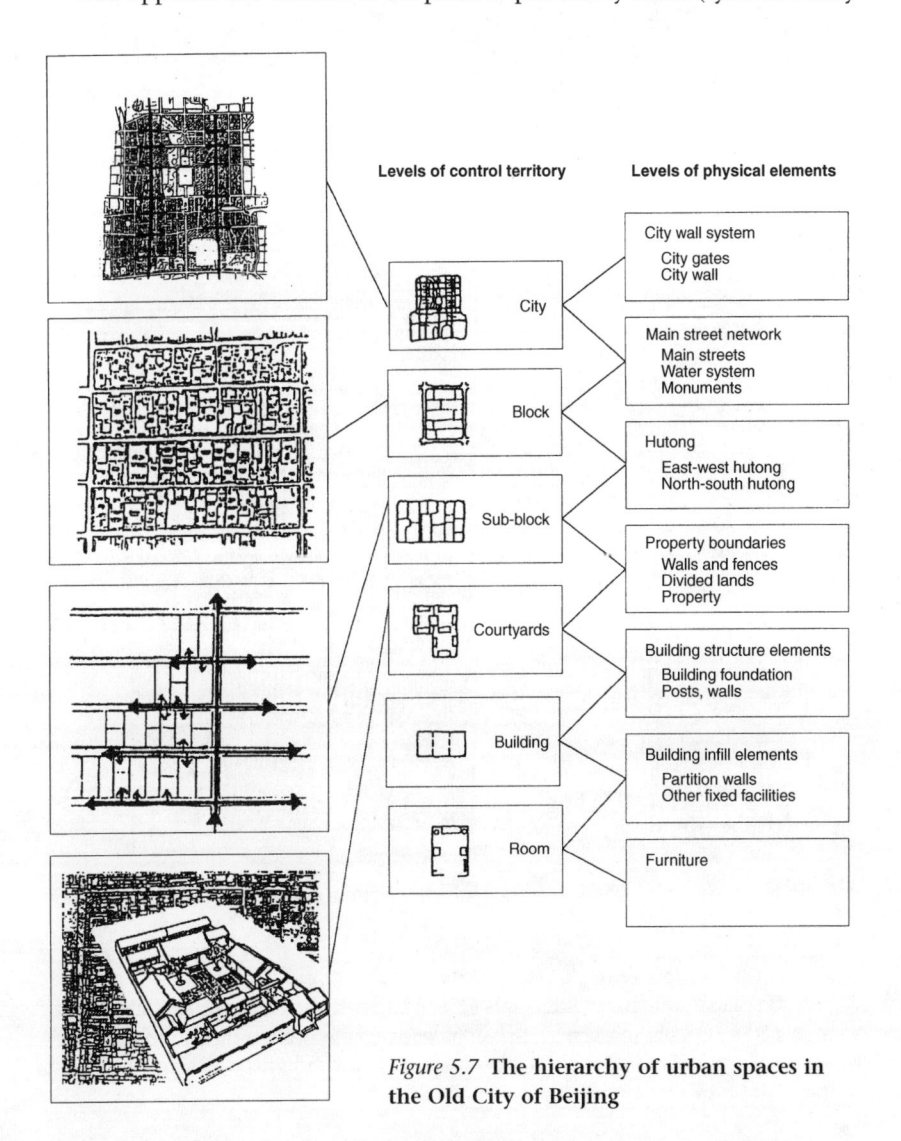

Figure 5.7 **The hierarchy of urban spaces in the Old City of Beijing**

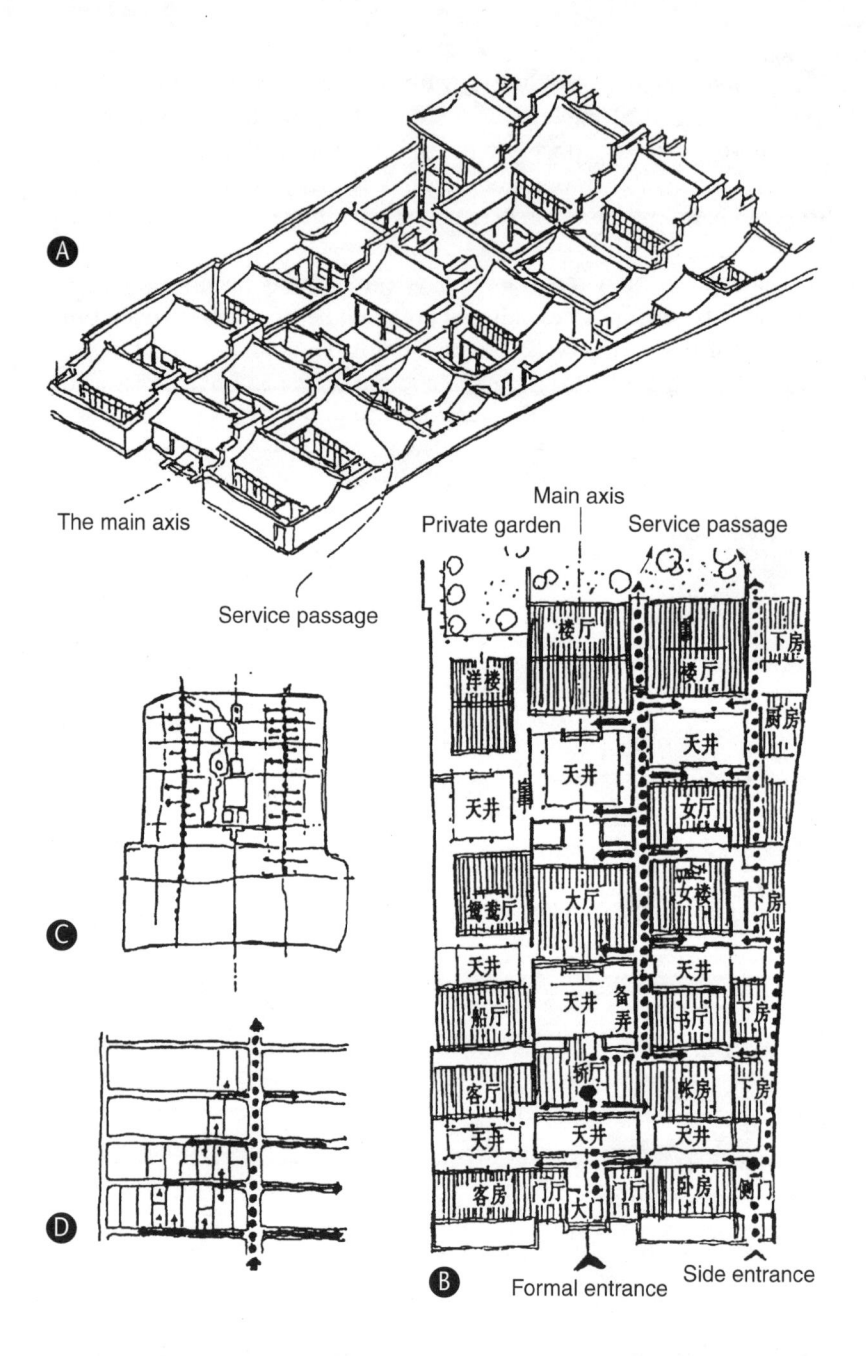

Figure 5.8 **Circulation routes in the courtyard houses and in the city.**
A and **B** A large residence in Suzhou. **C** The circulation system in the Old City of Beijing. **D** The circulation system in the *hutong* neighbourhood of Beijing. The fish-bone-like circulation system has been applied both in housing complexes and in the entire historic city.

flanked by chairs), if the room is more public, or the bed, if the room is more private.

A Classic Neighbourhood in Beijing: The Zhaohui-Jinggong Fang
The street system of the Zhaohui-Jinggong Fang, which contains the present Ju'er Hutong area, dates from the Yuan dynasty.[12] This neighbourhood block was essentially complete at the same time that Dadu was built, between AD 1267 and 1290, and its basic layout still remains. It has a typical plan, with nine parallel east-west *hutong* crossing one north-south street (Luogu Xiang), similar to that of the Song dynasty neighbourhoods of Kaifeng. The whole block measured 1,060 metres from east to west and 820 metres from south to north, covering an area of 84 hectares. The east half is the Zhaohui Fang, built at the beginning of the Yuan dynasty; the west half is the Jinggong Fang, built near the end of the Yuan dynasty. The typical distance between the *hutong* is 70 to 80 metres. The original size of the allotment in this block was determined according to the rank and status of the residents. As Hou Renzhi has described it:

> The size of the neighbourhood varied, and was not relevant to the allocation of house plots; what mattered to the allocation of house plots was the arrangement of *hutong*. When Dadu was built, a strict code was issued concerning the size of allotments for the houses of residents who were moving from the previous Jin dynasty capital, Zhongdu. The rich and highly ranked officials had priority. It was recorded in *Yuanshi-Shizubenji* that "up to the second month of the twenty-second year [of Shizu's reign] the affluent and the high-ranked were called first. Each unit was still 8 *mu*. Where the allotment was greater than 8 *mu* in size, or the household was not able to make full use of the allotment, the extra space had to be given to commoners who could then build their own houses."

We may still make some conjectures concerning the way in which the allotments were determined, based on the layout of a typical area. For instance, the area between the two *hutong* Dongsi Santiao and Dongsi Sitiao is exactly 80 *mu*, which may accommodate ten households. Eight *mu* is 4,320 square metres. A typical plot measures 73 by 60 metres or 62 by 63 metres. A *hutong* of 440 metres length may accommodate seven households. The layout would be modified where there were government offices, schools, and temples.

In Beijing, "the width of thoroughfares measured 24 paces, streets 12 paces; there were 30,084 fire alleys and 29 streets."[13] Much of the layout of the residential quarters in the city was similar to the Zhaohui-Jinggong Fang in the Yuan dynasty and was inherited through the Ming and Qing dynasties. The characteristics of this layout are:

1. The major thoroughfares determine the big street blocks, in which lanes and alleyways provide access to individual courtyard houses.
2. The blocks are of mixed land use, with a broad spectrum of building types, including shops, warehouses, offices, temples, mansions, and ordinary houses.
3. *Hutong* and courtyard houses form an integrated system.

This plan is highly logical and elegant and, on such a large scale, probably unprecedented in its time and even perhaps unique in all urban history. In eighteenth- and nineteenth-century Britain, the Georgian residential squares of Bath, London, Edinburgh, and Dublin shared something in common with this structure, restricting traffic to the main streets and back mews, and creating quiet, safe living environments for the aristocracy.[14] This English vision, however, was not a premise for the planning of an entire metropolis, and it was limited mainly to the service of the upper class. Only after the Second World War did modern planners like Tripp, concerned about the worsening impact of motor vehicle traffic, suggest that all existing urban neighbourhoods could be regrouped into distinct traffic-calmed precincts. This idea was adopted in Abercrombies's Greater London Plan and in the rebuilding of Coventry.[15] The "precinct" model of neighbourhood planning bears a remarkable similarity to some aspects of the traditional street structure in Beijing (Figure 5.9). Specifically, the clear hierarchy of Beijing's streets and lanes, as manifested in their length, width, and partial fish-bone layout, potentially fosters a pedestrian-friendly, traffic-calming residential environment. The traditional *hutong* layout of Beijing is thus a premodern legacy that could serve the needs of modern healthy urban living remarkably well.

The Courtyard House Type

The courtyard house is another important element in Beijing's urban form. Traditional Chinese architecture is generally based on the composition of various buildings around courtyards, and traditional Chinese cities are composed of such courtyard compounds (Figure 5.10). This can be seen in the Forbidden City and in most parts of the Old City of Beijing, but nowhere is it more clear than in the residential quarters where an endless variation of courtyard house arrangements has evolved (Figures 5.11 and 5.12). The typical courtyard house plan has buildings or pavilions placed along three or four sides of a building site, forming a courtyard in the middle; the whole complex is a basic courtyard house. The buildings face the courtyard, which provides outdoor space for family activities, circulation, ventilation, light, and drainage. The courtyard house is enclosed, and access is gained through an entrance normally placed on the south or the east side. A north entrance is rare, and, in such cases, an intermediate space is usually placed between

Traditional Courtyard Houses and a New Prototype   79

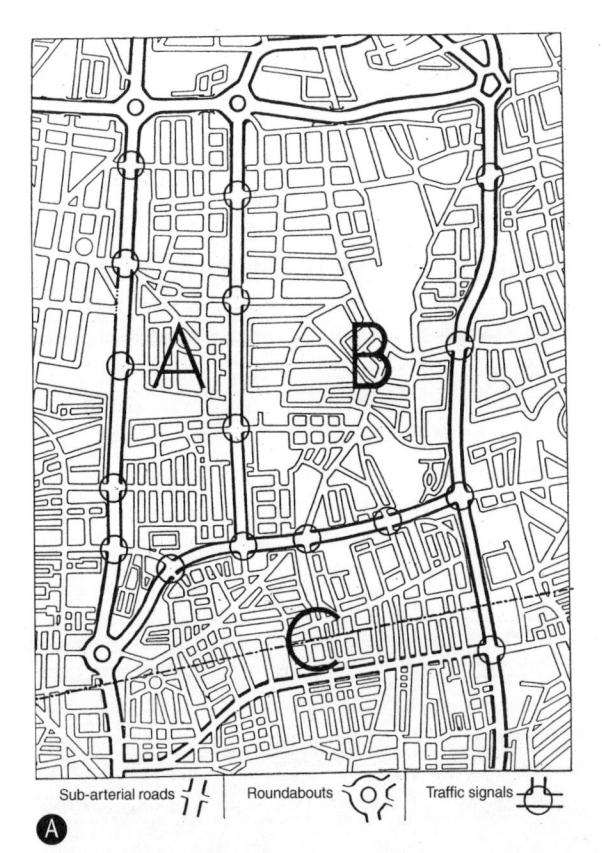

Figure 5.9
A comparison of Tripp's precinct plan and a plan of a Yuan dynasty Zhaohui-Jinggong Fang neighbourhood.
Ⓐ Tripp's residential precinct in between trunk roads. **Ⓑ** Plan of Yuan dynasty Zhaohui-Jinggong Fang (84 hectares). The Yuan dynasty neighbourhood, planned some 700 years ago, already showed a clear understanding of hierarchy in the urban road system.
Source: (A) Tripp 1942, 78.

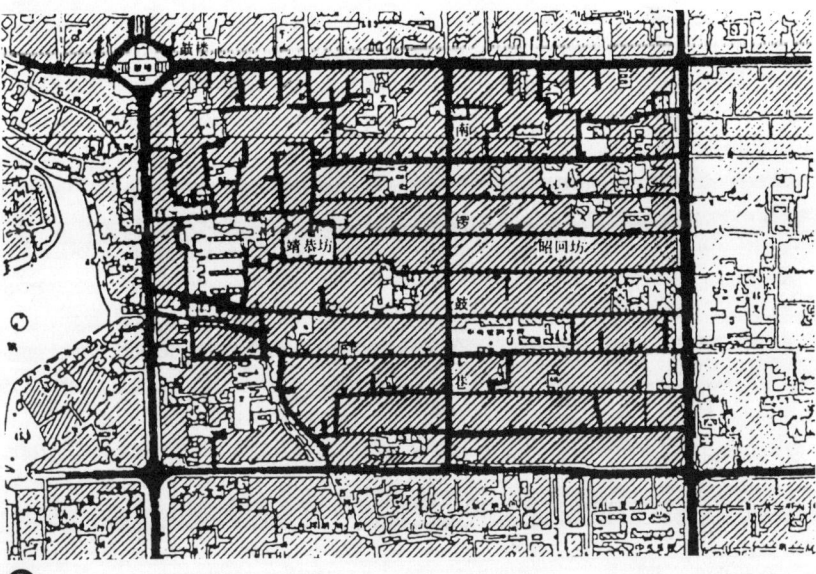

the entrance and the courtyard. The courtyard can be expanded whenever needed by adding more courtyards in front or at the back, or on either of the two wings. For a large complex, both methods are used (Figure 5.13). In fine weather, the uncovered courtyard may be used for circulation; corridors are built linking buildings to provide circulation in rain and snow. In south China, a complete daily service circulation system – called *huoxiang* (fire lane), *beinong,* or *binong* – is usually built (Figures 5.4 and 5.14). A courtyard complex ordinarily has an explicit longitudinal axis, upon which the whole building is organized. The main axis is also the ceremonial access to the house; this is usually reserved for important occasions, including weddings and funerals.

Characteristics of the Courtyard House Type
The plan and structure of the courtyard house prototype is highly modularized. The design and construction of the house is determined by the number of bays, the number of purlins, and the height of the columns. This building system began in the Han dynasty and matured in the Song dynasty, as is recorded in the Song treatise *Yingzao fashi.*

The simple plan of a courtyard house is, in fact, very flexible and may be adapted to a great variety of uses. A courtyard house may be occupied by one family or shared by a few. Some courtyard house complexes were adapted to temples in the past, and many have been turned into offices today, which exemplifies their versatility. In different regions in China, courtyard houses have been developed with their own characteristics according to regional conditions. In northern cities, such as Beijing, the courtyard is large in order to let in sufficient sunlight, while in southern cities it is much smaller in order to create more shade and better ventilation (Figure 5.15). Land use is economical in courtyard houses, since both inner and exterior space is usable. The courtyard is an outdoor living room in good weather, especially in the south where the climate is moderate, and the loosely defined indoor space is highly integrated with the courtyard. Courtyard houses are built with materials that are available locally. Lightness and flexibility also characterize windows and interior partitions, in the form of screens, and interior decoration, as in *cheshang luming zao*, a traditional Chinese wood structured design.

In short, the courtyard house and its distinctive features has a central role in the history of Chinese building. According to archaeologists, courtyard houses first appeared in China in the Zhou dynasty (1100-256 BC). A burial object in the Shaanxi Museum in Xi'an shows that as early as the Eastern Han dynasty (AD 25-220), courtyard houses of two or more storeys appeared (Figure 5.16). These types of houses have been widely adopted in many parts of China for a long time and are still the main type of housing in areas inhabited by the Bai and Naxi people of Southwest China (Figure 5.17, no. 6),

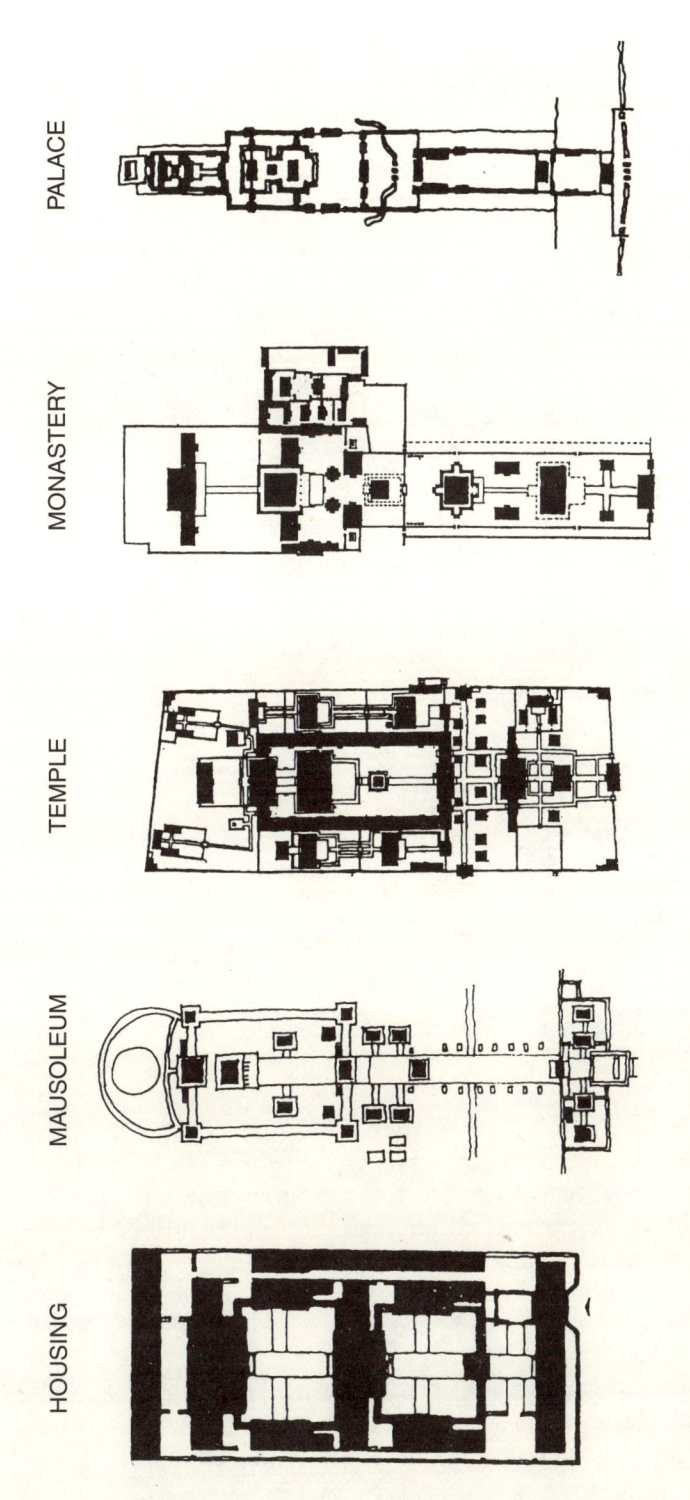

Figure 5.10 **A comparison of forms of building complexes.**
Most traditional Chinese building types, including houses, mausoleums, temples, monasteries, and palaces, are arranged around courtyards of varying shapes and sizes.

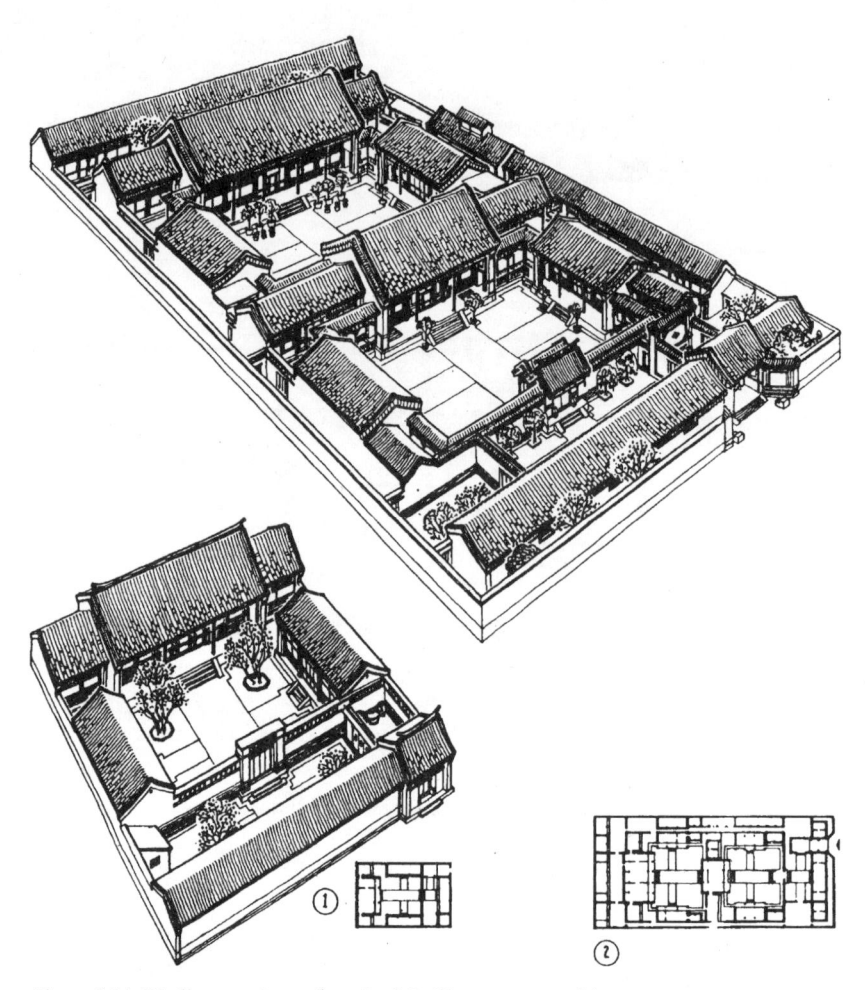

Figure 5.11 **Bird's-eye view of typical Beijing courtyard houses**
Source: Liu 1990, 210.

among others, while other variations have developed in other regions. Courtyard housing is, indeed, the basic building type of Chinese architecture, from which various building forms stemmed. From the social and technological points of view, courtyard houses – the artifacts of the hierarchical Chinese feudal society built with traditional technology – have lost their old reasons for existence in most regions of China. However, the concept still provides inspiration for current designs.

Emergence of a New Courtyard House Prototype
Since the late 1950s, the question of whether the traditional courtyard houses in Beijing should be preserved, adapted, re-invented, or replaced has been

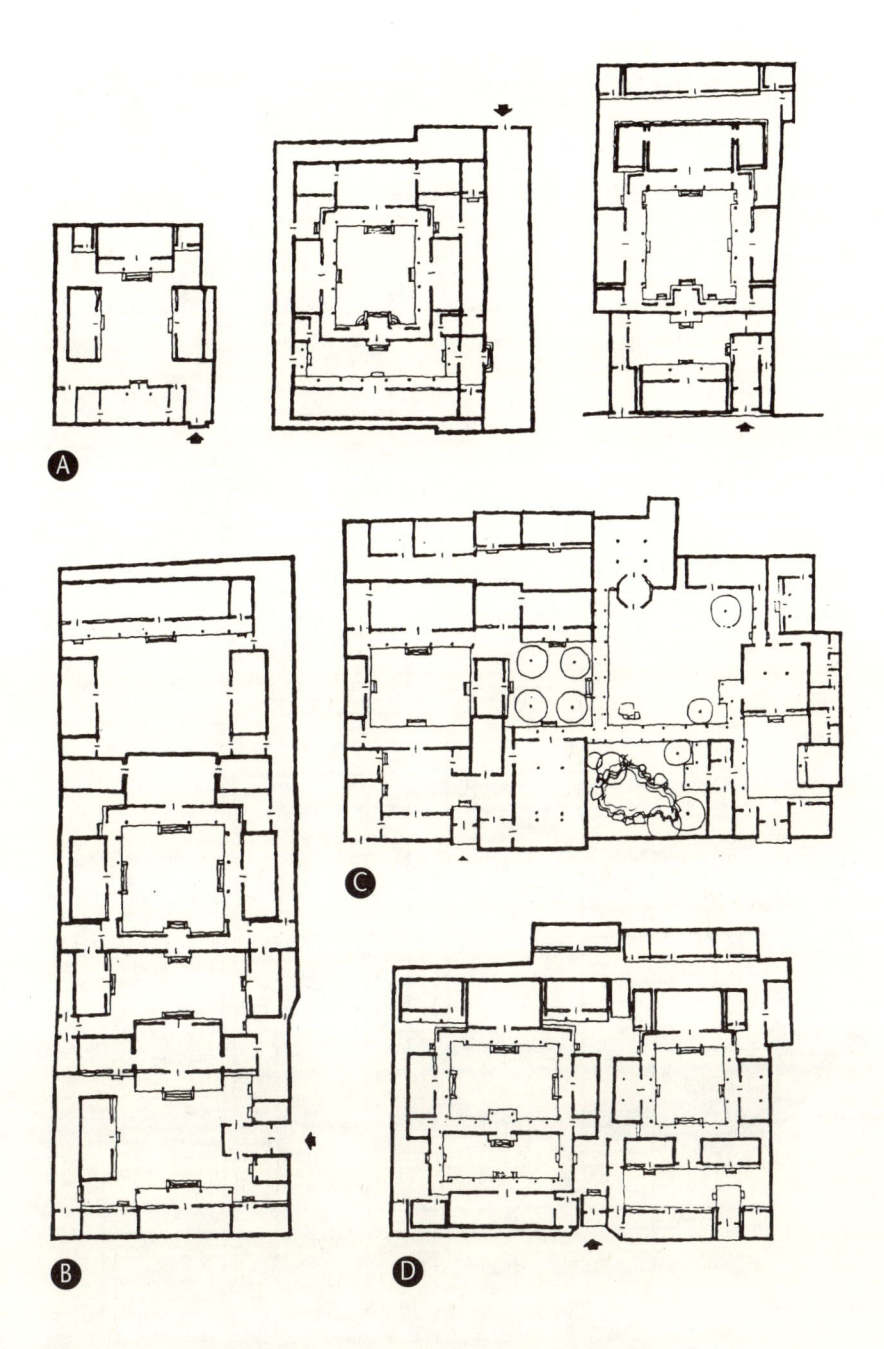

Figure 5.12 **Different compositions of courtyard complexes.**
A Basic one-courtyard complexes. **B** A longitudinal multi-courtyard complex.
C A latitudinal multi-courtyard complex. **D** Mixed multi-courtyard complex.
Particular site conditions and functional requirements have helped to generate a
rich variety of architectural spaces in the courtyard houses.

Figure 5.13 **Spatial organization in courtyard complexes.** In large courtyard complexes, the central axis is generally designed as the ceremonial passage. The passage between two parallel complexes is usually used as the daily circulation route. The arrangement is very land-efficient (as explained in Figure 5.20).

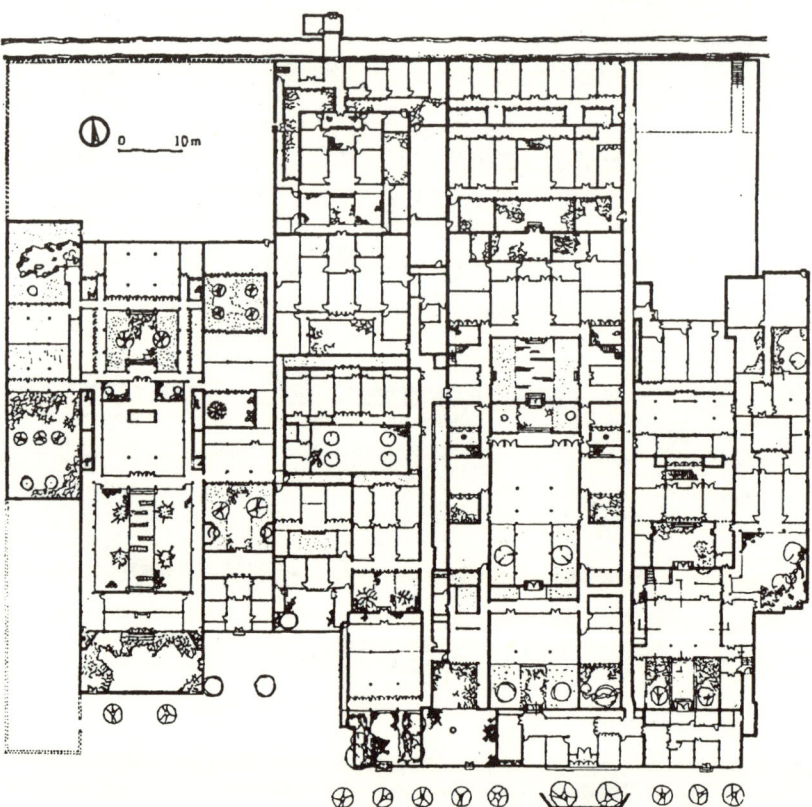

中路
中軸線
Central axis

Figure 5.14 **Plan of the residence of the Lu family in Tianguanfang Suzhou.**
Note the use of circulation passages between parallel courtyard complexes.
Source: Liu 1990, 229.

controversial. The introduction of the Soviet-style row and perimeter housing forms, which were highly regarded by Chinese city planning authorities, quickly replaced courtyard housing forms in Beijing as the model for new construction. To understand this phenomenon, it is necessary to look back at the history of modern urban planning and architectural thinking and to see how it ultimately affected residential building practice in China. The review offered here is cursory in the extreme: it is only an attempt to

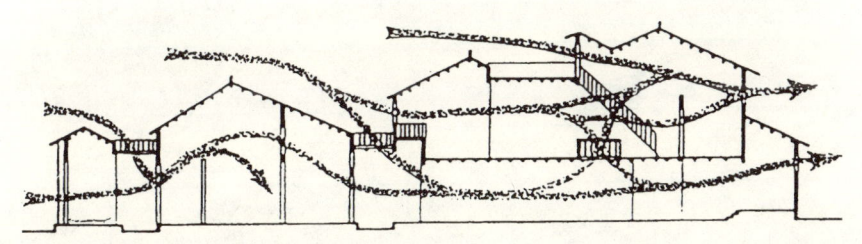

Figure 5.15 **Texture of the roofscape of traditional houses.** A moving rhythm is often composed in a traditional neighbourhood, which may be regarded as the fifth facade of the buildings. The organization of the roofscape is particularly interesting in southern China due to the small size of open courtyards and the complex arrangement of ventilation systems.
Source: Liu 1990, 276.

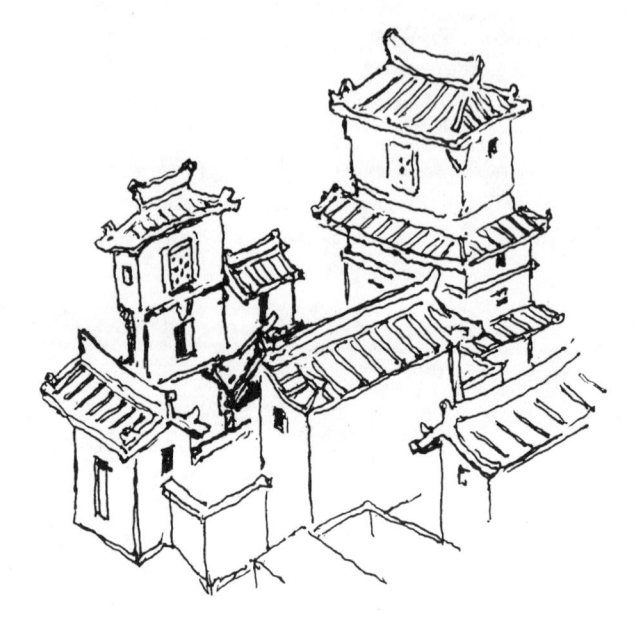

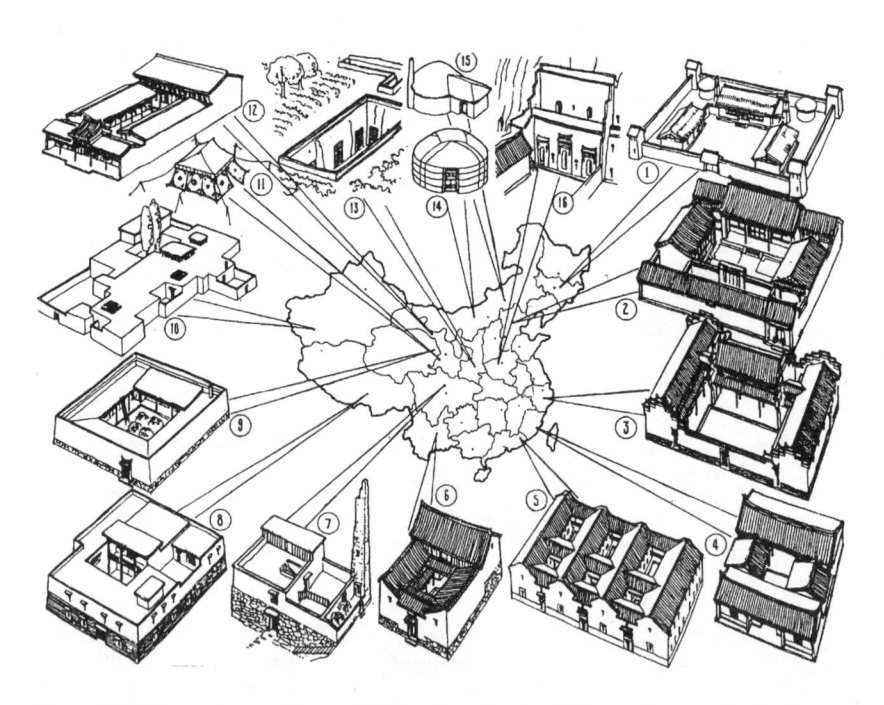

86 *Traditional Courtyard Houses and a New Prototype*

Figure 5.16 **Model of a multi-storey courtyard house**
Source: Sketch by Wu Liangyong based on an Eastern Han dynasty (AD 25-220) funeral object in Shaanxi Provincial Museum.

Figure 5.17 **House types all over China.** Despite the different forms of individual buildings, the courtyard composition is the most common.
Source: Diagram by Fu Xinian in Liu 1990, 206.

provide the basic background necessary in order to appreciate the architectural issues underlying the re-introduction of the courtyard house type to the Old City of Beijing.

New Housing and Urban Forms in the Twentieth Century

In the early period of the Industrial Revolution and throughout most of the nineteenth century, the rapidly growing cities of Europe and North America suffered serious housing shortages and an increase in slum areas. Low-cost housing for the working class was vigorously promoted. Some philanthropic industrialists later built new towns for workers in order to improve their living conditions. The Pullman Company Town in Chicago was one such example. Many important architects involved in housing design and new town planning also left a bold mark on the history of modern housing. The Dutch architect P. Berlage, for instance, prepared the development plan for Amsterdam South in 1917, using the basic nineteenth-century low-rise row house type but unifying the facade designs and introducing innovations to the overall site layout. Later, in Frankfurt in the 1920s, similar innovations were carried further by Ernst May, who also pioneered the use of large-scale prefabrication for housing. The result was housing that had a uniform appearance from unit to unit and that was separated from the street – a separation that was accelerated by the development of the motor car around the same time. As a result, the traditional urban tissue began to break down.

The development of modern technology had a strong impact on housing design and development, and it made possible the high-rise housing form. The work of Walter Gropius was especially significant for its use of technology. In 1928, his Dessau-Torten housing project was built in a completely new layout that was determined by the desire for more sunlight and open space, and by the use of a new building technology – tower crane tracks (Figure 5.18a). Two years later, Gropius demonstrated to a meeting of the Congrès Internationaux d'Architecture Moderne (CIAM) that, given the same area of land, more open space could be gained by increasing building height while retaining the same number of housing units and the same amount of sunlight penetration that occurred in row housing (Figure 5.18b). All of this facilitated the development of housing industrialization and the design of apartment blocks, which contributed a great deal to the improvement of housing conditions for the mass of working people. Indeed, socialist ideals drove much innovative modernist thinking, and when economic depression and fascist reaction began to oppress Europe in the 1930s, some of the innovators spent time in the Soviet Union testing their ideas further. It was from the USSR, then, that this influence on housing design and urban planning passed on to China in the 1950s.

The extreme of this trend towards integration of new technology into architecture and planning, and disregard for historically evolved urban

88 *Traditional Courtyard Houses and a New Prototype*

Figure 5.18
Achievements of modernist architecture.
A Gropius's rational housing at Dessau-Torten, 1926.
B Gropius's building height and building density analysis, 1926.
Source: Frampton 1980, 139-40.

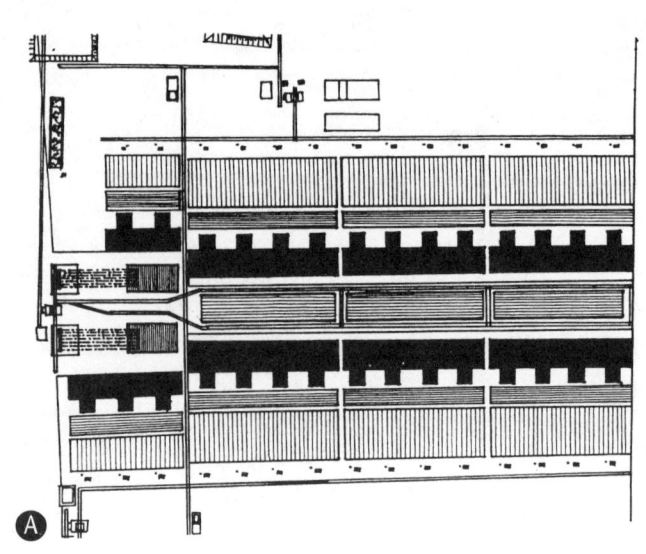

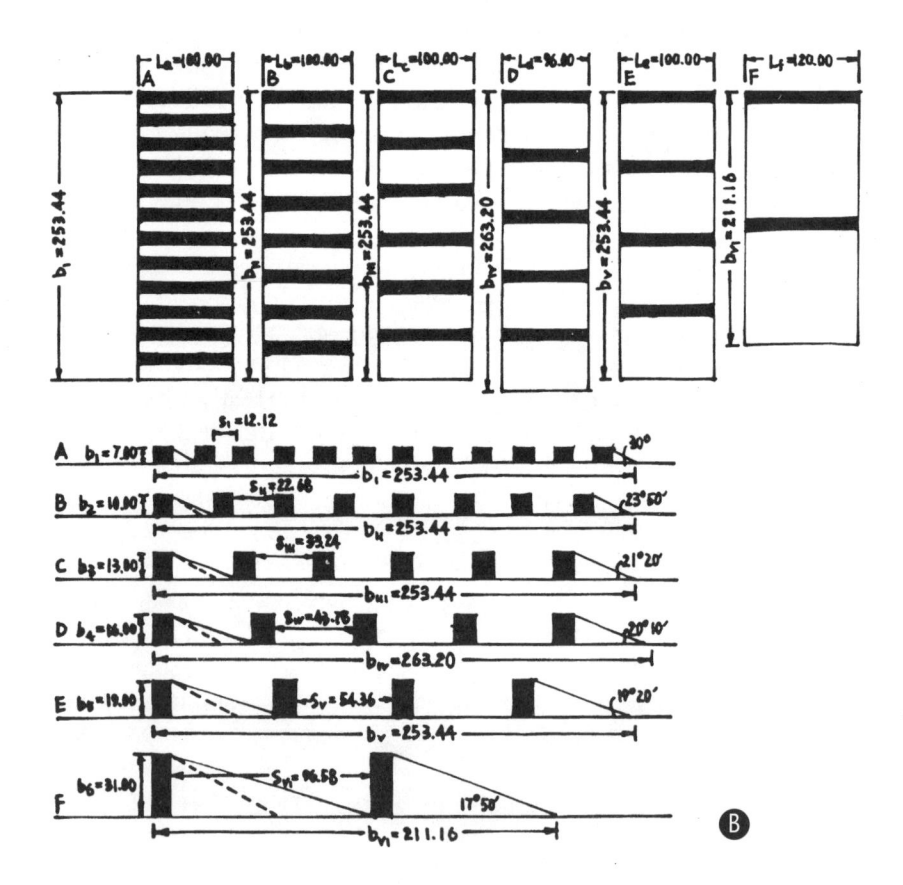

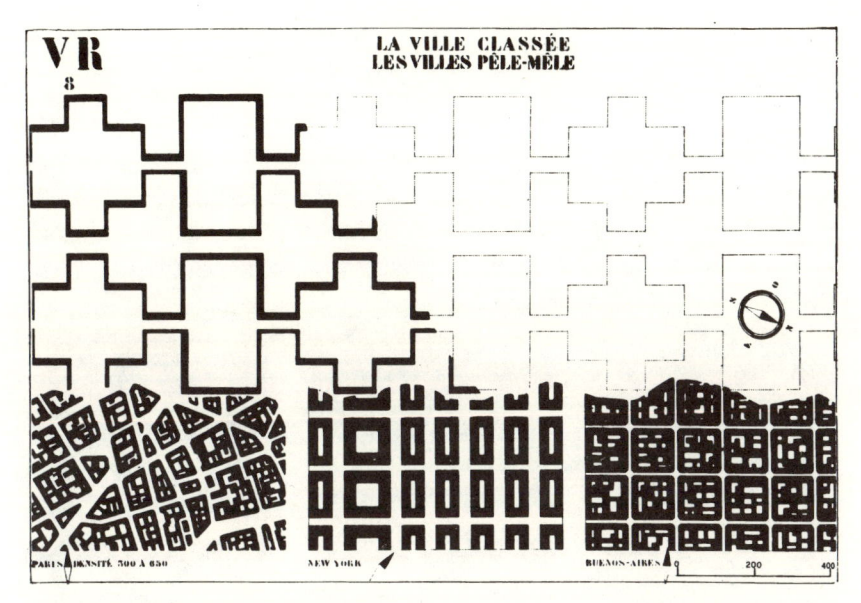

Figure 5.19 **Le Corbusier's scheme for the Ville Radieuse, compared with traditional urban fabric**
Source: Benevolo 1980, 864.

fabric, is exemplified in the visions of Ludwig Hilbersheimer and Le Corbusier – particularly in Le Corbusier's Plan Voisin proposal for Paris (1925). While Gropius concentrated on individual building design and was less concerned about urban space, Hilbersheimer and Le Corbusier proposed completely replacing the traditional city form with a utopian technology based form. As his Ville Radieuse vision (1930) showed, the city was to be built with high-rise buildings and was to be made accessible to fast modern transport (Figure 5.19). This allowed 95 to 100 percent of the ground space to remain open for maximum sunlight, fresh air, and green space. Three years later, much of this urban concept was incorporated into the milestone document of modern architecture and city planning – the Athens Charter – which simplified the city into four functional zones: dwelling, work, recreation, and transportation.[16] These ideas oversimplified architecture and planning and imposed monotonous forms on cities; consequently, they were criticized thirty years later.

Search for the Lost Order and Fabric

For many decades, buildings have been increasingly separated from the streets, open space increased but neglected, and the formal integrity and historic continuity of urban centres lost. The impact of modernist theories and methodologies on Chinese architecture and planning has been to produce even more simplistic attitudes towards the urban environment than was the case in the West. This was due to the extreme utilitarianism forced on the Chinese profession by poverty and political upheaval. Just as questions of architectural style were pushed into the background in the late 1950s, so too was urban design. In the West, alternatives to the modernist orthodoxy continued to be expressed, if not in building then at least in theory. At the turn of this century, Camillo Sitte noticed the lack of spatial artistic quality in many modern European cities and proposed a very human-scale approach to urban design that, in recent decades, has enjoyed a revival.

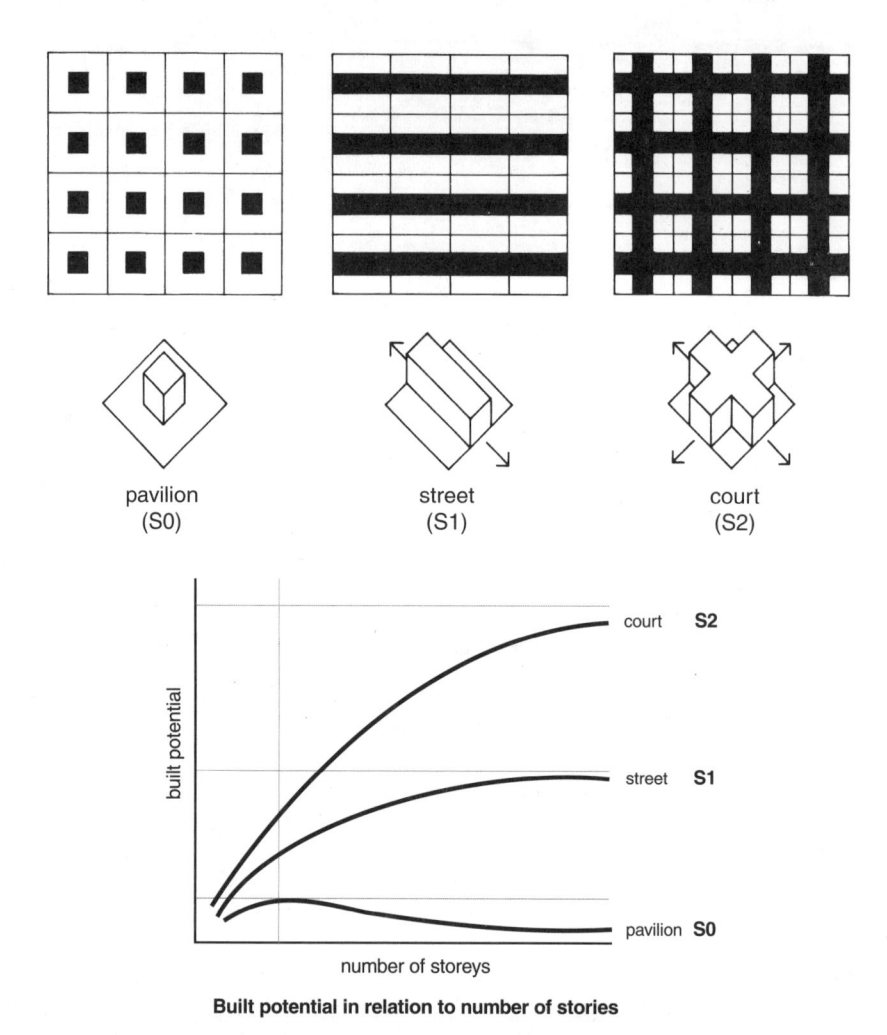

Figure 5.20 **Built potentials of pavilion, street, and courtyard forms.**
If density is kept the same, then S2 form has the best solar access; if solar access is kept the same, then S2 has the best density.
Source: Martin and March 1972, 36-7.

At the ninth CIAM meeting held in 1953, a young generation of architects responded to the simplistic model of the urban core by positing a more complex pattern that would be, in their view, more responsive to the need for identity. They argued that the sense of belonging was a basic emotional need, from which derived a feeling of neighbourliness, and that this was to be achieved in the narrow and short streets of slums rather than in spacious redevelopment.[17]

Following the mid-1960s, increasing numbers and types of studies began to revive interest in traditional housing and urban forms. The Martin Centre of Architectural and Urban Studies at Cambridge University carried out research on land use forms and came to the conclusion that, using the same area of land, the courtyard (or perimeter block housing) form is the most economical in terms of land use (Figure 5.20).[18] Some ten years later, Josef P. Kleihues began to reuse the perimeter block form for a housing project in West Berlin. The new perimeter block housing inherited the nineteenth-century city block form, but with much improved living conditions (Figure 5.21).[19]

By the late 1970s, Western architects and planners also gradually realized the negative effects of CIAM's zoning concepts, and they turned to mixed zoning in new developments. At the same time, some new concepts in urban morphology and building typology emerged. In 1967 Aldo Rossi's *The Architecture of the City* proclaimed both the autonomy of architecture from technology and the valid persistence of historic building types. In 1979 architect Rob Krier drew attention to the significance of the basic elements of urban space and city architecture; he called for a "formal response" to the existing urban space.[20] Leon Krier also presented the concept of a "city within a city," architecturally formed by quasi-nineteenth-century courtyard blocks.[21]

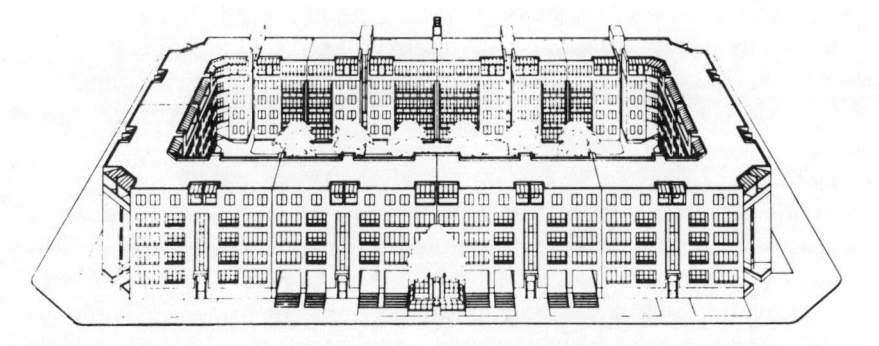

Figure 5.21 **Transformation of the neighbourhood built form in Western Europe.** Perimeter block housing in West Berlin, with both street and courtyard facade, by Kleihues (1978).
Source: Frampton 1992, 296.

One conclusion that can be drawn from the theoretical debates and actual experiences of this century of urban development is that the negation of traditional city form is part of the inevitable process of development, but it does not signify its end. Establishing a new city form is often more difficult than destroying the old. It suggests that now we need to reconsider the traditional relationship between building form and urban space. Unfortunately, in China, while much "postmodernist" thinking has emerged since the early 1980s with regard to individual building design, urban design has experienced no such theoretical evolution. Overwhelmed by the task of housing enormous urban populations, residential planning in China has continued along the path of industrialized, "standardized" apartment block types arranged in the form of large housing estates. While providing individual households with a very basic improvement in living conditions, this stereotyped housing form has created an unsatisfactory urban environment. Sadly, the resulting problems have not drawn enough attention either from professionals or from society at large. This is mainly due to the lack of appreciation for the artistic and social values of traditional cities; the younger generation in China has had little chance to experience the traditional urban environment, which has been so compromised in the last forty years.

Since the 1950s, planning policies for Beijing have been strongly influenced by the Master Plan of Moscow which, in fact, drew many ideas from the Greater London Plan. Ironically, the plans for Beijing treated the Old City as a backward area and neglected its rational city structure. Consequently, many streets were widened and reconstructed, and many valuable traditional neighbourhoods were damaged. It is time for us to rethink the value of the historic city of Beijing and to reconsider our planning policies for it. Lessons from the failures of pseudo-neighbourhood units invented by a modern architectural and planning philosophy, the recent concepts of the "city within the city," and the rediscovery of the value of urban blocks suggest that Beijing's traditional urban structure, which has lasted for over 800 years, may continue to be relevant to urban life in the future. What we must do is pay more attention to its valuable aspects and carefully improve its inadequate aspects.

Rediscovery and Redesign of the Courtyard House

In order to determine the features of a new courtyard housing form it is necessary to understand the conventional multi-storey and high-rise apartment buildings. Historically, the replacement of traditional street blocks with apartment blocks was a significant development. In Western European cities, the residential neighbourhood layout of apartment blocks, or slab-buildings arranged in parallel rows, emerged due to new industrialized building methods, increases in population density, requirements for privacy, and a desire for better light and ventilation.[22] It provided a solution to housing problems that had emerged since industrialization. This Western row housing form had a strong impact on China, especially in the late 1950s after the country had abandoned the former Soviet perimeter housing block design. The row-like layout soon became fashionable in most cities and towns; meanwhile, other housing forms were neglected. Apartment blocks have the advantage of providing every household with privacy, which is one of the basic needs of modern family life; however, they also create several problems.

First, the open space around the housing blocks is usually occupied by services such as parking, circulation, and rubbish collection. This space demands extensive landscaping, which, in most cases, has failed to materialize (Figure 5.22). Second, some outdoor space may be used by ground floor

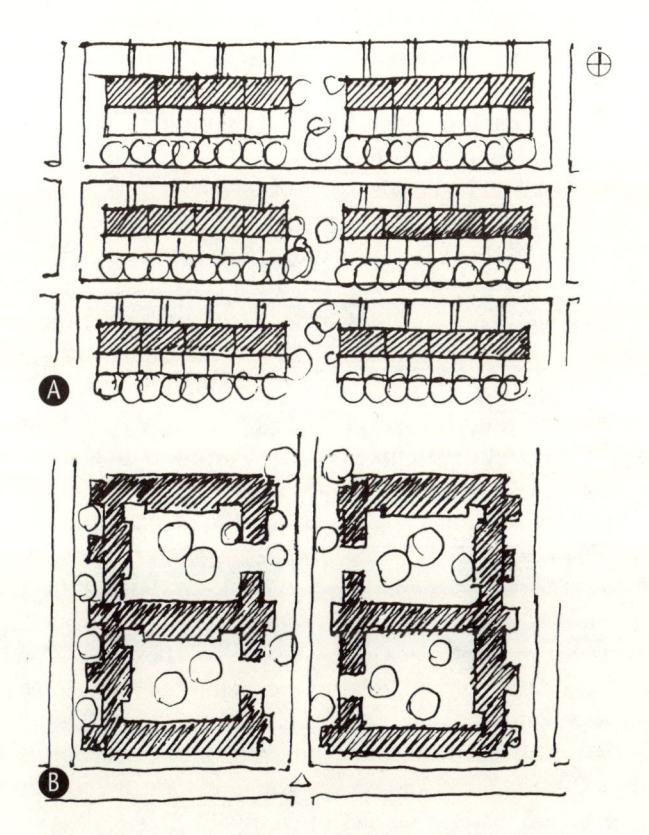

Figure 5.22 **A comparison of conventional apartment blocks with new courtyard-type houses.**
Ⓐ Spaces between the conventional apartment blocks are monotonous and difficult to use, except for parking and rubbish collection. Ⓑ The new courtyard-type houses create semi-public spaces that are easier for residents to identify with.

residents to plant gardens, but those living on the upper levels have no access to their own outdoor space other than a cramped balcony. Third, row housing blocks are similar in design, which makes it easy to guarantee every family equal conditions but creates a monotonous living environment devoid of identifiable features. Fourth, whether they are built in a planned manner or as infill, row housing and tower blocks can hardly fit into the existing traditional city fabric of Beijing (Figures 5.23, 5.24, and 5.25). Fifth, multi-storey and high-rise buildings challenge human scale in the urban environment. Finally, this form of housing discourages communication between neighbours. Over the years, some new designs have emerged that attempt to support residents' needs for variety and personalization as well as to brighten the appearance of the collective neighbourhood environment; "terraced garden housing" is one successful example (Figure 5.26), but it still does not address the problem of urban conservation and of building within an existing environment that has its own strong character.

In the Old City of Beijing, a special kind of community life has evolved in conjunction with the city's characteristic physical neighbourhood form. Neighbourhoods are an important locus of social life in all cities: the focal point for a community.[23] Such spaces are not only physically suited to neighbourhood social life, they are also reminiscent of how that life has been portrayed in literature and art. A great many literary works, as well as film, television, and stage dramas, have celebrated how these kinds of urban neighbourhood spaces have supported a social and cultural life that in many respects cuts across class, ethnic, and occupational lines and that is based on mutual respect, help, and sympathy. Just a few of the prominent modern Chinese works of this kind are Lao She's description of Xiaoyangjuan Hutong in *Si Shi Tong Tang [Four Generations Under One Roof]*, Xia Yan's *Shanghai Wuyanxia [Shanghai Under the Eaves]*, and the dramatizations *Chengnan Jiushi [Tales of the South City]*, *Xizhao Jie [Glow-of-the-setting-sun Street]*, and *Zhong Gu Lou [The Bell and Drum Towers]*. Works of classical literature and the lives of classical literati, too, often centre on a human-scale feature of the traditional urban landscape. One example would be the "Willow Spring" well and the teahouse built beside it in the vicinity of the eighteenth-century writer Pu Songling's family residence in Zibo, Shandong province.

On the scale of the individual dwelling, the traditional courtyard form, too, continues to have relevance in the contemporary city. Depending on their size, there are many examples of courtyards that serve very well as residences for one, two, or three families; indeed, their intimate scale and the close relation between indoor and outdoor spaces have an enduring attraction. Due to their close but secure relation with the public space of the lane, their hierarchy of access, and the clear separation of rooms within

Figure 5.23 **Conflict of different built forms.**
Ⓐ Conventional apartment blocks were designed with little sympathy and sensitivity towards traditional forms. **Ⓑ** With a little more thought, modern housing units can be built and integrated into the traditional setting.

96 Traditional Courtyard Houses and a New Prototype

Figure 5.24 Two further examples of how the new courtyard-type houses were integrated into the traditional settings of the neighbourhood

Figure 5.25 **A typical Beijing courtyard house.**
The courtyard of the Na family in Jinyu (Goldfish) Hutong in 1953. It has since been demolished.

Figure 5.26 **Terraced Garden Housing, designed by Lü Junhua, Tsinghua University**
Source: Lü 1991, 128.

them, courtyard compounds are also particularly adaptable as live-work spaces (for households engaged in intellectual, artistic, crafts, or small trade work) and as offices for small enterprises. This particular kind of adaptability is increasingly important in current economic restructuring, which has led to the proliferation of small companies and has led many households to engage in their own entrepreneurial activities. Moreover, if recent studies of the trend towards combining residence and workplace in the developed world are any indication of the future of China's cities, this kind of adaptability will only become even more useful.[24]

However, owing to the increase of population in the old neighbourhoods, most of the courtyard houses have degenerated from spacious abodes for single extended families to crowded multi-family compounds. Although strong community ties are still functioning, this is at the expense of privacy.[25] In some ways, this is the opposite of what is offered in the apartment blocks. Modern apartment buildings gain privacy and density, but they lose identity, adaptability, and neighbourliness. In modern life, the significance of neighbourhood may no longer be as important as it was, but that does not mean that it is no longer needed.[26] The negative impact of modern residential districts on cultural and social development and community life has to be rectified when planning and designing for the Old City of Beijing. It was in this context that the Ju'er Hutong courtyard housing experiment began.

Searching for new neighbourhood patterns has been one of the main concerns of modern planners. The origin of such attempts can be traced back to many utopian thinkers. Sociologist Clarence Perry's observations in the early 1900s first presented the concept of planning for community in a modern suburban context. He later collaborated with Clarence Stein and Henry Wright in producing the important plan for Radburn in Fairlawn, New Jersey, which used the pioneering concept of hierarchically structured "neighbourhood units." Essentially, the neighbourhood unit was an area of a size appropriate to a community of neighbours all sharing certain public facilities, such as schools, churches, community centres, and so on. It was assumed that geographical proximity would ensure a sense of community identity, and, in order to allow for the kind of social interaction that would follow from this, automobile access was limited to the periphery of the area while the centre was devoted to pedestrian space.

This became an extremely popular way of resolving conflicts between automotive and pedestrian traffic (the sketch in Figure 5.27 shows the neighbourhood unit concept as adopted in a scheme for the new British town of Hook). Unfortunately, Perry's concept was simplified in later town planning practice and is now criticized as an "abstract neighbourhood." In too many cases, residents relied almost completely on their cars for all types of activities, and the central pedestrian zones were left underused. The work of Jane Jacobs and many others put forward strong arguments against the abstract neighbourhood, claiming it was based on a simplistic and inaccurate concept of urban community relations and identity.[27] Christopher Alexander proposed that the city's structure is more complex than the hierarchical "tree" pattern of most modern neighbourhood plans; he proposed a more sophisticated "lattice"-type structure.[28] More recently, the "Neo-traditionalist" or "New Urbanist" planning movement is attempting to revive nineteenth-century-style street and block patterns as a way of promoting pedestrian activity and neighbourly sociability in new suburban and urban communities.[29] The advantages of the block system are that its high incidence of intersections encourages a greater number of encounters and that it is "permeable" to pedestrian traffic.[30] Its problems are with automobile traffic, and their solutions require measures other than the design of the overall street layout.

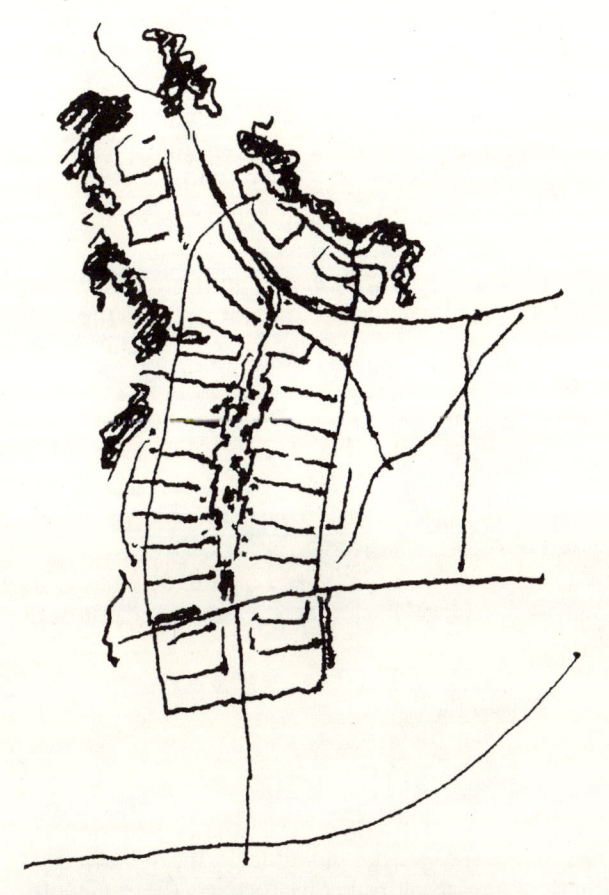

Figure 5.27 **Plan of Hook, Hampshire, England**
Source: Sketch by Wu Liangyong from the plan of Hook.
A fish-bone-like circulation system was used in the plan.

The Aesthetics of Courtyards, Houses, and Lanes

While this is not the place to dwell further on the complex issues raised by the arguments mentioned above, we can at least conclude that a satisfactory balance between privacy and communication among neighbours depends on the particular situation facing each environment and its inhabitants. In the case of Beijing, the neighbourhoods of the Old City possess a unique combination of the block-type layout and the hierarchical street network. One could say they possess the best of both worlds: the block system, with its high incidence of intersections and pedestrian permeability, and a precinct-like hierarchy that can control automobile traffic.

To be sure, this layout and network is closely integrated with the particular form of enclosure and privacy provided by the traditional courtyard house. The early twentieth-century scholar Wang Guowei pointed out that the layout of the courtyard is not only quite practical, but it is also one of the most elegant ways in which a complex of separate-but-related buildings can be arranged (Figure 5.28).[31] The many layerings of partial and strong enclosure achieved by the walls and trees of the *hutong* and courtyard environment is rarely seen in the West and is as important to the Old City's particular advantages as is the layout of streets and lanes.

One could say that there are five essential features of the relation between courtyard house and neighbourhood in Beijing:

1. *Clear distinction between private and common space*: With respect to the interiors of the buildings in the courtyard house, the saying is: "One

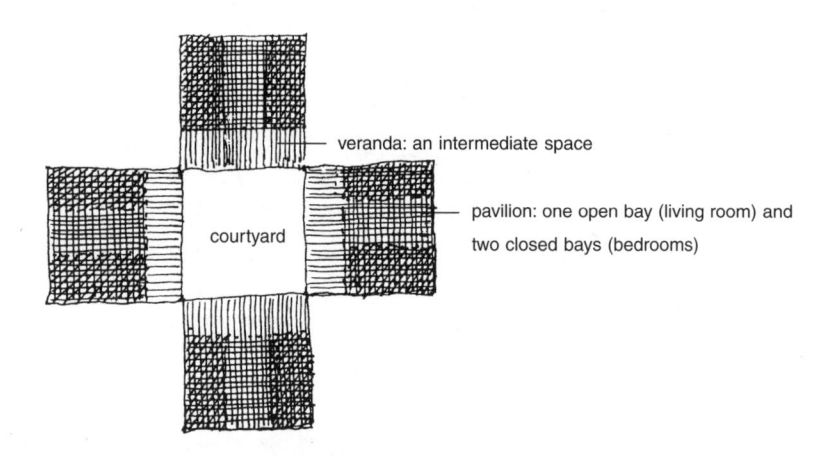

Figure 5.28 **Wang Guowei's description of the courtyard house.**
The courtyard is the most public part of the complex. The corridor is a grey traditional area between the courtyard and the rooms. There are usually one open and two closed bays in a room, for which different privacy levels were provided.

bright and two dark; one primary and two secondary [*yi ming er an, yi zhu er cong*]." This is to say that each of the pavilions on each side of a courtyard usually consists of three bays: the middle bay is the main hall or sitting room and is the only room accessible from the courtyard, and the two bays on either side of the hall are bedrooms or studies for private use and are accessible only from the hall. This principle in fact extends throughout the compound and between the compound and the *hutong*.
2. *Interrelation between interior and exterior*: There is a layering of indoor and outdoor spaces such that, viewed from the pavilions on its sides, the courtyard is a kind of extension of the building interior. Viewed from the public *hutong*, it forms a kind of roofless ante-room to the dwelling as a whole. This effect is multiplied by the addition of extra gates, courts, galleries, and verandas in more complex houses.
3. *Natural beauty in a human-made environment*: Courtyard houses are human-made, but nature is introduced in the form of various trees and flowers. Sophisticated gardens were created in some large courtyard house complexes in the past (Figure 5.29). However, even the humblest courtyards traditionally contain plants, fish tanks, and other small reminders of nature. The effect is to create in the neighbourhoods oases of tranquility and grace where residents can find relief from the stress and bustle of the city.[32]
4. *Residents' sense of identity and belonging to a local culture*: The courtyards' plants and flowers also highlight local culture and reflect the personality of the inhabitants. In Beijing, the courtyard houses contain local plants with special folk meanings. For example, pomegranate and date (fertility), magnolia and Chinese crab-apple (wealth), and wisteria and myrtle (official title). Gold fish symbolize abundance. This folk tradition has lost much of its original literal relevance, but the environment it has bequeathed us remains as aesthetically valuable as ever.
5. *Hierarchical structure of streets, lanes, and courtyards*: The city streets, lanes, courtyards, and rooms are structured in such a logical way that privacy increases as the living quarters are approached. The environment is easily accessible to pedestrians and cyclists but not to heavy automotive traffic. The hierarchy provides a rich variation of the experiences of urban space and creates a quiet, liveable environment with easy access to services. The city presents nature amidst human-made space; there is never a place that is too crowded or too quiet. There are trees, even in houses on the narrowest *hutong*, and it is never too far to walk to a marketplace, even from the innermost alleys.[33] After hundreds of years, Beijing's urban structure has become more and more diverse and complex because of the continuous inner growth of the old neighbourhoods. The city around them bustles ever more intensely. However, the various courtyards and lanes, often tree-shaded, still form quiet neighbourhoods

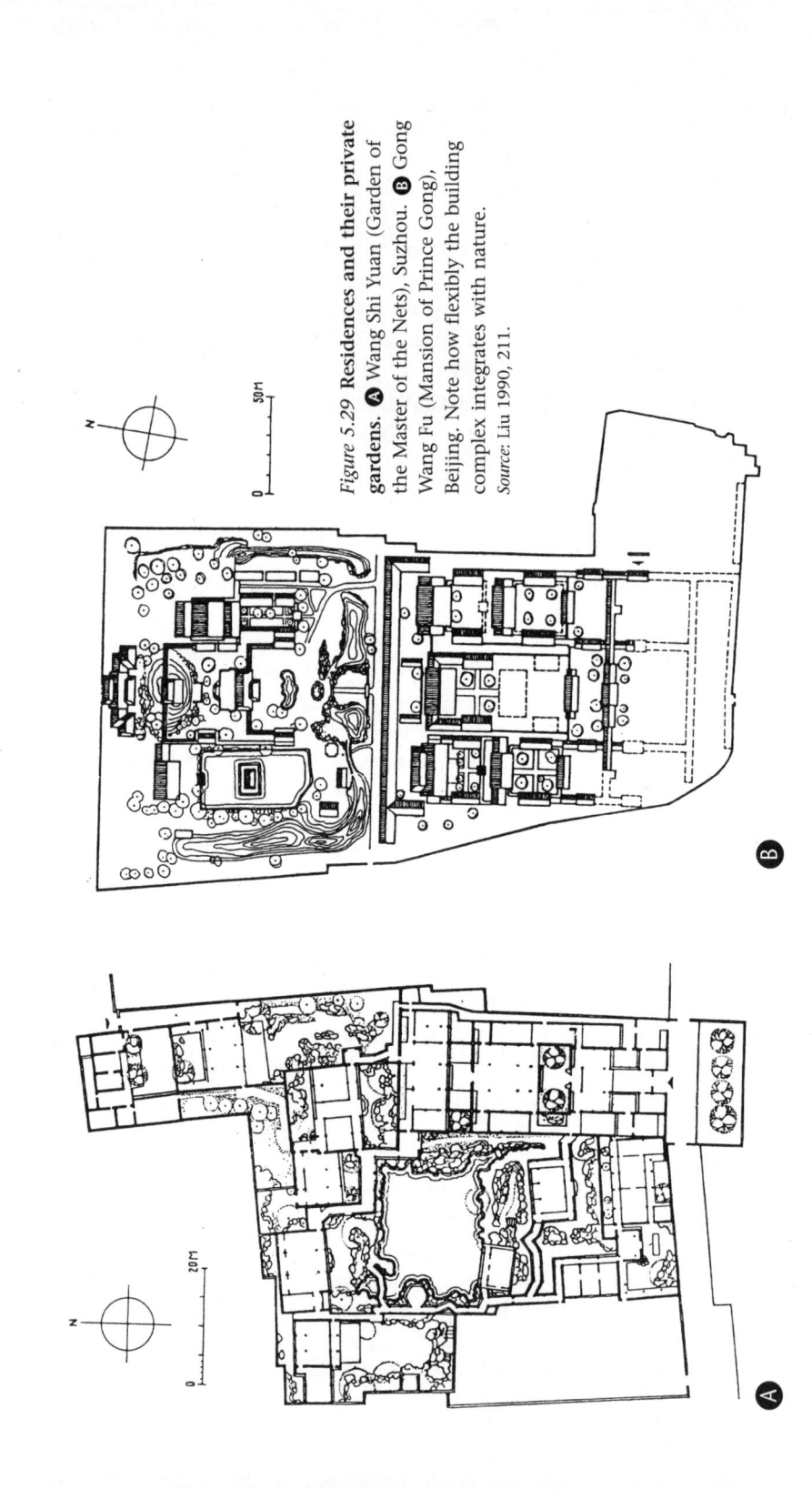

Figure 5.29 **Residences and their private gardens.** Ⓐ Wang Shi Yuan (Garden of the Master of the Nets), Suzhou. Ⓑ Gong Wang Fu (Mansion of Prince Gong), Beijing. Note how flexibly the building complex integrates with nature.
Source: Liu 1990, 211.

amenable to casual contact between neighbours. In fact, it is precisely this type of neighbourhood that is pursued by modern planners and architects in the city centres and suburbs of more developed societies.

Having thus summed up the aesthetic essence of the traditional residential environment of Beijing, we should be able to apply it to all new residential construction within the Old City. In other words, if new housing in the Old City can possess, support, and enhance the features outlined above, then it is worthy of its location and can be considered a continuation of Beijing's great tradition. This is the challenge facing any effort to create a new housing prototype for Beijing's Old City, and it is the goal of the particular project described in the remaining chapters of this book: the renewal of the Ju'er Hutong neighbourhood.

6
Planning and Design of the Ju'er Hutong Project

Earlier chapters in this book provide the theoretical premises for the attempt to develop a new courtyard house prototype. Their intent is to demonstrate the methodology of comprehensive consideration of urban form – from the largest to the smallest spatial scale, and from the most historic to the most immediate temporal scale – that should underlie the practice of design in the Old City. Unfortunately, this methodology is sadly lacking in current urban and architectural design practice in China, and so it is this methodology, more than any specific design outcome, that I hope will be appreciated.

The remainder of this book describes a case study concerned with rehabilitating the residential areas of the Old City of Beijing: the Ju'er Hutong project. The principles underlying the urban form of Beijing, as described in the previous chapters, served as the basis for the design of the Ju'er Hutong project carried out by a group under my direction at Tsinghua University. The following chapters describe in detail the progress of the project's design through different phases and its relation to the planning and design of the 8.2-hectare parcel in the northeast corner of the Nan Luogu Xiang area – the designated preservation district in which Ju'er Hutong is located (Figure 6.1). However, interwoven with the details of this case are further observations on general theories, principles, and methods of rehabilitation. These include:

- rediscovering the urban fabric of the Old City;
- establishing a new courtyard house prototype characterized by a series of courtyards with a system of internal access inspired by the "back alley" or "middle corridor" of the typical vernacular housing clusters in Suzhou;
- working out a standard courtyard house unit that achieves an ideal balance of sunshine, ventilation, lighting, and other environmental conditions on the one hand, and an intense use of land (floor-area ratio, or FAR) on the other;

Planning and Design of the Ju'er Hutong Project 105

[⌐ ⌐] Nan Luo Gu Xiang block   ■ 8.2 hectares of the Ju'er Hutong neighbourhood

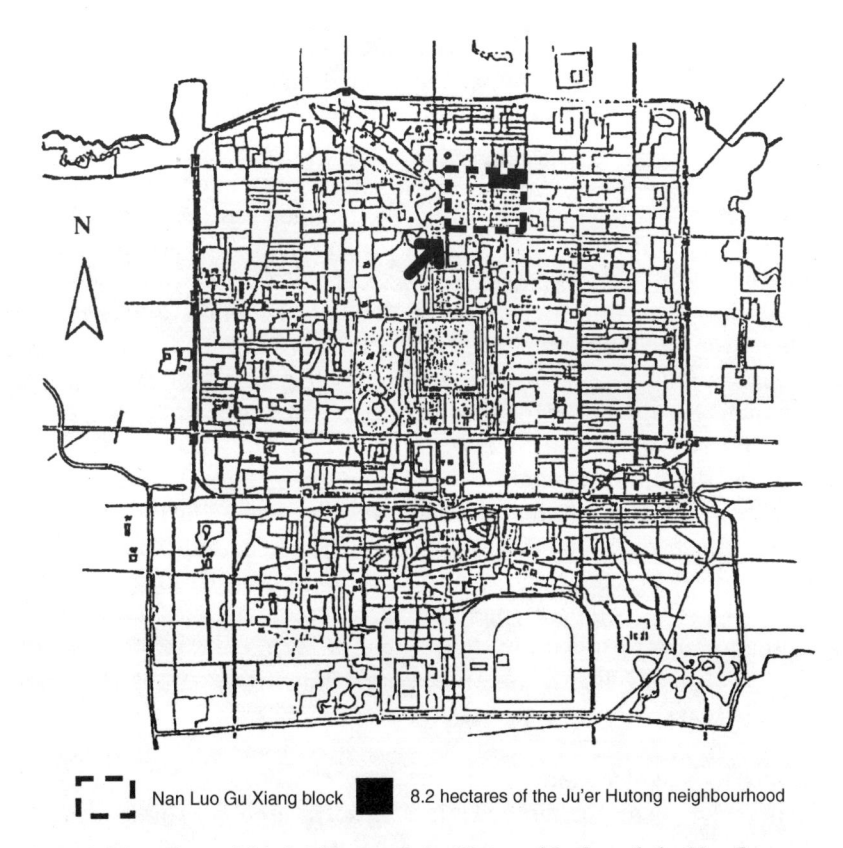

Figure 6.1 **Location of the 8.2-hectare Ju'er Hutong block and the Nan Luogu Xiang superblock in the Old City of Beijing**

- developing an alley-like system of access between courtyard units that recalls the age-old system of courtyards and *hutong*.

Development of a Design Idea

Early Studies
Since 1978, faculty and students in the School of Architecture at Tsinghua University have conducted studies for the Beijing Master Plan as well as for the urban design of particular neighbourhoods of the city. The Shichahai area around the three lakes north of Beihai was the most intensely researched by these many teams. Plans for the Shichahai area in 1979 precipitated the concepts of rehabilitation in traditional housing, organic renewal, and new courtyard housing design, and they led the way in establishing the relationship between Beijing's overall urban form and its neighbourhood structure, as described in the previous chapters (Figure 2.10).[1] Then, in 1983,

Professors Zhang Shouyi and Li Deyao led a team from Tsinghua University to survey the derelict housing in the Fahuasi area east of the Temple of Heaven. This work has had an important influence on subsequent studies of derelict housing.[2]

Research on an integrated strategy for conservation in Beijing's Old City continued from 1986 onwards, and some progress was made concerning old courtyard housing rehabilitation. Research findings and design proposals were presented in 1987 at a conference in London, and exhibitions were held in the United Kingdom, Germany, and Canada.[3] In the same year, the Beijing Municipal Government Housing Reform Office launched a pilot program to test, on a small scale, various approaches to renewing dilapidated neighbourhoods. Based on the Property Management Bureau's surveys of housing in particularly bad condition, each of the four districts that composed the Old City nominated a site for renewal. Ju'er Hutong was selected by the East City District, Xiaohoucang was selected by the West City District, Caochang Toutiao was selected by the Chongwen District in the southeast, and Dongnanyuan was selected by the Xuanwu District in the southwest. Each experimental project received some financial assistance from the municipal government. In the autumn of 1989, the first phase of the Ju'er Hutong new courtyard housing began, signifying a new phase of rehabilitation that combined experiment, research, and practice.

Site Survey and Selection

The Ju'er Hutong neighbourhood is located northeast of the Forbidden City, 600 metres east of the Drum Tower. It consists of an 8.2-hectare block bounded by Ju'er Hutong on the south, Nan Luogu Xiang on the west, Gulou Dong Dajie on the north, and Jiaodaokou Nan Dajie on the east (Figure 6.2). This block is crossed by two small winding lanes, Shoubi Hutong and Xiao Ju'er Hutong. The larger superblock, of which the Ju'er Hutong renewal site makes up the northeast corner, now takes its name from the street that bisects it, Nan Luogu Xiang. This superblock is the same Zhaohui-Jinggong Fang that dates from the Yuan dynasty, as described in Chapter 5. In 1982 the Municipal Master Plan designated it a Traditional Courtyard Housing Preservation District. The site is only one block away from the Di'anmen commercial street on the central axis of the city. It still contains many especially large and fine examples of old courtyard mansion compounds and gardens – architectural evidence of its former status as an aristocratic area – many of which were neglected or damaged outright during the Cultural Revolution.

In 1987, the planning team under my direction at Tsinghua University conducted a survey of twenty-four households in the courtyard compound at Numbers 41 and 99 (hereafter referred to as Number 41) Ju'er Hutong. This compound was originally a small temple named Hongdeshanlin. It is

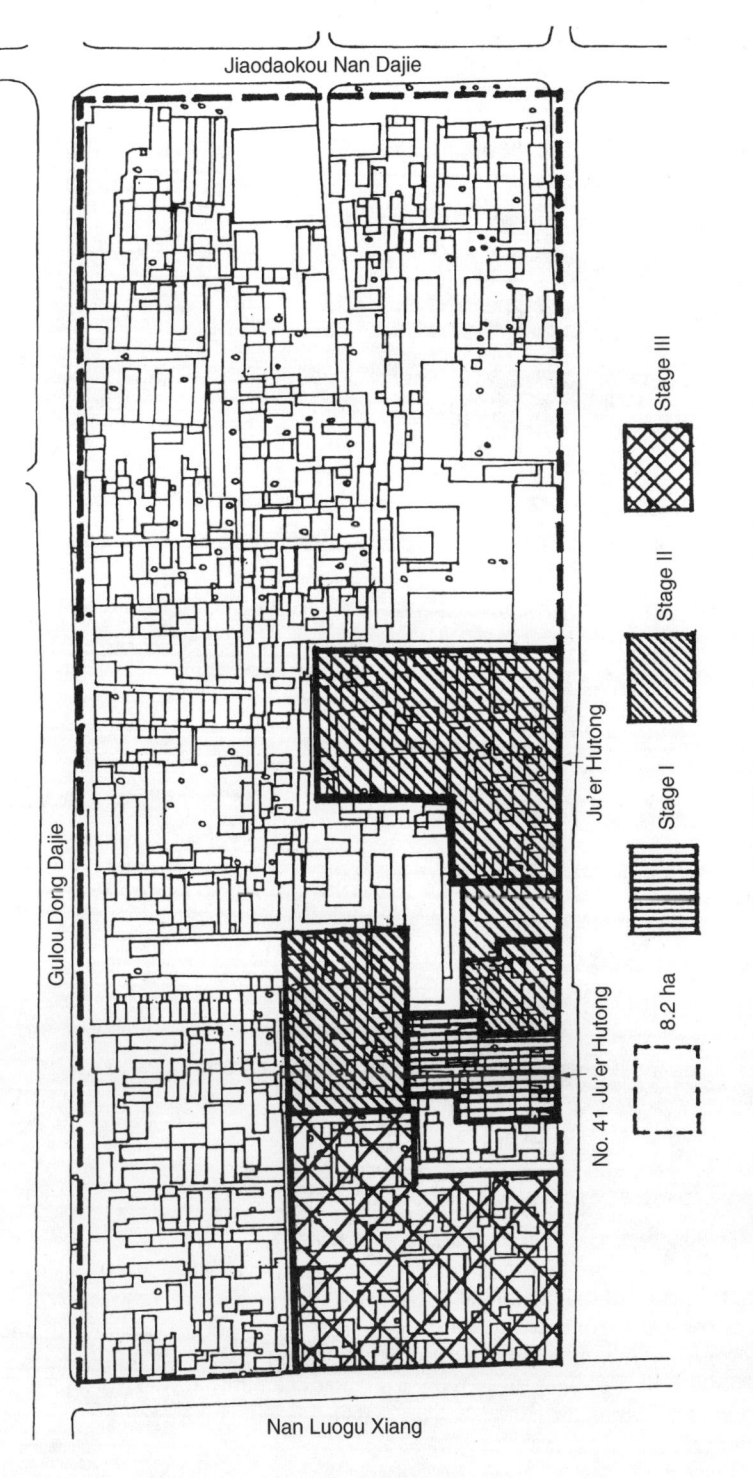

Figure 6.2 Location of the renewal parcels within the 8.2-hectare Ju'er Hutong block

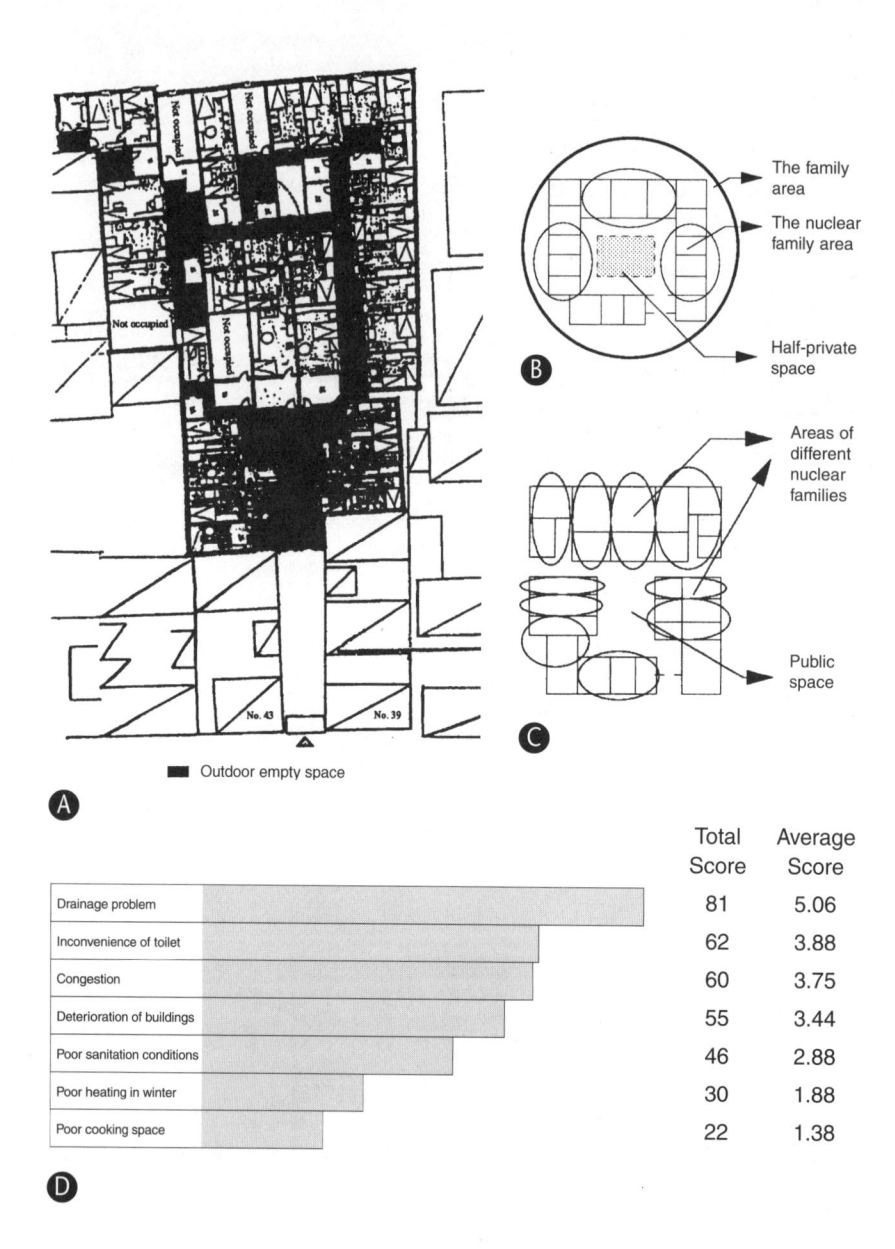

108 Planning and Design of the Ju'er Hutong Project

	Total Score	Average Score
Drainage problem	81	5.06
Inconvenience of toilet	62	3.88
Congestion	60	3.75
Deterioration of buildings	55	3.44
Poor sanitation conditions	46	2.88
Poor heating in winter	30	1.88
Poor cooking space	22	1.38

Figure 6.3 **Survey of courtyard at No. 41 Ju'er Hutong.**
Ⓐ Living conditions in the courtyard at No. 41 Ju'er Hutong prior to renewal.
Ⓑ Social structure of the traditional courtyard house: gradual gain of privacy inside the compound, and well-defined functional areas. **Ⓒ** Social structure of the typical courtyard house today: no gradual change of privacy; vague boundaries between different functional areas and possibilities of conflict among the residents.
Ⓓ Factors constituting the complaints of residents regarding their living conditions.

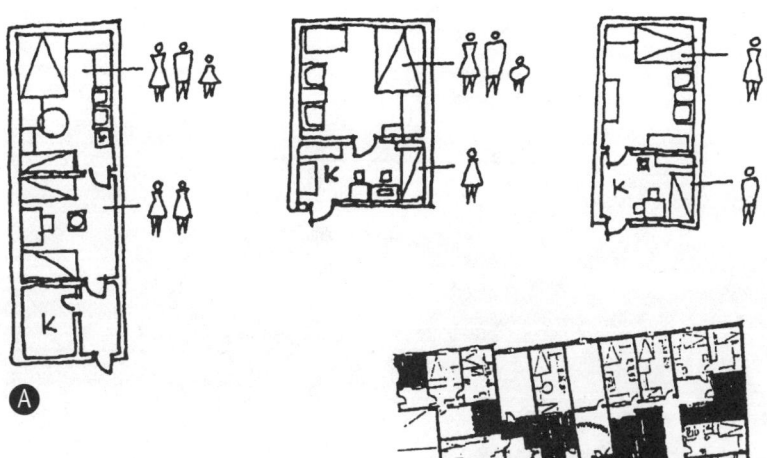

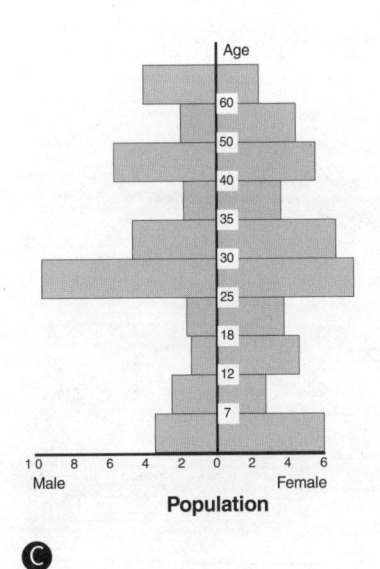

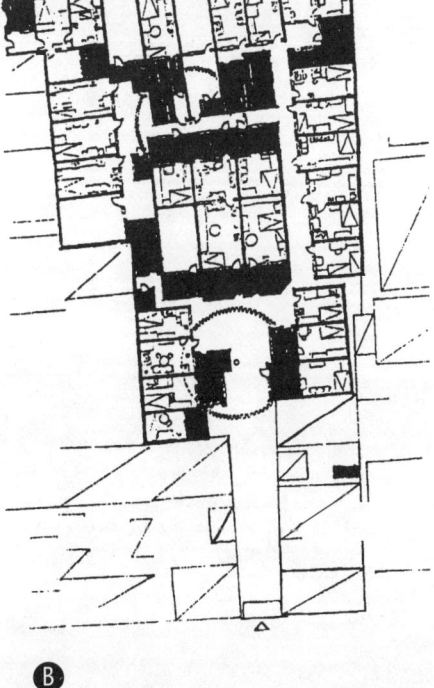

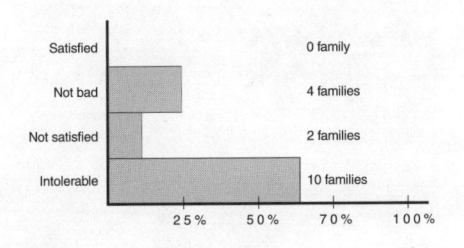

Planning and Design of the Ju'er Hutong Project   109

Figure 6.4 **Survey of courtyard at No. 41 Ju'er Hutong (continued).**
Ⓐ Selected household arrangements for different surveyed families. Ⓑ Residents' self-built extensions (shown in black). Ⓒ Population structure. Ⓓ General responses by residents regarding living conditions.

Figure 6.5 View over the courtyard at No. 41 Ju'er Hutong prior to renewal

Figure 6.6 Residents' self-built extensions filling in the courtyard

◄*Figure 6.7* **Remaining common circulation space within the courtyard**

▼*Figure 6.8* **Interior of one household, showing coal stove and tin chimney**

said that the temple once contained a broken stele dating from the Yuan dynasty, but this has long since disappeared. During the Japanese occupation of Beijing, it was used as a barracks for soldiers and then fell into disrepair as a *da za yuan*, or "big cluttered courtyard." After the Liberation, the general limitations of the economy prevented its reconstruction. The 1987 survey included residents' opinions, living habits, and potential post-renewal needs as well as the housing's physical condition (Figures 6.3 to 6.8, and Table 6.1).

The survey of the courtyard compound at Number 41 Ju'er Hutong identified a number of problems and conditions that ultimately led to its selection as the East City District's pilot renewal project (which, in turn, became Phase 1 of the entire Ju'er Hutong project):

1. *Extremely poor environmental conditions and facilities.* The existing courtyard ground level was 0.8 to 1.0 metres lower than the outside road and

Table 6-1

Survey of conditions before and after renewal at Ju'er Hutong Numbers 41 and 99

Situation before redevelopment	
Area (metres^2 excluding entrance passage)	1,000
Number of households	24
Number of persons with residential permit *(hukou)*	78
Number of persons normally in residence	85
Percentage of persons over 65 years	5
Percentage of persons under 14 years	15
Overall evaluation of conditions (percent)	
Satisfactory	0
Indifferent	25
Unsatisfactory	12
Intolerable	62
Overcrowding	
Original floor space of the courtyard (metres^2)	580
So-called temporary extensions (metres^2)	450
Percentage of total site covered	84
After redevelopment of Phase 1	
Area (metres^2)	2,090
Number of apartments	46
Number of households actually in residence	36
Number of households normally in residence	31
Number of persons normally in residence	91

was often flooded. Two-thirds of the households did not have direct sunlight, and there was only one water tap (installed before 1949) and one drain, which were shared by all eighty-plus residents. A shared public toilet was located about 100 metres away from the courtyard. Many buildings were either structurally hazardous, flooded, or leaking.
2. *Extreme crowding*. Population increase over the years forced the residents to build extensions into the courtyards. For example, in order to accommodate children over the age of fifteen in a separate bedroom from their parents, families generally had to build themselves an additional shelter in the courtyard space. These poor-quality buildings, initially approved on a temporary basis, had become permanent. At courtyard Number 41, as much as 84 percent of the site was covered by buildings, where originally only 58 percent was covered (the newer 26 percent was entirely self-built). The average sheltered area per household was 10.6 square metres, or 7 to 8 square metres per person, with the most crowded households only having 5.3 square metres per person. Moreover, the households were likely to grow even more, since a high proportion of them were made up of young married couples without children.
3. *Proximity to the traditional courtyard house protection zone*. Despite its severely dilapidated and crowded conditions, the Ju'er Hutong neighbourhood was located at the edge of the Nan Luogu Xiang Traditional Courtyard Housing Preservation District, which meant that the derelict housing could not be replaced by conventional five- or six-storey apartment blocks. It was therefore an ideal site for a new courtyard housing experiment.
4. *Support from the residents*. The residents were eager to improve their housing and environmental conditions. They supported the housing reform and were willing to purchase their own houses after the project was completed.

Inevitably, none of the residents living in the courtyard was happy with the housing conditions. However, the adverse physical conditions did not prevent close relationships from developing among the neighbours. They cooperated in a fashion that has become a hallmark of life in the crowded courtyards and *hutong*, as mentioned in the previous chapter. For example, if someone worked a night shift and needed to sleep during the day, he or she could ask the neighbours to keep quiet, and children were often looked after by neighbours while their parents were out. The average resident was in the habit of making unannounced visits to three to five neighbouring households. However, the most frequent visitors were not neighbours but work colleagues, relatives, friends, and old classmates. Residents kept the limited common space well, but, unfortunately, close relationships came at the expense of privacy, and, not surprisingly, quarrels over the common space did occur. When asked if they would prefer to have their own private, enclosed, small outdoor activity space (small court or terrace) or to share a relatively large court with a few other designated families, every resident chose the former.

In traditional courtyard houses, the many-layered transition from public to private domains, and the clear definition of these domains, has degenerated into the *da za yuan*. The current spatial structure of the courtyard house has diverged fundamentally from the traditional one. Domains are unclear and overlapping, and, consequently, residents easily come into conflict. Indeed, the relations among neighbours in Beijing's contemporary courtyard houses are very complex and are much closer than are those among residents of multi-storey apartment estates. The dozens of residents of a single courtyard compound generally all know each other's names, where each resident works, where their children attend school, whom they receive as guests, what intra-familial disputes they have: in short, they know each other nearly as well as they know themselves. Critics of high-rise apartment housing often point to the indifference that characterizes relations between their residents. However, it must be noted that in the one-storey courtyard houses, close relations among the residents do not necessarily mean intimate relations. Their interaction is forced upon them by tight circumstances and entails a fundamental disruption of privacy.

It is also important to point out that, unlike the residents of slums in many developing countries, most of the residents in these neighbourhoods have regular jobs and reliable incomes. The poor housing conditions are not necessarily signs of urban poverty, as most of the slum residents belong to local district-owned work units that often lack the funds to offer their workers new housing. As a result, they have to meet their increasing housing needs through adding extensions onto existing houses. Such self-help projects increase residents' attachment to the area where they live. They seek to improve their physical surroundings rather than to move out.

Therefore, the chief parameters of the renewal project were ultimately defined by the need to solve the basic physical problems listed above; to respect, support, and enhance the residents' attachments to each other and to their place; and to return to residents the original sense of privacy and spatial control that the traditional courtyard environment once provided.

Survey of Existing Conditions throughout the Neighbourhood (1989-90)

In total, seven courtyards, including Number 41, were chosen for the first phase. The project involved 44 households and 139 residents. However, the Tsinghua team anticipated the project expanding to include more of the neighbourhood and, therefore, conducted a wider survey of the surrounding 8.2-hectare block, investigating such issues as land use, road systems, building quality, and grouping of building clusters (Figures 6.9 and 6.10 and Table 6.2). This provided an overview on which the planning and design decisions for all the phases were based.

Community Facilities

The Ju'er Hutong neighbourhood is within close walking distance of abundant municipal facilities, shops, services, cinemas, hospitals, and primary and middle schools. Public bus lines link the area to all parts of the city. However, the neighbourhood lacks open space and social services such as day centres for the elderly, kindergartens, and playgrounds. Ju'er Hutong did have an elderly residents activity centre. On Sundays and on weekday

Table 6-2

A summary of basic statistics: A residential survey of the Ju'er Hutong neighbourhood before renewal (1988)

Total population (persons)	(4,800)*
Total residential population (persons)	3,180 (3,580)*
Total number of households	1,144
of 1 person	266
of 2-4 persons	752
of 5 or more persons	126
Average household size (persons per household)	2.79
Total land area within setback for new street widening (hectares)	6.76
Total residential land area (hectares)	5.47
Multi-storey buildings	0.42
Single-storey buildings	5.05
Total non-residential land area (hectares)	1.29
Retail services	0.14
Community services	0.01
Industry/warehousing	0.76
Streets and alleyways	0.38
Municipal utilities	0.00
Open space	0.00
Gross population density (persons per hectare)	408.8
Net population density (persons per hectare)	598.4
Seriously dilapidated residential area (square metres)	
Flooded (5 percent of total)	2,570
Poor building quality (11 percent of total)	5,401

* Figures in parentheses include residents of new multi-storey housing; all other population and household figures do not (because new multi-storey housing was not to be redeveloped).

116 *Planning and Design of the Ju'er Hutong Project*

Land Use

■ Retail and services
● Neighbourhood committee
⊤⊤ Hutong
☐ Single storey housing
▨ Institutions
▦ Factory
▩ Warehouses
⋮⋮ Apartment building

Residential building density

▦ > 60%
▨ < 60%

Residential population density

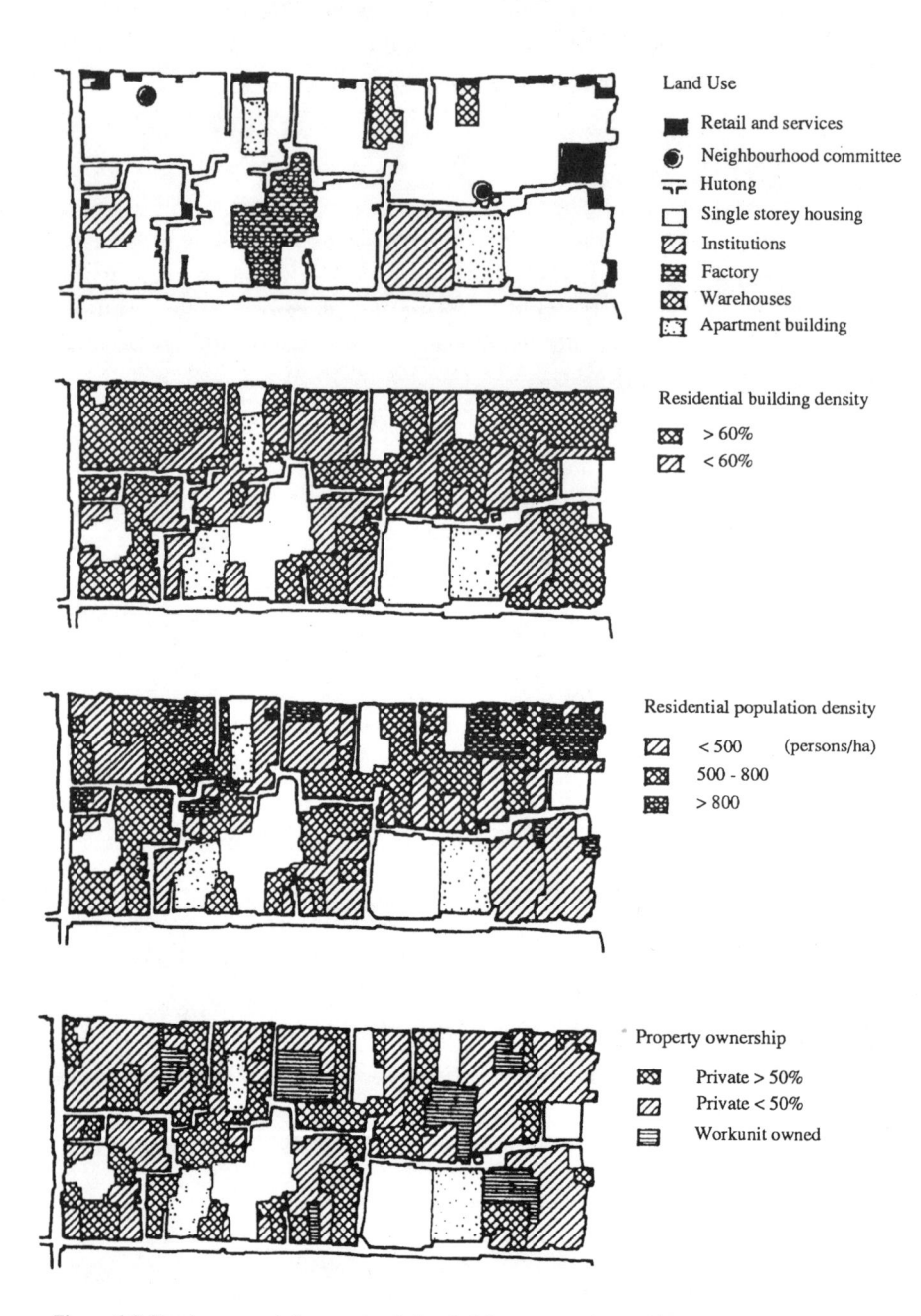

▨ < 500   (persons/ha)
▦ 500 - 800
▦ > 800

Property ownership

▦ Private > 50%
▨ Private < 50%
≡ Workunit owned

Figure 6.9 **Environmental survey of the 8.2 hectares of Ju'er Hutong neighbourhood: Basic indicators**

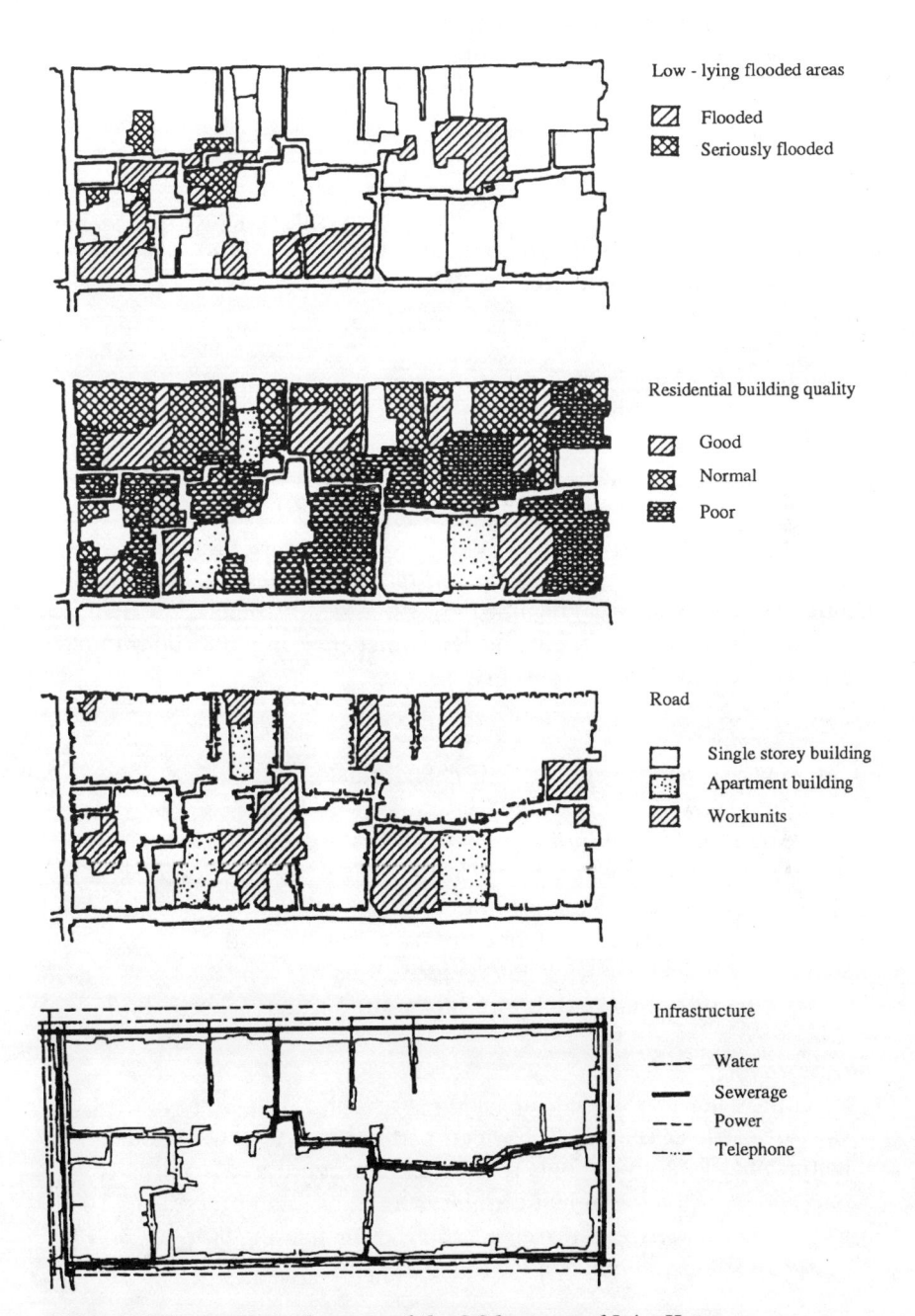

Planning and Design of the Ju'er Hutong Project 117

Figure 6.10 Environmental survey of the 8.2 hectares of Ju'er Hutong neighbourhood: Buildings and infrastructure

evenings, it was open for residents from this and other nearby *hutong*. The main activities were informal Peking Opera, chess, mah-jong, and so on. Elderly residents were relatively satisfied with this type of activity, but, given that 10 percent of the population in this 8.2-hectare block was over 65 years of age, the space provided was still too little. There was also a youth activity centre with a meagre library and two or three table-tennis tables, but it was much too small, and, after school, children were usually forced to play in the *hutong*. When housing conditions are so crowded, an adequate community centre is an absolute necessity.

Housing Conditions
Housing conditions in the Ju'er Hutong neighbourhood differ in terms of building type and period of construction. In addition to the traditional courtyard houses built over 100 years ago, there are brick-built multi-storey row-type apartments from the 1950s, low-cost buildings from the 1960s, and four- to six-storey apartment buildings from the 1970s. These buildings were mixed in terms of type and function. Except for a few protected historic houses and modern multi-storey apartment buildings, nearly all of the single-storey houses were hemmed in by a maze of temporary shelters recently built by residents. This made maintenance very difficult and hastened the deterioration of the environment.

Mixed Land Use
Land use was mixed within the neighbourhood and there was no overall planning. While the mix of land use was, in itself, not considered to be problematic – in fact, one of the eventual goals of the project was to accommodate a mix of residential and productive uses (see discussion below on Phase 2 of the development process) – the lack of a rational separation between certain industrial and residential uses created pollution and an intrusion on the residential living environment. This was combined with a lack of basic fire precaution measures, which caused serious concern.

Local Traffic
Street provision was inadequate and only occupied 3.5 percent of the total land area at Ju'er Hutong. The widest part of the system was about seven metres and the narrowest only two metres. The network of lanes was circuitous and carried a mixture of cars, bicycles, trucks, and pedestrians. There was no parking space, garbage collection, or firefighting facilities, and industrial loading and unloading were all difficult.

Physical Infrastructure
The infrastructure in the neighbourhood, including water supply, sewerage, power supply, and telecommunications, was obsolete and inadequate.

Gas supply would not be possible in the near future, and new development of any higher density would exacerbate existing problems. All of these problems are typical of the historic residential areas in Beijing. Realistically, these neighbourhoods required not only new housing, but also a comprehensive rehabilitation program. For this reason, from the point of view of design, it was essential to consider the housing as part of a larger urban spatial structure.

Search for a "New Courtyard System"

Having investigated the particular problems and needs of the neighbourhood as just described, the planning team at Tsinghua was ready to embark on the actual design work for Ju'er Hutong. In fact, however, design studies for the rehabilitation of courtyard-type housing had been carried out continuously since the first explorations in 1978. Many of the problems from one neighbourhood in the Old City to the next are similar, and so it was possible to use the early studies as the basis for introducing a new housing type in Ju'er Hutong. The following describes how that new type took shape.

Among the favourable comments received regarding the first phase of the Ju'er Hutong project are that it has an intimate atmosphere, a humane scale, and a strong local character – precisely the qualities that are now lacking in the modern apartment buildings found everywhere in Chinese cities. Indeed, these characteristics were derived directly from the historic courtyard houses of the old neighbourhoods and were the starting point of this experiment. Of particular importance is the retention of the courtyard space itself as a new communal space; this distinguishes the Ju'er Hutong design from that of conventional apartment blocks. The gardens and alleyways were laid out so as to preserve existing trees, and the second- and third-storey walls were whitewashed to contrast with the trees and their shadows. Socially, this new courtyard facilitates neighbourhood communication through the provision of intimate and well-defined communal space, while retaining privacy and supplying the amenities available in modern apartment blocks. The Ju'er Hutong project thus aimed to combine the benefits of the two housing forms.

However, although the design work for the Ju'er Hutong project began with an architectural concept inspired by the traditional courtyard form as modified to serve modern households, it very quickly also had to take into consideration the issue of density, or, more precisely, land-use intensity. Without a floor-area ratio comparable to that of conventional multi-storey buildings, the new housing type would not be viable under the intense pressure to use land efficiently. The design process proceeded through three stages, each dealing with successively larger-scale issues. Since actual construction was also phased, this allowed some of the smaller-scale issues to be resolved and tested in construction before the larger-scale issues had to be resolved. But before this process can be described, it is necessary to discuss the issue of land-use intensity, since this has been such a central concern in the debate over the conservation, redevelopment, and rehabilitation of Beijing's Old City.

Debate over the Floor-Area Ratio

Definition of Floor-Area Ratio

Floor-area ratio is related to environmental quality. Defined as the amount of floor area built on a certain area of land, floor-area ratio reflects the intensity of that site's use with regard to building. Planning for floor-area ratio can, therefore, control building density (or ground coverage); population density; and, ultimately, environmental quality. Other factors being equal, the higher the floor-area ratio, the greater the profits the developer can make. A careful balance between environmental quality and profit making is one of the basic goals of the Ju'er Hutong project.

Relaxation of central planning in China's economy has created leeway for developers to bargain for more profitable floor-area ratios. Consequently, over the past year or two, speculators in the newly opened land market have had the opportunity to manipulate the floor-area ratio. Some local authorities have lifted the upper limit of approved floor-area ratios, and others have leased land recklessly to developers for quick profits. Some architects have sacrificed their professional integrity to meet the developers' excessive demands. The result too often has been the destruction of China's historic cities and their replacement with "concrete jungles."

Floor-Area Ratio in the Old City Areas

Floor-area ratio in the Old City of Beijing is a complicated issue. Before deciding on a reasonable figure for any particular situation, several points must be considered. To begin with, redevelopment has to be based on the principle of conservation. There is no doubt that the Old City needs renewal, but views differ as to what would be an appropriate approach. Some believe that it should be developed into a central business district for its spatial and economic advantages; others are interested in modelling it on the modern Western city. Purely commercial interests could destroy the historic element completely, and copying Western design could conflict with Beijing's special physical and social structures. In my view, a better idea is to conserve the Old City so as to encourage tourism and recreation; this could be regarded as a "cultural investment" in the city. Additionally, a comprehensive development policy has to be pursued in order to balance the interests of residents and developers with traffic and infrastructure concerns and environmental quality. Sensitive areas with historical, cultural, or environmental significance should be made priorities for conservation, and a special budget should be established to guarantee financial resources for this purpose.

It is also important to refute the presumption that the taller the building, the higher the building density; when carefully designed, low-rise buildings can reach a comparable density. In the case of Beijing, low-rise buildings raise the floor-area ratio and also create a more desirable visual impact than do high-rise buildings. As described below, the Ju'er Hutong experiment proves that this approach is feasible (Figures 6.11 to 6.13). Furthermore, in the Old City residential land use is decreasing while the area given for roads and other infrastructure, as well as for institutions and commerce, is increasing. Given this reality, a reasonable number of residents should be

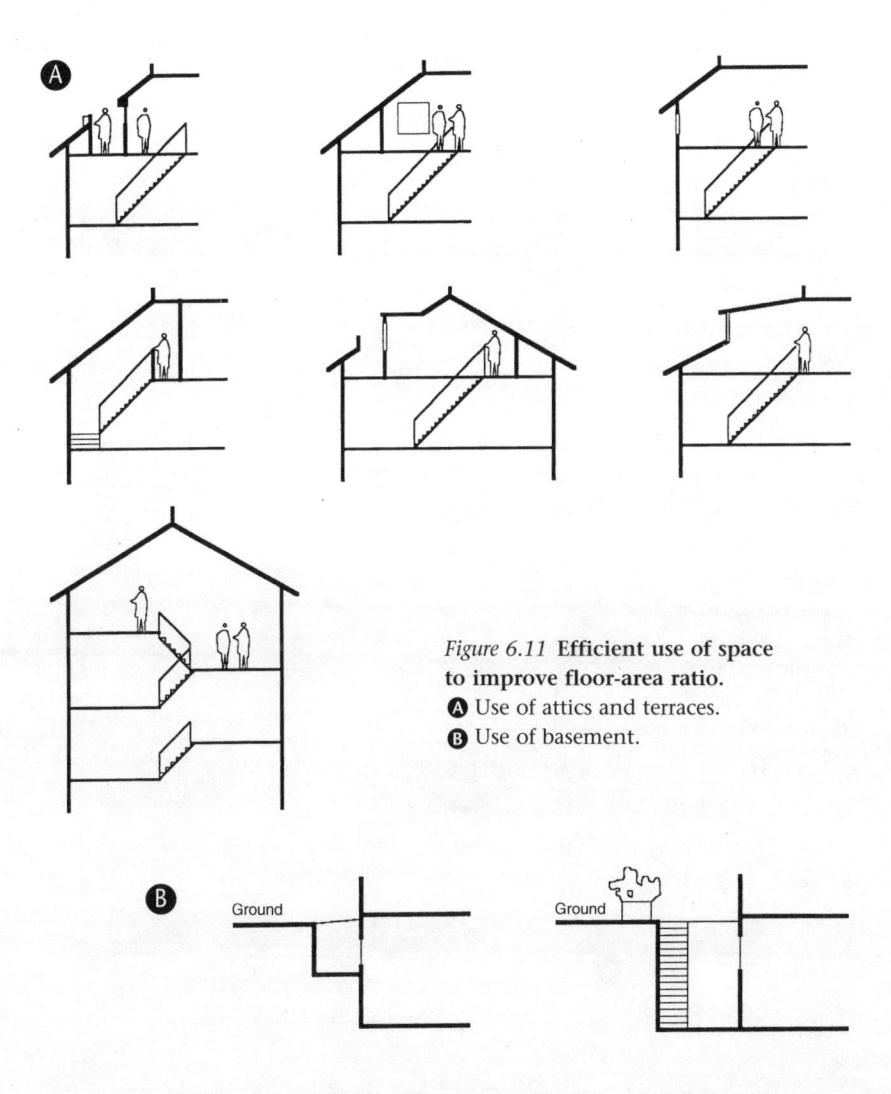

Figure 6.11 **Efficient use of space to improve floor-area ratio.**
Ⓐ Use of attics and terraces.
Ⓑ Use of basement.

122 *Planning and Design of the Ju'er Hutong Project*

housed outside the Old City in order to ease the pressure for a higher floor-area ratio. If this were done, then environmental quality could be safeguarded through a reasonable floor-area ratio and inventive design.

The Design Process

Stage One: The Courtyard Compound

A typical traditional courtyard house in Beijing has one courtyard and an overall form that has evolved to house an extended family (which is much larger than an average modern family). Also, past land-use intensity was much lower than today's land-use intensity – the buildings of most courtyard compounds covered only 50 to 60 percent of the plot and were only

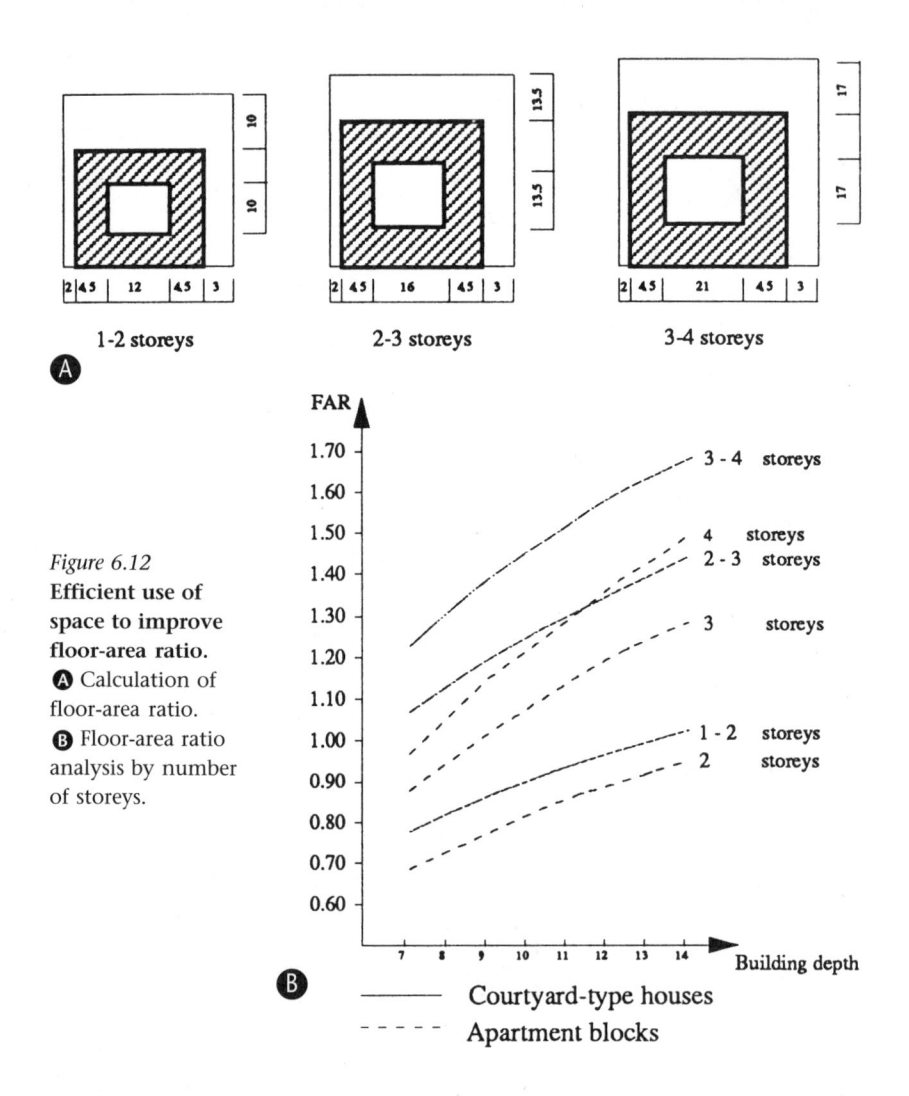

Figure 6.12
Efficient use of space to improve floor-area ratio.
Ⓐ Calculation of floor-area ratio.
Ⓑ Floor-area ratio analysis by number of storeys.

Planning and Design of the Ju'er Hutong Project   123

Fixed building depth

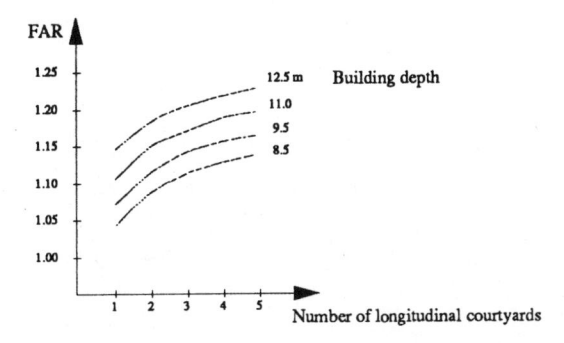

[FAR vs Number of longitudinal courtyards, curves for Building depth 12.5 m, 11.0, 9.5, 8.5]

Fixed number of longitudinal courtyards

[FAR vs Building depth, curves for Number of longitudinal courtyards 5, 4, 3, 2, 1]

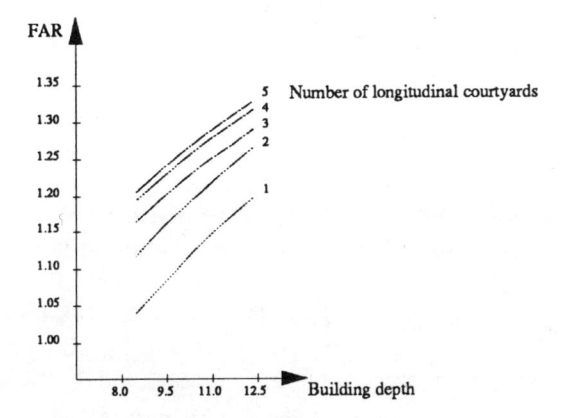

It can be seen from this figure that the increase of FAR is no longer obvious when the buildings are higher than 4 storeys.

Comparison with apartment blocks with similar conditions

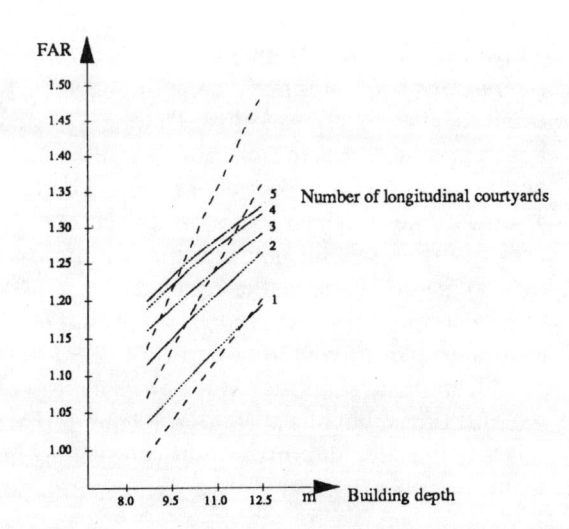

[FAR vs Building depth, curves for Number of longitudinal courtyards 5, 4, 3, 2, 1]

Figure 6.13 **Efficient use of space to improve floor-area ratio.**
Floor-area ratio analysis by number of longitudinal courtyards.

one-storey. It is therefore quite difficult to transform this kind of single-courtyard compound into a modern courtyard serving many families. However, the courtyard complexes of large palaces and mansions can serve as meaningful models today. In these cases, a long corridor, which is called *yongxiang* in palaces and *jiadao* in mansions, facilitates circulation in the complexes, which were composed of many self-contained courtyard enclosures (Figures 5.8a and 5.8b). The *beinong* in courtyard compounds in Suzhou plays the same role. In the early plans of the new courtyard houses, different courtyard sizes were combined with one- to three-storey buildings using two corridors similar to those in the large traditional complexes (Figure 6.14).

The above scheme, however, was unrealistic because it occupied too large an area of land per unit. In order to raise the floor-area ratio, the size of the courtyard was reduced – an unavoidable but far from ideal solution (Figures 6.15 and 6.16).

Stage Two: The Standard New Courtyard Cluster
At stage two, the design work focused on developing a standard new courtyard cluster with a reasonable density and floor-area ratio that also met requirements for sunlight, ventilation, and privacy. Houses of different heights and orientation were put together first. The relationship between building height and courtyard size was determined in order to meet standard sunlight requirements; courtyards of different sizes were then fit into the redevelopment sites (Figures 6.17 and 6.18). Previously known as "quasi-courtyard houses," such designs are now called "new courtyard houses." A cluster of two large courtyards and two small ones became the basis for Phase 1 of the Ju'er Hutong project construction (Figure 6.37).

The research in these first two stages led to several conclusions, which provided new insights into courtyard housing. First, it is possible to achieve a high floor-area ratio with a two- to three-storey courtyard building form even in this height-restricted zone (nine metres is the maximum building height in the block around Ju'er Hutong). This confirms what Martin and March proposed.[4] As Lin Hok Leung has also said, "a medium-rise courtyard house of 4-5 storeys can provide as much floor space as an 8-10 storey highrise apartment" and can have several advantages over the latter.[5] The Ju'er Hutong experiment proves this point for the first time in China. Second, by forming roof garden terraces, the combination of two- and three-storey buildings creates more private outdoor space than do the balconies on ordinary apartment blocks, which lie in a row. Third, the use of pitched roofs to provide more useable space in the attics increases the floor-area ratio without affecting sunlight penetration (Figure 6.11a). The result of these factors is that a two- and three-storey courtyard compound system can reach higher densities than can ordinary row apartment buildings with the same

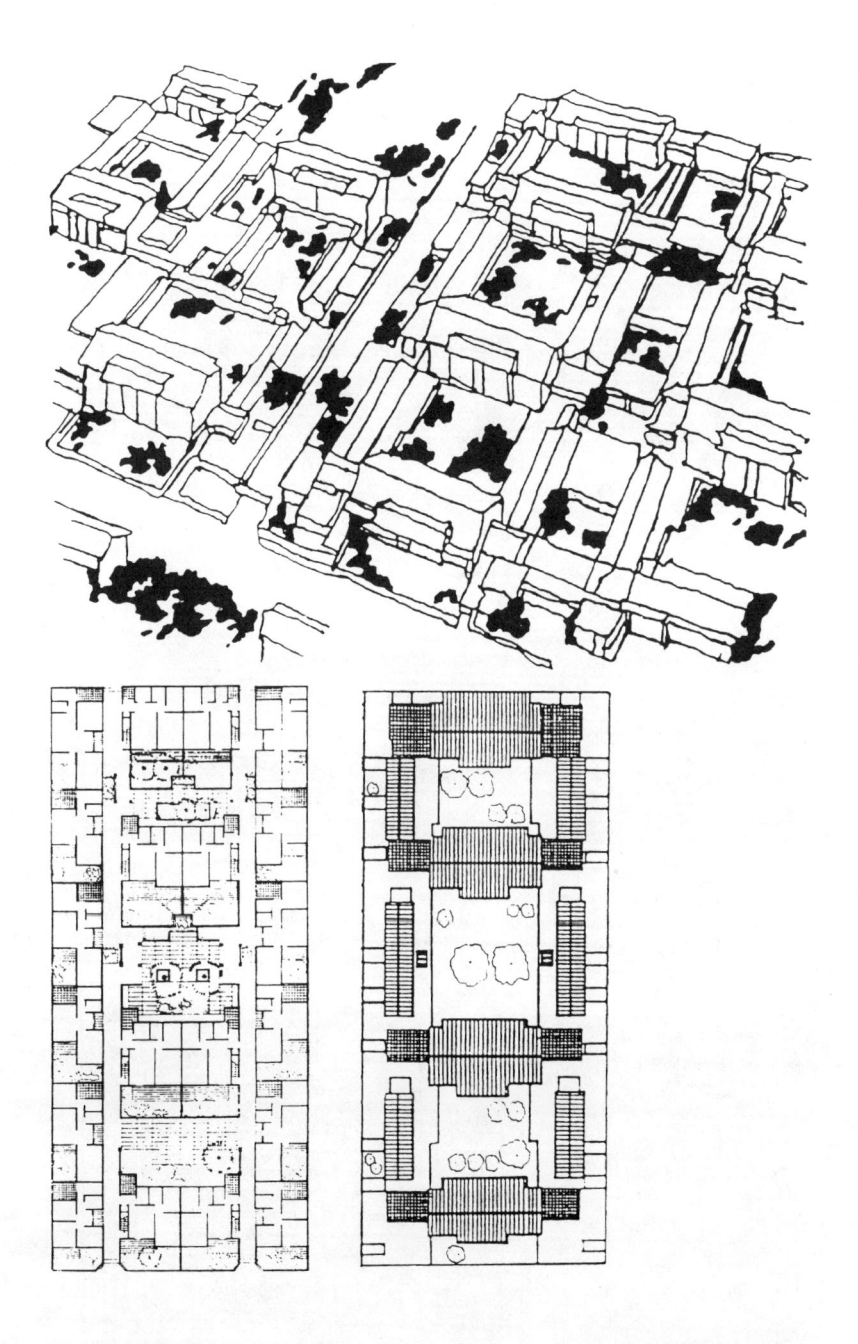

Figure 6.14 **Early studies (Design Process Stage 1): Courtyard complexes in the 1979 proposal.** Each standard courtyard complex consists of thirty units, including eight two-bedroom units (53 m^2/unit), eighteen three-bedroom units (60-70 m^2/unit), and four six-bedroom units (120 m^2/unit). Each hectare of land accommodates 115 households, or 540 residents.

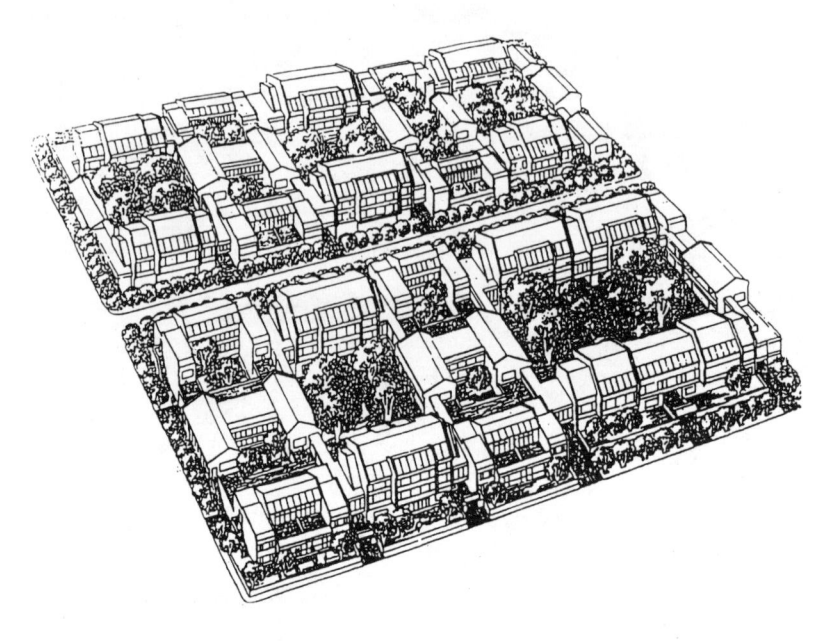

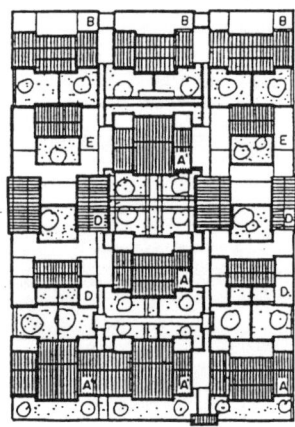

126 *Planning and Design of the Ju'er Hutong Project*

Varied courtyard organization

- A Unit type A
- B Unit type B
- C Unit type C
- D Unit type D
- E Unit type E

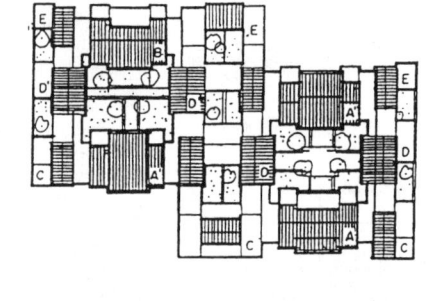

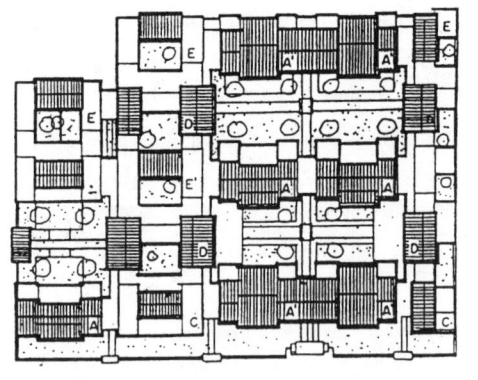

Figure 6.15 **Early studies (Design Process Stage 2): Small courtyard clusters in the 1987 proposal**

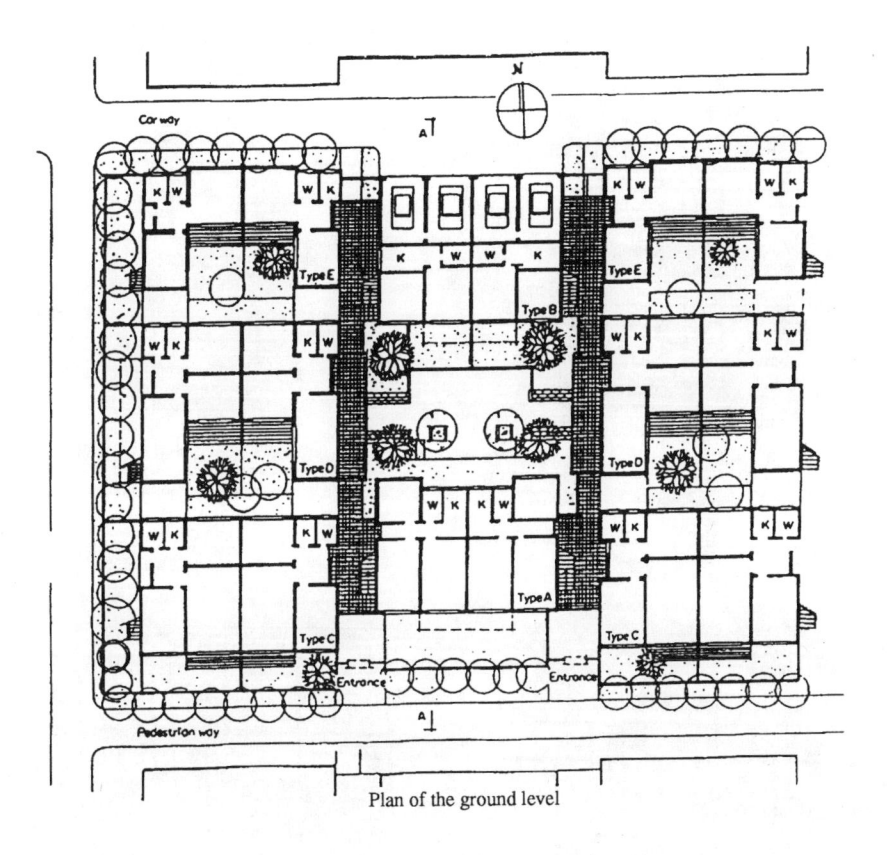

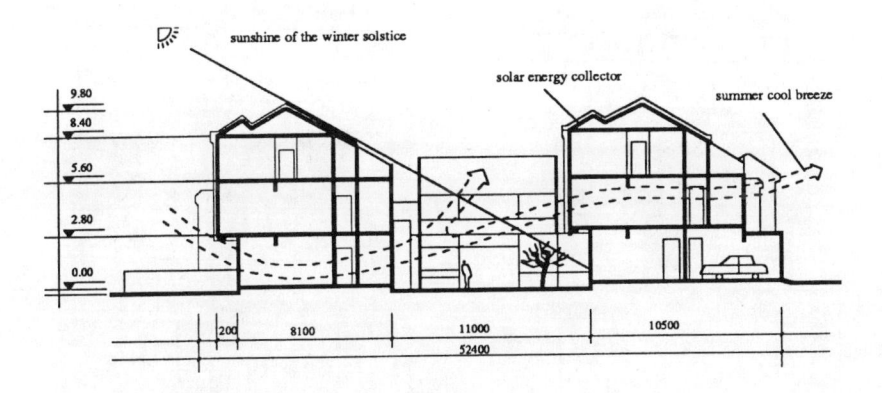

Planning and Design of the Ju'er Hutong Project 127

Figure 6.16 Early studies (Design Process Stage 2): Plan and section

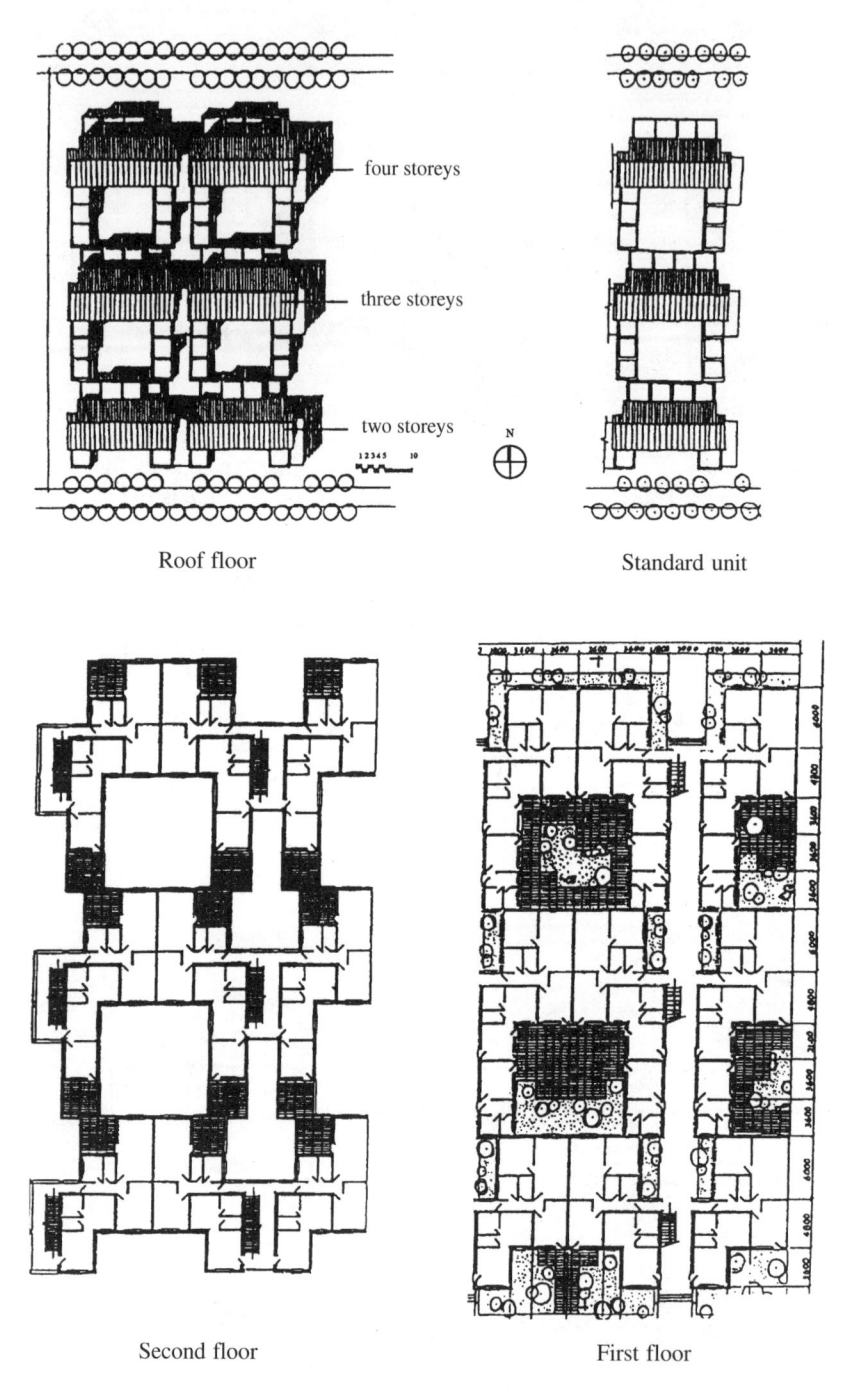

128 *Planning and Design of the Ju'er Hutong Project*

Roof floor

Standard unit

Second floor

First floor

Figure 6.17 **Early studies (Design Process Stage 3): Plan of courtyard complexes**

Figure 6.18 **Standard new courtyard-type house.** To compare with a standard traditional courtyard house, see Figure 5.25.

building depth. Additional advantages, not directly related to density, are that low-rise courtyard housing forms can help to create a more energy-efficient micro-climate and that the courtyard locations and sizes are quite variable, allowing for the preservation of existing trees and other irregular features on the site. Finally, two- and three-storey buildings require only light construction techniques, reducing capital costs and allowing for more flexible construction procedures, which is of primary importance when trying to respect the existing context of a historic area. Very often, the rigidity of conventional design and construction is the main reason given for *not* preserving local features in redevelopment projects.

Stage Three: The Courtyard-Alleyway System
Finally, having satisfactorily dealt with the density issue in the design of the standard courtyard cluster, the process could turn to the design of the access system of lanes linking these clusters (Figure 6.19). These lanes enable the circulation of pedestrians, emergency vehicles, and other services within the complex. They can be marked by different archways to enhance the identity of each courtyard unit or cluster of units and to recall the old *fangli* system of distinguishing neighbourhoods. At this stage, the lanes were moved outside of the courtyard to avoid traffic disturbance too close to the

residences. At this stage, too, we considered the location of the community centre, which had to meet the needs of increasing community activities in the neighbourhood, particularly for the elderly (10 percent of the residents of the 8.2-hectare parcel of Ju'er Hutong are over sixty-five) (Figure 6.20).

The use of habitable basement space was also tested in Phase 2 of the project. In the old residential areas, the street level is generally higher than the building sites, and normally the ground level courtyards are lower than the streets. Often redevelopment of these areas requires a great volume of earthwork because the existing courtyards are lower than the streets, which have been built up with new paving over the centuries. One of the most pressing goals of the redevelopment program has been to remedy the drainage problems that result from this difference in ground level. The introduction of a basement not only increases floor space, but it also eliminates the need to bring in extra fill. Well designed basement apartments with adequately large windows, light-wells, and sunken outdoor patios have proven to be very satisfactory dwellings in Phase 2 (Figure 6.11b).

Architectural Aesthetics and Creativity
The following were the main aesthetic considerations concerning the design of the new courtyard housing at Ju'er Hutong.

Comfortable Courtyards
To make the new courtyards comfortable, the design carefully controlled the height of the surrounding buildings to avoid creating the feeling of being in a well-like hollow. The use of grey brick only up to the top of the ground floor, and the use of whitewash above, both recalls the traditional scale and colour of the old-style courtyards and reduces the sense of being overshadowed by the higher storeys. Where possible, gaps were opened to allow occasional views. Careful furnishing with trellises, benches, lamps, paving, and patio spaces improved the function of the courtyards as outdoor living and social spaces (Figures 6.21 through 6.25). The project rigorously preserved existing trees (Figure 6.26) and planted new trees of different types to create varied scenery in miniature.

Views from Attics and Terraces
To maximize both the indoor and outdoor space, lofts and roof terraces were used. Residents in the third-floor duplex or loft apartments have the pleasure of living conditions that are comparable to those in two-storey villas; some enjoy views of the Old City's roofscape, the Jingshan Hill, the White Pagoda, and the Drum Tower. The roof terraces provide additional space for residents to engage in planting – an important traditional pastime, as described in Chapter 5. They also enhance the building's image by forming a rich roofline (Figures 6.27 through 6.29).

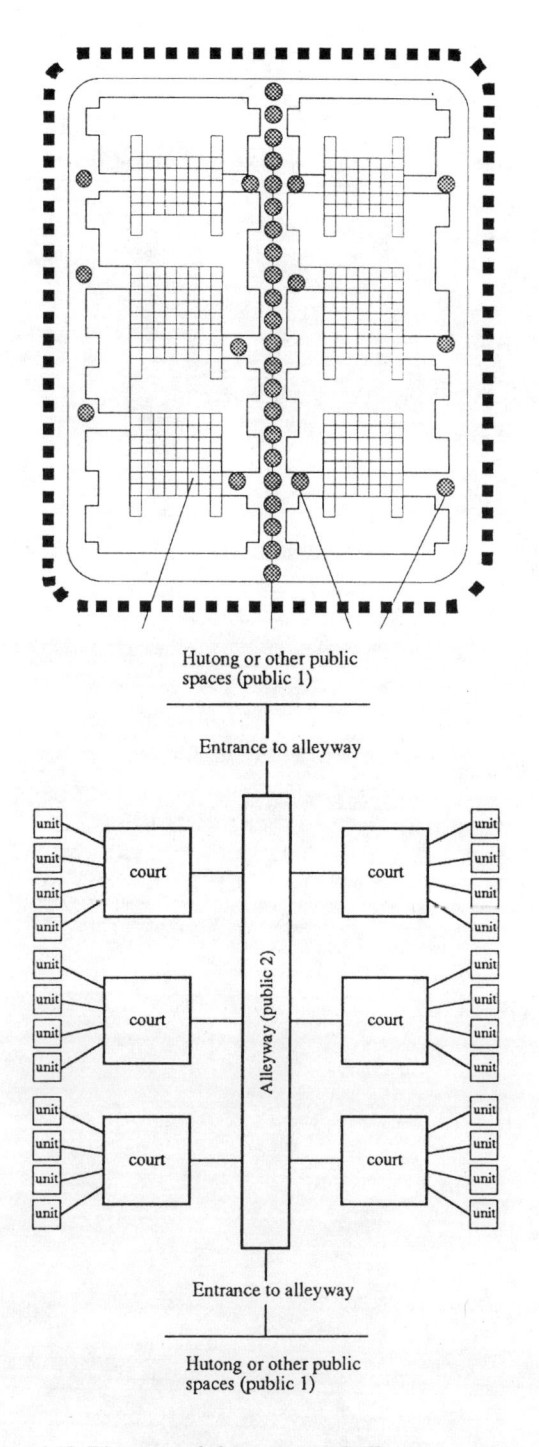

Planning and Design of the Ju'er Hutong Project   131

Figure 6.19 **Diagram of the courtyard-alleyway system**

132 *Planning and Design of the Ju'er Hutong Project*

▲ *Figure 6.20* **New community centre**

▶ *Figure 6.21* **Rooftop trellises for vines**

Planning and Design of the Ju'er Hutong Project 133

▲ *Figure 6.22* **Interior of a new courtyard, with clearly delineated semi-private realms in a small space, including balconies, trellises, and patio spaces behind fences**

◄ *Figure 6.23* **The courtyard itself is intimate enough to accommodate household activities and children's play without jeopardising privacy**

134 Planning and Design of the Ju'er Hutong Project

Figure 6.24 The relatively small courtyards are more easily furnished than are the amorphous spaces that flow between the typical row-type apartment buildings, and thus they more easily become outdoor rooms

Figure 6.25 The courtyard pavement itself is decorative, adding to the amenity of the furnishings

Figure 6.26 **Foundation work, showing the effort made in design and construction to preserve existing trees**

Figure 6.27 **Roofscape of the new courtyard houses**

136 *Planning and Design of the Ju'er Hutong Project*

Figure 6.28 **View from one roof terrace, towards the Drum and Bell Towers**

Figure 6.29 **Planting on a roof terrace**

Use of Traditional Language
The design of the new courtyard housing is inspired by traditional architecture. The choice of materials and colour schemes allowed the new buildings to blend in with the traditional courtyard house area. The roofs are partially pitched and shaped in a traditional grey-tiled pattern (Figure 6.30). Along the *hutong*, which is traditionally lined only by one-storey buildings, the design of the new housing at Ju'er Hutong minimizes the impact of the extra height of two, three, or four storeys by setting the buildings back from the *hutong* and placing in front of them lower garden walls of grey brick and wrought iron (Figure 6.31). The use of traditional Chinese architectural elements like the articulated gate; the *yingbi* and *zhaobi*, or entrance screen; and ornate door knockers has helped to create a sense of belonging and a home-like atmosphere for residents and visitors (Figure 6.32). Such features support the continuation of traditions that are still common in the *hutong*, like the posting of Spring Festival paper mottoes around the gate. Moreover, these features give the buildings an individuality utterly lacking in conventional modern apartment complexes.

Searching for Peace and Quiet
Novelist Lao She wrote in *Xiang Feng Shi Sheng [Country Wind and City Sound]* that "the good thing about Beiping [Beijing] is not its having perfect design everywhere, but its having space everywhere for one to breathe freely." Indeed, the beauty of Beijing does not rest solely on its architecture; rather, it

Figure 6.30 **Traditional tile pattern on the roofs**

138 *Planning and Design of the Ju'er Hutong Project*

Figure 6.31 **Ⓐ** Grey brick garden walls provide a sense of continuity along the *hutong* and **Ⓑ** help to break up the mass of the multi-storey housing

Planning and Design of the Ju'er Hutong Project 139

Figure 6.32 **Ⓐ** Ornamental doorways, **Ⓑ** screens, and **Ⓒ** door-knockers recall the details of the traditional Beijing vernacular

is the spaces around the buildings that make the buildings stand out beautifully – not grand spaces such as one finds in European cities, but intimate spaces in scale with intimate architecture. In the modern city, this uniquely intimate spaciousness and its accompanying sense of peace and quiet has long been lost. The new courtyard design tries to reintroduce it, especially for the sake of the children and the elderly in Ju'er Hutong.

As John Habraken, among others, has proposed, true vernacular building types are the result of an unspoken social agreement.[6] Such types need little or no explicit professional intervention in order to persist. The new courtyard housing experiment is still at the testing stage; it is still a prototype rather than a mature type that has been adopted by society at large. Nevertheless, it conveys two important experiences. First, the new courtyard housing form has emerged from the logic of Beijing's traditional urban form and from the challenge of rehabilitating that form. Second, it has helped to break down the "old" stereotypes of modern housing design and to stimulate new ideas. In an era of increasing social and economic improvisation, such new ideas are sorely needed.

The Development Process
The following sections summarize the actual physical development of the Ju'er Hutong renewal project as it has proceeded through four phases of planning and construction (Figures 6.2 and 6.33). Further details are provided in Appendix 2, which includes the project goals and statistics as submitted to the Beijing Municipal Planning Bureau for development approval.

Phase 1 (1989-90)
The first phase of the Ju'er Hutong new courtyard housing project began in October 1989 and was completed in August 1990. The site of the first phase covered seven old courtyards and a total of 2,090 square metres. Sixty-four bays of old housing were demolished. The new housing had forty-six apartment units, and the total building floor area was 2,760 square metres; this is 2.5 times the space that existed before renewal. The new units included a variety of types in order to suit different households (Figure 6.34). Each household was provided with some outdoor floor space, either a patio, balcony, or roof terrace. The new housing layout was built on the "standard new courtyard system," as described near the beginning of this chapter. The courtyards were formed by placing the two-storey buildings on the east and west sides and the three-storey buildings on the north and south sides.

A housing cooperative was set up for the first phase of the experiment in order to provide adequate housing units in which to settle the original households. The cooperative also managed the financing; income was obtained from the members of the original resident households, who each paid 350 *yuan* per square metre, while their employers paid 250 *yuan* per square

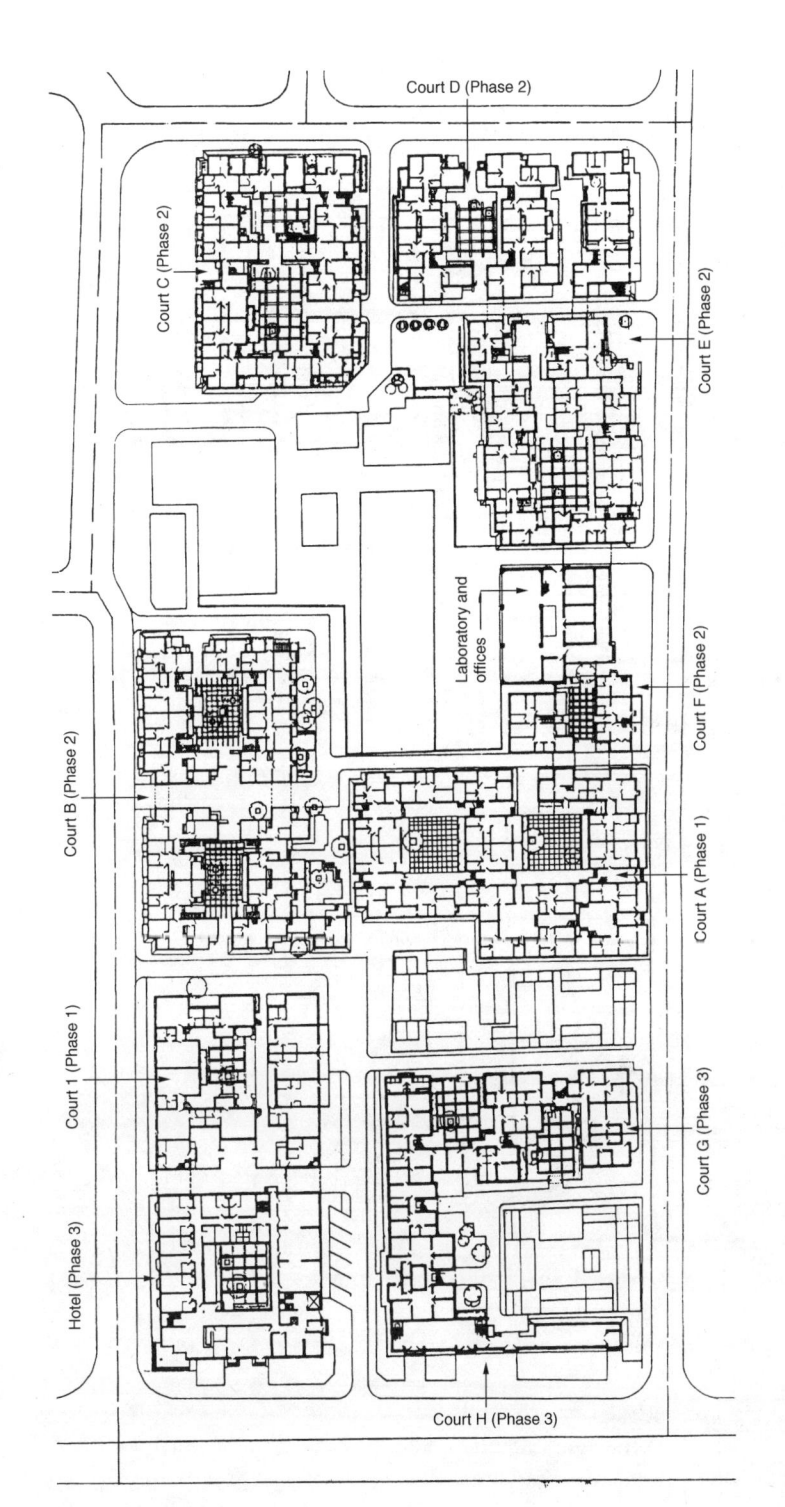

Figure 6.33 **Floor plan of Phases 1, 2, and 3**

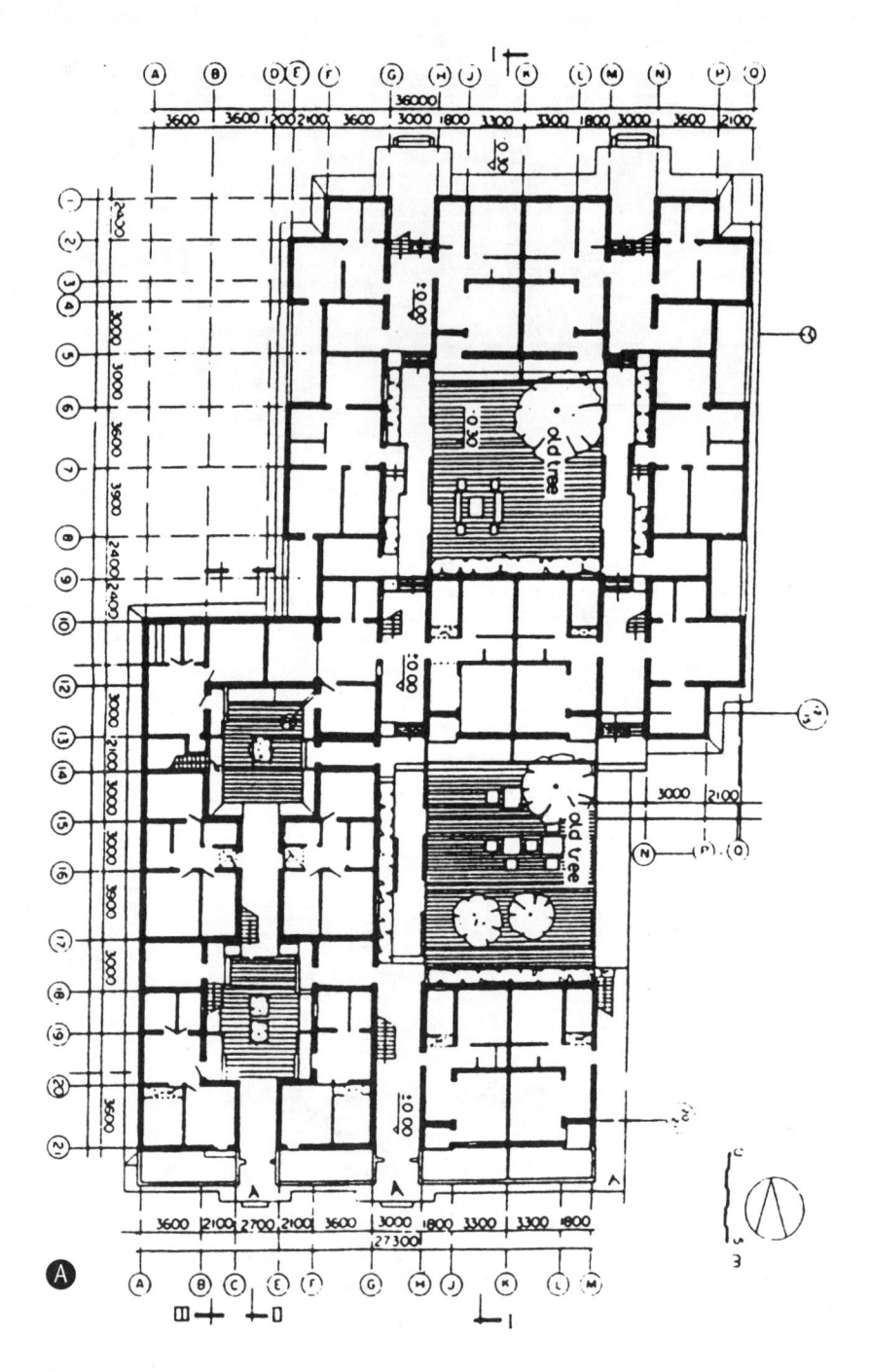

142 *Planning and Design of the Ju'er Hutong Project*

Figure 6.34 **Design of Ju'er Hutong Phase 1.**
Ⓐ Plan of ground floor level. Ⓑ Context plan. Ⓒ Elevations. Ⓓ Sections.

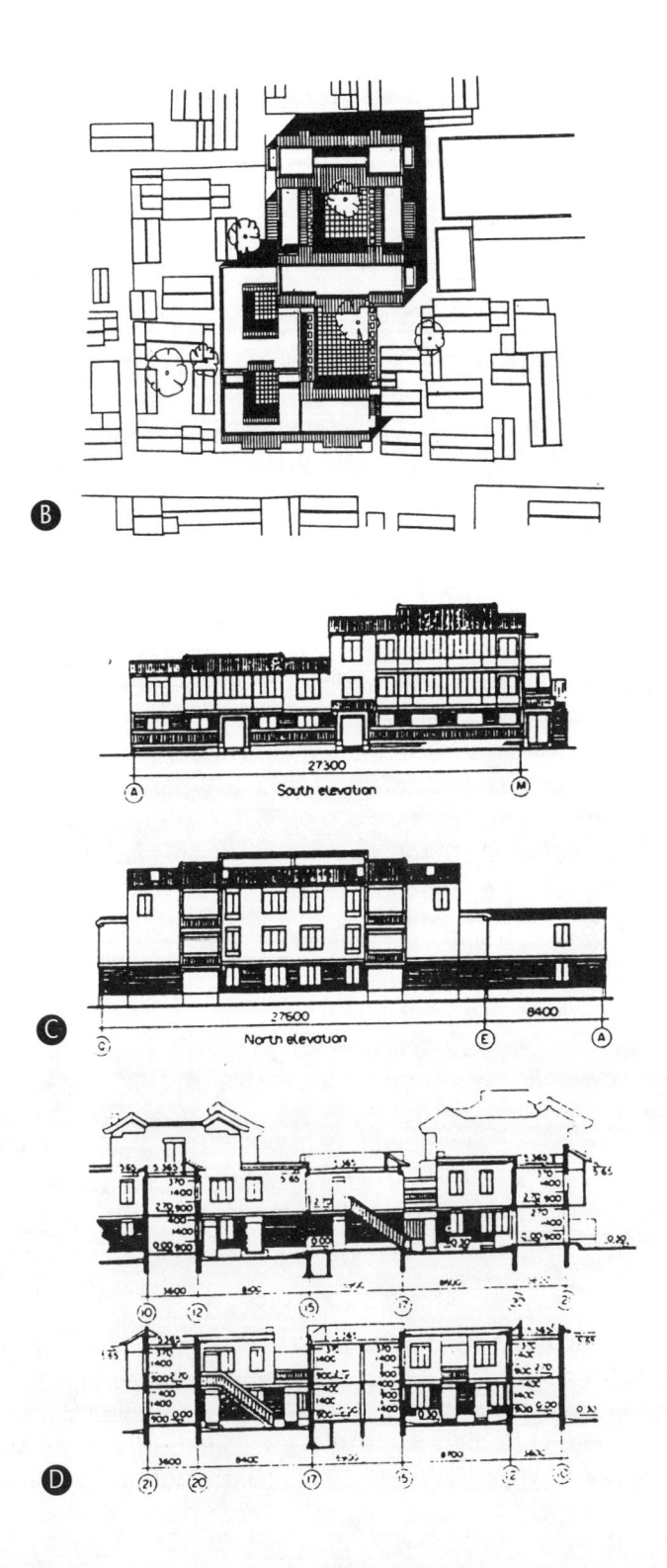

Planning and Design of the Ju'er Hutong Project 143

metre. The local government also provided some subsidies. For the sum paid, the residents obtained the right of use, which was transferable five years after the purchase. The cooperative also oversaw improvements in housing conditions. The project increased the average living space from 7 or 8 to 12.4 square metres per person. Residents who could not afford to buy, or who were unwilling to move back to, the new units were helped by the cooperative to exchange their units with residents in other areas. After the original residents were resettled, the cooperative sold the remaining units in order to recover the remainder of the development costs. Approval for the first phase came from the Beijing Municipal Government. Mayor Chen Xitong, speaking in 1990, further confirmed the intention of the government to coordinate renewal projects in the Old City with the development of new areas, housing reform, real estate management, and historic conservation.

Phase 2 (1990-3)
The design of the second phase began as soon as the drawings for the first phase were completed. A prime objective was to follow up on the problems of Phase 1 and select 1.14 hectares from the 8.2 hectares surveyed as the site for the second phase, which involved another 192 households. The design of the basic courtyard system was improved. The shape of the courtyard was no longer solely rectangular; instead, a more flexible form was devised to accommodate the location of the entrances and existing trees. The circulation passage was taken to the outside of the courtyard to reduce intrusion, while forming a complete pedestrian alleyway system. A master plan for the whole 8.2-hectare block was issued. A service road was planned along the perimeter of the redeveloped area. Since the redevelopment site encircled a factory that was difficult to relocate, it was incorporated into the redevelopment scheme because it generated little pollution. Part of the factory premises that had derelict single-storey buildings was to be redeveloped. In fact, the factory would become part of the mixed zoning concept in planning. A community centre of 300 square metres was also included.

Construction began in 1991. With the exception of one court and the factory, the bulk of the project was completed in 1992. The remaining sections were held up by difficulties in basement construction and were finished in 1994 (Figures 6.35 through 6.40).

Phase 3 (1992-ongoing)
Immediately after the approval of the second phase development, the planning and design work for the third phase got under way. A site to the west of the first two phases was chosen. Due to changes in housing standards and complications in land use and land ownership, the third phase would take longer to complete. The scheme was finalized and the construction

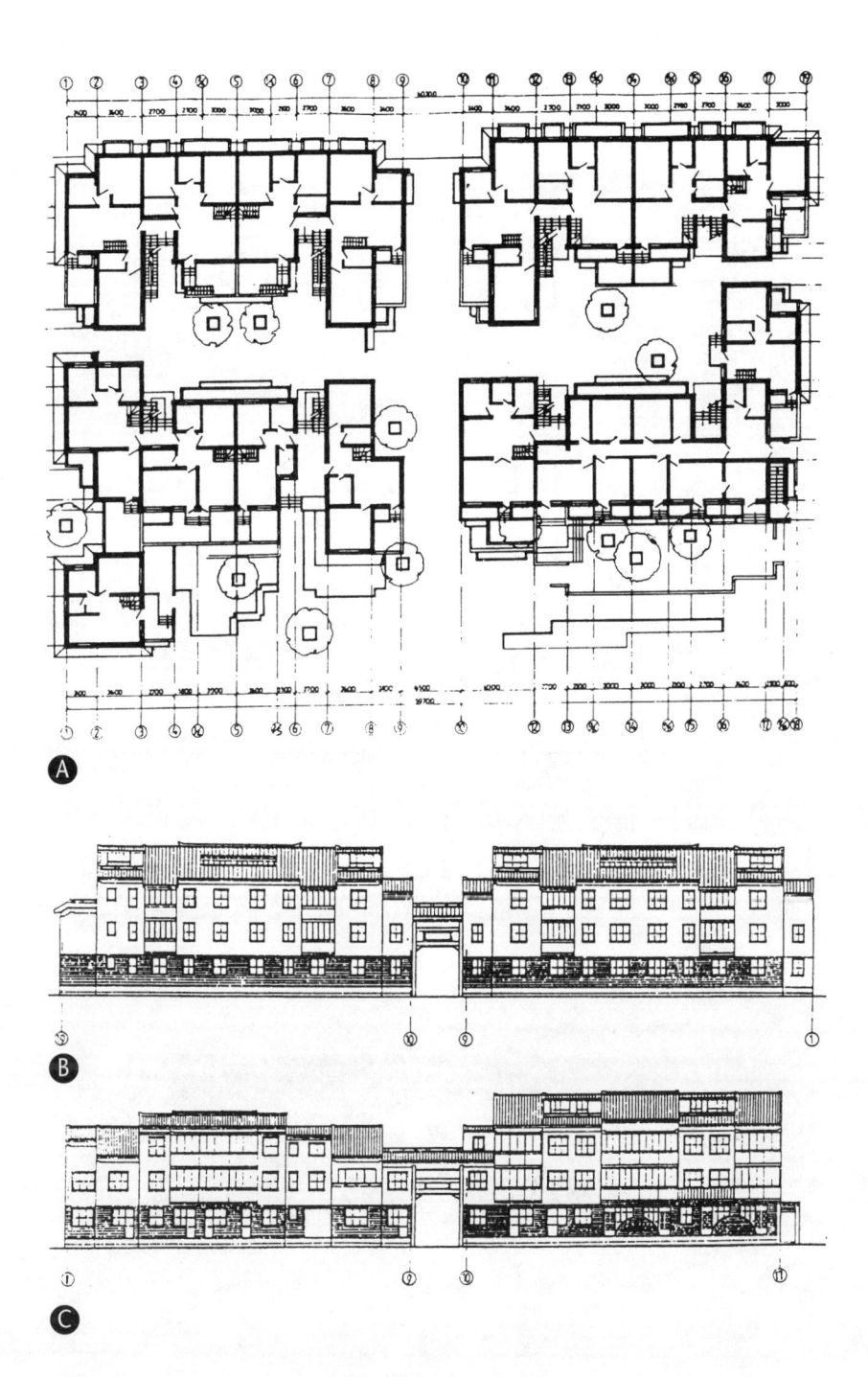

Planning and Design of the Ju'er Hutong Project 145

Figure 6.35 **Design of Ju'er Hutong Phase 2: Court B.**
Ⓐ Plan of floor level 1. Ⓑ North elevation. Ⓒ South elevation.

146 *Planning and Design of the Ju'er Hutong Project*

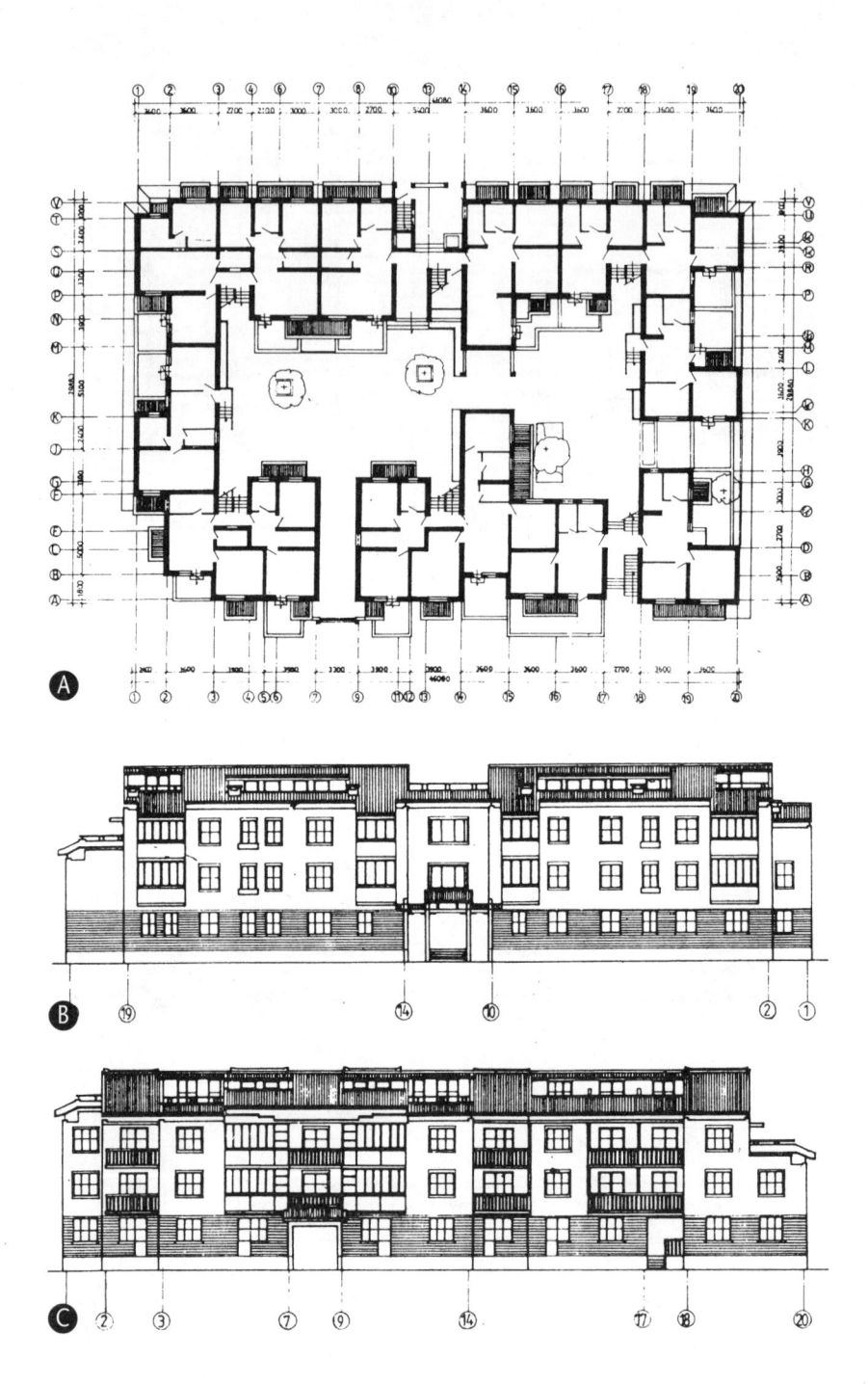

Figure 6.36 **Design of Ju'er Hutong Phase 2: Court C.**
Ⓐ Plan of floor level 1. **Ⓑ** North elevation. **Ⓒ** South elevation.

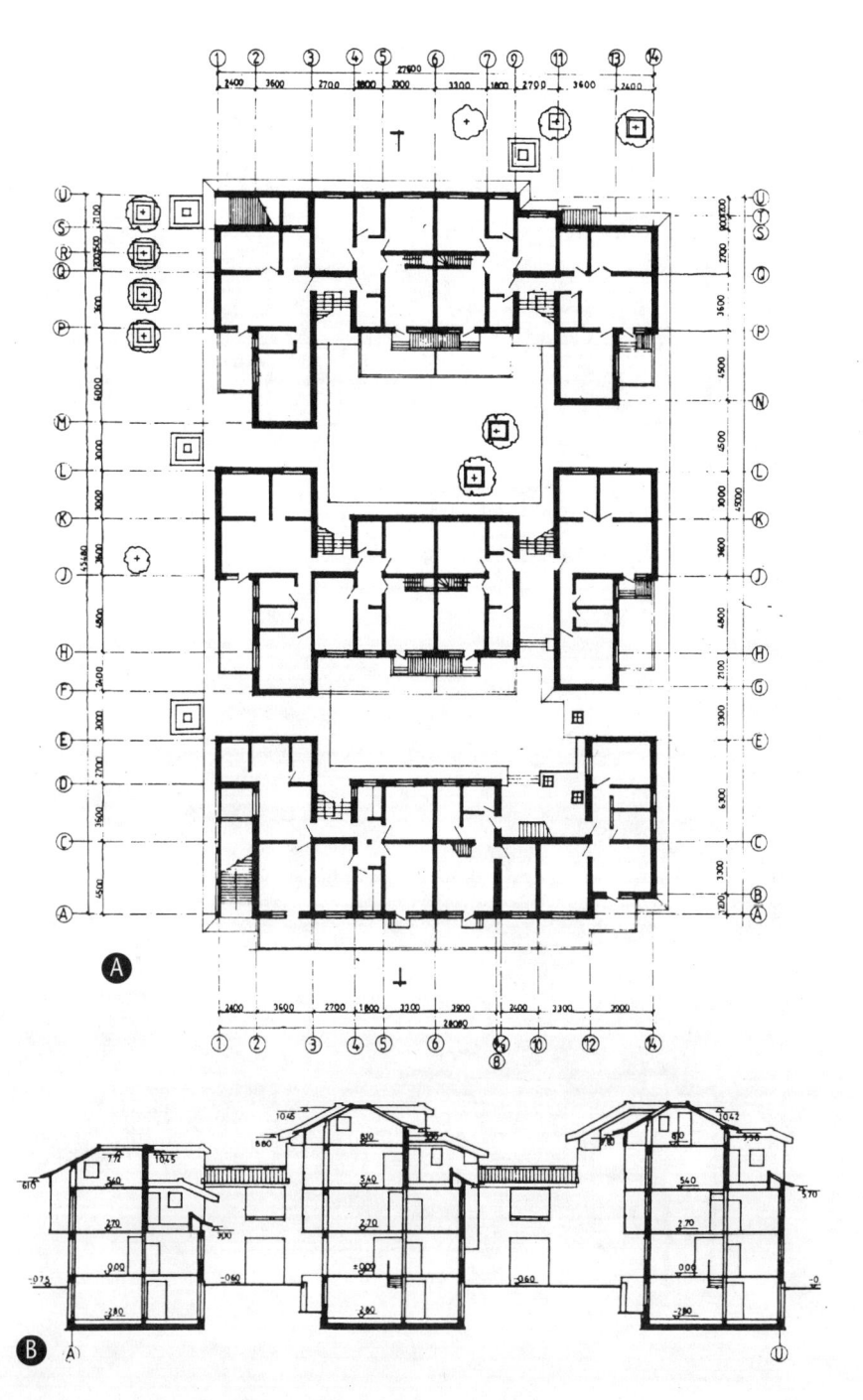

Planning and Design of the Ju'er Hutong Project 147

Figure 6.37 **Design of Ju'er Hutong Phase 2: Court D.**
Ⓐ Plan of floor level 1. Ⓑ Section.

148 *Planning and Design of the Ju'er Hutong Project*

Figure 6.38 **Design of Ju'er Hutong Phase 2: Court E.**
Ⓐ Plan of floor level 1. **Ⓑ** Section.

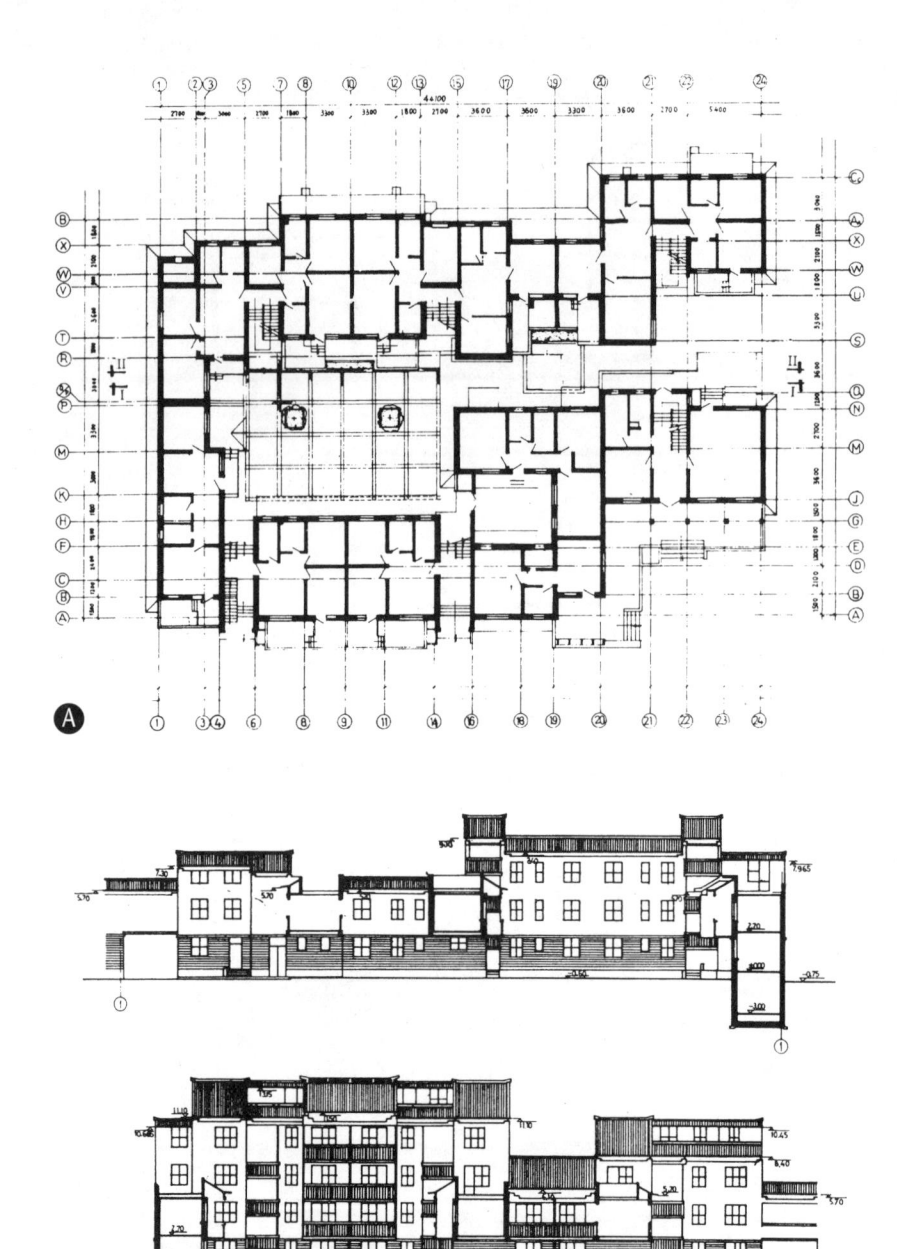

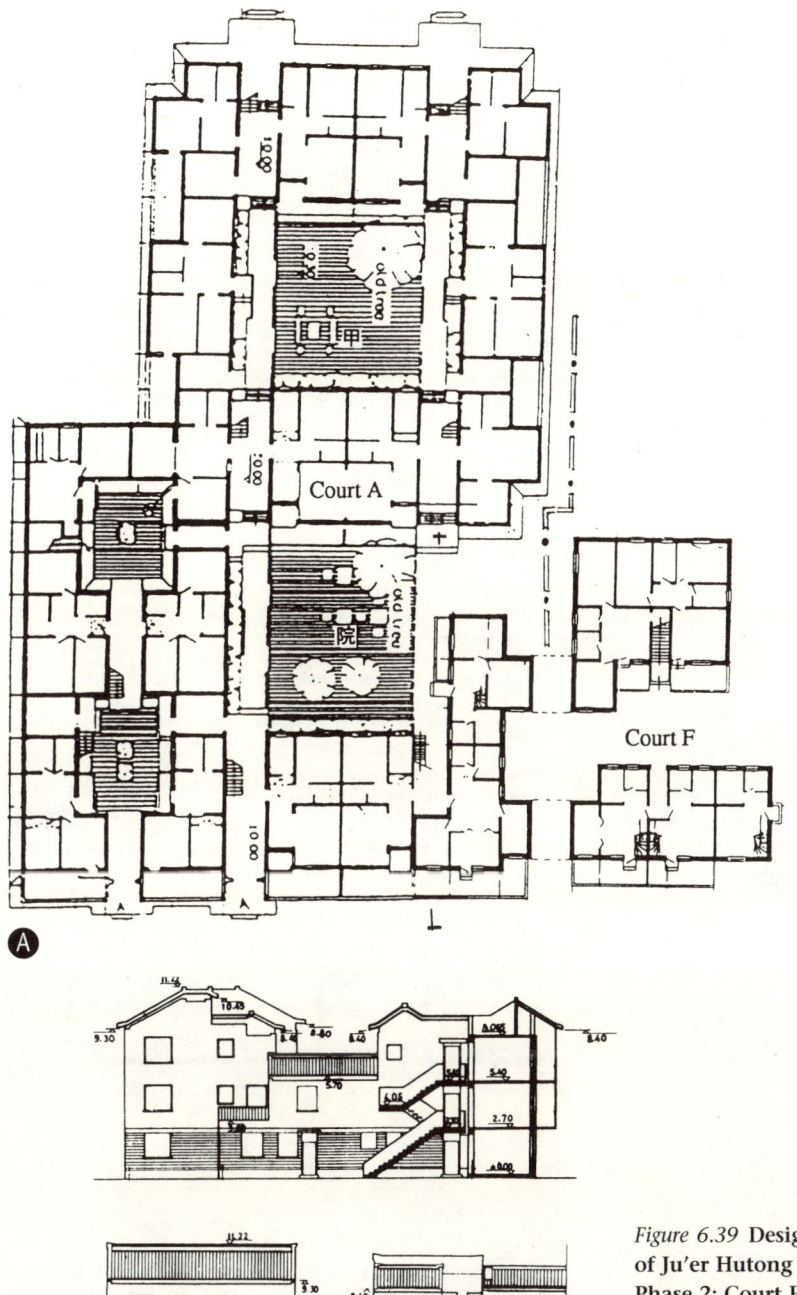

Planning and Design of the Ju'er Hutong Project   149

Figure 6.39 **Design of Ju'er Hutong Phase 2: Court F.**
Ⓐ Plan of floor level 1: courts A and F.
Ⓑ North elevation.

150 *Planning and Design of the Ju'er Hutong Project*

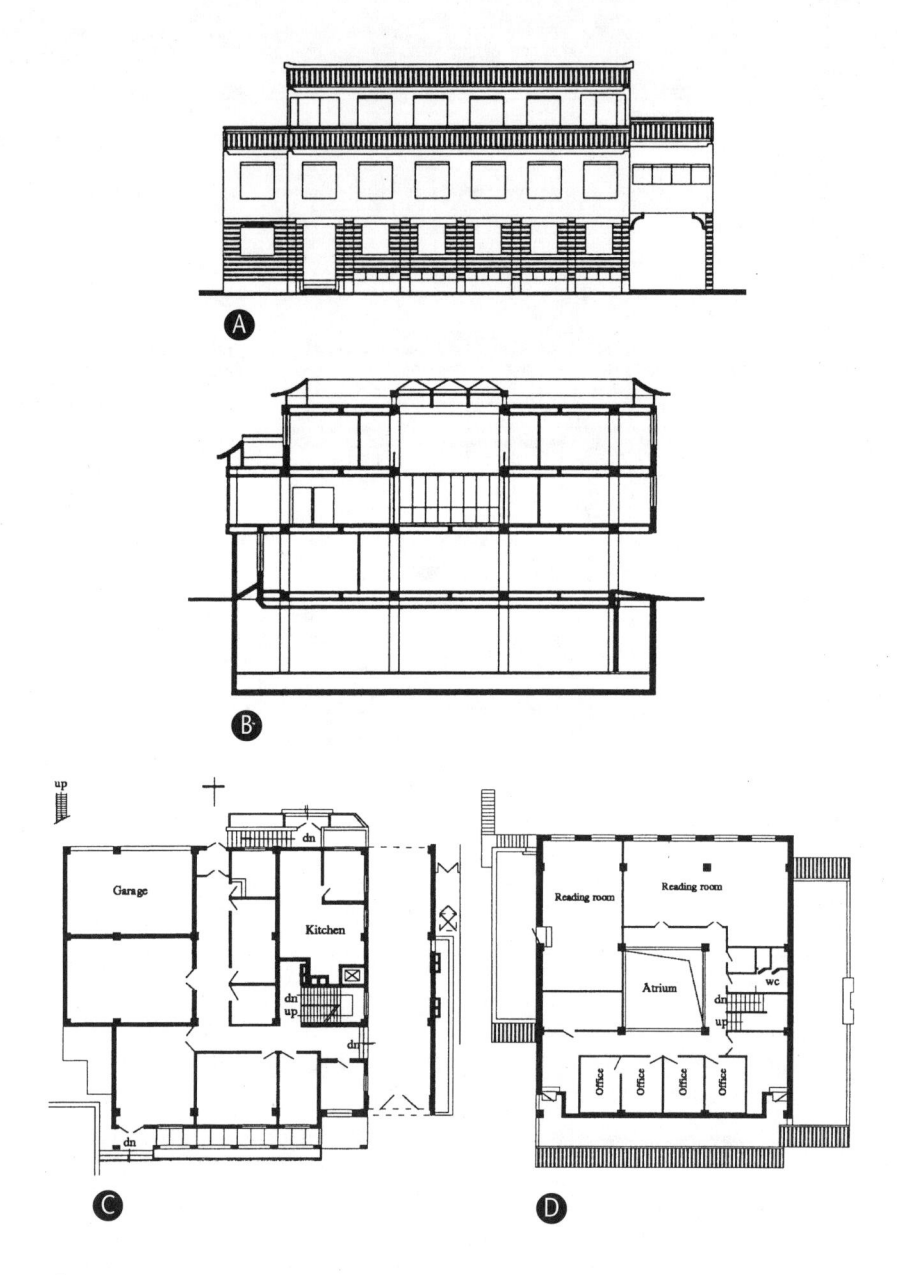

Figure 6.40 **Design of a factory laboratory and office building.**
A South elevation. **B** Section. **C** Plan of floor level 1. **D** Plan of floor level 3.
An existing factory within the Phase 2 parcel was rehabilitated into laboratory and office space. The original plan layout was retained, with new spaces arranged around a central atrium. This design attempted to obtain the maximum FAR given the building height.

planned for 1994, but it has been suspended primarily due to rising land prices (Figures 6.41 through 6.43).

This phase of development involved a small area but many more building types. There were four main improvements. First, the courtyard design became even more flexible. Courtyards were designed with one side open, and large, deep units with small courtyards were also proposed. Thirty-seven apartments – totalling 2,269 square metres and averaging 61.3 square metres per household – were designed to use movable partitions. These units had bays wide enough – from 5.4 metres to 6.3 metres – to be partitioned into two rooms of flexible size.

Also, for the first time, the courtyard form was applied to a non-residential use: a courtyard was designed around an existing tree to accommodate a small hotel (Figure 6.44). Third, shops were designed along the street front at the northern end of Nan Luogu Xiang. Finally, a complex of traditional courtyard houses at one end of Ju'er Hutong, which was still in good condition, was to be rehabilitated. When the third phase is completed, the southern and western parts of Ju'er Hutong will join together, and the effect of the new courtyard-*hutong* system will be clear.

Phase 4 (1993-ongoing)
The fourth phase will complete the whole Ju'er Hutong block experiment (Figures 6.45 and 6.46). As only 6.31 hectares of the 8.2 hectares are within the property line that can be used for redevelopment (due to road widening), the actual remaining area is 4.44 hectares. While this fourth and last phase is similar to the first three in many ways, it must also resolve the most complex and difficult issues of the project. These include rationally completing the circulation system within the block while preserving the original location, scale, and character of the *hutong*; completing a sensible land-use pattern that balances residential, industrial, institutional, and commercial needs; redeveloping the infrastructure; and establishing an overall identity for the block. Also, and perhaps most challenging of all, there is a need to set up a financial scheme that makes use of real estate development on the north edge of the block fronting on the major street, Gulou Dong Dajie, in order to raise revenue for the renewal of the interior of the block. The architectural implications of this challenge are that commercial development along this edge will come under the most intense pressure to raise densities and building heights. The true success of the Ju'er Hutong experiment will surely hinge on Phase 4.

Studies of the Nan Luogu Xiang Traditional Housing Protection Area
The first three phases of the Ju'er Hutong experiment provided a sound foundation on which to proceed with a rehabilitation study for the entire

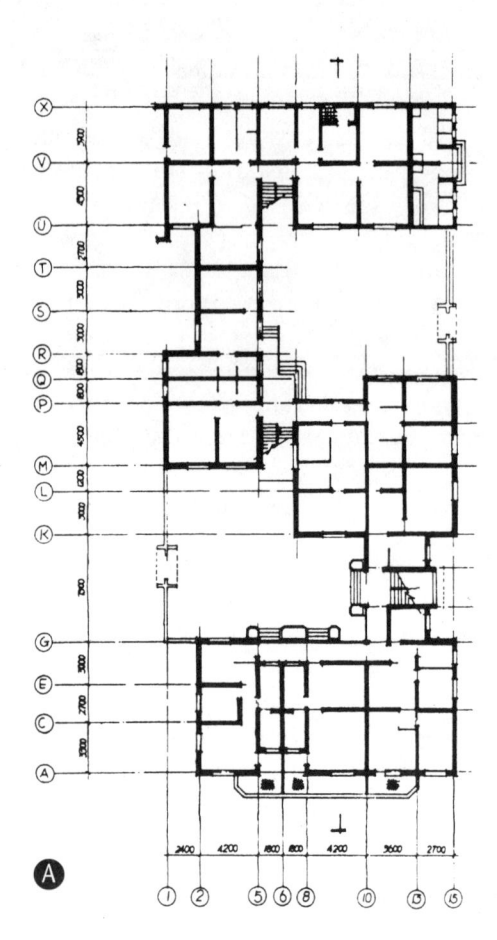

152 *Planning and Design of the Ju'er Hutong Project*

Figure 6.41 **Design of Ju'er Hutong Phase 3: Court G.**
A Plan of floor level 1.
B East elevation. **C** Section.

Planning and Design of the Ju'er Hutong Project 153

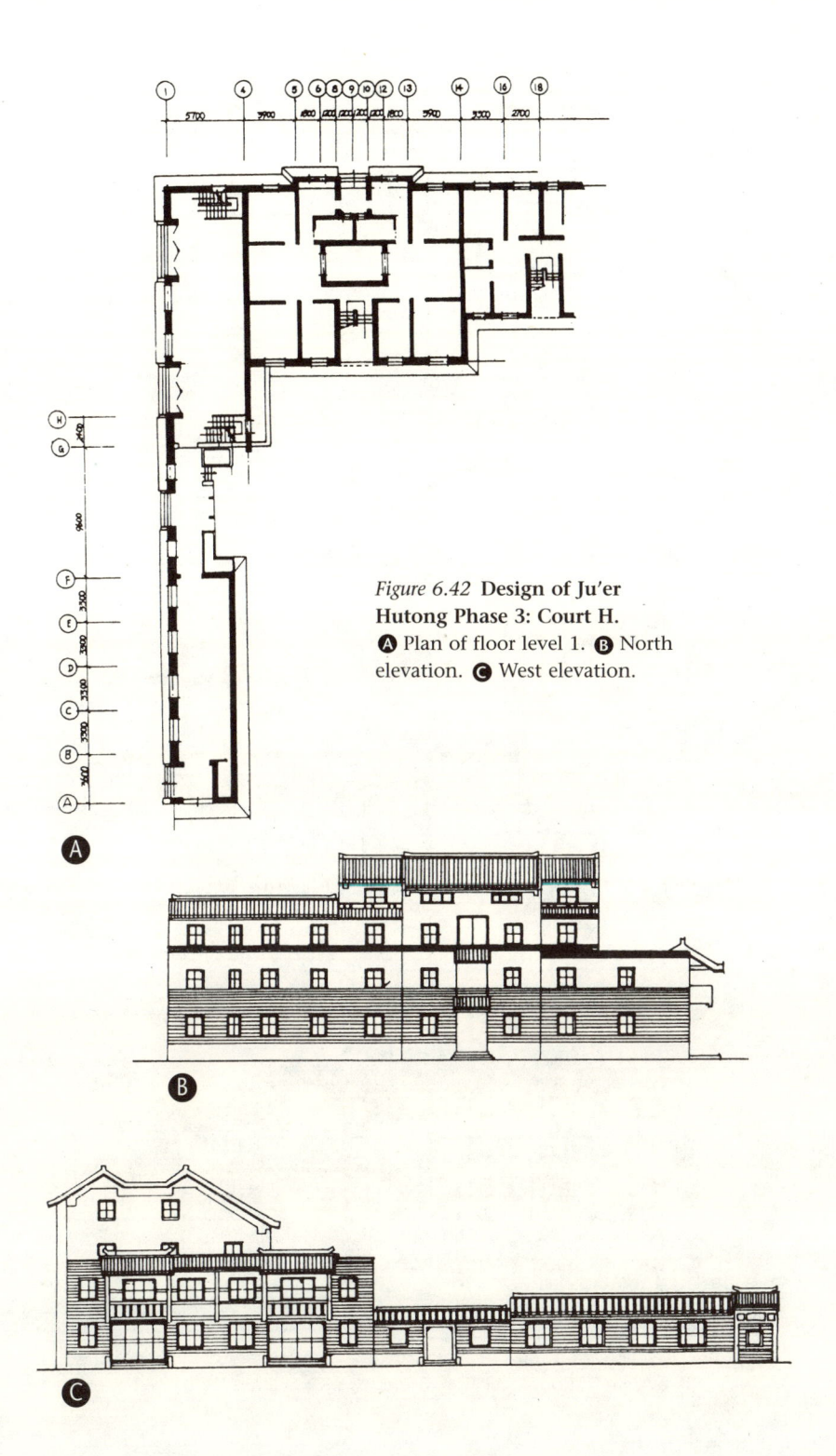

Figure 6.42 **Design of Ju'er Hutong Phase 3: Court H.**
Ⓐ Plan of floor level 1. **Ⓑ** North elevation. **Ⓒ** West elevation.

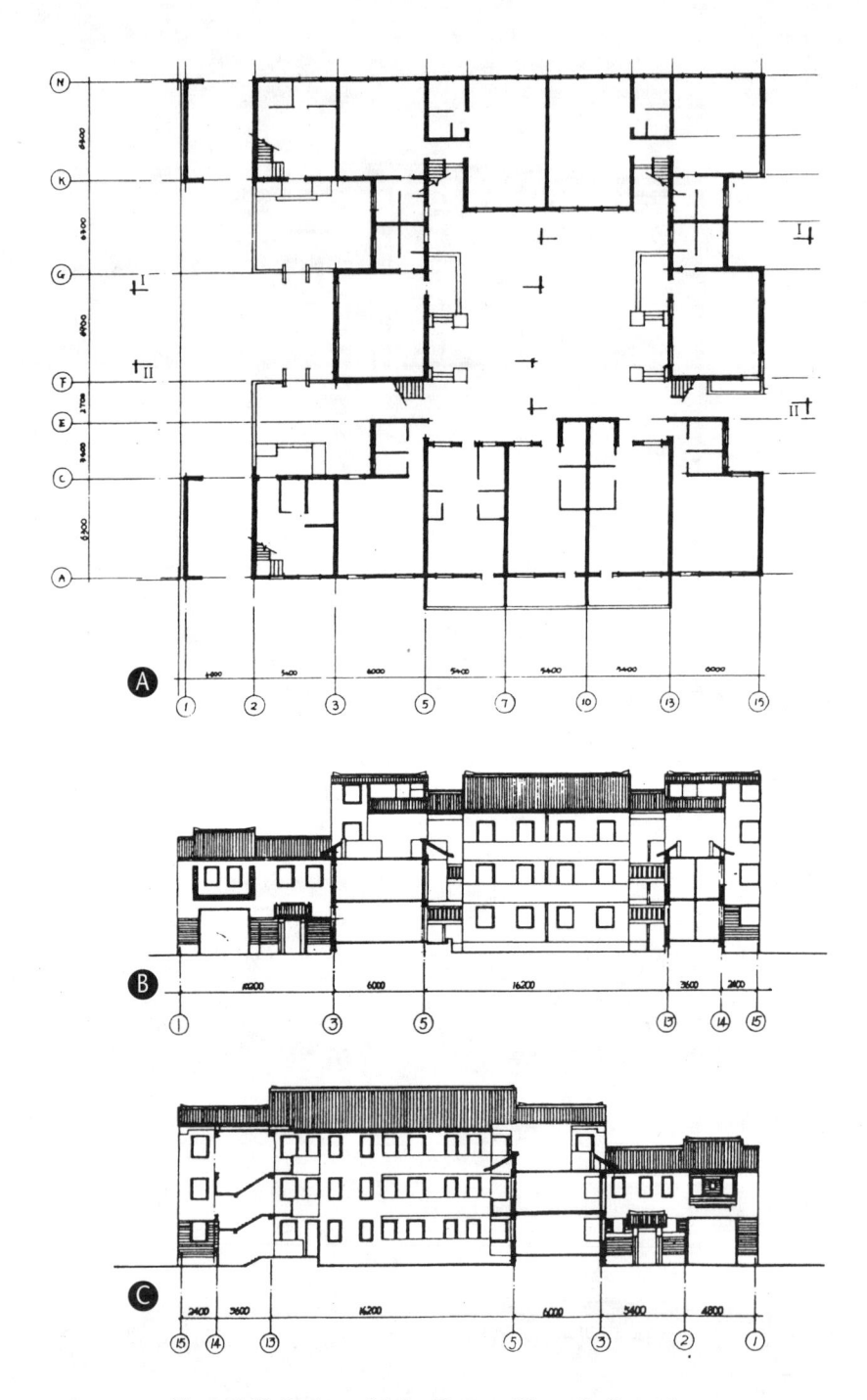

154 Planning and Design of the Ju'er Hutong Project

Figure 6.43 **Design of Ju'er Hutong Phase 3: Court I.**
Ⓐ Plan of floor level 1. **Ⓑ** Section I-I. **Ⓒ** Section II-II.

Planning and Design of the Ju'er Hutong Project 155

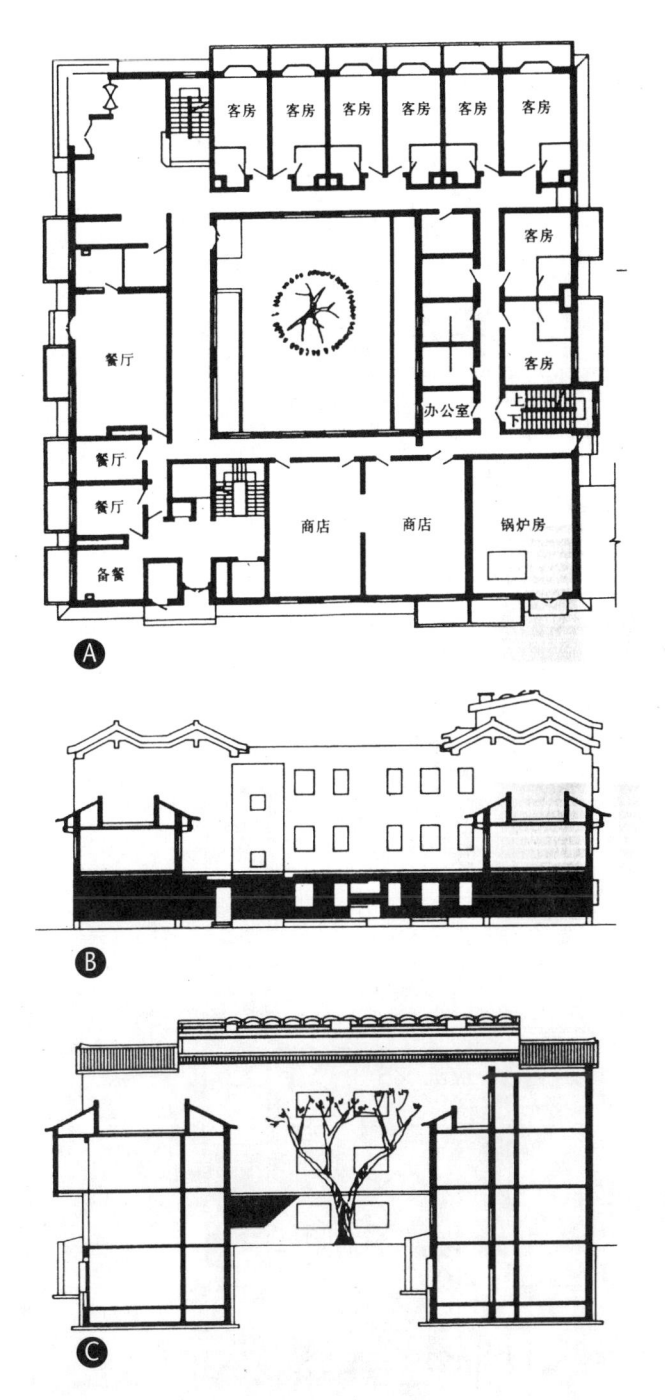

Figure 6.44 **Design of Ju'er Hutong Phase 3: Hotel building.**
Ⓐ Plan of floor level 1. Ⓑ West elevation. Ⓒ Section.

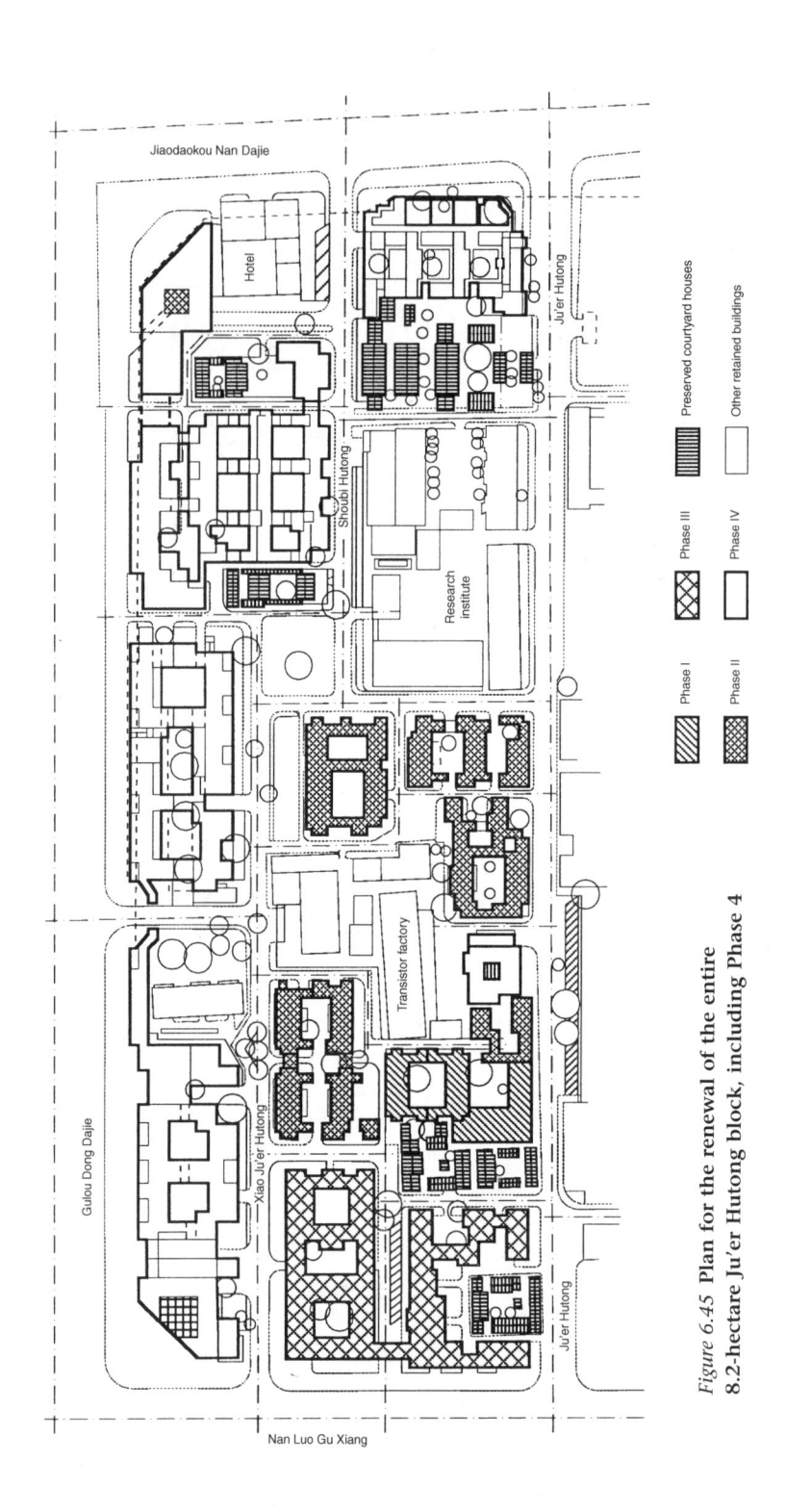

Figure 6.45 **Plan for the renewal of the entire 8.2-hectare Ju'er Hutong block, including Phase 4**

84 hectares of the Nan Luogu Xiang Traditional Courtyard Housing Preservation District, which contains many important examples of historic courtyard housing complexes (Figure 6.47). Fifteen historic sites in the district are currently designated at national, municipal, or district levels of protection. A preliminary survey was carried out in 1991-2, and again in 1993, to study the existing conditions of the neighbourhood (Figure 6.48). A detailed planning and urban design proposal arising from it may be carried out in parallel with the fourth phase of the Ju'er Hutong project and may be used as the basis for zoning codes and other legislation in rehabilitation areas. Once the proposal is accepted, the area may be divided into additional rehabilitation units for detailed design (Figure 6.49).

As described in the previous chapter, the Nan Luogu Xiang area is laid out in a classic fishbone pattern, with a central north-south street (the street after which the district is named) and seventeen main smaller east-west *hutong* running off either side of it. It is a classic Beijing "superblock" bounded on the west by Di'anmen Wai Dajie, on the north by Gulou Dong Dajie, on the east by Jiaodaokou Nan Dajie, and on the south by Di'anmen Dong Dajie. Like the 8.2-hectare Ju'er Hutong block within it, the Nan Luogu Xiang block holds a very advantageous position in the Old City with regard to access to shopping, services, parks, and cultural and recreational facilities. There are four primary schools and two secondary schools within the block.

The main problems facing Nan Luogu Xiang are similar to those facing the Ju'er Hutong neighbourhood, with the additional challenge that among the dilapidated houses and backward infrastructure are many gems of classical architecture that must be restored in some fashion. Although the Beijing Master Plan has designated the Nan Luogu Xiang block a "Traditional Courtyard Housing Preservation District," it makes no reference to detailed architectural or functional guidelines or regulations for preservation, restoration, or adaptive reuse. Indeed, detailed guidelines and regulations do not exist for this kind of environment. The problem is compounded by the master plan's own requirements for the improvement of traffic through the area, largely by enlarging the road area, which currently occupies only 5 percent of the total land area of the block.

Despite the increased complexity of developing and conserving the Nan Luogu Xiang block, its difference with regard to Ju'er Hutong is mainly one of size rather than of kind. I firmly believe that the experience of renewing Ju'er Hutong offers most of the answers to the planning of Nan Luogu Xiang. While the details of design should continue to evolve and take new forms, the principles of comprehensive planning combined with gradual intervention, care to maintain the existing community, and respect for the local street pattern and architectural scale and vocabulary (e.g., the large gates, grey roof tiles, etc.) should remain constant.

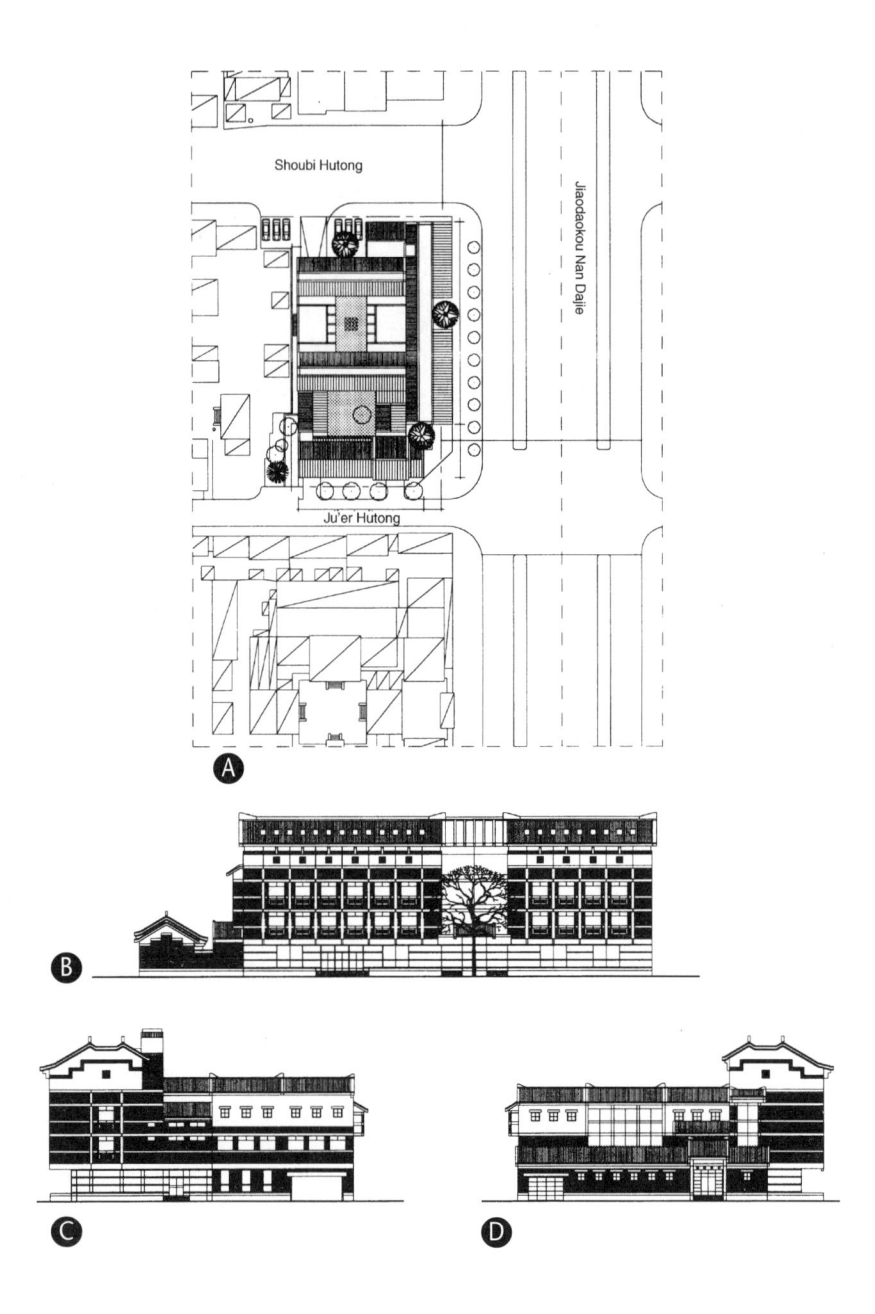

Figure 6.46 **Design of new housing, retail shops, and offices for Phase 4, at the corner of Ju'er Hutong and Jiaodaokou.**
Ⓐ Plan. **Ⓑ** East elevation. **Ⓒ** North elevation. **Ⓓ** South elevation. **Ⓔ** Plan of floor level 1. **Ⓕ** Section. **Ⓖ** West elevation. Special attention was paid to the architectural design in order to keep this higher, denser building in harmony with the traditional neighbourhood. An old tree on the site was also carefully preserved.

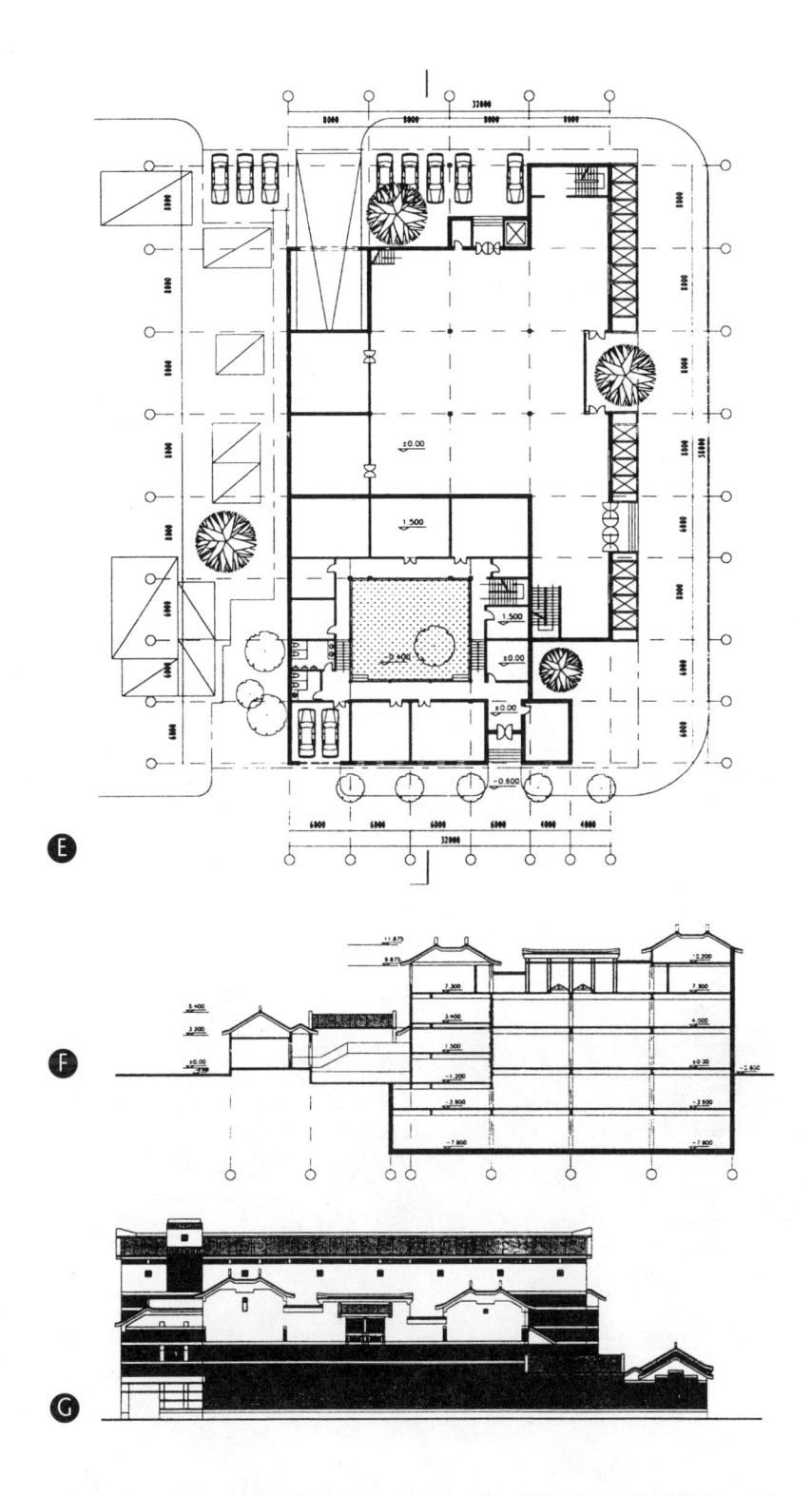

Planning and Design of the Ju'er Hutong Project 159

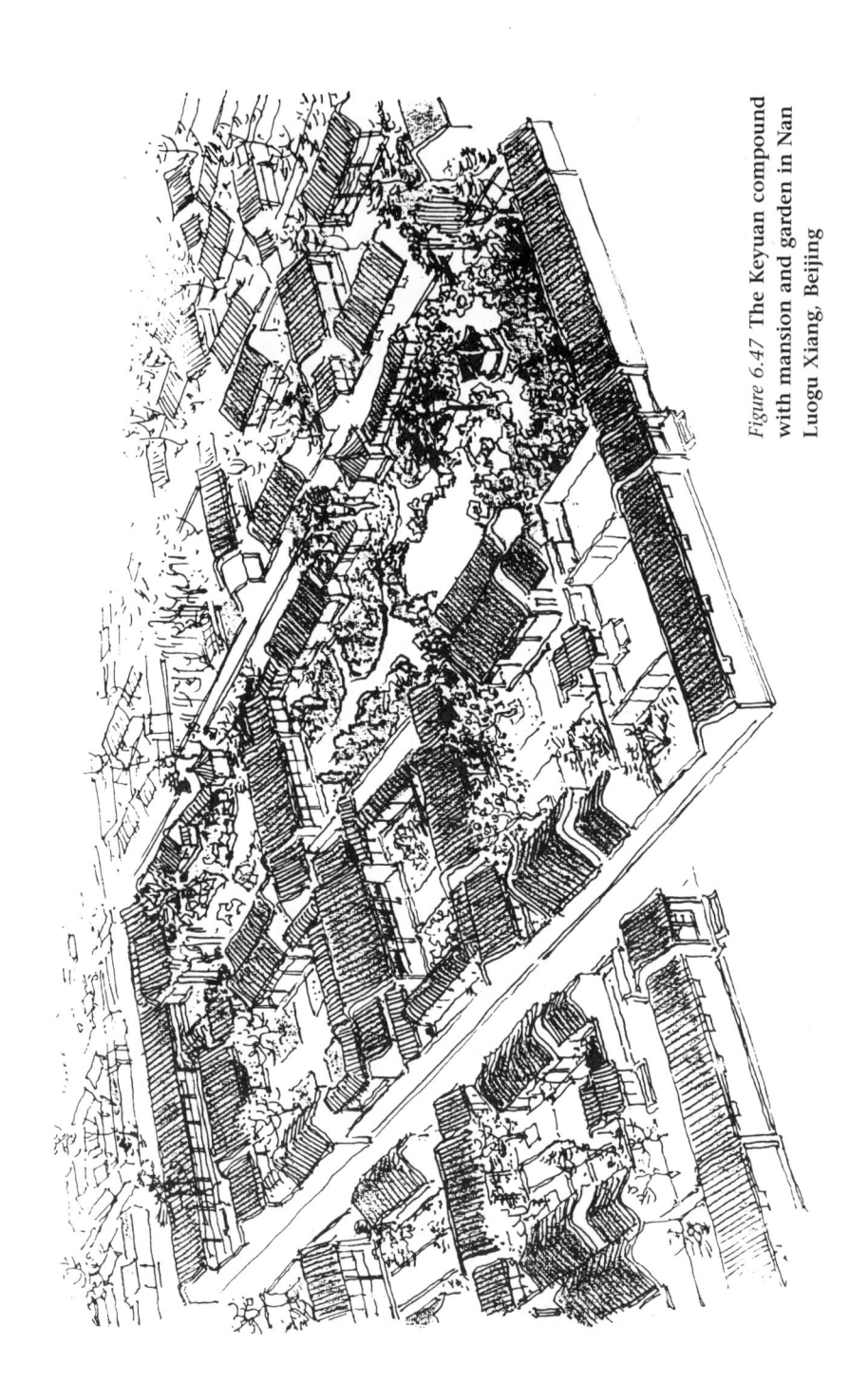

Figure 6.47 The Keyuan compound with mansion and garden in Nan Luogu Xiang, Beijing

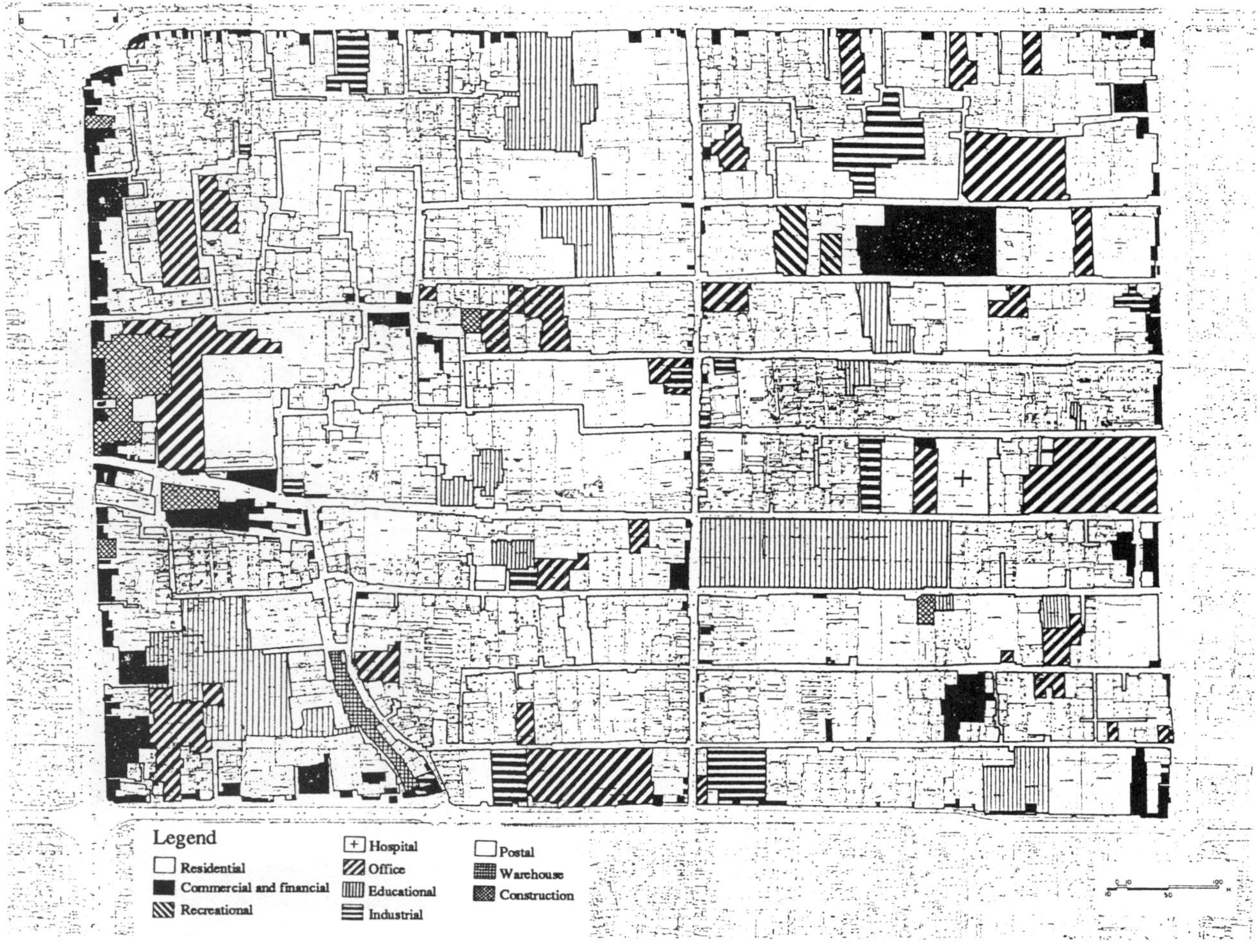

Figure 6.48
Existing land use in the Nan Luogu Xiang area, 1994
Source: Institute of Architectural and Urban Studies, Tsinghua University

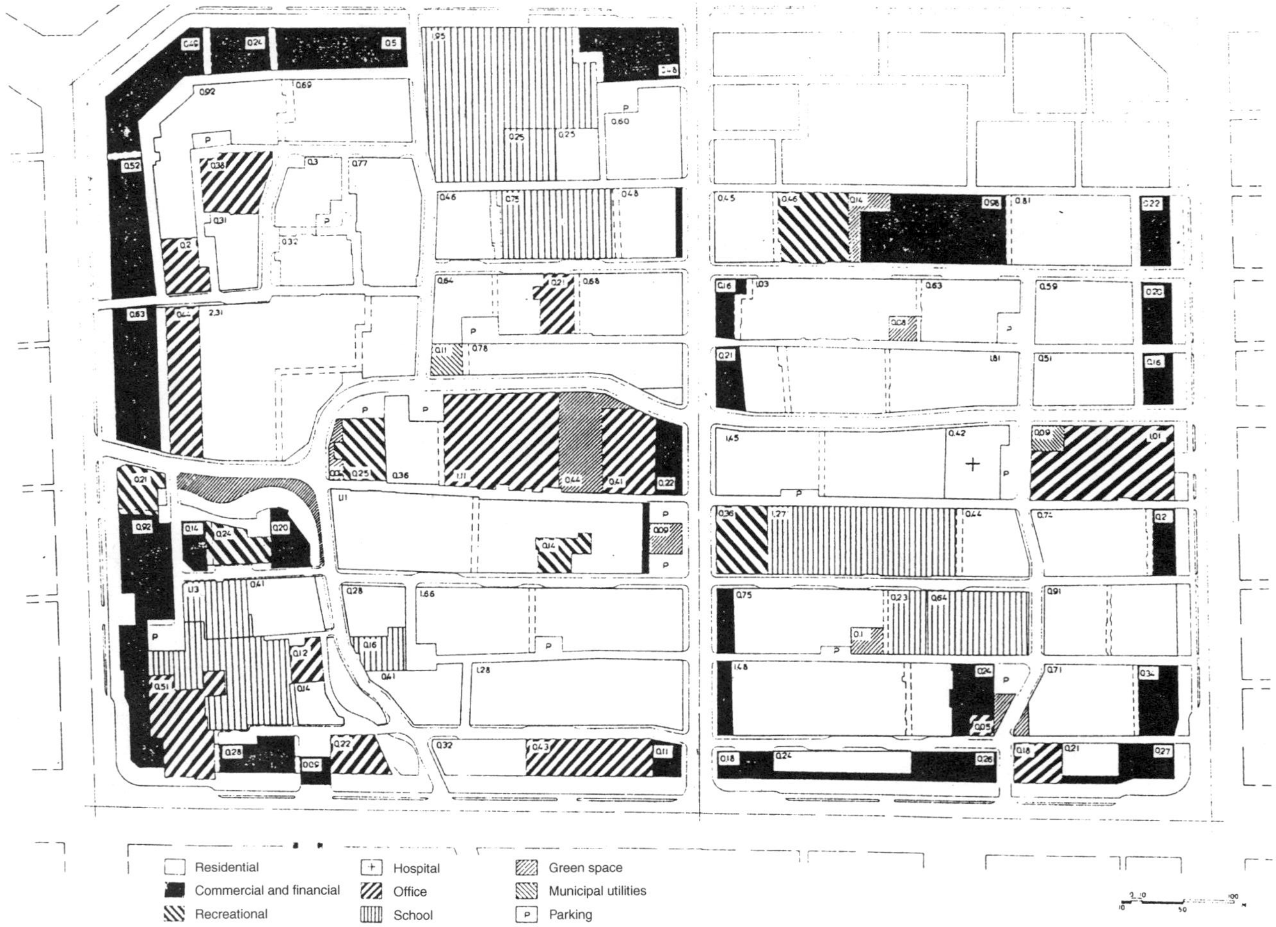

Figure 6.49
Planned land use in the Nan Luogu Xiang area, 1994
Source: Institute of Architectural and Urban Studies, Tsinghua University

7
Post-Occupancy Evaluation and Lessons from the Planning and Design Experience

In 1992, two years after the Phase 1 housing units were occupied, and five years after the residents on the site were first surveyed, a survey was conducted among the original residents in order to obtain input for future planning and design projects. The survey included both those who were rehoused on the site and those who relocated. The conclusion was favourable in general, but some problems were also noted. Since the Ju'er Hutong project was only an initial experiment to rehabilitate the residential areas of the Old City of Beijing, it was difficult to bring theoretical concepts and design visions into effect. However, the more difficulties one confronts, the more gains one may expect to make when attempting to overcome them. This is the ultimate point of Chapter 7. I reached the following preliminary conclusions after my study, and they are further elaborated upon at the end of this chapter:

- A feasibility study is difficult, but it is indispensable to a practical project.
- The key to the rehabilitation of the Old City of Beijing lies in the comprehensive improvement of its environment.
- Instead of accomplishing the whole task at one stroke by means of large-scale clearance and complete rebuilding, the comprehensive rehabilitation of the Old City can only be accomplished in phases, through organic renewal and sustained progress.
- During the long process of execution, it is necessary to have repeated discussions concerning different problems. These discussions must encompass the views of urban planning, urban design, architectural design, and civil engineering, and a consensus must be reached.
- The design of the New Courtyard House type is a problem of great importance, and it still remains to be studied. Further progress may be made by deriving inspiration from the traditional Chinese design system established by Yangshi Lei and by applying the modern Design Knowledge System. This would call for more attention to the standardization and

modularization of single buildings and their structural components, combined with more imagination devoted to the spatial composition of buildings and gardens.

Post-Occupancy Evaluation

Residents who Returned to the Neighbourhood after Renewal

Redevelopment in the first phase completely transformed the area of Number 41 Ju'er Hutong, apart from the preservation of two trees. The new housing provides 2,760 square metres of floor space, more than 2.5 times the amount of space that existed previously (1,085 square metres). The project houses forty-six households: two more than before (Figure 7.1). As described in the previous chapter, the 1987 survey of the courtyard at Number 41 revealed six serious problems that were typical in the old neighbourhoods: threat from structural failure, frequent flooding, roof leakage, lack of light, poor ventilation, and overcrowding. That survey also uncovered some less quantifiable, but equally important, problems of social interaction; while existing residents benefited in many respects from their close contact with neighbours, they suffered from the constant lack of privacy. The post-construction, post-occupancy evaluation aimed to determine the extent to which these problems were resolved. More specifically, the survey also sought to determine the suitability of the New Courtyard House type to the lives of the resident population with regard to the quality of their living space and the mode of their social interaction. With these goals in mind, the planning team at Tsinghua University interviewed thirty-one households in the new housing development. The survey work consisted of face-to-face interviews (conducted according to a questionnaire) and the observation both of interior space and exterior space and the use to which each was put (Figure 7.2 and Table 7.1).

Regarding interior space, the design of apartments was oriented mainly towards the needs of the original population (as opposed to the needs of newcomers purchasing the units at market rates). Existing residents tend to use their bedrooms throughout the day for various activities and do not keep separate parlours especially for visitors. Therefore, the new suites generally included large or mid-size bedrooms (no smaller than 12 square metres) and a small or mid-size hall (10 square metres or more). The average number of bedrooms per household was 2.13. The average bedroom slept 1.28 residents, whereas before renewal there were approximately two residents per bedroom. Eighty percent of the households after renewal were able to accommodate different generations in separate bedrooms. Overall, the new housing provided 12 square metres of living space per resident (not including kitchens, toilets, and hallways), while before renewal each resident had, on average, only 7 to 8 square metres of all kinds of shelter.

Kitchens and toilets were about 4 and 2.5 square metres, respectively, and were of the same standard as were those provided in typical multi-storey apartment buildings built in new estates, except that no gas for heating stoves or water could be piped in. This is because the natural gas network has not yet been extended into the central Old City. However, a local hot-water heating plant was hooked up to provide heat to the new housing.

Regarding exterior space, 83 percent of the respondents approved of the atmosphere created by the courtyard space. No one felt that there were too many households or that the space was excessively crowded. Ninety-six percent responded either that it was not crowded or that it was only sometimes crowded (mainly on the weekends when children – many of them

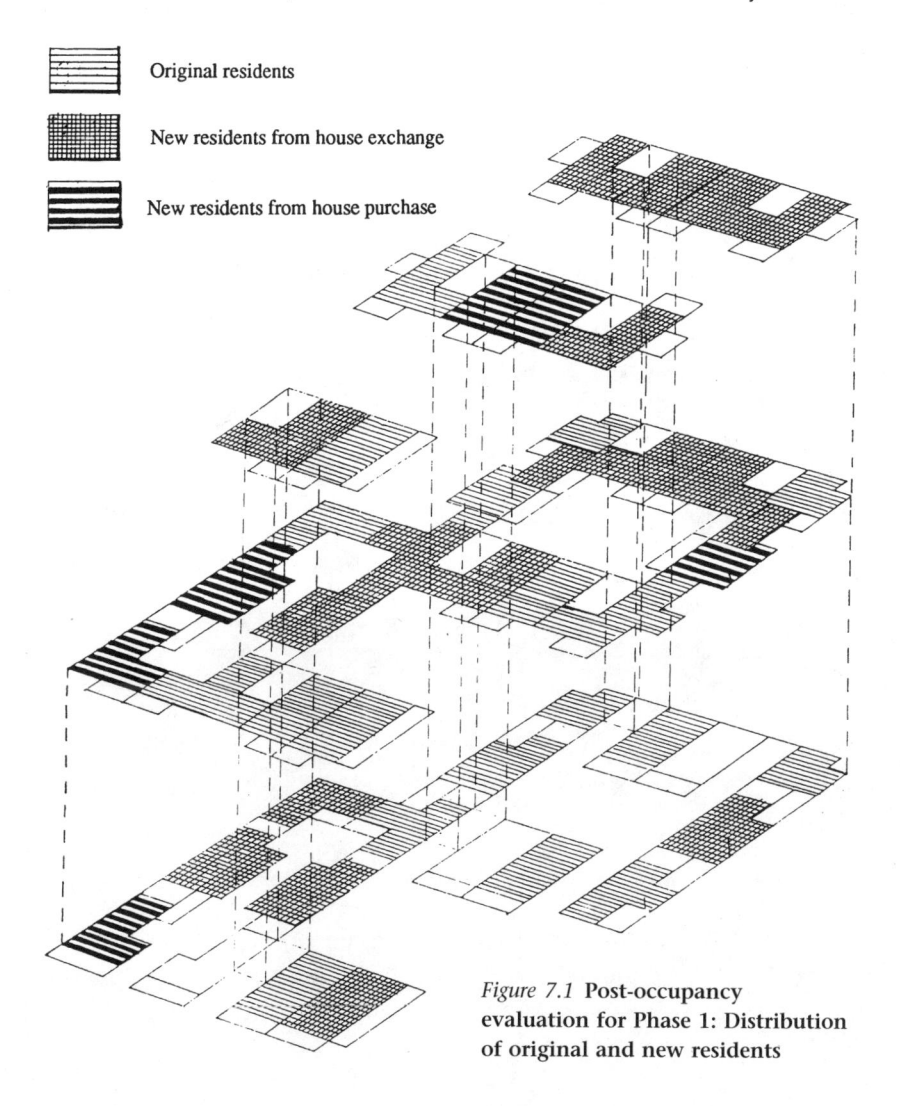

Figure 7.1 **Post-occupancy evaluation for Phase 1: Distribution of original and new residents**

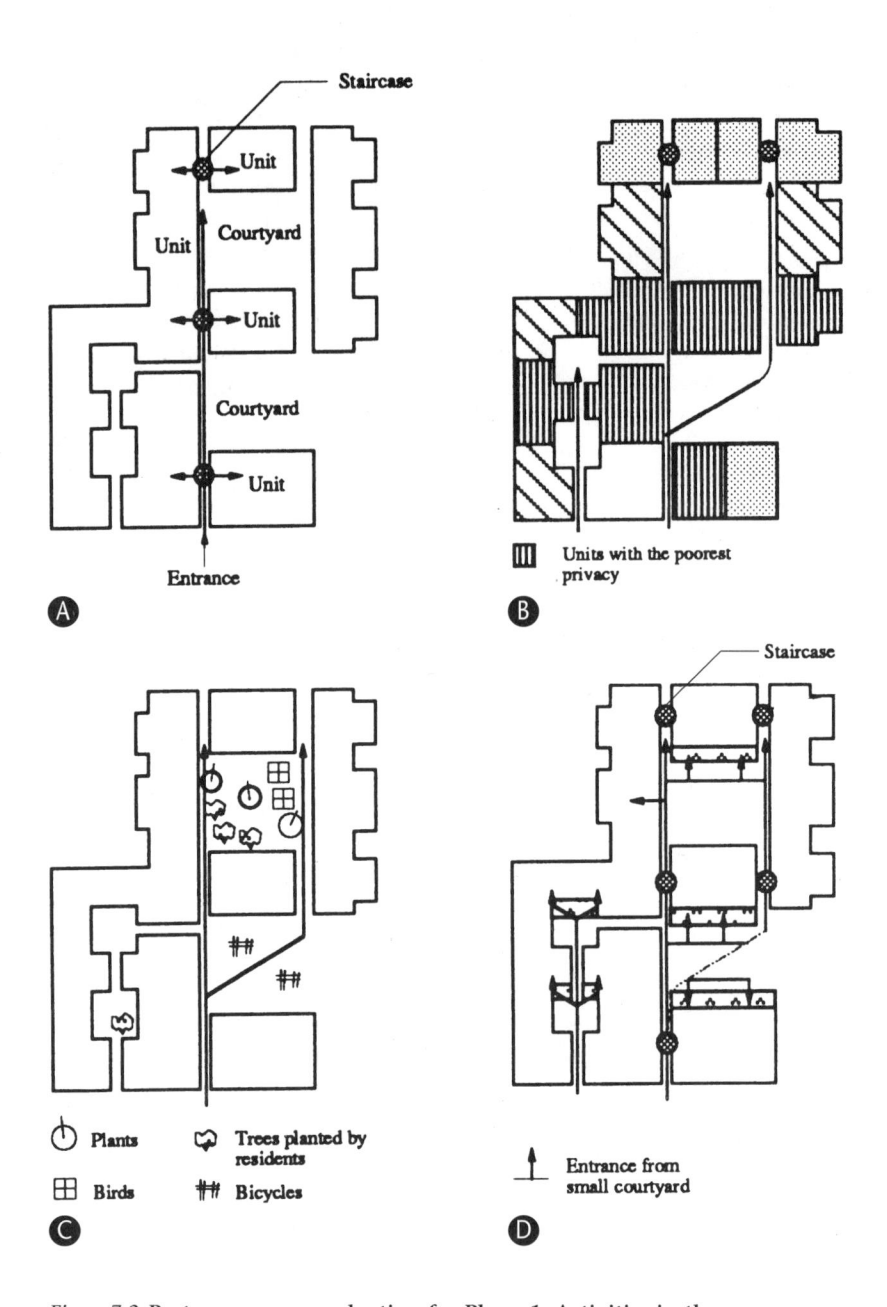

Figure 7.2 **Post-occupancy evaluation for Phase 1: Activities in the neighbourhood.** Ⓐ Circulation of the new courtyard house. Ⓑ Level of privacy on ground floor. Ⓒ Residents' adaptation of the courtyard. Ⓓ Use of entrances on the ground floor.

Table 7-1

Post-occupancy evaluation for Phase I:
A survey of residents in the new courtyard-type houses at Ju'er Hutong

Question		Percent
Neighbourliness		
1. For all of your neighbours in this courtyard, you:		
1. Are very familiar with	0- 3	46
	4- 6	19
	7-10	6
	10-	6
2. Are quite familiar with	0- 3	23
	4- 6	41
	7-10	0
	10-	13
3. Only say hello to	0- 3	17
	4- 6	19
	7-10	26
	10-	7
4. Seldom communicate with and know little about		9
2. For all the people in this courtyard, you:		
1. Are familiar with most of them		46
2. Know some of them		29
3. Don't know most of them		26
3. The approaches for you to get to know your neighbours mainly include:		
1. Meeting them when you enter and leave home		64
2. Asking them for help quite often		33
3. Discussing interior finishing together		6
4. Working together for neighbourhood interests		13
5. Through the contact of the elderly and children		26
6. Others		16
4. Your comment on the number of households in this courtyard is:		
1. Too many and very crowded		0
2. Moderate. Crowded sometimes		16
3. Ok. Not crowded		81
4. Too few and too quiet		3
5. Your comment on the building form of this new courtyard house is:		
1. Nice living environment and thus you like it		83
2. You are indifferent to it		0
3. Uncomfortable and thus you don't like it		17

▶

◀ *Table 7-1*

Question	Percent
6. Your comment on the plantation in this new courtyard house is:	
1. Pretty and practical	62
2. Visually pretty only	29
3. Neither visually pretty nor practical	9
7. How do you usually use your platform, balcony, and courtyard?	
1. As storage space	71
2. As leisure space	23
3. As sightseeing sites	9
4. As communicating places with your neighbours	9
5. Others	16

Sense of Security

8. You think a reinforced anti-burglar door:	
1. Unnecessary	68
2. Improves security	19
3. Not even enough	13
9. You think courtyards, balconies, and terraces:	
1. Improve sense of security	71
2. Are not good for security	16
3. Are very bad for security	13
10. You think the shared courtyards:	
1. Provide mutual protection	89
2. Are of no benefit for security even when locked	11
3. Need further supervision for security	0
11. You think locking the entrance in the evening:	
1. Necessary	81
2. Indifferent	16
3. More locks need to be added between courtyards	3

Sense of Territory and Privacy

12. At what point do you feel "at home" when you come back from work?	
1. Jiaodaokou / Nan Luogu Xiang	6
2. Ju'er / Shoubi hutong	29
3. The new courtyard complex	46
4. Inside door of apartment	19
13. When at home, you feel it is:	
1. Intolerably noisy	9
2. Sometimes noisy. Bearable	23
3. Relatively quiet	68

▶

◄ *Table 7-1*

Question	Percent
14. Your bedroom curtain is:	
1. Often drawn	16
2. Drawn in the evening and sometimes during the day	4
3. Drawn only in the evening	74
4. Others	6
15. Your living room curtain is:	
1. Often drawn	16
2. Drawn in the evening and sometimes during the day	6
3. Drawn only in the evening	64
4. Others	14
16. When you feel it is noisy outside your apartment, you usually:	
1. Put up with it	38
2. Go to a quiet room	13
3. Exchange bedroom with living room	0
4. Go out	0
5. Others	23
17. When it is warm, you open windows:	
1. Often for ventilation	78
2. When it is quiet	0
3. Seldom because of the noise	13
4. Others	9

from the surrounding neighbourhood – would play in the courtyards). The provision of balconies and roof terraces as outdoor or semi-outdoor spaces for the upper-storey apartments considerably reduced the pressure to use the ground space in the courtyards. Sixty-seven percent of the residents considered the courtyard to be a quiet place, and only 70 percent drew their curtains in the evening. This response indicated to the design team that problems of noise and overlooking in the courtyard were not as bad as expected. Eighty-nine percent of the residents felt that the courtyard was safe, though it was still necessary to lock the main gate to the *hutong* at night.

On the whole, the New Courtyard House type seems to have provided a special balance between the privacy and anonymity of walk-up apartment dwellings on the one hand, and the close but sometimes intrusive relations of one-storey courtyard housing on the other hand. Nearly half of the Phase 1 residents replied that they knew most of their neighbours, and 60 percent of all respondents said that they knew their neighbours primarily through encountering them while passing through the common space. Thus physical design has played a significant role in supporting neighbourliness. Moreover, the standard courtyard unit seems to have been more than just a design convenience: it truly has social meaning for the residents. After returning from work, more residents felt they had "reached home" when they entered the courtyard cluster than when they entered their own apartments. Indeed, more residents felt this way upon entering the *hutong* than upon entering their own apartments – another strong indicator that the original sense of neighbourhood spatial community has persisted.

Some interesting conclusions may also be drawn about how the particular layout and size of the courtyards affects the social life of residents. Breaking down resident responses according to the location of their homes within the complex, it becomes clear that residents of the innermost large courtyard enjoyed both the strongest social relations as well as the cleanest and best kept environment. The courtyard nearest the *hutong*, on the other hand, became too much of a through-passage and was used by too many people. The residents whose apartments abutted it were thus discouraged from taking care of it and using it as an "outdoor living room." However, residents of both of the large courtyards enjoyed stronger relations than did residents of the two small courtyards on the side. This seems to be due to the inability of the small courtyards to accommodate much outdoor activity.

In sum, residents gave a very positive overall response to many of the ways in which the project affected their lives. This was a very encouraging outcome.

Residents Who Relocated outside the Neighbourhood after Renewal

Of all the pilot neighbourhood renewal projects initiated in Beijing during the late 1980s, Ju'er Hutong was the only one that promoted the Housing Reform policy to the extent of requiring that all residents who returned to the neighbourhood after renewal had to purchase their units. This meant that many residents either could not afford to return or, for other reasons, chose a less expensive alternative. Before construction began, residents were shown plans and models of the new housing and, according to their original living space and number of household members, were offered new units of various sizes at preferential rates. Those who chose not to buy were given the options of (1) moving to other government-owned housing elsewhere (generally old, one-storey buildings in the Old City); (2) moving to new housing that was either provided by the government or offered at a lower market price (generally well outside the Old City); or (3) exchanging their right to purchase at the preferential rate for a house elsewhere. In total there were thirty-one resettled households, of which twenty-six were surveyed by the planning team at Tsinghua (Figure 7.3).

On average, the relocated households enjoyed an increase of 20 square metres of built area in their new homes. In terms of living rooms (i.e., living or bedrooms but not kitchens, toilets, or halls), only three households did not receive an increase over what they had in their original situation; the

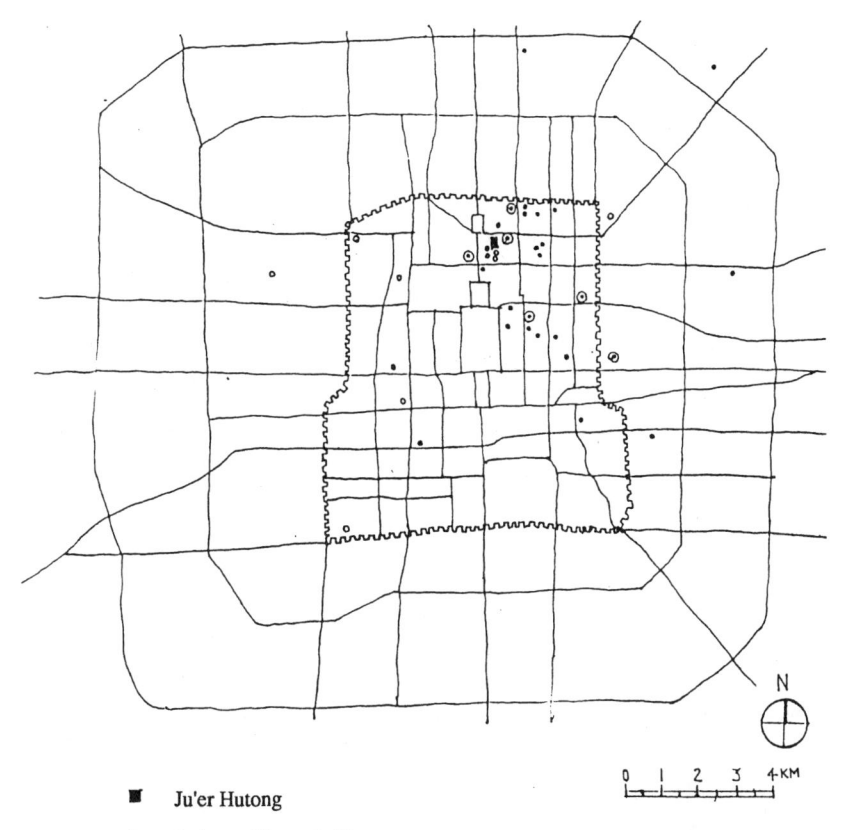

- ■ Ju'er Hutong
- ▼ Relocated households
- ▫ Original locations of some new residents from house purchase
- ◎ Original locations of some new residents from house exchange

Figure 7.3 **Resettlement and relocation of residents in the city**

majority received two additional rooms. Indeed, five families received an extra apartment in order to house separate generations. Of the thirteen households that originally did not have a south-oriented dwelling, ten enjoyed an improvement in access to sunlight. Seventy percent were able to move to other housing in the same district of the city (the East City District). Only four households moved outside the Second Ring Road, and these enjoyed the greatest improvement in physical housing conditions (on average, their new apartments had three living rooms and were located in new buildings).

In sum, physical housing conditions improved significantly for those households that did not return to Ju'er Hutong, especially in proportion to the distance they moved. On the whole, residents of the Old City are not happy to move out. However, given the higher-quality living conditions at relatively lower rents in the suburbs, many residents are willing to move if they can bicycle to work within half an hour and if adequate schools and other services are available. The relocation problems that have more recently emerged with other renewal projects stem from a lack of resettlement options and the great distances that relocated residents have had to move. The result has been a growing resentment towards a situation in which "the wealthy stay and the poor must go." At Ju'er Hutong, however, the developers and the district government's various property management offices took great care to help residents find adequate alternative housing sites, both within and without the Old City. In the end, residents were able to feel that, given their resources, they had received a fair opportunity to exercise their preferences. None of those surveyed expressed regret over the choices they had made.

Lessons Learned from the Design, Construction, and Management Experience

As a result of (1) the post-occupancy survey, (2) various other communications between the project planning team at Tsinghua and the residents and management of Ju'er Hutong, and (3) the general experience of implementing Phase 1, we became aware of a few difficulties that had to be addressed in later phases of the project. These are outlined below.

Design Issues

Rubbish Disposal Chute

The first problem was whether or not there was a need for a rubbish disposal chute, and the third-floor residents wrote to the city government requesting a solution to this problem. The design team argued that there would be no need for a rubbish chute in a three-storey apartment house. The opening of a chute would have to be placed at the platform level between the second and third floors, and the residents on the second floor would have to go up a flight of stairs to use it. Thus, a chute of this kind would only serve two or three families on the third floor while causing extra work to keep it clean. Rubbish disposal is not inconvenient at the moment, and after the service road is finished it will become even easier. Gradually, the residents have accepted this idea.

Sunlight Conditions

Despite careful calculations in the original design, slight alteration of building sizes during construction resulted in insufficient sunlight for the ground floor apartments during some winter periods. The rooms in the east and west wings are also darker than was expected on overcast days because of the particular local surroundings. Altogether, about 15 percent of the households experienced occasional inadequate daylight. Larger windows, higher ceilings, and more careful siting reduced these problems in later designs. However, the interior of courtyard housing always has uneven daylighting.

Kitchen and Toilet
Rising living standards have increased the demand for higher-quality kitchen and toilet designs. In the second and third phases, these utilities have been upgraded.

Construction Issues
The small scale of redevelopment of each phase generated extra difficulties in construction. In the second phase, the finished ground level of the courtyard was higher than it was in the first phase, and this caused drainage difficulties. Temporary drainage was provided, but a systematic solution will be possible only after completion of the alleyway system.

Management Issues
Since the residents have moved in, the property has been managed by a newly formed real estate development company. Despite its efforts, many problems remain unsolved, such as control of irregular construction on the balconies and terraces, and change of property use from residential to commercial. In order to meet the increasing management challenges, a community committee was set up for the Ju'er Hutong neighbourhood by the East District City Council in September 1992. Due to the number of issues raised by the residents, a neighbourhood management policy seemed necessary in order to cope with the many post-occupancy problems.

Experience Gained
The post-occupancy evaluation reveals some of the effects of the new living environment on the daily lives of the residents as well as the complexity of the factors involved. It also helps to solve many post-occupancy problems and to provide a better understanding of the directions that should be taken by future redevelopment projects. Architects can contribute to the improvement of people's living conditions through better housing design. Even under intense land pressure, such as occurs at Ju'er Hutong, architects can still find ways to create more indoor and outdoor space to reduce the social and psychological pressures caused by overcrowding. This contributes positively to the interaction between people and their environment.

Main Obstacles to Progress in Planning and Design

Conceptual Design
Although substantial research had been conducted before the project was

commissioned, the team members were still apprehensive. There was uncertainty about the new housing type in its embryonic form. Committed to designing a comfortable new courtyard housing form, the team made several architectural models in order to examine the effects of courtyard sizes formed by buildings of similar height. Specialists were consulted on questions such as sunlight penetration, and the issues of privacy and floor-area ratio were dealt with when the design concept was improved. As the scale of investment and resettlement varied throughout the early stages, the conceptual design was modified to adapt to changing circumstances.

Planning Permission

Because of the unorthodox housing form, there was some initial difficulty with regard to obtaining planning permission from the government. The design had to be improved in order to meet statutory requirements. Some innovation was also necessary in order to preserve the character of the design. For example, the new courtyard housing form does not comply with conventional firefighting regulations, which require straight roads, large curb radii, and simpler building forms. To solve the problem, fire hydrants were placed in the courtyards, and this, combined with clear passages along the perimeter of the building complexes, met the requirements. Another example of needed innovation concerned the width of the *hutong*; it was impossible to find space to widen the lanes, and, in any case, the resulting increase in traffic through the middle of the neighbourhood would be undesirable. Consequently, after consulting with the traffic management authorities, we added a *hutong* of variable width. This *hutong* would meet the needs of occasional two-way traffic but would discourage through traffic.

Resettlement

The resettlement program was probably the most difficult part of the renewal project. When the housing renewal program began, there was no resettlement precedent to study. Inevitably, residents misunderstood the redevelopment policies. Initially, they were allowed to take part in the housing reform voluntarily. It was a major decision for families to participate; as a result, some families changed their minds quite a few times based on various rumours concerning amount of compensation, property rights, and so on. It was only after the East City District Development Company declared clear and sound resettlement policies that the program began to progress more steadily. The complexity of resettlement and the indecision of the residents caused some alteration in the design. The lesson learned from this was that renewal policies must be financially acceptable to ordinary residents with limited funds. It was also critical that the living environment be attractive to residents after redevelopment and that the developer have an opportunity to make a reasonable profit. The picture became clearer and more predictable in the second phase of the project.

Project Drawings and Documents
Because the project was innovative, it was not surprising that the volume of drawings and documentation was massive. Due to the complicated conditions of the site, as many as ninety-five drawings were prepared. Although the first stage of the project covered only 2,760 square metres, 10,000 *yuan* was spent on design fees. The fees were insufficient for the amount of work completed by the design office, although the sum was finally accepted because of the project's social benefits.

Construction
The small site developed during the first phase made building work more difficult. There was simply insufficient space, not only for construction work, but also for modern machinery to be moved to the site and stored. The decision to preserve the existing trees made construction work even harder: it was a miracle that the first phase was completed in ten months. Much praise is owing to the designers and to the developers, who were to receive awards from the Beijing Municipal Government for their efforts. The good craftsmanship of the builders should be recognized for its enduring quality.

Real Estate Management
Financially, the project was initiated by the newly founded "housing cooperative" established by the Housing Reform Office. This new government program was designed to gradually change the existing welfare housing to private housing. This, in fact, has marked a shift in housing management from the conventional work-unit based, low-rent system to a market-based system. However, the efficiency and effectiveness of the new real estate management system have yet to be tested.

Comments on Crucial Aspects

Programming
A sound program was the key to the success of this project. In conventional construction, architects carry out the design according to a brief issued by the clients. However, past experience shows that clients often have little understanding of architectural design, and this benefits neither themselves nor the general public. Moreover, a client's design brief may not involve innovation in design and building technology. Planning authorities are also more concerned with macro management than with small-scale innovation. The burden, therefore, rests with architects when specific problems need creative solutions. This requires a detailed study – "project programming" – in order to understand the nature and goals of the projects and to uncover possible solutions. In the Ju'er Hutong project, three proposals were produced based on this study. These did not replace the design brief but

provided an opportunity for the design to be considered in the light of more adequate information.

Improvement through Comprehensive Environmental Rehabilitation
It is a popular view that renewal in the Old City can be accomplished simply by demolishing the old housing and building new housing. Without comprehensively rehabilitating the infrastructure, however, it would be impossible to improve environmental quality. At Ju'er Hutong there was, for example, the problem of supplying central heating in the first phase. No space was available for a new boiler house, nor was it practical to use the coal-based local heating system. It was only after negotiation that it was decided to expand the existing boiler house in a nearby factory. Infrastructure problems will become more acute when the expansion of the project overloads the existing system. Therefore, infrastructure, and, by extension, the whole environment, must be considered prior to any specific plan to replace buildings.

Necessity of Phasing
As in the case of the Ju'er Hutong project, all inner-city housing renewal involves issues of housing reform, development of new housing forms, and conservation of the urban fabric. These are complicated issues that also affect other parts of the neighbourhood. Building quality, ownership, and the urgency for redevelopment vary from compound to compound. As developer investment is limited, it is necessary to divide the project into phases so that each area can be looked at as thoroughly as possible. This does not mean that larger-scale development is not possible in the future, only that more development experience and financial support are required in order for it to proceed.

Interaction Between Planning and Design
Although design is carried out in stages, an overall plan that considers land use, infrastructure, and architectural design is necessary. Any successful solution to inner-city housing renewal, especially to conservation issues, requires intensive interaction between planning and architectural design.

Reflections on the *Yangshi Lei* Approach[1]
Looking back over the history of housing development in Beijing, two established types of housing and one potential type can be identified. The first is the traditional courtyard house; the second is industrialized apartment housing, which contradicts the first; and the third is new courtyard housing, which fuses the first two and attempts to better fit the historic context. In traditional Chinese architecture, a simple typological classification was used in conjunction with a sophisticated modular system. The

number of bays, the height of the columns, and the height of the roof determined the dimension of the rest of a building's components. This led to the standardization, typification, and modularization of individual buildings. Freed from the need to attend to the details of building construction, the creativity of traditional architects in China was mainly expressed in the mastery of the composition of building complexes, courtyards, and garden making. This classical architectural principle is still applicable today, particularly with the help of computer-aided design.[2] In the new courtyard

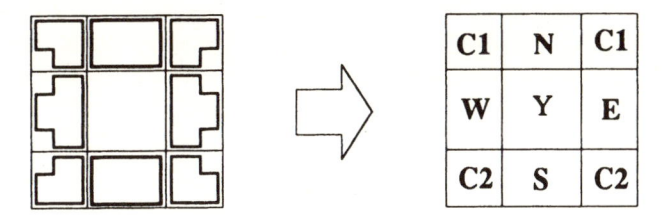

Figure 7.4 **Studies of the elementary forms of the courtyard-type house: Basic courtyard – nine-square composition.**

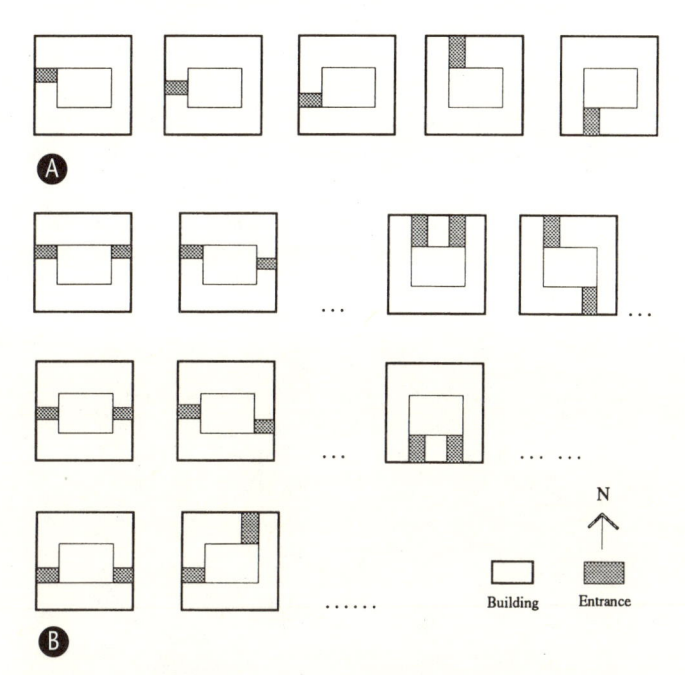

Figure 7.5 **Studies of the elementary forms of the courtyard-type house: Standard courtyards with different entrance locations.** Ⓐ One entrance to courtyard. Ⓑ Two entrances to courtyard.

house, it may also be possible to standardize the building blocks, courtyard types, apartment units, and construction components so that the drafting tasks can be simplified in order to achieve efficiency. Variations in the sizes of the sites may be resolved by finding the best composition of different standardized units, which will allow designers to spend more time on the master plan. Such extended classical design procedures will no doubt contribute to the harmony of physical forms in the organic renewal process (Figure 7.4 through Figure 7.10).

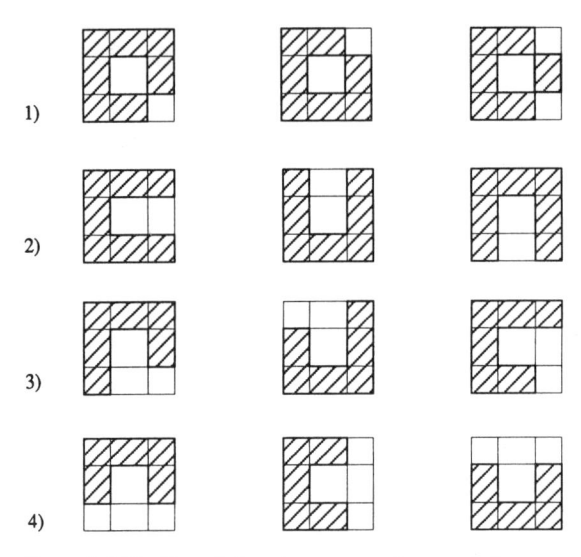

Figure 7.6 **Studies of the elementary forms of the courtyard-type house: Derived courtyard with modifications of units** (west and east units in c-1 and c-2 are difficult to handle with regard to solar access, light, and ventilation).

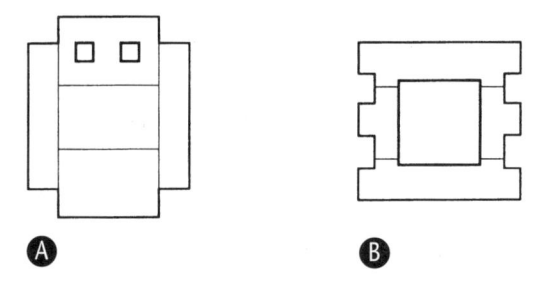

Figure 7.7 **Studies of the elementary forms of the courtyard-type house: Other variations through bulk and form modifications.** **A** Small light wells inside units to increase FAR. **B** Modifications for better north-south orientation.

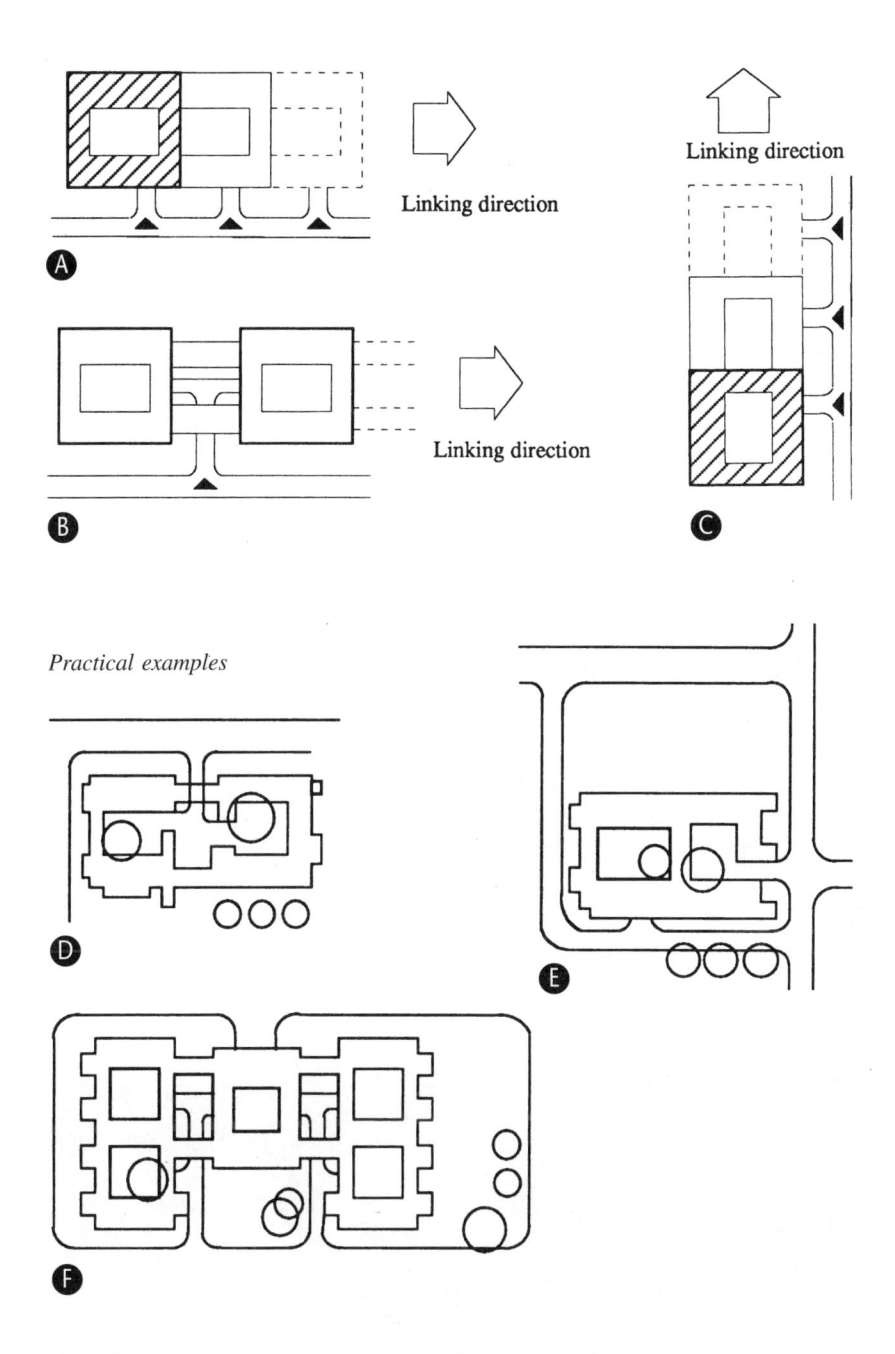

Post-Occupancy Evaluation and Lessons from the Planning and Design Experience   179

Practical examples

Figure 7.8 **Studies of the elementary forms of the courtyard-type house: Articulation of courtyards.** **Ⓐ** Direct latitudinal combination. **Ⓑ** Indirect latitudinal combination. **Ⓒ** Longitudinal combination. *Practical examples*: **Ⓓ** Court B [Phase 2]. **Ⓔ** Court C [Phase 2]. **Ⓕ** Phase 3.

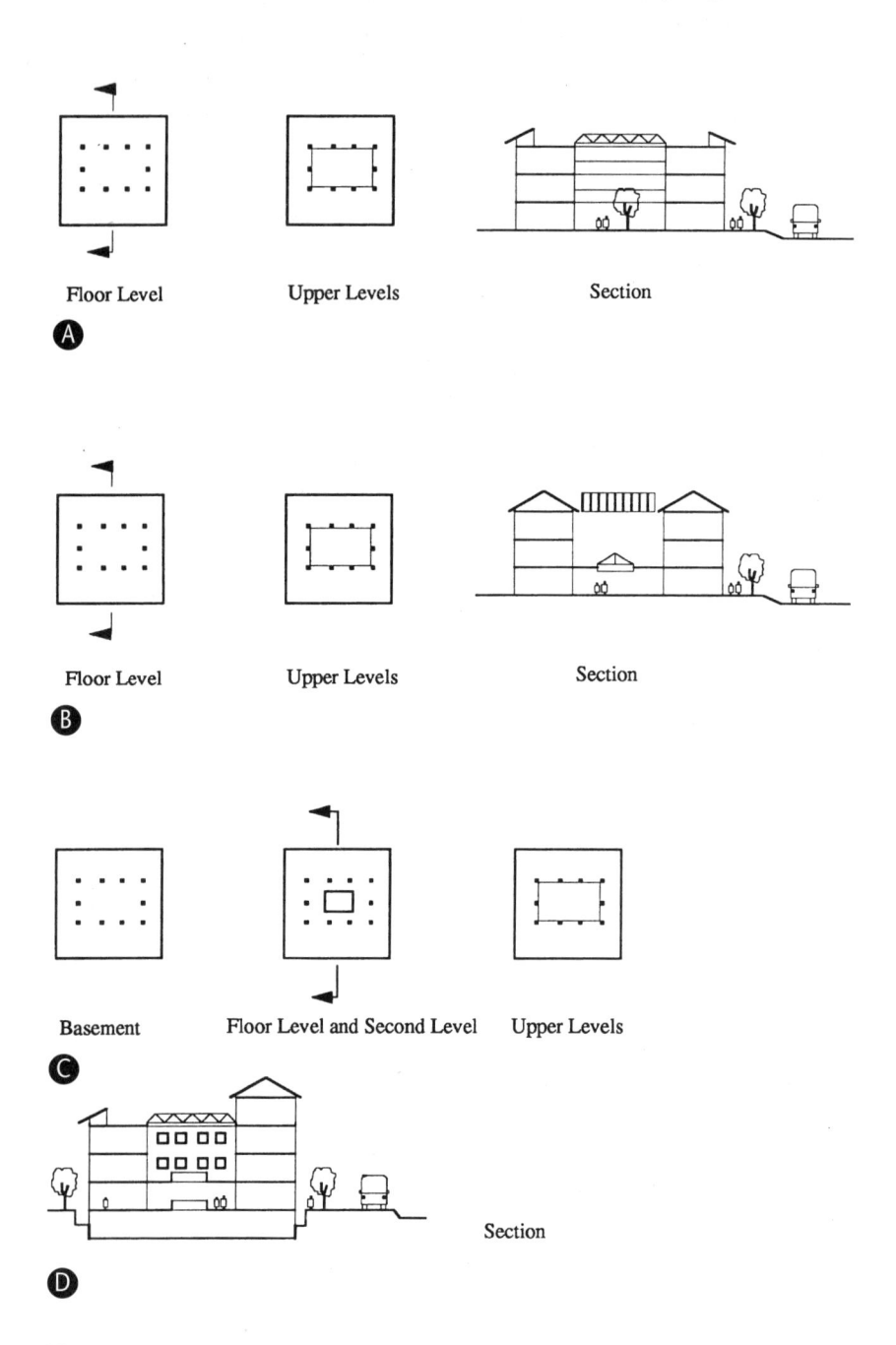

180 Post-Occupancy Evaluation and Lessons from the Planning and Design Experience

Figure 7.9 **Studies of the elementary forms of the courtyard-type house: Non-residential buildings.** Ⓐ Courtyard type [similar to residential buildings]. Ⓑ Atrium type. Ⓒ Roof-terrace type. Ⓓ Mixed type.

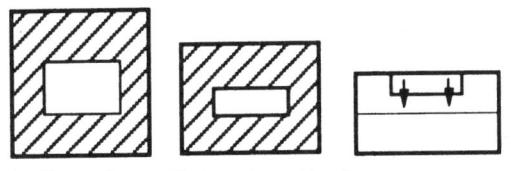

1. Front shop with housing at back

2. Ground floor shop with housing on upper floors
   a. Shop + housing
   b. Shop + housing + other

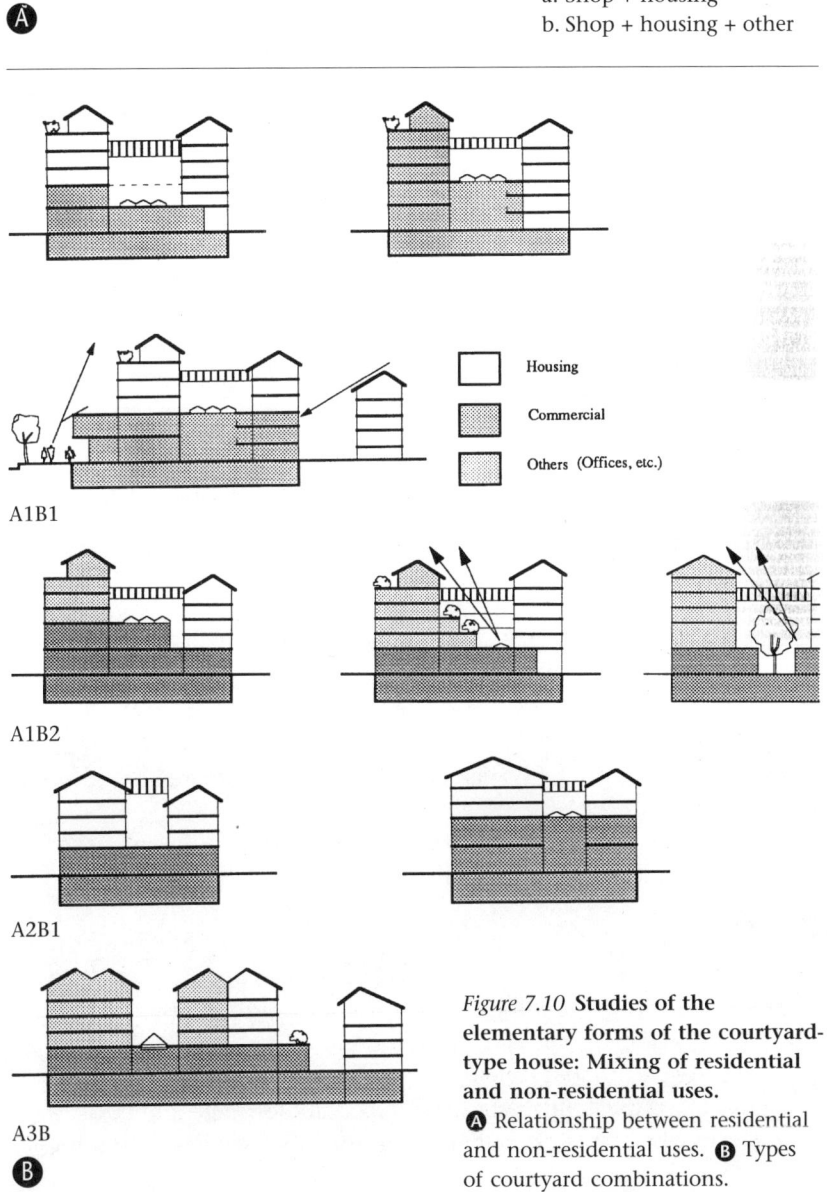

Ⓐ

A1B1

A1B2

A2B1

A3B

Ⓑ

Housing

Commercial

Others (Offices, etc.)

Figure 7.10 **Studies of the elementary forms of the courtyard-type house: Mixing of residential and non-residential uses.**
Ⓐ Relationship between residential and non-residential uses. Ⓑ Types of courtyard combinations.

8
The Continuing Debate over Redevelopment

Opposing Views on Housing Standards

The first phase of the Ju'er Hutong renewal project generated discussion on several issues that require further examination. One of the most contentious is housing standards. Many Chinese and international experts would have preferred higher standards for the first phase of the project. They argued that a low standard that meets short-term needs will quickly fall shy of the residents' expectations. The fact that the Ju'er Hutong project is located in an important conservation area is also a powerful reason to raise the standards. There are those, however, who feel the existing building standard is already above what the average person can currently afford. Standards for social housing have long been the subject of debate in both China and the West, and they are the crux of the contradiction between short- and long-term goals. As Peter Hall put it, "Should public housing ... be built to reflect the standards and aspirations of the first generation of occupiers, or the second or third? If it is built merely to minimal contemporary standards, the risk is that it will be regarded as substandard within a generation or two; and it may not be possible then to redesign it except at unacceptable cost. But if it is built in advance to satisfy the standards of tomorrow, then less resources will be available to satisfy the pressing housing needs of today."[1]

Although there are no easy answers to this problem, future designs should take the following aspects into consideration:

1. *Multiplicity of socio-economic groups:* Household income has become more diverse in recent years; therefore, flexible policies are required to supply different socio-economic groups with housing to suit their respective needs. Rigid limits on housing standards should not be set, as the economy is in a period of rapid development. The Ju'er Hutong neighbourhood requires a relatively high standard, especially for the commodity housing units, the sales of which are used to finance affordable housing for

ordinary residents. At the same time, too obvious a difference between the standard of housing units offered on the market at high prices and the standard of units offered to lower-income groups at preferential prices runs the risk of segregating different income groups and stigmatizing the poorer ones. The design of Ju'er Hutong struck a delicate balance between these two concerns and has avoided the kind of spatial segregation of market-rent-paying residents from original residents that one sees in other renewal projects in Beijing.[2]

2. *Flexible design:* Housing units should be flexibly designed so that future alterations and extensions can be easily accommodated.
3. *Continual review:* The housing stock should be viewed in the context of continual renewal. The city will always have a certain percentage of medium- to low-standard housing units that will need future upgrading.

Opposing Views on Resettlement

The way in which the original residents are resettled is another point of sharp debate. There is an argument for rehousing all of the original residents in their old neighbourhoods after renewal. There is also an argument that supports relocating all original residents in order to have flexibility in the design, redevelopment, and allocation of the units. Most of the residents hold the former view, which was adopted in the other initial pilot renewal projects in the Old City. However, even if all original residents remain in the neighbourhood, the degree to which the local community can remain unchanged in the fast-developing economy is questionable. At Ju'er Hutong, many of those original residents who were offered preferential prices to return to the neighbourhood after renewal have since sublet their units to newcomers and found housing for themselves elsewhere. Resettlement may be unavoidable in most cases, but measures can be taken to minimize its negative impact.

Those who support the complete relocation of the existing community are divided on the form of renewal that should take place. Some would like to restore the old courtyard-type houses to their original condition, but with improved infrastructure, and then rent or sell them to the highest bidder. They would have to be very expensive to cover the improved infrastructure costs. This approach may be appropriate in tightly regulated preservation districts, but it could not be used in the renewal and rehabilitation of the Old City as a whole. Others prefer to redevelop large areas with modern, higher-density luxury-standard housing that could also be sold on the market. While this approach is clearly the most profitable, it is socially and politically controversial because it would involve rehousing the original residents en masse in order to cater to a much more privileged group. Not all inner-city gentrification projects in developed countries have been good experiences, and in this case it is necessary to prevent the underprivileged from suffering further because of renewal.

In short, neighbourhood housing and rehousing standards involve a web of economic and social issues that are associated with housing needs and social stability. A balance between social and financial gain is recommended. For example, some residents could remain in their renovated houses to maintain neighbourhood continuity, while other redeveloped houses could be sold so that the renewal program is self-financing. Otherwise, the renewal program will fail to meet its original goal.

Cost and Economy

The Call to Reduce Costs

The Ju'er Hutong approach has been criticized for being too expensive to be applied broadly throughout the Old City. If a building design incurs costs that are too high for ordinary residents, then the project will eventually fail. The primary goal of the Ju'er Hutong experiment was to explore a new courtyard-type housing form. The first consideration was the rationality and practicality of a new housing form and whether a reasonable floor-area ratio could be reached while offering proper sunlight conditions, privacy, and high-quality indoor and outdoor living space. The result of the first phase of the project proved satisfactory; however, the issue of costs had to be dealt with. The cost of building the first phase was estimated at 600 *yuan* per square metre at the design stage. According to the contractor, the construction cost was 555 *yuan* per square metre, but when this was combined with the price of the boiler (50,000 *yuan* to be shared with Phase 2) and other infrastructure facilities, a higher cost than that associated with conventional apartment housing resulted.

Ways to Reduce Costs

Redevelopment costs consist of several components. First, complex building forms contribute to high construction costs. In future designs, the building forms may be standardized and designed systematically in order to reduce costs. Second, construction management was difficult for this project because of its small scale and the awkward site conditions. Increasing demand for a more intense use of land than originally existed led, in turn, to the need for complex engineering work at the perimeter of the site. As the scale of redevelopment increases, such difficulties will tend to diminish and costs will be reduced.

Third, at Ju'er Hutong the high-quality landscaping was expensive; this component can be scaled down to suit smaller budgets in other projects. Fourth, some of the interior decoration was wasted after some returning residents renovated their units with higher-quality work; this waste may be avoided in the future through user-specific programming. Finally, the use of traditional building materials added to the cost. In order to fit into the existing architectural environment, traditional grey bricks and tiles were used. Production of these building materials ceased long ago, and purchasing them added extra costs to the construction. Cheaper alternatives can be used in the future.

Comparability of Costs

The building costs for courtyard-type housing tends to be unfairly judged against those of conventional apartment blocks. In fact, they are two different housing forms, and, in many respects, the costs are not comparable. Conventional apartment blocks have very simple plans, with little variation between floors except for small balconies on the second floor and above. Within the new courtyard-type housing, a variety of designs are possible through the use of balconies and terraces as outdoor living space. The open space around a conventional apartment block is often difficult to use except for parking and rubbish collection; the open space around the courtyard-type houses is a much more liveable place. The apartment blocks can hardly suit the traditional urban environment of Beijing, but courtyard-type housing forms can be comfortably integrated into it. Moreover, the conventional apartment block building structure is simple, whereas courtyard-type housing forms are complex and, inevitably, more expensive.

The Use of East and West Wings in Courtyard-Type Housing

Apartment blocks can all have a southern orientation and guarantee every household equal sunlight conditions; this obviously cannot be achieved in courtyard-type houses. Having east- and west-facing units is often regarded as a shortcoming of courtyard-type housing, and under the public housing distribution policy, housing often has to be designed in an equitable manner. In the Ju'er Hutong project, the new courtyard-type housing form makes various housing conditions available in terms of orientation, location, floor level, courtyard size, and so on. Therefore, rents or selling prices vary to suit different needs.

Finally, in housing renewal projects, infrastructure charges are significant. In the first phase of the Ju'er Hutong project, new infrastructure work was limited to the installation of a septic tank and the improvement of the existing boiler house; thus, the costs were not critical. But with further redevelopment of the neighbourhood, there must be more investment in infrastructure, which will inevitably increase costs.

Housing Reform

The Ju'er Hutong project was born out of the current housing reform, without which it would have remained an idea on paper. One of the main features of the reform was, for the first time, the establishment of a housing cooperative in Beijing. The residents in the neighbourhood have shown great enthusiasm for it, but there is still a need for future improvement.

The fundamental idea behind housing reform in the Ju'er Hutong project was to find a new way to fund housing redevelopment. Since the state is no longer the sole contributor of funds, local governments, work units, and individuals all have to pay their share. The crucial point here is to decide how much of the cost individuals should bear. In the first phase of the project, it was decided that the buyers from the original neighbourhood would pay 350 *yuan* per square metre, while their employer would pay 250 *yuan* per square metre. If a resident's employer could not pay the subsidy, as was usually the case, the buyers could make use of a special low-interest bank loan and the remainder of the cost was paid by the government. Consequently, about one-third of the original residents were able to move back after redevelopment.

Those who could not pay have moved out to other areas and to improved housing conditions. Guaranteeing to residents that their housing conditions would be improved was very important to the renewal program. The proportion of original residents returning to the redeveloped houses should also be kept at a reasonable level – one-third should be the minimum. Such a policy can also create interest and gain the support of the developers. In Beijing, in order to encourage the Old City renewal, the city government issued a policy that requires the developers to subsidize renewal through the use of profits made in suburban development. This policy has not yet been implemented in the East City District where the Ju'er Hutong project took place.

These types of measures are broadly recognized as the direction in which Chinese urban housing policy should proceed. In 1991, the Beijing Municipal Housing Reform Policies Office started to consider using World Bank loans to create a housing development and management company in order to form a new housing development system. This idea still has relevance for current housing issues in the city. The following general recommendations should receive further consideration:

1. Local authorities, work units, and individuals should be encouraged to set up housing associations in order to develop affordable housing for ordinary people. This will help to improve the efficiency of housing investments.
2. The current vertical housing allocation system should be changed to one that involves horizontal collaboration among various property ownerships on the same land plot for the purpose of forming a unified development.

3. A cross-subsidy policy should be set up in the Old City areas to better finance projects that redevelop dilapidated housing units.

In short, under the socialist market economic system, it is very important to get the government, developers, and communities working together to solve housing problems. Presently, the newly established housing cooperative in the Ju'er Hutong neighbourhood is only playing a limited role. It is not yet the economic entity it should be: finance for redevelopment is controlled by the developer and the District Property Management Office. After the first phase was completed and the residents had moved in, the housing cooperative did not take over responsibility for service, property management, or maintenance in the neighbourhood. An effective mechanism for resident participation and management has yet to be found. Housing cooperatives are a new option in housing provision, and their development will require participation from other related organizations. The establishment of housing cooperatives is one way of achieving housing reform; others should also be explored.

9
Future Prospects

Multidimensional Redevelopment in Historic Cities

Since the 1950s, "old city reconstruction" (*jiucheng gaijian* or *gaizao*) was the popular term used by Chinese planners for the renewal of historic cities. This was an unfortunate term because it implied large-scale demolition and rebuilding, which proved to be disastrous when applied. In 1983, I recommended that the term be replaced by "urban renewal" or "urban regeneration" (*chengshi gengxin*), which involves three main components:[1]

1. *redevelopment* or *rebuilding* of areas where the building stock and infrastructure are in extremely poor condition;
2. *rehabilitation* of areas where some of the building stock is run down but the overall layout and building quality is still in reasonably good shape; and
3. *conservation* in areas with great historic importance and value.

Such a three-pronged approach, known in some Western countries as "careful urban renewal,"[2] was attempted by the Ju'er Hutong project, wherein selective redevelopment at the scale of the individual building or compound is the means through which rehabilitation and conservation are achieved at the scale of the neighbourhood.

Urban renewal may mean different things according to particular conditions in each neighbourhood, city, or country. Beijing needs to renew the Old City area because it is one of the most important historic cities in the world and the last example of traditional Chinese city planning, as described in Chapter 1. Its unique physical structures and comprehensive urban design require careful consideration and a positive attitude towards conservation and redevelopment in order to avoid damage such as that caused by the development of the past forty years. Beijing is also facing new opportunities and challenges brought about by economic and housing reform. Housing policies should be based on the city's problems; however, lessons from other countries where the housing market is more developed can provide useful references.

Towards a Comprehensive Approach

Physical Context

Regeneration of the Old City must bring benefits on all fronts – social, cultural, environmental, and economic. The ultimate task of urban renewal is to improve the city's living environment. The Ju'er Hutong project revealed a number of issues that warrant further research. First, there is a need for standardized design and the construction of a courtyard-type housing system. So far, the project has experimented with different courtyard forms. To meet the needs of larger-scale future development, it is necessary to identify some basic courtyard-type housing forms and their possible modifications so as to cope with various housing standards and densities. This could be facilitated by computer-aided design.

There is also the task of rehabilitating the traditional Beijing street block, of which the Ju'er Hutong area is a typical example. This block is a clearly defined neighbourhood in physical terms and is a coherent part of the historic street system of the Nan Luogu Xiang area (formerly the thirteenth-century Zhaohui-Jinggong Fang). The Ju'er Hutong project will be complete when the whole block is renewed. A comprehensive assessment of the layout and structure of the street block is required, including: integration of courtyard-type housing with the traditional circulation network, addition of residential-area amenities, creation of public and semi-public space, reduction of overcrowded housing, establishment of a local architectural image, and implementation of sustainable development policies. Furthermore, a systematic evaluation of the plan is necessary in order to incorporate mixed land use, the combination of different building types, service facilities, and infrastructure. A review of this kind will help to form a general redevelopment policy for similar neighbourhoods in the city.

Social Context

In China, housing is regarded as part of the social welfare system, and the government has taken full responsibility for its provision; however, the government alone cannot solve the enormous housing problems in a country with more than one billion people. Housing reform is necessary in order to bring market forces into play. The aim of housing reform in the Chinese context is to improve living standards and to create prosperity. It would be inappropriate to use housing reform merely to increase floor-area ratio regardless of the unique environment of historic areas. In the future, the government's job will be to guide housing reform while safeguarding societal needs. Examples of non-profit housing in developed countries are also useful to China.

In order to provide a socially and culturally balanced living environment, a proportion of the original residents should be guaranteed a return to the redeveloped old neighbourhood. This requires that there be a certain amount of affordable housing in the project, cross-subsidized by a commercial component. From a planning point of view, the Old City of Beijing is overpopulated and decentralization is necessary. Current housing redevelopment in the Old City provides such an opportunity, but in order for this to happen not all of the original residents can be rehoused in their redeveloped old neighbourhoods. This type of change in the community social structure has to be monitored carefully in order to minimize negative effects. In the first phase of the Ju'er Hutong project, one-third of the original residents were successfully rehoused in the redeveloped neighbourhood. This figure may serve as a reference for other similar projects.

Economic Context

Attracting investment and managing finance for real estate development are difficult issues in Beijing. The Ju'er Hutong project is one of the earliest experiments in housing development funded jointly by the state, work units, and individuals. Less than a year after the completion of the first phase, one-third of the new residential units were resold to the original residents at a price subsidized by the sale of the commercial units. It is possible to make a small profit on a site similar to this one.

Due to the increasing complexity of housing redevelopment, especially in terms of infrastructure, there are several concerns that need to be addressed. The intrinsic value of city-centre land dictates a high land-use intensity in the Old City. It is crucial to increase housing density so as to match the land value in the central areas and, at the same time, to create an agreeable living environment. Ju'er Hutong is located in a nine-metre height-controlled zone, and buildings have a three-storey height maximum. In order to increase density in the first two phases of the project, attics and basements were designed, and this proved to be practical. Occasionally, four-storey buildings may be permitted, and with careful planning and design they can block the view of nearby dilapidated or neglected buildings. Various design devices, including landscaping and the manipulation of courtyard space, can also be applied to improve environmental quality.

Traditionally, Chinese cities have a mixed land-use pattern. In the commercial areas, most city blocks have shops fronting on the main streets around the perimeter and residential houses fronting on the lanes within. In the residential areas, such as Ju'er Hutong, institutional and religious buildings mix with houses to form a sophisticated neighbourhood pattern based on a simple courtyard-type system. The traditional mixed land-use pattern was earlier decried by modern planners, but it is now considered valuable by planning professionals in many countries. Mixed land use in redevelopment areas not only helps to generate a healthy community economy, but it also opens up more ways of financing redevelopment projects.

Inner-city redevelopment and new suburban area development are inseparable; the Beijing Municipal Government has already set up a mechanism to cross-subsidize the former with the latter. The high cost of redeveloping housing in the Old City suggests that it should be commercialized in order to make development of infrastructure and public service improvement financially feasible.

Urban renewal needs to take place at a considerable scale in order to include infrastructure and other public services in the budget: but this does not mean the larger the scale of renewal the better. Large-scale renewal requires a big investment in infrastructure, not to mention considerable housing space for relocation. In the first phase of the Ju'er Hutong project, most of the relocation housing space was provided within the Old City. The second phase was larger, however, and relocation became more difficult; some of the families had to be accommodated in new housing areas far from the site. The complexity of renewal work in the existing neighbourhood not only requires prior careful planning and design, but also a long process of land acquisition and construction. The larger the scale, the longer and more complicated the process becomes and, thus, the more difficult it is to handle.

In recent years, many cities in China have gradually realized the problems of hasty renewal programs, and some of them have already begun to bring land and real estate development under stricter control. Economic assessment of renewal programs should consider not only short-term costs, but also long-term costs (such as maintenance). As any urban renewal project has an impact on its neighbouring areas and on the city as a whole, economic assessment should take into account the wider context.[3]

Cultural Context

Another important goal of the Ju'er Hutong project was to foster a new culture within the traditional urban environment. Housing is not only intended to meet people's material needs, but also to play an important role in their social and cultural lives. The Ju'er Hutong project attempts to create an environment in which the inhabitants can enjoy a new kind of privacy as well as have access to their neighbours in natural surroundings. From the perspective of the wider culture, the architecture of Ju'er Hutong explored the meaning of "a sense of place" in the context of Beijing's modernization. All of these objectives will be further examined in the extended redevelopment of the surrounding Nan Luogu Xiang area.

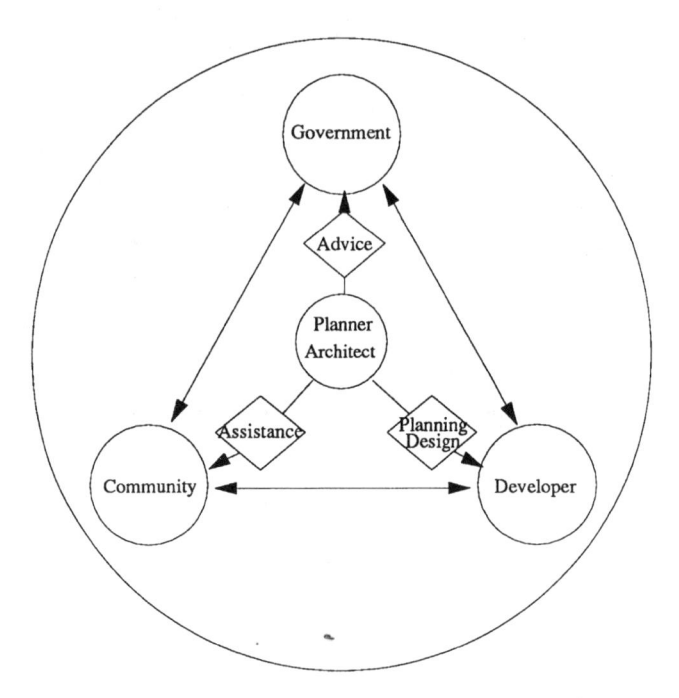

Figure 9.1 **The role of the planner and architects in the Ju'er Hutong rehabilitation project.** Interaction of the Tsinghua team with other participants of the rehabilitation project.

A "Three-in-One" Process of Planning, Design, and Management

In response to current housing requirements, the Ju'er Hutong experiment provides a new model for planning, design, and management in the Old City residential areas (Figure 9.1). A new management system has emerged in urban housing redevelopment in the form of the Housing Reform Office created by the Beijing Municipal Government. This office is responsible for general policy making on housing and has authorized each city district government to designate its own housing redevelopment areas. In the case of Ju'er Hutong, it was the East City District Property Management Office that, for this purpose, appointed the East City Development Company. These two bodies have been working together with the community for a long time and have a sound knowledge of the local housing situation. The neighbourhood committees in the East City District have also organized a non-government body, the Housing Co-operative, to accelerate the progress of the project; the three bodies work in coordination. The district government and the property management office are the decision makers, and the District Development Company, with the support of the neighbourhood committee, carries out the actual work, including planning and design brief preparation, relocation, construction, marketing, and so on.

To assist in the establishment of the housing cooperatives, our team acted as a consultant to the municipal and district authorities, as a planner and designer to the development company, and as a coordinator to the new Ju'er Hutong Community Management Committee. In China, as in other countries, it is common practice for architects to serve only their clients, who are usually either public or private developers. The job of an architect is simply to design; normally, no extra effort is put towards worrying about broader social and economic issues. The role of the architects in the Ju'er Hutong project reached far beyond that conventionally set out by the profession. And, given the socio-economic circumstances in China, this seemed only appropriate.[4] The "three-in-one" system is very promising for architects, despite the heavier workload it entails.

Community Participation

The "three-in-one" system needs to be refined, as rapid development has put more pressure on all participants involved in urban renewal. The government should maintain authority over the newly funded development companies in order to encourage them to improve their performance. Various new regulations are also required: there are no formal government policies to guide the commercial housing market, and some of the Ju'er Hutong housing has been changed to non-residential use despite management policies to prevent this. However, legislation can only be effectively implemented through the participation of the entire neighbourhood.

Improving Standards in Housing Redevelopment

An Interdisciplinary Approach

Urban renewal in China is directly affected by government policies as well as by changing social and economic structures. And renewal will have a strong impact on the physical environment. Housing is one of the most important components of urban renewal and involves city planning, urban and architectural design, building materials and technology, and the implementation and management of housing reform policy. The Ju'er Hutong project is a vivid example of an interdisciplinary approach in which architects and planners have taken a comprehensive view of urban development. Such an approach widens the scope for finding the most appropriate solutions to existing problems.

Extending Research and Design to Development

Research on housing renewal in the Old City and the potential role of new courtyard-type housing began in 1978, and a special program on derelict housing was initiated at the School of Architecture at Tsinghua University in 1982. This continuous research gave the team a strong foundation upon which to base its work for the municipal government on the Ju'er Hutong project in 1987. Housing experimentation and renewal is an ongoing process that requires careful study, long-term planning, and a symbiotic relationship between research and practice. Two German examples – the 1925 Wiessenhof exhibition in Stuttgart and the 1987 International Berlin Architectural Exhibition (IBA) – illustrate how specific well planned events can contribute to this process and, thus, can have a wide-ranging impact on housing design and development. In comparison, housing renewal in China generally lacks the necessary foundation of research and systematic analysis. The Ju'er Hutong research team strongly feels that the current housing renewal programs urgently need better overall planning and management strategies as well as a stronger link to research.

The involvement of professionals in housing research in China is not new; however, the effects are limited because of the lack of opportunities for experimentation under a planned economy. With housing reform in place, opportunities are emerging. Many land development companies have been set up, and they need guidelines for action. Therefore, research is becoming more and more relevant. The Ministry of Construction and other related organizations should pay more attention to research in order to improve housing development.

A Special Example with General Significance

The Ju'er Hutong project was a solution to a problem presented by a specific site. It was a design constrained by its location in the central area of historical Beijing, its proximity to an important conservation area with restrictive building height limits, and its neighbouring structures (which vary in terms of their physical condition). Based on many years of research and exchanges with planning practitioners and scholars around the world, the team at Tsinghua University introduced a philosophy of organic renewal and raised awareness of the value of continuity in the urban fabric, which led to the development of the new courtyard-type housing prototype. The experiment also tested a new pattern of housing development in the context of rapid economic, social, and cultural changes in Beijing. It should be remembered that this new courtyard-type housing form is only one of a number of possible forms that the renewal of old neighbourhoods in Beijing could take: other housing forms, including tower blocks, could be appropriate within the Old City.

As an experiment, the project has touched upon many facets of urban renewal in China. It demonstrated the need to develop distinct building forms for specific settings. China is a large country with many different regions, and within each of these there are local styles and traditions to be identified and preserved. Vernacular architecture is deeply rooted in local life, and an understanding of daily life can create suitable new architectural forms within the local context. In this respect, sociology, economics, and other relevant fields become more important in architecture. Thus, we need an interdisciplinary approach to urban renewal. In a sense, the Ju'er Hutong experiment raised a very large set of issues within a very tiny space. However, I believe that the basic design philosophy applied in this small project is not limited to its specific situation but is relevant to the renewal of historic cities in general. As "every painting strives to create or express a unique idea," the creativity of today's architects and planners will surely be nourished by an understanding and inheritance of our architectural tradition.[5]

10
Conclusion

Four years have passed since the first draft of this book was completed, and many new problems and conditions have emerged in the urban planning and development of Beijing. While it is impossible here to review the changes in great detail, they are so closely related to the issues discussed throughout this book that it is necessary to touch upon them briefly. In so doing, I hope not only to bring some closure to this account of the Ju'er Hutong project, but also, and more important, to show how the project is part of a dynamic situation and a continuing debate.

Further Development of Organic Renewal Theory and Its Application to Neighbourhood Conservation in the Old City of Beijing

The Ju'er Hutong project was only the beginning of a series of efforts to apply the principles of organic renewal to the planning of the Old City of Beijing. Once Phase 2 of the project was under way, my research team developed the approach not only in the later phases of Ju'er Hutong's planning, but also in the planning for several other historic areas in Beijing (Figure 10.1).

Conservation and Rehabilitation of the Nan Luogu Xiang Area (1994)
Since Chapter 6 included a detailed description of the conservation and rehabilitation of the Nan Luogu Xiang area, no further elaboration is necessary here. However, it is important to emphasize that this area, historically named the Zhaohui-Jinggong block, is one of the oldest existing examples of Yuan dynasty urban street layout, and it has been listed as one of Beijing's traditional courtyard preservation areas. Therefore, the key issue of its planning lies in the protective control of development throughout the entire block so as to avoid destruction of the existing residential character and spatial layout. The plans for other historic areas, as described below, vary in the relative emphasis they put on conservation or redevelopment, respectively.

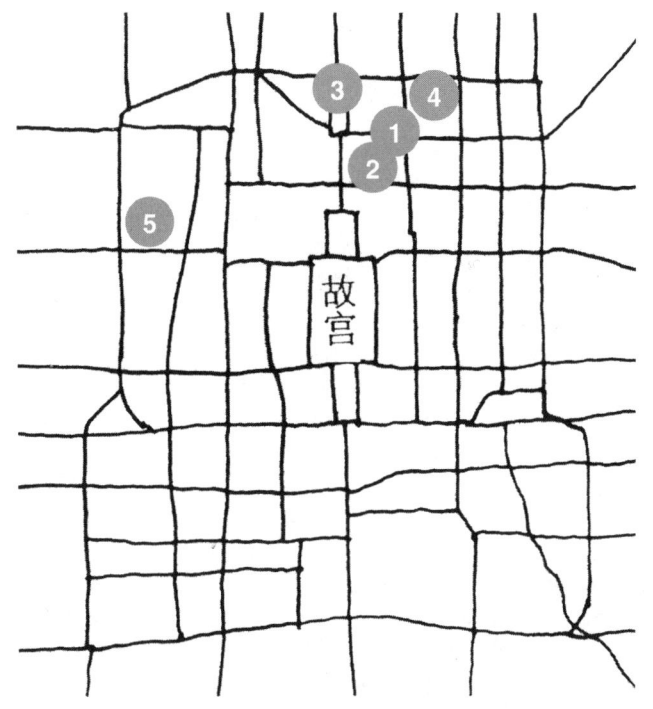

1 Ju'er Hutong (8.2 ha)   4 Guozijian
2 Nanluoguxiang   5 Baitasi (White Pagoda Temple)
3 Northern Central Axis Area

Figure 10.1 Map of Beijing's Old City showing the location of neighbourhood rehabilitation planning projects undertaken by the author's team

Urban Design Study of the Northern Central Axis Area (1995)

Bounding the west of the Nan Luogu Xiang block is the Northern Central Axis. Located in the northern part of the Old City, it features a high population density and a backward basic infrastructure, but, because it is an essential element in Beijing's historic city form, its redevelopment is very restricted. Even though it has been on the list of areas to be renewed for many years, no renewal has been carried out. Passive conservation, instead of rehabilitation, has resulted in the decay of the buildings and the deterioration of the environment in this neighbourhood.

In order to regenerate this area while respecting its traditional cultural importance, my team at Tsinghua University began in July 1995 to carry out an in-depth urban survey of the area and proposed an urban design scheme, which aimed at stimulating its development by defining its historic heritage and highlighting its cultural value.

Our scheme has the following characteristics:

- Before making a proposal, we worked with the government to formulate a series of detailed planning control policies on adjacent areas, including the Zhonggulou area, the Shishahai area, the entire Luogu Xiang area, and the Jingshan area. Based on these, we tried to complete a comprehensive urban design study on the Northern Central Axis area.
- Taking into special consideration the influence of inter-area and intra-area traffic upon urban form, we conducted a detailed study of the organization and the arrangement of the transportation system, and proposed a number of alternative plans.
- The proposal consists of two aspects; namely, conservation and redevelopment. The conservation part extends to various levels, including historic relics; townscape; urban fabric; local identity, conventions, and customs; architectural fragments and details; and traditional urban life. The redevelopment aspect, on the other hand, is based on the area's history as well as its present status. Considering the type and mode of the spatial development of this area, the plan attempts to exploit the area's humanistic, historic, and geographical characteristics through small-scale and mixed land uses, thus enhancing the diversity of functions and stimulating development step-by-step through the whole area.

Conservation and Rehabilitation of the Guozijian Area (1996)
The Guozijian area is located in the northeastern part of Beijing's Old City, also quite close to the northern Luogu Xiang block. Established in the Yuan dynasty (1206-1368), it enjoys a history of more than 700 years and contains three of the city's most important historic sites: the nationally protected Confucius Temple and Guozijian (Imperial Academy), and the municipally protected palace Xunjunwang Fu. Leading to these sites, Chengxian Jie still passes under four Yuan dynasty symbolic archways (*pailou*) and is the only four-archway street in Beijing. In addition, the area also contains a number of traditional courtyard houses with good layout and construction quality. Together with the temples at Yonghegong and Bailin Si, which border its east side, the Guozijian area is listed as one of Beijing's key conservation areas.

In late 1995, my team worked with the East City District government, the Municipal Bureau of Historic Relics, and the City Planning Bureau on a detailed survey of the area, and then it began a conservation and rehabilitation plan for it. This plan has several characteristics:

- After thorough investigation of various aspects of the neighbourhood's environment and community, we clarified the boundary of the conservation area and identified areas within it for potential development, thus

facilitating the implementation of conservation by the government departments concerned.
- Through a survey of the historic sites and traditional architecture in general, we clarified the historic and cultural significance of this area, thus establishing the principle of development centring on conservation and rehabilitation.
- According to the priority of conservation needs, we divided the whole area into segments of differing urgency for conservation, rehabilitation, and redevelopment, and then we formulated detailed modes of implementation.
- In the identified redevelopment areas, small-scale redevelopment is permitted.

Conservation and Rehabilitation of the Baita Si Area (1997)
Located within the old Fuchengmen Gate, with an area of around forty hectares, the White Pagoda Temple (Baita Si) area is another place where the old urban environment has been well preserved. However, it is also an area in which housing is hazardously dilapidated; that is, where buildings of Grade 4 and 5 construction quality constitute more than 80 percent of the total housing area.[1]

The Baita Si (formally named Miaoying Si) was constructed in the Jin dynasty (1115-1234). The 52.37-metre-high brick and stone White Pagoda within this temple was built under the direction of a Nepalese artisan, Anige, in the Yuan dynasty and remains the largest Tibetan-and-Nepalese-style pagoda in China. It not only marks one of the city's liveliest grounds for religious activities, but it is also a striking landmark in the majestic capital's cityscape.[2] From the maze of winding *hutong* in the neighbourhood there are countless picturesque views of the towering pagoda.

The Baita Si temple fair was, historically, the most important urban cultural activity in this area. Originating in the Ming dynasty and continuing through the Qing dynasty, it was one of the city's "Four Great Temple Fairs" and a classic venue for Beijing's traditional trade and entertainment culture. When old Beijingers said "go to the Baita temple," they didn't mean to worship; rather, they meant to watch Peking operas, take tea, buy and sell things, and visit relatives and friends. This kind of fair lasted until the 1970s.

In April 1997 my team began to survey the conservation and rehabilitation of the Baita Si area. The survey and the Detailed Control Plan (a plan similar in scope and type to that shown for Nan Luogu Xiang in Chapter 6) is now basically complete, and some preliminary architectural designs have been developed on the basis of this planning. The team's basic principle in this plan is, first, to make full use of the Baita Si, enhancing its influence as the area's landmark and, second, to preserve and redevelop the residential neighbourhood and enhance its unique identity within the Old City. Thus the plan consists mainly of two parts: (1) revival of the temple fair and (2) rehabilitation and redevelopment of the residential neighbourhood.

Revival of the Temple Fair

As a means of maintaining and making full use of the landmark status of the Baita Si and its importance to the environment, revival of the temple fair is a timely idea. At a time when spaces for traditional trading and cultural activities within the Old City are decreasing, many residents and tourists feel a renewed interest in these activities. A revival of the temple fair not only preserves culture, but also creates economic resources for the entire area.

In Beijing's Master Plan, the area around Baita Si is designated as an open green area – a determination I cannot quite agree with. On the one hand, it is too impractical to realize: the demolition of so many houses and the relocation of so many residents in order to create an open public park would be prohibitively expensive. Moreover, it would destroy the city fabric around the temple, cutting its connection with the surroundings and making the cityscape bare and monotonous. On the other hand, if the low courtyards are retained and a small plaza is opened to hold temple fairs, then both the historic scenery and the social economy will benefit.

Considering the "small and diversified" nature of the traditional trading activities,[3] my team proposed that the revival of the temple fair should involve small-scale redevelopment. The first phase of the project includes two parts. One is to rehabilitate the Baita Si by rebuilding its *shanmen* (front gate) (which was demolished in the 1970s) and so enable it to re-initiate religious activities, attract tourists, and so on. The second part is to rehabilitate the present commercial street, including pulling down several factory warehouses and eyesore buildings, refurbishing the old stores, and building new mix-used courtyard houses. The second phase of the project plans to extend the commercial street to the north and rearrange some *hutong* in adjacent areas (e.g., adding a few new east-west *hutong*) so as to improve the link between the commercial street and the adjacent residential neighbourhood. The third phase of the project will depend on further developments. By rehabilitating the courtyard houses to the east of the Baita Si, the space for the temple fair can be extended towards the east along the street and would be able to accommodate temple fairs as large as those of the Qing Dynasty.

Rehabilitation and Reconstruction of the Residential Area

In order to maintain the unique *hutong*-centred residential environment around the White Pagoda, the spatial features of the existing *hutong*, including their scale and orientation, must be largely preserved. At the same time, a number of new *hutong* can be opened up, both to facilitate access and to add new view corridors.

Since the existing courtyard houses in this area are of low quality, most of them will have to be pulled down and rebuilt. However, in the process of rebuilding we must maintain (or at least not ruin) the original neighbourhood fabric. The new buildings should remain courtyard-style residences for different classes of people; or they can be public buildings with traditional cultural functions, such as traditional trading places for the temple fair, flower and bird markets, antique markets, or museums of historical culture. In the course of this new construction there will be an opportunity to create sufficient open space for viewing of the White Pagoda itself.

In addition, the whole area should retain low building heights, featuring mainly courtyard houses of two to three storeys. In order to obtain more useable floor area, the following approaches can be adopted:

- Considering the low level of the ground in this area (1.5 to 2.0 metres lower than the streets around it), the new buildings can adopt the form of "sinking" courtyard houses with sub-basements.
- In certain places one more storey may be added to buildings, as long as the sense of scale of the *hutong* and views of the White Pagoda are not affected.
- Since the White Pagoda is already invisible from the Second Ring Road north of the Fuchengmen Bridge, in certain of the areas more distant from the Pagoda, especially to the northwest, four-storey courtyard houses may be built. A terraced structure can be adopted so there will be decks from which residents can view city sights to the east (such as the Coal Hill and the Beihai Qiongdao Island).

Further Understanding of the Concept of Organic Renewal

Through more explorations of the concept of organic renewal in the planning and design of the above-mentioned areas, we have come to the following conclusions:

- The concept of organic renewal is applicable to Beijing's Old City. It accords with the laws of urban development and satisfies the special needs associated with the conservation and redevelopment of historic cultural areas.
- The possible modes of organic renewal are not fixed. For different areas, based on their own special conditions, the goals, means, and phasing of renewal should vary. In all cases, however, the process of planning should involve a stronger emphasis on urban design so as to create more amenable urban spaces.
- In historic cultural areas, especially those that reflect the essence of the city, only small-scale rehabilitation and careful renewal should be attempted,

with conservation being a precondition of all such work. The renewal process should adopt appropriate technology whenever possible.
- It is worthwhile to point out that the concept of organic renewal has already been accepted with regard to the renewal of other historic cities in China, such as Suzhou and Jinan. Of course, different modes of organic renewal are appropriate to different local conditions.[4]

Problems Now Facing the Renewal of Beijing's Old City

Since the completion of the second phase of the Ju'er Hutong project in 1994, the situation for redevelopment in Beijing has undergone great changes. On the one hand, Beijing's municipal government has highly praised the Ju'er Hutong project; on the other hand, it has not promoted the use of organic renewal. The general outlook for the renewal of Beijing's Old City, as well as for progress on the later phases of the Ju'er Hutong project, are far from satisfactory. My perspective on this more general situation, and some possible solutions, is the subject of the rest of this chapter.

Old City Renewal and Beijing's Real Estate Development

The most unavoidably pressing issue is real estate development. In the late 1980s, urban land leasing and housing privatization were introduced as part of China's economic reform. As a result, real estate development was increasingly drawn into the city's building and renewal processes. As a mode of financing, real estate development made positive contributions to early dilapidated housing renewal. For example, in the first and second phases of the Ju'er Hutong project, a balanced budget was ensured by allowing the developer to sell off extra units. At that time, Beijing's real estate industry was just starting, the scale of development was small, and real estate development companies were still subsidiaries of government organizations and were largely under direct government control. The company involved in the Ju'er Hutong project has reported a "slight profit" from it. We must point out that all renewal projects at that time, including Ju'er Hutong, Xiaohoucang, and Chunfeng Hutong, stressed social benefits and aimed at immediate reconstruction or rehabilitation of the most dilapidated houses. It was a fundamental premise that the majority of the original residents should move back afterwards.

In 1992, Beijing issued a policy statement, *Methods for Implementing the Central Government's Provisional Regulations for Leasing and Transfer of State-Owned Urban Land-Use Rights*, and began the practice of land leasing. The emergence of this policy greatly stimulated the development of Beijing's real estate industry; at the same time, it revealed the value of urban land, especially of the land inside the Old City. Soaring land prices have led to an increase in the size of renewal projects and have made them increasingly market-driven. Many newer dilapidated housing renewal projects, such as at Baoguo Temple and Taoyuan, were no longer based on residential redevelopment but, instead, accommodated mainly commercial uses, such as office towers and retail spaces. Few if any original residents could move back.[5]

Some purely commercial real estate developments have demolished even more of the Old City in the name of dilapidated housing renewal (although they have nothing to do with it) and have obtained subsidies from government policies intended to support housing renewal, not commercial development. Moreover, commercial real estate companies, after obtaining large parcels of land inside the Old City in the name of dilapidated housing renewal, have continued to negotiate with the government over such issues as permissible land use or construction objectives, exceeding the limits on building heights and permitted floor-area ratios, in order to increase profits. If their demands are not met, or when they sense market changes, these developers use the excuse of insufficient funds either to delay construction or to cease work, thus tying up idle land and inconveniencing the city and residents. One study has shown that of all the lands allocated to developers inside the Old City, on two-thirds of it construction has not yet begun. While this land amounts to eighteen years of construction work for the developers (at today's construction capacity), they are still applying for development rights over more land within the Old City.[6] At the same time, many areas, although they have long been designated as dilapidated housing renewal areas, are denied redevelopment, and even normal maintenance is not carried out, thus causing quickened deterioration of good-quality houses along with the bad-quality ones. In their pursuit of profits, developers first develop areas that have either good access and infrastructure along major roads and streets or lower population densities (so that relocation is less expensive). Areas that are removed from major thoroughfares, with high population densities, poor basic infrastructure, and high concentrations of dilapidated houses, are left untouched because there is less profit to be made there.[7]

It is clear that commercial real estate development as a market behaviour aiming at the highest possible returns on investment is inconsistent both with dilapidated housing renewal, which emphasizes social benefits, and with the principles of conserving the cultural and historic heritage of the city. Therefore, with the increase of commercial real estate development, conflicts between real estate developers and residents are mounting. In particular, relocation of large numbers of residents to distant outskirts of the city has aroused strong resentment among residents. According to some reports, since 1995 relocation-related disputes have sharply increased and have become a political problem deserving of serious attention.

Seen from the present situation, Beijing has not been able to establish a healthy, regulated real estate market (especially at the level of land development). The relevant laws and policies are still vague and riddled with loopholes. Most transactions are carried out "in the dark," lack sufficient transparency, and are determined by non-market "interference."

Renewal of the Old City and Beijing's Infrastructure Construction
Beijing's basic infrastructure construction has been unable to match its growth for many decades. The city's especially rapid urban expansion since the early 1980s has highlighted the problems of poor public infrastructure, irrational transportation networks, and inadequate road surface areas. Increasing complaints from the populace have put great pressure on the municipal government. Each administration has resolved to do something about the city's backward infrastructure and has committed large sums of money to the problem.

However, construction of infrastructure has its own internal logic and cannot be developed arbitrarily. Development of infrastructure in a city requires not only an enormous financial investment, but also a complete overall plan to maintain relative unity through different stages of development. Currently there is little coordination among different districts and projects, especially in redeveloping the Old City. On the one hand, huge sums of money were invested in high-profile infrastructure projects to meet the publicized goal of "eliminating backwardness in 20 years,"[8] only to find that within a few years this new infrastructure already needed reconstruction due to not having considered the development needs of adjacent areas. On the other hand, many areas inside the Old City still do not even have basic sewage pipes. The sharp contrast is quite disturbing.

Second, the construction of infrastructure is not an isolated issue. Its solution is dependent on comprehensive consideration of the development of the whole city, and so sporadic and short-term expedients should be avoided. Experiences at home and abroad have long shown that simple, or leap-frog, constructions of new basic infrastructure cannot solve problems in the long run. For example, simply widening streets cannot possibly solve the city's traffic congestion problem. We must have a comprehensive traffic and transport development and management policy, which would include understanding the causes of traffic congestion, limiting the number of vehicles, adjusting the road network, providing parking spaces, developing public transportation, and improving traffic management.[9] Bai-Yi Lu was widened in 1997, after many shops were demolished and many trees were cut down along the old road, and now it is just as congested as it was before.[10]

Finally, infrastructure development should pursue practical goals rather than attempt to meet unrealistic standards. The problems of financing infrastructure development should be addressed by better management of infrastructure construction, by pay-for-use policies, and by providing government funds through taxation. Beijing still lacks such policies, but the municipal government blindly continues to launch large-scale infrastructure projects. As a result, the government has had to lease off land adjacent to the infrastructure projects to developers, who then develop profitable buildings in order to finance the infrastructure (so-called "in-kind" leasing).[11] Currently, the most dramatic example of this practice is seen in the widening of the so-called Ping'An Dajie, the streets that run across the Old City from east to west, north of the former Imperial City.[12] This street passes some of Beijing's most treasured historic landscapes and architecture, including Beihai Park and the Shishahai Lakes; its widening threatens access to these sites and will also damage the scale of their environment. Generally, all construction of this type results in situations in which the developers have an undue advantage in negotiating with the government, making urban planning difficult and leading to loss of state property.[13]

Renewal of the Old City and Macro-Scale Regulation of Beijing's Urban Development

Since the 1990s, an important aspect of China's administrative reform has been the delegation of administrative power to lower-level governments. The central government has given provincial and municipal governments greater power to manage their local economies. At the same time, district and county governments also obtained greater powers from municipal governments. In 1994, Beijing Municipality delegated the dilapidated housing renewal project-granting rights to district governments, which became the guiding actors in housing renewal, real estate development, and other urban construction projects in the city.[14] District governments, as a result, have gained considerable financial benefits.

For example, the West City District government has been developing its own financial district, which occupies 103 hectares of land within the Old City, with more than 3 million square metres of business and commercial space.[15] The construction of this "Financial Street" project has done great damage to the Old City of Beijing: it not only affects the ancient city's architectural character through its great height and bulk on an axis with the Forbidden City's west flank, but it will also create tremendous traffic problems along the west Second Ring Road and in the entire Old City once it is completed. By then, will we have to build another east-west thoroughfare to cut across the Zhongnanhai Compound and the Forbidden City? Even that would not be enough to solve the traffic problems that will result.[16]

In the mid-1980s, before the Financial Street project got under way in 1992, while attending a meeting to decide whether to allow the construction of the first high-rise building in Beijing (the Jingcheng Tower), I pointed out that since more and more high-rise buildings and a central business district (CBD) would be inevitable in Beijing, the planning authorities should research their locations in advance. The best choice, I suggested then, was the district outside the Chaoyang Gate of the Old City, which has already had many high-rise office buildings and a convenient connection with the airport. After several rounds of studies, the 1991 Master Plan of Beijing accepted this suggestion and planned a CBD outside the Old City in the Chaoyang District and provided a design for it. The 1997 Development Control Plan for the Urban Centre of Beijing reconfirmed this location for Beijing's CBD.

From the very beginning the Financial Street project, as a duplicate CBD in both function and content, was in direct conflict with the master plan. Moreover, since it was located inside the Old City of Beijing, many planning professionals strongly opposed it.[17] Unfortunately, the West City District Government, following its own economic interests, not only allowed the project to go ahead, but also made it a key construction project of the district, listed it in the ninth Five-Year Plan of Beijing, and rushed the construction through at great speed.

Following this example, the other three city-centre districts all started their own competing CBD-scale construction projects. The East City District launched the Oriental Plaza project (with a total built area of over 1 million square metres) in Wangfujing, and Xuan Wu District started the International Financial Centre (with a total built area of over 1.7 million square metres). These projects are not only a waste of investment and require redundant infrastructure construction (which will remain incomplete long after the buildings themselves are finished), but they have also to some extent prevented the development of a suitably scaled CBD for Beijing, leaving many foreign companies to wonder where to set up their branch offices.[18] Without effective macro-scale regulations and strong planning control, developments motivated by local interests will contradict and conflict with the interests of the city as a whole.

So, much more emphasis should be put on macro-scale regulations and their legal enforceability. The emergence and development of modern urban planning was itself originally a response to blind urban growth, and it is one of the most important means of macro-control the government can use in a market economy. At the same time, a market economy should be governed by laws. Only after urban planning has the effect of law can urban development itself find a legal footing. The present planning system depends entirely on the administrative orders of various levels of government and is, therefore, prone to be influenced by individual government leaders, who are in a poor position to handle conflicts of interests caused by the decentralization of administrative power or to deal with greedy real estate developers.

In addition, it is necessary to reform urban planning practice and management. Whereas urban planning in China has conventionally been viewed as a technical field akin to architecture or engineering, the American planning theorist Jonathan Barnett has described urban planning as public policy, needing special emphasis on the coordination of the functions and the integration of the interests of various levels of government and business in a market economy.[19] Some say that the present planning system in Beijing is still a product of a planned economy, basically involving a "top-down" process. It is in fact not so. Urban planning and management have actually long been weak, and the municipal government lacks the means for providing necessary policy guidance, macro-regulations, and methods of cross-district coordination. The municipality is unable to use urban planning to turn the motivations of district governments for local development into a driving force for the development of the whole city. For example, the policy of "combining new district development with Old City renewal" was originally a good way to solve the conflicts between preservation and development, and it was carried out in practice in the 1980s. That is, developers were given preferential access to suburban sites in exchange for the low-profit development of central sites. Similarly, the development of suburban sites was arranged partly to facilitate the reduction of city-centre densities. But it became a hollow principle in the present situation due to a lack of effective measures to coordinate the interests of urban and suburban districts. If every district must satisfy its own developmental needs within its borders, then it will be impossible to limit real estate redevelopment in the Old City. The consequences will be stark indeed.

General Thoughts on the Planning and Construction of Beijing[20]

The Old City of Beijing is now facing problems of "thousands of heads and tens of thousands of strands," some of which have accumulated through the years and are seemingly impossible to tackle. On the other hand, Beijing's municipal government administrations are too eager to make their mark, often setting their eyes on near-term effects and focusing too much attention on the Old City. Without an integrated strategy for the Old City, the situation is like "shooting ten thousand arrows all at once," with the Old City being the target of each. It is very worrisome indeed. As Beijing is a mega-regional centre, the preservation and development of its Old City is tightly connected not only to the development of the entire city, but also to the strategic development of the Beijing-Tianjin-Hebei region. An overall review of the problems of Beijing's planning and construction is of immediate urgency.

The Integrity of the Beijing-Tianjin-Hebei Regional Development

In order to research Beijing's economic development needs, a clear concept of the greater Beijing-Tianjin-Hebei economic region needs to be established. This will enable us to study the region as a whole: the distribution of its productive forces, how to make each city benefit from its relative advantages, and how to promote the coordinated economic development of the whole region.

Beijing is the political and cultural centre of the country; at the same time, it is a mega-city with acute water shortage problems and grave levels of pollution. Beijing should accelerate the readjustment of its industrial structure with foresight, orienting it towards administrative and tertiary economies. It should restrict its rapid population explosion to prevent overcrowding. And it should leave room for the future development of its political, cultural, and international activities.[21] Beijing's development should avoid placing too much focus on Beijing itself and, instead, should emphasize comprehensive development in a fan-shaped plane towards the sea to the southeast of the city, seeking a sensible distribution of urban functions within the Beijing-Tianjin-Hebei region (Figure 2.4).

In recent years, with the construction of highways connecting Beijing, Tianjin, and Tangshan, the necessary prerequisites for development are provided for some areas, laying down the opportunities for the coordinated development of the whole region. For example, it takes only half-an-hour to drive between Beijing and Langfang, and between Langfang and Tianjin, while driving from Langfang to Tangshan takes only one hour. The time scale of spatial distance has been shortened dramatically. At present, between the central towns within the region, a grape-like linear city has taken preliminary shape, with much more convenient connections between Beijing and the new Tanggu Harbour, all of which will benefit and support the dispersion of Beijing's functions.

Seeking a Suitable Regional and Urban Structure for Greater Beijing

Since the early 1950s, the municipal jurisdiction of Beijing has encompassed 16,800 square kilometres. We call this area "Greater Beijing," which is composed of the Old City, the planned urban districts (the built area), and the municipally administered rural areas (municipal territory). To promote the formation of a more manageable and efficient regional and urban structure, the area adjacent to the municipal territory, towns like Zhuozhou and Langfang, could provide land to industrial enterprises that would not be permissible within Beijing municipality itself. These towns could then take advantage of the dispersal of Beijing's growth to assist their own development. As for the areas within the municipal territory but outside the inner and planned urban districts, development is now feasible because the transportation system to these satellite settlements has been much improved. The infrastructure of some satellite cities or towns, including Changping, Huairou, Shunyi, and Tongxian, have assumed a scale suitable to support even more development. The focus of most future development should gradually move to these areas. The intensive development of peripheral areas will surely provide opportunities to disperse pressure on the Old City.[22]

Seeking a Polycentric Urban Layout
At the end of the 1950s, Beijing's government committed itself to plan the city's development according to the "dispersed groups" model, which is a model that would limit the central city's growth and channel it to suburban clusters of development separated by green belts (somewhat as Abercrombie proposed for London in the 1940s). However, owing to the lack of concrete measures of enforcement, it has never been effectively applied. In particular, the continued focus of development on the Old City led to the decline of the peripheral clusters' attractiveness and caused the current inefficient concentric development around the Old City. In order to avoid the further development of this phenomenon and the over-concentration of development in the Old City, special effort should now be put towards the planning and construction of "multi-core" development outside the Old City. The Second and Fourth Ring Roads should be used as main express trafficways, while the Third Ring Road should be developed as a boulevard-type "circular axis." Development should concentrate at nodes along the Third Ring Road, like Gongzhufen, Madian, and Chaowai, thus forming several secondary urban centres (relative to the Old City) and attracting urban activities to these areas (Figures 2.5 and 10.2).

More Careful and Effective Preservation of the Old City
If the above advice were to be adopted, it would, on the one hand, generate a healthier way of developing Beijing and, on the other, make possible a more careful and effective strategy for preserving the Old City. Relative to the 16,800 square kilometres of municipal territory, the 62.5 square kilometres of the Old City (where the Forbidden City and historic lakes take up one-third of the total area) is an insignificant amount of land indeed. And yet the preservation of the Old City is such a difficult and serious task. Further emphasis on the cultural value of the Old City is needed in order to induce a more positive strategy for its preservation.

At present, with a density of 28,000 people per square kilometre, the Old City is already overcrowded. However, it is not difficult to predict that it has many latent development tendencies. These tendencies cannot be left uncontrolled. It is unacceptable to use the Old City as the source of land for urban development and allow it to be swallowed up and destroyed by

210 *Conclusion*

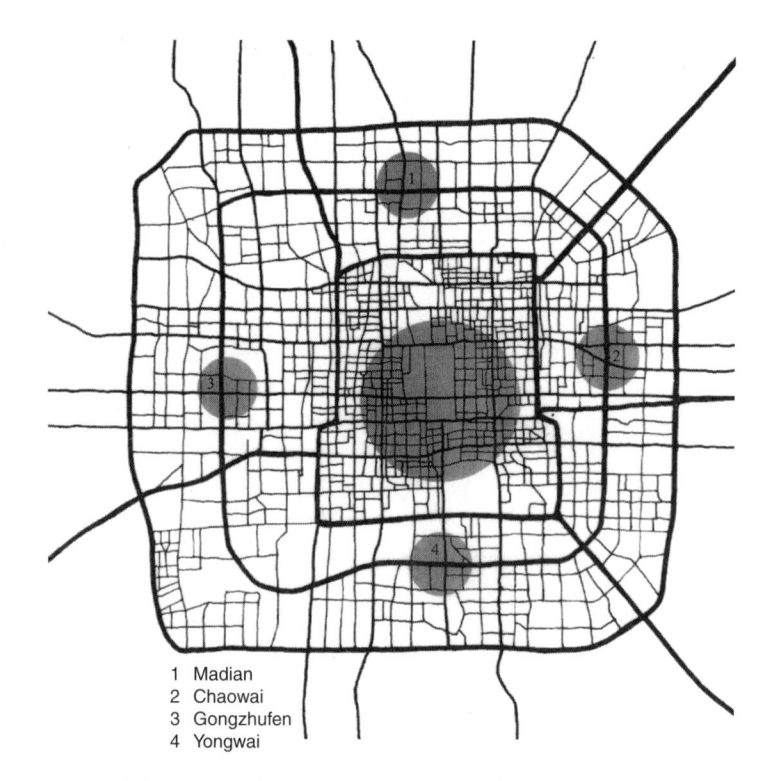

Figure 10.2 **Proposal for a polycentric urban layout for Beijing, based on the city's current development (compare with Figure 2.5)**

1 Madian
2 Chaowai
3 Gongzhufen
4 Yongwai

commercial, entrepreneurial, and financial projects. The key is dispersion: otherwise there will be neither preservation nor improvement of the Old City's environmental quality. Functions like the central business district should be located outside the Old City, while its residential, political, and cultural functions should be preserved and its environment improved.

Even though the Old City has already changed a great deal, I still think that the principle of integrated preservation is both feasible and necessary. This does not mean that we should restore everything to its original state but, rather, that we should develop the Old City as a "growing whole" based on an "integrated" concept. By adhering to the intrinsic urban fabric, adopting good urban design during renewal, and strictly controlling the volume and height of new buildings, the integrity of space and the organic order of buildings can be preserved.

Conclusions

Based on this research and thinking, my team has developed some suggestions for the urban renewal of the Old City of Beijing:

- Reduce the speed and scale of urban renewal. In some very important historical neighbourhoods, even though there may be many dilapidated houses to be rebuilt, without the certainty of success it is better to use utmost caution in granting approvals for renewal projects. Caution will be beneficial in the long run.[23] This, indeed, is the attitude endorsed by the new mayor of Beijing. The government has strengthened its review procedure for old and dilapidated housing renewal projects and has slowed redevelopment in the Old City. However, renewal currently takes the form mainly of large-scale redevelopment projects, and this must be completely changed.
- Seek new ways to develop real estate in the Old City, including reinforcing the openness of the land development and oversight systems, curtailing quick profits in development, and inducing the land market to develop in a more healthy direction (this will involve regulation).
- Continue the original small-scale renewal policy; enhance the definition and safeguarding of historical and cultural districts; establish districts based on current conditions where commercial redevelopment will be forbidden (but allow suitable organic renewal) as early as possible.
- Urban design should be emphasized in drawing up planning regulations. Especially in the most valuable historic districts, there is a special need for specific planning standards and guidelines based on thorough urban design studies.
- In sum, the land redevelopment rights to which developers are entitled should be re-examined. The policy of "combining new district development with Old City renewal" is still applicable today, but governments must provide more concrete measures and methods for its implementation, especially in making appropriate adjustments to management mechanisms.

For architects who are devoting their work to the preservation of history and culture in the face of a resurgent market economy, there will be many difficulties, but they should not abandon their responsibilities. They should enlarge their understanding of society and find a way of employing new technical possibilities. They should maintain their ideals and be practical at the same time.

To some extent, our current work is like firefighting: it cannot be delayed for even a second. Through experiments in Ju'er Hutong and other places, we realize that the preservation of the Old City is an extremely difficult task; however, at the same time, we gain confidence through our work, for if we stick to the principles of careful and incremental renewal, we are sure to find a technical solution to the problem.[24]

If we say that the debate taking place between 1949 and 1950 concerning where to locate the new central government's administrative centre (i.e., inside the Old City or in the western suburbs) was, in essence, a debate over preservation and development, then our opposition to the endless sprawl of commercial and office buildings in the historic centre of the Old City and our advocacy of a CBD outside it is the continuation of that debate under new circumstances. It is a pity that, for political reasons, this scholarly question, very meaningful to urban planning studies, was not debated sufficiently in those early years (even today, some people will spring to defend one or the other side whenever they hear it mentioned). Just as history itself shows, the Old City of Beijing needs more careful preservation, control, and dispersion, while more centralized new development should be located in the Greater Beijing area outside the Old City. We can say that we have paid a high price to learn these lessons.

Now, the twenty-first century is nearly upon us, and the city of Beijing is facing even greater development. Challenges and opportunities coexist, and historic experiences cannot be ignored. A new mode of development calls out to us. The question now is whether we can seize it and work with it.

Appendix 1

Chronology of major Chinese dynasties and their capitals

Dynasty	Period	Capital city
Xia	2100-1600 BC	unknown
Shang	1600-1028 BC	Erlitou (near Luoyang), Ao (near Zhengzhou), etc.
Zhou	1027-256 BC	
Western Zhou	1027-771 BC	Feng and Hao (near Xi'an)
Eastern Zhou	770-256 BC	
Spring and Autumn Period	770-475 BC	Luoyang
Warring States	475-221 BC	Lüdu, Anyi, Jiang, Xiadu, Handan, Linzi, etc.
Qin	221-206 BC	Xianyang (near Xi'an)
Han	206 BC - AD 220	
Western Han	206 BC - AD 8	Chang'an (Xi'an)
Xin	9-23	
Eastern Han	25-220	Luoyang
Three Kingdoms	220-265	
Wei	220-265	Ye, Luoyang
Shu	221-263	Chengdu
Wu	222-280	Jianye (Nanjing)
Jin	265-420	
Western Jin	265-317	Luoyang
Eastern Jin (and southern dynasties)	317-587	Jiankang (Nanjing)
Northern Dynasties	386-581	
Northern Wei	386-534	Pingcheng (near Datong), Luoyang
Eastern Wei, etc.	534-550	Ye, etc.
Sui	581-618	Yangzhou, Luoyang, Chang'an (Xi'an)

◀ Appendix 1

Dynasty	Period	Capital city
Tang	618-907	Chang'an (Xi'an)
Five Dynasties	907-960	various
Song	960-1279	
Northern Song	960-1127	Bianliang (Kaifeng)
Southern Song	1127-1279	Lin'an (Hangzhou)
Liao (Khitan semi-nomadic empire)	907-1211	five northern cities including Liao Nanjing (Beijing)
Jin (Jurchen semi-nomadic empire)	1115-1234	five northern cities including Zhongdu (Beijing) and Bianliang (Kaifeng)
Yuan (Mongol)	1206-1368	Khara-Khorum (in Mongolia), Shangdu (in Inner Mongolia), Dadu (Beijing)
Ming	1368-1644	Nanjing, Linhao (Fengyang), Beijing
Qing	1644-1911	Mukden (Shenyang), Beijing

Appendix 2
Planning Statistics for the Ju'er Hutong Project

Table 1

Land use and population in the 8.2-hectare Ju'er Hutong block,[a] before and after renewal

	Before renewal			After renewal		
	Amount (hectares)	Proportion (%)	Average (m^2/person)[b]	Amount (hectares)	Proportion (%)	Average (m^2/person)[b]
Land use						
Total area of block	8.2	100		6.3	100	
Residential[c]	6.32	77.1	17.65	3.34	53.0	14.5
Road area	0.3	3.6	0.84	0.76	12.1	3.3
Retail, offices, and services[d]	0.48	5.9	1.34	1.16	18.4	5.0
Concentrated green space	0	0	0	0.22	3.5	0.96
Other	1.1	13.4		0.82	13.0	
Population						
Total population		4,800			4,500	
Residential population		3,580			2,300 (770 households)	
Population density		585 persons/ha			714 persons/ha	
Residential pop. density[e]		504 persons/ha			420 persons/ha	

a Does not include road area surrounding the block.
b Average per capita land area = total land area / residential population.
c Includes neighbourhood services.
d Yards that combine commerce and residence are split evenly between these categories.
e Residential population density = residential population / (total land area - all other land area).

Table 2

Main master planning statistics for the 8.72-hectare Ju'er Hutong block[a]

	Prior to Phase 4	Master planning	Condition prior to Phase 1
Total land area (hectares)	8.41	8.72	8.41
Total floor area (10,000m^2)	7.72[b]	11.2[c]	5.85
Floor-area ratio	0.92	1.28	0.7
	(0.84 above ground)	(1.15 above ground)	
Population (persons)[d]	3,570	2,300	3,580
Number of households	1,210	770	1,270
Average persons per household	2.95	2.98	2.82
Population density (persons/ha)[d]	425	264	426
Housing floor area			
Floor area (10,000m^2)	4.3	5.5	3.2
Percent of total floor area	55.6%	49.1%	54.7%
Average floor area per person	12.05	23.91	8.94
Average floor area per household	35.5	71.43	25.2
Non-housing floor area (10,000m^2)			
Office	0.9 (11.7%)	1.2 (10.7%)	0.8 (13.7%)
Factory	1.1 (14.2%)	1.1 (9.8%)	0.9 (15.4%)
Retail	1.1 (14.2%)	2.8 (25%)	0.9 (15.4%)
Public utilities, etc.	0.33 (4.3%)	0.6 (5.4%)	0.05 (0.8%)
Subtotal	3.43	5.7	2.65
Percent of total floor area	44.4%	50.9%	45.3%

a Includes half of road area surrounding the block.
b 71,000m^2 above ground and 6,200m^2 below ground, including Phases 1, 2, and 3, and existing apartment buildings and conserved courtyard houses.
c 100,000m^2 above ground and 12,000m^2 below ground.
d Residential population only; does not include retail, factory, and office staff who live elsewhere.

Table 3

Consolidated planning statistics for the entire redeveloped area of Ju'er Hutong Phases 1 and 2

	Before renewal	After renewal	Notes
Total land area (m²)	12,550	12,550	
Total floor area (m²)	7,235	20,657.33	16,565.92 above ground + 4,091.41 below ground
Floor-area ratio	0.58	1.65	1.32 above ground
Building footprint area (m²)	7,235	5,707.45	
Ground coverage	57.7 %	45.5 %	
Average building height (storeys)	1	3.62	2.9 above ground
Ratio of demolished to built floor area		1 : 2.86	
Housing			
Land area (m²)	11,450	11,450	
Floor area (m²)	6,785	15,542.83	14,889.59 above ground + 653.24 below ground
Number of households	245	210	
Population (persons)	634	620	
Average persons per household	2.59	2.95	
Population density (persons/ha)	535	523	calculation includes road area
Average floor area per person	10.7	25.07	
Average floor area per household	27.69	74.01	
Return rate of original households		24.9 % (61 households)	
Other land uses			
Road area (m²)	400	400	
Factory land use area (m²)	700	700	
Other floor areas			
Factory buildings (m²)	450	1,994.6	1,454.33 above ground + 540.27 below ground
Public buildings (m²)		2,750.3	222 above ground + 2,528.3 below ground
Civil defence (m²)		369.6	all below ground

Table 4

Planning statistics for Phase 1 of the Ju'er Hutong project

	Before renewal	After renewal
Total land area (m^2)	2,050	2,050
Total floor area (m^2)	1,085	2,760
Floor-area ratio	0.53	1.35
Building footprint area (m^2)	1,085	1,079.3
Ground coverage	53 %	53 %
Average building height (storeys)	1	2.56
Ratio of demolished to built floor area	1 : 2.54	
Housing		
Land area (m^2)	2,050	2,050
Floor area (m^2)	1,085	2,760
Number of households	41	46
Population (persons)	138	133
Average persons per household	3.14	2.89
Population density (persons/ha)	673	649
Average floor area per person	7.86	20.75
Average floor area per household	24.66	60
Return rate of original households	31.7 % (13 households)	

Table 5

Planning statistics for Phase 2 of the Ju'er Hutong project

	Before renewal	After renewal	Notes
Total land area (m²)	10,500	10,500	
Total floor area (m²)	6,150	17,897.33	13,805.92 above ground + 4,091.41 below ground
Floor-area ratio	0.59	1.71	1.31 above ground
Building footprint area (m²)	6,150	4,628.15	
Ground coverage	58.57 %	44.08 %	
Average building height (storeys)	1	3.87	2.98 above ground
Ratio of demolished to built floor area	1 : 2.91		
Housing			
Land area (m²)	9,400	9,400	
Floor area (m²)	5,700	12,782.83	12,129.59 above ground + 653.24 below ground
Number of households	204	164	
Population (persons)	496	487	
Average persons per household	2.43	2.97	
Population density (persons/ha)	506	497	calculation includes road area
Average floor area per person	11.49	26.25	
Average floor area per household	27.94	77.94	
Return rate of original households	23.5 % (48 households)		
Other land uses			
Road area (m²)	400	400	
Factory land use area (m²)	700	700	
Other floor areas			
Factory buildings (m²)	450	1,994.6	1,454.33 above ground + 540.27 below ground
Public buildings (m²)		2,750.3	222 above ground + 2,528.3 below ground
Civil defence (m²)		369.6	all below ground

Table 6

Planning statistics for Phase 3 of the Ju'er Hutong project

	Before renewal	After renewal	Notes
Total land area (m^2)	8,320	8,830	
Total floor area (m^2)	5,182.3	10,937.87	includes 300m^2 of conserved courtyard houses
Floor-area ratio	0.62	1.24	1.31 above ground
Building footprint area (m^2)	4,554	3,236.8	
Ground coverage	54.74 %	36.66 %	
Average building height (storeys)	1.14	3.38	2.98 above ground
Ratio of demolished to built floor area	1 : 2.18		
Housing			
Land area (m^2)	6,600	4,230	
Floor area (m^2)	3,460	6,116.95	
Number of households	94	71	
Population (persons)	349		
Average persons per household	3.71		
Population density (persons/ha)	499		calculation includes road area
Average floor area per person	9.91		
Average floor area per household	36.81	86.15	
Other uses			
Hotel land use area (m^2)	1,320	1,300	
Hotel floor area (m^2)	1,704.3	3,601.9	
Retail land use area (m^2)		450	
Retail floor area (m^2)		886.76	
Road area (m^2)	400	1,100	
Public toilet floor area (m^2)	18	32.77	

Table 7

Planning statistics for Phase 4 of the Ju'er Hutong project

	Before renewal	After renewal	Notes
Total land area (hectares)	6.32	6.58	Overall total land area (Table 2), less the total land areas of Phases 1, 2, and 3 (Tables 3 and 6)
Total floor area (10,000m^2)	4.6	8.1	Includes 29,000m^2 of conserved work unit buildings
Floor-area ratio	0.73	1.23	
Ratio of demolished to built floor area	1 : 3.33		Not counting 2,000m^2 of preserved courtyards
Housing			
Total floor area (10,000m^2)	2.43	3.5	After renewal includes 26,000m^2 new apartments + 9,000m^2 conserved courtyards
Total number of households	930	500	After renewal includes 370 households in new apartments + 130 households in conserved courtyards
Resident population (persons)	2,600	1,400	Includes about 400 residents of conserved apartment buildings
Average persons per household	2.8	2.8	
Population density (persons/ha)	411	213	
Average floor area per person (m^2/person)	9.35	25	
Average floor area per household (m^2/household)	26.13	70	
Other floor areas			
Community centre (10,000m^2)		0.1	
Infrastructure (10,000m^2)			Includes heating plant enlargement, public toilet, etc.
Commercial (10,000m^2)		1.6	
Work unit enlargements (10,000m^2)		0.2	
Civil defence (10,000m^2)		0.63	

Appendix 3

Wu Liangyong's Acceptance Speech on the Presentation of the World Habitat Awards on World Habitat Day, 4 October 1993

Mr. President of General Assembly, Mr. Secretary-General, United Nations, Mr. Peter Elderfield, Director, Building and Social Housing Foundation, Ladies and Gentlemen:

On behalf of the Work Team of the Ju'er Hutong Courtyard Housing Project, may I first thank the Building and Social Housing Foundation and all the distinguished participants for giving such an honourable international award to a Chinese housing project for the first time.

We appreciate the significance of this award. This award is given to a country with the largest population in the world. Over the last decade, China has made magnificent strides in housing developments. With a total urban housing construction of more than 10 billion square metres between 1979 and 1990, the average floor area per person was significantly increased from about four to more than seven square metres. However, tremendous efforts still are required to meet the increasing housing needs and improve the living standards of the people.

This award is given to a country with several thousand years of civilization. In China's hundreds of important historic cities, one of the most pressing tasks is how to create social housing that not only provides modern amenities, but also fits into the existing historic environment.

As is pointed out in the Press Release, "The world can no longer afford the luxury of endless pontification, debates and conferences on the world's shelter problems, what it needs now are solutions." The Ju'er Hutong Courtyard Housing Project is one of our contributions to such solutions. Searching for a new housing model is difficult, but developing and promoting a new housing model is even more so. In a big country such as China, it is necessary to explore many more new housing approaches to solve shelter problems.

There is a Chinese saying that ninety miles is only half way to a hundred because the last ten miles is more difficult and important. We are facing glorious and arduous tasks, great responsibilities, and a long march. We are greatly encouraged by this award and commit ourselves to continuing our contribution to the world in the future.

Finally, I would like to take this opportunity to invite any comments or suggestions from our professional colleagues. Thank you.

Notes

Chapter 1: The City of Beijing in Historical Perspective

1. For prominent English-language descriptions, see Wu Liangyong, "A Brief History of Ancient Chinese City Planning," *Urbs et Regio* 38 (Kassel: Gesamthochschulbibliothek, 1986); see also Hou Renzhi, "The Transformation of the Old City of Beijing, China: A Concrete Manifestation of New China's Cultural Reconstruction," in *World Patterns of Modern Urban Change*, ed. Michael P. Lanzen (Chicago: University of Chicago, Geography Department Research Papers, 1986); Victor F.S. Sit, *Beijing: The Nature and Planning of a Chinese Capital City* (Chichester: Wiley, 1995); Nancy S. Steinhardt, *Chinese Imperial City Planning* (Honolulu: University of Hawaii Press, 1990); Paul Wheatley, *The Pivot of the Four Quarters: A Preliminary Enquiry into the Origins and Character of the Ancient Chinese City* (Chicago: Aldine, 1971); Arthur F. Wright, "The Cosmology of the Chinese City," in *The City in Late Imperial China*, ed. G.W. Skinner (Stanford: Stanford University Press, 1958).
2. Wu, "A Brief History of Ancient Chinese City Planning," 79-80.
3. Barclay G. Jones, "Chinese among the Largest World Agglomerations: An Historical Analysis," paper presented at the Conference on Planning for Human Settlements: China and the United States, Tongji University, Shanghai, 29 June to 1 July 1987.
4. Liang Sicheng, "Beijing, Dushi Jihua de Wubi Jiezuo [An Unparalleled Masterpiece of Urban Planning]," in *Liang Sicheng Wenji [The Collected Papers of Liang Sicheng]*, vol. 4 (Beijing: Zhongguo Jianzhu Gongye Chubanshe [China Construction Industry Publishing House], 1987 [1951]).
5. Steen Eiler Rasmussen, *Towns and Buildings* (Cambridge: MIT Press, 1983).
6. Edmund N. Bacon, *Design of Cities*, rev. ed. (London: Thames and Hudson, 1975).
7. Henry S. Churchill, *The City Is the People* (New York: Peynal and Hitchcock, 1945).
8. Ibid.
9. Ibid.
10. Ibid.
11. Osvald Siren, *Walls and Gates of Peking* (London: John Lane, 1924).
12. Bacon, *Design of Cities*, 244.
13. Liang, "Beijing."
14. For a classic graphic survey of Chinese monumental architecture, see Liang Ssu-ch'eng (Liang Sicheng), *A Pictorial History of Chinese Architecture: A Study of the Development of Its Structural System and the Evolution of Its Types*, ed. Wilma Fairbank (Cambridge, MA: MIT Press, ca. 1984). For vernacular housing construction techniques in Beijing, see Lu Xiang and Wang Qiming, *Beijing Siheyuan* (Beijing: Zhongguo Jianzhu Gongye Chubanshe [China Construction Industry Publishing House], 1996); Liu Dunzhen, *Zhongguo Zhuzhai Gaishuo [General Description of Chinese Houses]* (Beijing: Jianzhu Gongcheng Chubanshe [Architectural and Engineering Publishing House], 1957); Andrew Boyd, *Chinese Architecture and Town Planning: 1500 B.C.-A.D. 1911* (New York: Transatlantic Arts, 1962).
15. Liang, "Beijing."

Chapter 2: Planning and Development in Beijing since 1949

1. Hou Renzhi, "The Transformation of the Old City of Beijing, China: A Concrete Manifestation of New China's Cultural Reconstruction," in *World Patterns of Modern Urban Change*, ed. Michael P. Lanzen (Chicago: University of Chicago, Geography Department Research Papers, 1986).
2. Liang Sicheng and Chen Zhanxiang, "Guanyu Zhongyang Renmin Zhengfu Xingzheng Zhongxinqu Weizhi de Jianyi [Proposal for the Administrative Centre for the People's Central Government]," in *Liang Sicheng Wenji [The Collected Papers of Liang Sicheng]*, vol. 4 (Beijing: Zhongguo Jianzhu Gongye Chubanshe [China Construction Industry Publishing House], 1987, [1951]).
3. I attended a meeting in early 1951 at which Mr. Xue Zizheng from the Beijing Municipal Government announced Mao Zedong's ideas concerning the design of Tiananmen Square.
4. Wu Liangyong, "Lishi Wenhua Mingcheng de Guihua Jiegou, Chengshi Gengxin yu Chengshi Sheji [Planning Structure, Urban Renewal and Urban Design in Historic Cities]," in Wu Liangyong, *Chengshi Guihua Sheji Lunwenji [Selected Papers on Urban Planning and Design]* (Beijing: Yanshan, 1988). Paper originally published in 1983.
5. The *Tuancheng*, a round miniature citadel within the Imperial Park around Beihai, includes an exceptional Qing dynasty pavilion and occupies a site that was first developed during the Yuan dynasty. The structure was to be demolished according to plans to widen and straighten the street and bridge across the Beihai-Zhonghai waterway. Liang Sicheng's persistent protests succeeded in having the street diverted and in preserving the Tuancheng.
6. Dong Guangqi, "Zongjie Lishi Jingyan, Jiakuai Jiucheng Pojiuweifang Gaijian Bufa [Learn from Past Experience and Accelerate the Renewal of Derelict Housing]," *Beijing Guihua Jianshe [Beijing Planning and Construction]* 4 (1989): 11-3.
7. This proposal was supervised by Wu Liangyong and Cheng Yingquan. In early 1951, considering the current situation, I suggested to Professor Liang Sicheng that, since the plan to centre the government within the Old City seemed about to prevail over the plan for a new centre, the group should attempt to find a compromise between the two. Liang supported this idea. At that time, seven students, including Li Daozeng and Wang Zhaotuo, joined the team. Many senior civil engineers, historians, architects, and planners were invited to give lectures to the team to help with problems and to provide technical information for the project, including Cao Yanxing (Director of the Water Authority, formerly Director of the Construction Bureau), Wang Mingzhi (Director of the Construction Bureau), Chen Mingshao (Vice Director of the Water Authority), Hou Renzhi (Professor at Peking University), Lin Chao (Professor at Tsinghua University), and Li Songchen (Professor at Peking University School of Engineering).
8. Wu Liangyong, "Xin de Qidian [A Starting Point]," in Wu Liangyong, *Chengshi Guihua Sheji Lunwenji [Selected Papers on Urban Planning and Design]* (Beijing: Yanshan, 1988). (Paper originally published in 1985.)
9. *Demographic Yearbook* (New York: Department of Economic and Social Affairs, Statistical Office, United Nations, 1991); see also United Nations *Prospects of World Urbanization*, 1987.
10. Ibid.
11. Lewis Mumford, *Architectural Record* (March 1965).
12. Tsinghua University Urban Planning Group, "Dui Beijingshi Guihua de Jidian Shexiang [Some Visions for the Urban Planning of Beijing]," *Jianzhu Xuebao [Architectural Journal]* 5 (1980): 6-15.
13. Walter Bor, "Recommendations for the Plan of Beijing," in *Chengshi Guihua [City Planning]* (September 1992): 38-42.
14. Wu Liangyong, "Beijingshi Guihua Chuyi [On City Planning in Beijing]," *Jianzhushi [Architect]* 2 (1979): 1-8; and Wu Liangyong, "Beijingshi Gucheng Baohu de Shidai Shiming [The Mission of Our Age in the Protection of Beijing's Historic City]," in *Chengshi Guihua Sheji Lunwenji [Selected Papers on Urban Planning and Design]* (Beijing: Yanshan, 1988). (Paper originally published in 1984.)
15. Ibid.
16. Ibid.
17. Wu Liangyong, "Beijingshi de Jiucheng Gaizao ji Youguan Wenti [Renewal in the City of Beijing and Related Issues]," *Jianzhu Xuebao [Architectural Journal]* 2 (1982): 8-11.

18 Wu Liangyong, 1992. "Beijing Lishi Wenhua Mingcheng Baohu yu Jianzhu Chuangzao [Architectural Creativity and the Protection of the Historic City of Beijing]," *Beijing Guihua Jianshe [Beijing Planning and Construction]* 3 (1989): 4-8.
19 Tsinghua University Urban Planning Group, "Dui Beijingshi Guihua de Jidian Shexiang [Some Visions for the Urban Planning of Beijing]," *Jianzhu Xuebao [Architectural Journal]* 5 (1979): 6-15.
20 Wu Liangyong, *Chengshi Guihua Sheji Lunwenji [Selected Papers on Urban Planning and Design]* (Beijing: Yanshan, 1988).
21 To my knowledge, this idea was first advocated for Beijing in a proposal by a team from the Massachusetts Institute of Technology's School of Architecture and Planning in a 1987 collaborative studio with the Tsinghua University School of Architecture.
22 Dong Guangqi, "Beijing Jiucheng Baohu yu Gaizao de Huigu yu Zhanwang [A Look Back and a Look Forward at Urban Conservation and Redevelopment in Beijing]," *Beijing Guihua Jianshe [Beijing Planning and Construction]* 5 (1993): 14-6.
23 Wu Liangyong, "Cognition in Urban Aesthetics," in *Aesthetics of the Urban Environment*, 1-4 (Beijing: China Social Press, 1991).
24 According to the Municipal Property Management Bureau's survey of housing conditions, all housing falls within one of five grades: Grade 1 is new and in good condition; Grade 2 is structurally sound and weatherproof but in need of repair; Grade 3 is structurally sound (i.e., columns, beams, and bearing walls are intact) but suffers from leaking roofs, crumbling masonry, and/or broken windows or doors; Grade 4 is structurally unsound but not in imminent danger of collapse; Grade 5 is hazardously dilapidated.
25 This point is also emphasized in Sir Bernard M. Fieldon, *Conservation of Historic Buildings* (London: Butterworth, 1982).

Chapter 3: Residential Development and the Renewal of Derelict Houses
1 Beijing Statistics Bureau, Beijing Yearbook 1992 (Beijing: Beijing Statistics Press, 1993).
2 The four central districts, which include the Old City, are the East City, the West City, Chongwen, and Xuanwu; the four near-suburban districts are Chaoyang, Haidian, Shijingshan, and Fengtai.
3 See Chapter 2, Note 24.
4 Data supplied by Beijing Municipal Property Management Bureau, January 1991.
5 Xicheng Qu Weijiufang Gaizao Zhihui Bu [West City District Housing Renewal Headquarters], "Xicheng Qu Zhufang Tekunhu de Diaocha ji Jiejue Fangan [A Survey of Overcrowded Households and a Scheme for Their Relief in the West City District]," in *Xicheng Qu Weifang Gaizao Yantao Cailiao [Discussion Materials on Old and Dilapidated Housing Redevelopment in the West City District]*, 5 October 1991.
6 Ibid.
7 Lu Xiaoxiang, "Beijing Jiucheng Gaijian ji Weijiufang Gaizao [The Rebuilding of the Old City and the Redevelopment of Old and Dilapidated Housing in Beijing]," in *"Jiuchengqu yu Weijiufang Gaizao" Yanxiuban Jiangyi [Proceedings of the Inner City Housing Redevelopment Workshop]* (Beijing: The Information Centre of the Ministry of Construction, October 1991).
8 Planned housing estates of this size in China are called *xiao qu* ("small district"), a term translated from the Russian Soviet planning term *mikro rayon*.
9 Wang Ruisheng, "Chengshi Jiujuzhuqu de Gaizao ji Duice [Inner City Neighborhood Redevelopment Policies]," *Jiuchengqu yu Weijiufang Gaizao Yanxiuban Jiangyi [Proceedings of the Inner City Housing Redevelopment Workshop]* (Beijing: Information Centre of the Ministry of Construction, October 1991).
10 "A Survey of the Poor Housing Areas."

Chapter 4: Organic Renewal in Historic Cities
1 Quoted in E.R. Trincanato, *Houses of Venice* (Venice: Canal, 1980), 1-10.
2 In Beijing, there are 3 architectural sites listed as UN World Cultural Heritage sites; 36 are listed at the national level, 209 at the municipal level, and 777 at the district level.
3 Liu Xiaoshi, "Dui Beijing Lishi Wenwu Baohu he Xiandaihua Wenti de yixie Yijian [Comments on the Protection of Cultural Relics and Issues of Modernization]," paper presented at the International Symposium on Historic Cities and Modernization (Beijing, 1989).

4 Dong Guangqi, "Zongjie Lishi Jingyan, Jiakuai Jiucheng Pojiuweifang Gaizao Bufa [Learn from Past Experience and Accelerate the Renewal of Derelict Housing]," *Beijing Guihua Jianshe [Beijing Planning and Construction]* 4 (1989): 11-3.
5 Liu Yan, "Beijing Jiucheng de Zhengti Baohu [On Integrated Conservation in the Old City of Beijing]," (Master's thesis, Tsinghua University, 1986).
6 Jane Jacobs, *The Death and Life of Great American Cities* (New York: Random, 1961); and *The Economy of Cities* (New York: Random, 1969).
7 William Rees, *Planning for Sustainable Development: A Resource Book* (Vancouver: University of British Columbia Centre for Human Settlements, 1989); see also Shridath Ramphal, *Our Country, the Planet: Forging a Partnership for Survival* (London: Lime Tree, 1992).
8 Sun Guoting, "Shupu [On Calligraphy]," in *A Dictionary of the Best Chinese Calligraphy* (Beijing: Da Di [Great Earth], 1989).
9 Wu Liangyong, "Urban Development and Cultural Continuity," paper presented at the International Symposium on Cultural Tradition and Modernization (Hong Kong, 1987).

Chapter 5: Traditional Courtyard Houses and a New Prototype
1 Professor Zheng calls this "the root in the square motif," Zheng Xiaoxie, "The Protection of the Characteristics of Historic Chinese Cities," *Architectural Journal* 12 (1983): 4-13.
2 Zhu Zhixin, Hu Shi, et al., "Jingtian Zhidu You wu Zhi Yanjiu [A Study on the *Jingtian* System]" (Taibei: Zhongguo Wenxian Chubanshe [China Literature Press], 1965), 4-13.
3 Leonardo Benevolo, *The History of the City*, trans. Geoffrey Culverwell (Cambridge, MA: MIT Press, 1980).
4 "*Tianxia Junguo Libishu*" is a multivolume work on Chinese history and geography. It was written by Gu Yanwu in the seventeenth century during the Qing dynasty.
5 15 *mu* = approximately 1 hectare.
6 Zhao Lisheng, "Youguan Jingtianzhi de yixie Bianxi [Some Analytical Distinctions Concerning the *Jingtian* System]," *Lishi Yanjiu [Historical Studies]* 4 (1980): 77-91.
7 Fan Wenlan, *Zhongguo Tongshi Jianbian [A Brief History of China]*, rev. ed., vol. 1 (Beijing: People's Press, 1964).
8 Zhang Jichang, "Hutong yu Shuijing [*Hutong* and Wells]," in *Hutong ji Qita: Shehuiyuyanxue de Tansuo [Hutong and More: An Exploration Into Social Linguistics]* (Beijing: Yuyan Xueyuan Chubanshe [College of Languages Publishing House], 1990).
9 Ibid.
10 According to a note by Yan Shigu (Sui-Tang dynasty) in *Shiji Benyi*, the word *shijing*, or "market-well," is explained thus: "In antiquity there were no markets; every morning people went to the well for water, and exchanged goods by the well. This is why it was called *shijing*." See also "Pingzhun Shu [History of Pingzhun]" in *Shiji [Records of the Historian]*, by Sima Qian (Han dynasty), reprinted by Shangwu Publishing House.
11 Fu Xinian, "A Study on the Architecture at the Qishanfengchu Archaeological Site, Shan'xi Province," *Wenwu [Cultural Relics]*, nos. 1, 2, and 3 (1981).
12 Hou Renzhi, *Lishidilixue: Lilun yu Shixian [Historical Geography: Its Theory and Practice]* (Shanghai: Shanghai Renmin Chubanshe [Shanghai People's Publishing House], 1979), 157.
13 *Xijinzhi*. This was first written in the thirteenth century and is the first comprehensive series of books on the geography of Beijing and its surrounding regions. There were about 100 volumes, some of which were lost during the Ming dynasty. The Beijing Library has republished some of the remaining volumes.
14 Lewis Mumford, *The City in History: Its Origins, Its Transformations, and Its Prospects* (London: Penguin, 1991), 452-6.
15 H.A. Tripp, *Town Planning and Road Traffic* (London: Arnold, 1946), 78.
16 Kenneth Frampton, *Modern Architecture: A Critical History* (London: Thames and Hudson, 1980).
17 Ibid.
18 Sir John Leslie Martin and Lionel March, *Urban Space and Structures* (Cambridge, UK: Cambridge University Press, 1972).
19 Frampton, *Modern Architecture*.
20 Rob Krier, *Urban Space* (London: Academy Editions, 1979).
21 Leon Krier, *Rational Architecture* (Bruxelles: Archives D'Architecture Moderne, 1978).

22 Jean Castex, *Formes urbaines: de l'isle à la barre* (Paris: Dunod, ca. 1977).
23 Mumford, *The City in History*.
24 An empirical survey and references to the general literature on the subject of current home-based employment trends are provided in Penny Gurstein, Principal Investigator, *Planning for Telework and Home-based Employment: A Canadian Survey on Integrating Work into Residential Environments* (Vancouver: University of British Columbia Centre for Human Settlements, prepared for the Canada Mortgage and Housing Corporation Centre for Future Studies in Housing and Living Environments, March 1995).
25 See Chapter 6 for details concerning the resident social survey at Ju'er Hutong.
26 *Shehuixue Gailun [An Introduction to Sociology]* (Tianjin: Tianjin People's Press, 1984).
27 Jane Jacobs, *The Death and Life of Great American Cities* (New York: Random, 1961). See also Tridib Banerjee and William C. Baer, *Beyond the Neighborhood Unit: Residential Environments and Public Policy* (New York: Plenum, ca. 1984).
28 Christopher Alexander, "The City Is Not a Tree," *Architectural Forum* 4 (1965): 58-62; Ibid., 58-61.
29 Andres Duany and Elizabeth Plater-Zyberk, *Towns and Town-making Principles* (Cambridge, MA/New York: Harvard University Graduate School of Design/Rizzoli, 1991).
30 This is Jane Jacobs's argument and is also the argument of Ian Bentley et al. in *Responsive Environments: A Manual for Designers* (London: Architectural Press, 1985).
31 Wang Guowei, *Guantanjilin*, vol. 3 (Beijing: Zhonghua, 1959).
32 Zheng Banqiao, "Bamboos and Rockery," in *Zheng Banqiao Ji* (Shanghai: Shanghai Ancient Books, 1979), 168-9.
33 Lao She, "Xiang Beiping [Thinking of Beiping]," in *Xiangfeng Shisheng [Village Scenes and City Sounds]*, ed. Qian Liqun (Beijing: People's Literature Publishing House, 1982).

Chapter 6: Planning and Design of the Ju'er Hutong Project

1 The work on Shichahai that led ultimately to the design of the Ju'er Hutong project was directed by Wu Liangyong and Guan Zhaoye. Wang Weiyu, Gu Chuanhui, Chang Youshi, and postgraduate students Huang Hanmin, Wang Diemin, and Hu Zhengfan formed part of the team. Subsequent studies on this area have been conducted by Zhu Zixuan and Li Daozeng.
2 Zhang Shouyi and Li Deyao, "Beijingshi Wei, Ji, Lou Diqu Zhufang Jianshe Wenti [The Problems of Hazardous, Crowded, and Leaky Housing Areas in Beijing]," in *Beijing Chengshi Guihua Yanjiu Lunwenji [Collected Research Papers on the Urban Planning of Beijing] 1946-1996*. Beijing: Zhongguo Jianzhu Gongye Chubanshe [China Construction Industry Publishing House], 1996.
3 The presentation and exhibitions were directed by Wu Liangyong and compiled by Wu Menglin, Wang Yi, and Chen Zhihua. The contents were published in *Beijing Lishi Wenhua Mingcheng de Wenwu Baohu [Heritage Preservation in the Historic City of Beijing]* (Beijing: Yanshan, 1990).
4 See Sir John Leslie Martin and Lionel March, *Urban Space and Structures* (Cambridge, UK: Cambridge University Press, 1972), Ch. 5.
5 Lin Hok Leung, "A Modern Chinese Cityscape," *China City Planning Review* 3 (December 1987): 52.
6 N.J. Habraken, *Transformations of the Site*, 3rd rev. ed. (Cambridge, MA: Awater, 1988), Sec. 3.3, "Signs of Structure."

Chapter 7: Post-Occupancy Evaluation and Lessons from the Planning and Design Experience

1 *Yangshi Lei* ("Pattern-master Lei") was the title given to the court-appointed master of imperial architectural projects in the Qing dynasty. By the end of the dynasty, the master had become one of a number of generations of the Lei family, who passed down from father to son a mastery of the principles of classical Chinese architecture and the ability to classify all buildings according to a few standard types and their variations.
2 Nan Fang, "A Knowledge-Based Computational Approach to Architectural Precedent Analysis" (Delft, the Netherlands: PhD diss., Technical University of Delft, 1993). A design knowledge-system has been developed that makes use of the Ju'er Hutong project in order to conduct an "architectural precedent analysis" with the aid of the computer. Although this

method is still under development, it does show that a foundation has been laid for the further computer-aided design of new courtyard house types based on the Ju'er Hutong project.

Chapter 8: The Continuing Debate over Redevelopment
1 Peter Hall, *Urban and Regional Planning*, 3rd ed. (London and New York: Routledge, 1992).
2 Daniel Abramson, "New Housing in Old Beijing: A Comparative Survey of Projects Completed to Date," *China City Planning Review* 10 (September 1994): 42-56.

Chapter 9: Future Prospects
1 Wu Liangyong, "Planning Structure, Urban Renewal and Urban Design in Historic Cities," in Wu Liangyong, *Chengshi Guihua Sheji Lunwenji [Selected Papers on Urban Planning and Design]* (Beijing: Yanshan, 1988). Paper originally published in 1983.
2 *Careful Urban Renewal in Krenzberg Berlin: Step by Step*, Proceedings of the Conference held to review the progress of the European Campaign for Urban Renaissance, 1982.
3 Wu Liangyong, *A General Theory of Architecture* (Beijing: Tsinghua University Press, 1989).
4 Ibid.
5 Rao "Ziran" (Song Dynasty), "Twelve Common Mistakes in Painting," *Fine Arts Critiques* (Beijing: People's Fine Arts Press, 1900).

Chapter 10: Conclusion
1 According to the Beijing Municipal Property Management Office, buildings in Beijing are structurally classified into five grades. Grades 1 and 2 are structurally sound; Grade 3 is structurally safe but requires major repair; while Grades 4 and 5 are structurally unsafe (see Chapter 2, note 24).
2 Yu Minzhong, Qing Dynasty, *Ri Xia Jiu Wen Kao* (Beijing: Beijing Ancient Books, 1981), vol. 51, 72.
3 Zhang Yan, Fang Ke, "Tanqiu 'Xiao er Duoyanghua' de Shangye Fazhan Moshi: Beijing Guozijian Diqu Shangye Guihua de Xianzhuang Diaocha yu Fenxi [Searching for Small-Scale and Diversified Commercial Development: Survey and Analysis for the Planning of Retail in the Guozijian District of Beijing]," *Chengshi Guihua [Urban Planning]* 4 (1998): 47-50.
4 Geng Hongbing, "'Jiucheng Gengxin' Xueshu Yantaohui Zongshu [A Summary of 'the Conference on Inner City Redevelopment']," *Chengshi Guihua [Urban Planning]* 1 (1996): 10-2; see also "Dui Suzhou Jiucheng Gaizao de Ruogan Renshi [Some Understandings Regarding the Renewal of Suzhou's Old City]," *Chengshi Guihua [Urban Planning]* 3 (1996): 13-5; Zhang Jie, Fang Yiping, "Jinan Furong Jie Qushui Jie Diqu Baohu Zhengzhi Guihua Yanjiu [A Conservation Study of the Furong Street-Qushui Street District in Jinan]," *Chengshi Guihua Huikan [Urban Planning Forum]* 3 (1996): 45-8.
5 At the end of 1994, the Hengji commercial development project was sold at US$ 6,700/square metre at the Second Real Estate Trade Fair in Beijing, which brought real estate to its highest recorded value. See *Beijing Fangdichan [Beijing Real Estate]* 1 (1995): 21-2.
6 Zhong Jianwei, Wei Ke, "Dongcheng Qu Tudi Kaifa Zhuangkuan, Wenti ji Duice [Land Development in the East City District: Its Situation, Problems and Counter Policies]," *Beijing Guihua Jianshe [Beijing City Planning and Construction]* 5 (1995): 53-5.
7 Fang Ke, "Beijing Weijiufang Gaizao Zenmole? [What's Wrong with Beijing's Old and Dilapidated Housing Renewal?]," *Beijing Fangdichan [Beijing Real Estate]* 3 (1998): 39-40.
8 "Ershi nian bu luohou."
9 See the special section on urban transport in *China City Planning Review* 12, no. 1 (June 1996): 6-42.
10 Jin Jingyuan, "Bai-Yi Lu Kaishi Duche [Bai-Yi Road Iss Becoming Congested]," *Chengshi Guihua [Urban Planning]* 4 (1998): 61. The so-called Bai-Yi Road is the old imperial highway running from the Baishiqiao (White Stone Bridge) just outside the northwest corner of the Old City out to the Yi He Yuan (Summer Palace). Until it was widened, this road was famously shaded by rows of poplar trees and was featured in Allan Jacobs's *Great Streets* (Cambridge, MA: MIT Press, ca. 1993).

11 Cheng Rong, "Zhongguo Xiandai Chengshi Kaifa de Yunxing yu Tiaokong Lilun Yanjiu [Theoretical Research on the Momentum and Control of Urban Development in Contemporary Chinese Cities]" (Nanjing: PhD diss., Dongnan University, 1996), 66-7.
12 Fang Ke, "Cong Ping'An Dajie Gaizao kan Beijing Chengshi Guihua Jianshe Zhong de jige Tuchu Wenti [Some Prominent Problems of Beijing's Urban Planning and Construction as Seen in the Redevelopment of Ping'An Street]," *Chengshi Wenti [Urban Issues]* 5 (1998): 25-9.
13 Wang Jun, "Chengshi Jianshe Ruhe Zoushang Fazhi Guidao: Beijing Dongfang Guangchang Gongcheng Yinfa de Sikao [How Urban Construction Can Get on the Legal Track: Thoughts on the Oriental Plaza Development Project]," *Liaowang [Overview]* 3 (1996): 7-9.
14 See Beijing Municipality, file 44: transfer of the dilapidated housing renewal project power-of-approval to the district governments, thereby allowing district governments the power to review and approve such projects in their districts. See Fang Ke, "Shiyi Gaijian: Tansuo Beijing Jiucheng Juzhuqu Youji Gengxin de Yi Zhong Shiyi Tujing [Appropriate Rebuilding: Searching for a Method of Organic Renewal of the Old City of Beijing]" (Beijing: MA thesis, Tsinghua University, 1997), 17-25.
15 Wang Gongwei, "Kaifa Jianshe Zhong de Beijing Jinrong Jie [Beijing's Financial Street Under Construction]," *Beijing Guihua Jianshe [Beijing's Planning and Construction]* 5 (1995): 32-4.
16 Fang Ke, "Cong Chengshi Guihua Jiaodu Kan 'Jinrong Jie' Xianxiang: Jianlun Beijing Chengshi Guihua yu Jianshe Mianlin de jige Tuchu Wenti [Reviewing the 'Financial Street' Phenomenon from the Perspective of Urban Planning: Some Critical Problems in the Urban Planning and Construction of Beijing]," *Jianzhushi [Architect]* 83 (1998): 19-22.
17 Among the most respected of these critics are Zhou Ganzhi, Zou Deci, and Dong Guangqi.
18 Xinhua News Agency, *Cankao Xiaoxi [Reference News]*, 24 February 1998, 4.
19 Jonathan Barnett, *Urban Design as Public Policy* (New York: Harper and Row, 1978).
20 Wu Liangyong, "Dui Beijing Guihua Jianshe de Zhengti Sikao [General Thoughts on the Planning and Construction of Beijing]," *Beijing Guihua Jianshe [Beijing Planning and Construction]* 3 (1996): 1-3.
21 Wu Liangyong, "Beijing Shi de Jiucheng Gaizao ji Youguan Wenti [Beijing's Urban Renewal and Related Questions]," in *Chengshi Guihua Sheji Lunwenji [Collected Papers on Urban Planning and Design]* (Beijing: Yanshan, 1988).
22 Wu Liangyong, "Beijing Shi Guihua Chuyi [A Modest Proposal for the Planning of Beijing]," speech given at the planning forum held by the Beijing Academy of Science, April 1979, *Chengshi Guihua Sheji Lunwenji [Collected Papers on Urban Planning and Design]* (Beijing: Yanshan, 1988). See also Wu Liangyong, "Guanyu Yuanjiaoqu Fazhan Weixingcheng Wenti [The Questions on Developing Satellite Cities in the Far Suburbs]," in *Chengshi Guihua Sheji Lunwenji [Collected Papers on Urban Planning and Design]* (Beijing: Yanshan, 1988).
23 Wu Liangyong, "Guanyu Beijing Shi Jiucheng Qu Kongzhixing Xiangxi Guihua de Jidian Yijian [Some Opinions on the Detailed Development Control Plan for the Old City District of Beijing]," *Chengshi Guihua [Urban Planning]* 2 (1998): 6-9.
24 "Careful" urban renewal and "step-by-step" urban renewal have already been accepted as effective principles by Western European countries. See European Parliament, *Files on the Urban Renewal Movement in Europe*, 1981; *Careful Urban Renewal in Krenzberg Berlin: Step by Step*, Proceedings of the Conference held to review the progress of the European Campaign for Urban Renaissance, 1982.

Glossary of Chinese Terms

bei	"North," as in *Bei Luogu Xiang* [North Gong-and-Drum Lane], *Beijing* [Northern Capital], or *Beihai* [North Lake]
beinong	circulation system or fire lane
Bishu Shanzhuang	Mountain Resort to Flee the Summer Heat, the Summer Palace of the Qing dynasty in Chengde
cheng	"city walls," or simply "city"
cheshang luming zao	an exposed interior wood pitch roof structure without ceiling, applied in traditional Chinese architecture in South China
dajie	"Big street," or Avenue
da za yuan	"Big cluttered court," the slang term for overcrowded traditional courtyard houses
dong	east
dougong	the brackets that join beams to posts in traditional Chinese architecture
fangli	the basic unit of the residential quarters in the city
fu	noble mansion
gong	palace
gulou	drum tower
hai	"sea," often poetically used for "lake"
hukou	household registration, the required legal document allowing a person to reside at a particular address
hutong	lane or alleyway in Beijing, supposedly from an old Mongolian word for "well"
jiadao	a long corridor in mansions, facilitating circulation
jiaguwen	the ancient Chinese language carved on animal bones
jie	street
jing	meaning "of well," forms part of the word "*jingtian*"
Jingji Shanzhuang	Mountain Resort of Tranquil Living
jingtian	"well and field," a gridiron land division system formed by roads and dikes in ancient China
jiucheng gaizao	"old city renewal." In this text, *gaizao* is translated as "renewal" when it refers to a general program to improve old areas of the city; *gaizao* is translated as "redevelopment" when it refers to the actual replacement of old buildings and streets with new ones
juanmen	entrance arches
Ju'er Hutong	Chrysanthemum Lane
Kaogongji (*Zhou Li*)	The Artificers Record (from the Rites of the Zhou dynasty)
li	a group of courtyard houses aligned in some regular form
lüli	residential quarter in the city

Luogu Xiang	Gong-and-Drum Lane
men	Gate, as in *Tiananmen* [The Gate of Heavenly Peace]
menlou	gate house
mu	system of measurement (1 *mu* = 0.067 hectares)
nan	"South," as in *Nan Luogu Xiang* [South Gong-and-Drum Lane] or *Nanjing* [Southern Capital]
pailou	free-standing high-bracketed post-and-beam structure straddling a way
pingjiangfutu	the historic plan of Suzhou in the Song dynasty
shan	mountain or hill
shanmen	the front gate of a temple
si	temple
siheyuan	the basic courtyard house of quadrangular shape
wai	"Outside," as in *Chongwenmen Wai* [Outside the Gate of Praising-the-Arts]
Wangcheng	The "Royal City," the legendary prototype of Chinese imperial capitals
weijiufang gaizao	"Old and Dilapidated Housing Renewal," the program to improve old neighbourhoods; see also *jiucheng gaizao*
xi	west
xiang	a more classical word for "lane"
xiao qu	"small district," translated from the Russian Soviet planning term *mikro rayon*, and referring to a residential district of about 10,000 people
Yangshi Lei	Pattern-master Lei appointed by the Qing emperors. The Lei family members were in charge of all the imperial architectural projects and knew the principles of classical Chinese architecture
yingbi	screen walls
Yingzao fashi	the Song dynasty manual of architectural building standards and methods
yongxiang	a long corridor in palaces, it facilitates circulation
yuan	Chinese currency
yuanmen	side gates of government offices
zhaobi	in traditional Chinese architecture, a decorated wall facing the main entrance
zhonglou	bell tower

Bibliography

Abramson, Daniel. 1994. "New Housing in Old Beijing: A Comparative Survey of Projects Completed to Date." *China City Planning Review* 10, no. 3 (September): 42-56.
Alexander, Christopher. 1965a. "The City Is Not a Tree [First part of two-part article]," *Architecture Forum* 4: 58-62.
–. 1965b. "The City Is Not a Tree [Second part of two-part article]," *Architecture Forum* 5: 58-61.
–. 1979. *A Pattern Language*. New York: Oxford University Press.
–. 1985. *The Production of Housing*. New York: Oxford University Press.
Bacon, Edmund N. 1975. *Design of Cities*. Rev. ed. London: Thames and Hudson.
Banerjee, Tridib, and William C. Baer. 1984. *Beyond the Neighborhood Unit: Residential Environments and Public Policy*. New York: Plenum.
Barnett, Jonathan. 1978. *Urban Design As Public Policy*. New York: Harper and Row.
Beijing Fangdichan [Beijing Real Estate]. 1995. 1: 21-2.
Beijing Municipal Institute of Urban Planning and Design. June 1990. *Beijing Lishi Chengshi de Baohu he Xiandaihua Fazhan [Beijing: Preservation and Modernization of the Historic City]*. [Promotional Brochure].
–. 1991. Unpublished statistics.
Beijing Statistics Bureau. 1993. *Beijing Yearbook 1992*. Beijing: Beijing Statistics Press.
Benevolo, Leonardo. 1980. *The History of the City*. Trans. Geoffrey Culverwell. Cambridge, MA: MIT Press.
Bor, Walter. 1992. "Recommendations for the Plan of Beijing," in *City Planning*. Beijing. September.
Boyd, Andrew. 1962. *Chinese Architecture and Town Planning: 1500 B.C.-A.D. 1911*. New York: Transatlantic Arts.
Cankao Xiaoxi [Reference News], 24 February 1998, 4.
Careful Urban Renewal in Krenzberg Berlin: Step by Step. 1982. Proceedings of the Conference held to review the progress of the European Campaign for Urban Renaissance.
Castex, Jean. 1977. *Formes urbaines: de l'isle a la barre*. Paris: Dunod.
Cheng Jingqi. 1981. "Traditional Street Conservation in Beijing." *Architectural History Studies* 2: 73.
Cheng Rong. 1996. "Zhongguo Xiandai Chengshi Kaifa de Yunxing yu Tiaokong Lilun Yanjiu [Theoretical Research on the Momentum and Control of Urban Development in Contemporary Chinese Cities]." PhD diss., Dongnan University.
China City Planning Review. 1996. Special section on urban transport. 12, no. 1 (June): 6-42.
Churchill, Henry S. 1945. *The City Is the People*. New York: Peynal and Hitchcock.
Demographic Yearbook. 1991. New York: Department of Economic and Social Affairs, Statistical Office, United Nations.
Dong Guangqi. 1989. "Zongjie Lishi Jingyan, Jiakuai Jiucheng Pojiuweifang Gaizao Bufa [Learn from Past Experience and Accelerate the Renewal of Derelict Housing]." *Beijing Guihua Jianshe [Beijing Planning and Construction]* 4: 11-3.

–. 1993. "Beijing Jiucheng Baohu yu Gaizao de Huigu yu Zhanwang [A Look Back and a Look Forward at Urban Conservation and Redevelopment in Beijing]." *Beijing Guihua Jianshe [Beijing Planning and Construction]* 5:14-6.
Duany, Andres, and Elizabeth Plater-Zyberk. 1991. *Towns and Town-making Principles*. Cambridge, MA/New York: Harvard University Graduate School of Design/Rizzoli.
Fan Wenlan. 1964. *Zhongguo Tongshi Jianbian [A Brief History of China]*. Vol. 1. Rev. ed. Beijing: People's Press.
Fang Ke. 1997. "Shiyi Gaijian: Tansuo Beijing Jiucheng Juzhuqu Youji Gengxin de Yi Zhong Shiyi Tujing [Appropriate Rebuilding: Searching for a Method of Organic Renewal of the Old City of Beijing]." MA thesis, Tsinghua University, Beijing.
–. 1998. "Beijing Weijiufang Gaizao Zenmole? [What's Wrong with Beijing's Old and Dilapidated Housing Renewal?]." *Beijing Fangdichan [Beijing Real Estate]* 3: 39-40.
–. 1998. "Cong Chengshi Guihua Jiaodu Kan 'Jinrong Jie' Xianxiang: Jianlun Beijing Chengshi Guihua yu Jianshe Mianlin de jige Tuchu Wenti [Reviewing the 'Financial Street' Phenomenon from the Perspective of Urban Planning: Some Critical Problems in the Urban Planning and Construction of Beijing]." *Jianzhushi [Architect]* 83: 19-22.
–. 1998. "Cong Ping'An Dajie Gaizao kan Beijing Chengshi Guihua Jianshe Zhong de jige Tuchu Wenti [Some Prominent Problems of Beijing's Urban Planning and Construction as Seen in the Redevelopment of Ping'An Street]." *Chengshi Wenti [Urban Issues]* 5: 25-9.
Fang Nan. 1993. "A Knowledge-Based Computational Approach to Architectural Precedent Analysis." PhD diss., Technical University of Delft, the Netherlands.
Fieldon, Bernard M. 1982. *Conservation of Historic Buildings*. London: Butterworth.
Frampton, Kenneth. 1992. *Modern Architecture: A Critical History*. 3rd ed. New York: Oxford University Press.
Fu Xinian. 1981. "A Study on the Architecture at the Qishan Fengchu Archaeological Site, Shan'xi Province." *Wenwu [Cultural Relics]* 1, 2, and 3.
–. 1998. *Essays on Architectural History*. Beijing: China Antique Press.
Geng Hongbing. 1996. "'Jiucheng Gengxin' Xueshu Yantaohui Zongshu [A Summary of 'the Conference on Inner City Redevelopment']." *Chengshi Guihua [Urban Planning]* 1: 10-2.
Greater London Council. 1978. *A GLC Study: An Introduction to Housing Layout*. London: Architectural Press.
Gurstein, Penny. Principal Investigator. March 1995. *Planning for Telework and Home-based Employment: A Canadian Survey on Integrating Work into Residential Environments*. University of British Columbia Centre for Human Settlements, Vancouver, British Columbia. Prepared for the Canada Mortgage and Housing Corporation Centre for Future Studies in Housing and Living Environments.
Habraken, N.J. 1988. *Transformations of the Site*. 3rd rev. ed. Cambridge, MA: Awater.
Hall, Peter. 1992. *Urban and Regional Planning*. 3rd ed. London and New York: Routledge.
He Yejü. 1985. Kaogongji *Yingguo Zhidu Yanjiu [Research on the System of Building in the* Kaogongji*]*. Beijing: Jianzhu Gongcheng Chubanshe [Architectural and Engineering Publishing House].
Hou Renzhi. 1979. *Lishi Dilixue de Lilun yu Shijian [The Theory and Practice of Historical Geography]*. Shanghai Renmin Chubanshe [Shanghai People's Press].
–. 1986. "The Transformation of the Old City of Beijing, China: A Concrete Manifestation of New China's Cultural Reconstruction." In *World Patterns of Modern Urban Change*. Ed. Michael P. Lanzen. Chicago: University of Chicago, Geography Department Research Papers.
–. 1988. *Beijing Lishi Dituji [An Historical Atlas of Beijing]*. Beijing: Beijing Chubanshe [Beijing Press].
Jacobs, Allan. 1993. *Great Streets*. Cambridge, MA: MIT Press.
Jacobs, Jane. 1961. *The Death and Life of Great American Cities*. New York: Random.
Jin Jingyuan. 1998. "Bai-Yi Lu Kaishi Duche [Bai-Yi Road Is Becoming Congested]." *Chengshi Guihua [Urban Planning]* 4: 61.
Jones, Barclay G. 1987. "Chinese among the Largest World Agglomerations: An Historical Analysis." Paper presented at the Conference on Planning for Human Settlements: China and the United States. Tongji University, Shanghai, 29 June to 1 July 1987.

Krier, Leon. 1978. *Rational Architecture*. Bruxelles: Archives d'Architecture Moderne.
Krier, Rob. 1979. *Urban Space*. London: Academy Editions.
Lao She. 1982. "Thinking of Beiping." In *Xiangfeng Shisheng*. Ed. Qian Liqun. Beijing: People's Literature.
Leung, Lin Hok. 1987. "A Modern Chinese Cityscape." *China City Planning Review* 3 (December): 52.
Liang Sicheng. 1984. *A Pictorial History of Chinese Architecture: A Study of the Development of Its Structural System and the Evolution of Its Types*. Ed. Wilma Fairbank. Cambridge, MA: MIT Press.
—. 1986. *Liang Sicheng Wenji [The Collected Papers of Liang Sicheng]*, vol. 4. Beijing: Zhongguo Jianzhu Gongye Chubanshe [China Construction Industry Publishing House].
Liu Dunzhen. 1957. *Zhongguo Zhuzhai Gaishuo [General Description of Chinese Houses]*. Beijing: Jianzhu Gongcheng Chubanshe [Architectural and Engineering Publishing House].
Liu Xiaoshi. 1989a. "Comments on the Protection of Cultural Relics and Issues of Modernization." Paper presented at the International Symposium on Historic Cities and Modernization, Beijing.
—. 1989b. "Dui Beijing Lishi Wenwu Baohu he Xiandaihua Wenti de yixie Yijian [Comments on the Protection of Cultural Relics and Issues of Modernization]." Paper presented at Lishi Mingcheng yu Xiandaihua Jianshe Guoji Xueshu Taolunhui [International Symposium on Historic Cities and Modernization], Beijing, May.
Liu Yan. 1987. "Beijing Jiucheng de Zhengti Baohu [On Integrated Conservation in the Old City of Beijing]." MA thesis, Tsinghua University, Beijing.
Liu Zhiping. October 1990. *A Brief History of Chinese Residential Architecture: Cities, Houses, Gardens*. Beijing: Zhongguo Jianzhu Gongye Chubanshe [China Construction Industry Publishing House].
Lü Junhua. 1991. "Towards New Urban Housing Design." *Habitat International* 3: 125-31.
Lu Xiang, and Qiming Wang. 1996. *Beijing Siheyuan*. Beijing: Zhongguo Jianzhu Gongye Chubanshe [China Construction Industry Publishing House].
Lu Xiaoxiang. 1991. "Beijing Jiucheng Gaijian ji Weijiufang Gaizao [The Rebuilding of the Old City and the Redevelopment of Old and Dilapidated Housing in Beijing]." *"Jiuchengqu yu Weijiufang Gaizao" Yanxiuban Jiangyi [Proceedings of the Inner City Housing Redevelopment Workshop]*. Beijing, Information Centre of the Ministry of Construction, 5 October.
Martin, Sir John Leslie, and Lionel March. 1972. *Urban Space and Structures*. Cambridge: Cambridge University Press.
Morris, A.E.J. 1979. *History of Urban Form: Before the Industrial Revolutions*. 2nd ed. Harlow, Essex, England: Longman Scientific & Technical.
Mumford, Lewis. 1961. *The City in History: Its Origins, Its Transformations and Its Prospects*. New York: Harcourt, Brace.
—. 1965. "New Regional Plan to Arrest Megalopolis."*Architectural Record*. March: 147-54.
Ramphal, Shridath. 1993. *Our Country, the Planet: Foregoing a Partnership for Survival*. London: Lime Tree.
Rao Ziran (Song Dynasty). 1900. "Twelve Common Mistakes in Painting." In *Fine Arts Critiques*. Beijing: People's Fine Arts Press.
Rasmussen, Steen Eiler. 1983. *Towns and Buildings*. Cambridge: MIT Press.
Rees, William. 1989. *Planning for Sustainable Development: A Resource Book*. Vancouver: University of British Columbia Centre for Human Settlements.
Shehuixue Gailun Editing Group. 1984. *Shehuixue Gailun [An Introduction to Sociology]*. Tianjin: Tianjing Renmin Chubanshe [Tianjin People's Publishing House].
Sima Qian (ca. 145 BC-ca. 86 BC). *Shiji [Records of the Historian]*. Beijing: Shangwu.
Siren, Osvald. 1924. *Walls and Gates of Peking*. London: John Lane the Bodley Head.
Sit, Victor F.S. 1995. *Beijing: The Nature and Planning of a Chinese Capital City*. Chichester: John Wiley and Sons.
Steinhardt, Nancy S. 1990. *Chinese Imperial City Planning*. Honolulu: University of Hawaii Press.
Sun Guoting. 1989. "Shupu [On Calligraphy]." In *A Dictionary of the Best Chinese Calligraphy*. Beijing: Great Earth.

Trincanato, E.R. 1980. *Houses of Venice.* Venice: Canal.
Tripp, H.A. 1942. *Town Planning and Road Traffic.* London: Edward Arnold.
Tsinghua University. 1983. *Studies Into Derelict Housing.*
Tsinghua University Urban Planning Group. 1980. "Dui Beijingshi Guihua de Jidian Shexiang [Some Visions for the Urban Planning of Beijing]." *Jianzhu Xuebao [Architectural Journal]* 5.
–. 1996. *Beijing Chengshi Guihua Yanjiu Lunwenji [Collected Research Papers on the Urban Planning of Beijing] 1946-1996.* Beijing: Zhongguo Jianzhu Gongye Chubanshe [China Construction Industry Publishing House].
United Nations. 1987. *Prospects of World Urbanization.*
Wang Gongwei. 1995. "Kaifa Jianshe Zhong de Beijing Jinrong Jie [Beijing's Financial Street Under Construction]." *Beijing Guihua Jianshe [Beijing's Planning and Construction]* 5: 32-4.
Wang Guowei. 1959. *Guantanjilin.* Vol. 3. Beijing: Zhonghua.
Wang Jun. 1996. "Chengshi Jianshe Ruhe Zoushang Fazhi Guidao: Beijing Dongfang Guangchang Gongcheng Yinfa de Sikao [How Urban Construction Can Get on the Legal Track: Thoughts on the Oriental Plaza Development Project]." *Liaowang [Overview]* 3: 7-9.
Wang Ruisheng. 1991. "Chengshi Jiujuzhuqu de Gaizao ji Duice [Inner City Neighborhood Redevelopment Policies]." *Jiuchengqu yu Weijiufang Gaizao Yanxiuban Jiangyi [Proceedings of the Inner City Housing Redevelopment Workshop].* The Information Centre of the Ministry of Construction, Beijing, 5 October.
Wheatley, Paul. 1971. *The Pivot of the Four Quarters: A Preliminary Enquiry into the Origins and Character of the Ancient Chinese City.* Chicago: Aldine.
Wright, Arthur F. 1958. "The Cosmology of the Chinese City." In *The City in Late Imperial China.* Ed. G.W. Skinner. Stanford: Stanford University Press.
Wu Liangyong. 1982. "Beijingshi de Jiucheng Gaizao ji Youguan Wenti [Renewal in the City of Beijing and Related Issues]," *Jianzhu Xuebao [Architectural Journal]* 2: 8-11.
–. 1986. *A Brief History of Ancient Chinese City Planning: In Urbs et Regio.* Kassel: Gesamthochschublibothek.
–. 1987. "Urban Development and Cultural Continuity." Paper presented at the International Symposium on Cultural Tradition and Modernization, Hong Kong.
–. 1988. *Chengshi Guihua Sheji Lunwenji [Collected Papers on Urban Planning and Design].* Beijing: Yanshan.
–. 1989. *Guangyi Jianzhuxue [A General Theory of Architecture].* Beijing: Tsinghua University Press.
–. 1991. "Cognition in Urban Aesthetics" In *Aesthetics of the Urban Environment,* 1-4. Beijing: China Social Press.
–. 1992. "Beijing Lishi Wenhua Mingcheng de Baohu yu Jianzhu Chuangzao [Architectural Design and the Protection of the Historic City of Beijing]." *Beijing Guihua Jianshe [Beijing Planning and Construction]* 3: 4-8.
–. 1996. "Dui Beijing Guihua Jianshe de Zhengti Sikao [General Thoughts on the Planning and Construction of Beijing]." *Beijing Guihua Jianshe [Beijing Planning and Construction]* 3: 1-3.
–. 1998. "Guanyu Beijing Shi Jiucheng Qu Kongzhixing Xiangxi Guihua de Jidian Yijian [Some Opinions on the Detailed Development Control Plan for the Old City District of Beijing]." *Chengshi Guihua [Urban Planning]* 2: 6-9.
Wu Liangyong, Menglin Wu, Yi Wang, and Chen Zhihua. 1990. *Beijing Lishi Wenhua Mingcheng de Wenwu Baohu [Heritage Preservation in the Historic City of Beijing].* Beijing: Yanshan.
Yu Minzhong (Qing Dynasty). 1981. *Ri Xia Jiu Wen Kao.* Vol. 51. Beijing: Beijing Ancient Books.
Zhang Jie, and Yiping Fang. 1996. "Jinan Furong Jie Qushui Jie Diqu Baohu Zhengzhi Guihua Yanjiu [A Conservation Study of the Furong Street - Qushui Street District in Jinan]." *Chengshi Guihua Huikan [Urban Planning Forum]* 3: 45-8.
Zhang Qingchang. 1990. *Hutong ji Qita: Shehuiyuyanxue de Tansuo [Hutong and More: An Exploration Into Social Linguistics].* Beijing: Beijing Yuyan Xueyuan Chubanshe [Beijing Institute of Languages Press].

Zhang Shouyi and Li Deyao. 1996. "Beijingshi Wei, Ji, Lou Diqu Zhufang Jianshe Wenti [The Problems of Hazardous, Crowded, and Leaky Housing Areas in Beijing]." *Beijing Chengshi Guihua Yanjiu Lunwenji [Collected Research Papers on the Urban Planning of Beijing 1946-1996]*. Beijing: Zhongguo Jianzhu Gongye Chubanshe [China Construction Industry Publishing House].

Zhang Yan, and Ke Fang. 1998. "Tanqiu Xiao er Duoyanghua de Shangye Fazhan Moshi: Beijing Guozijian Diqu Shangye Guihua de Xianzhuang Diaocha yu Fenxi [Searching for Small-Scale and Diversified Commercial Development: Survey and Analysis for the Planning of Retail in the Guozijian District of Beijing]." *Chengshi Guihua [Urban Planning]* 4: 47-50.

Zhao Lisheng. 1980. "Youguan Jingtianzhi de yixie Bianxi [Some Analytical Distinctions Concerning the *Jingtian* System]." *Lishi Yanjiu [Historical Studies]* 4.

Zheng Banqiao. 1979. "Bamboos and Rockery." In *Zheng Banqiao Ji*, 168-9. Shanghai: Shanghai Ancient Books.

Zheng Xiaoxie. 1983. "The Protection of the Characteristics of Historic Chinese Cities." *Jianzhu Xuebao [Architectural Journal]* 12: 4-7.

Zhong Jianwei, and Ke Wei. 1995. "Dongcheng Qu Tudi Kaifa Zhuangkuan: Wenti ji Duice [Land Development in the East City District: Its Situation, Problems and Counter Policies]." *Beijing Guihua Jianshe [Beijing Planning and Construction]* 5: 53-5.

Zhu Jiaguang and Fu Zhijing. 1988. "De-Nei Dajie 265 hao Gengxin Guihua Sheji Gousi [Planning and Design Concept for the Renewal of Number 265, Deshengmen Nei Dajie]." *Beijing Guihua Jianshe [Beijing Planning and Construction]* 3: 18-21.

Zhu Zhixin, Hu Shi, et al. 1965. "Jingtian Zhidu You wu Zhi Yanjiu [A Study on the *Jingtian* System]." Taibei: Zhongguo Wenxian Chubanshe [China Literature Press] 4-13.

Index

Architects, role in Ju'er Hutong project, 192-3
Architectural awards, Ju'er Hutong project, xviii, 222
Architecture: in Beijing, 13-4; of houses in China, 86; modern, 87-92; and natural landscape, 14-5, 29; new courtyard house prototype, 82-103; in Old City, 38-9; of traditional courtyard houses, 137, 139
Asian Urban Research Network (AURN), xiii

Baita Si area, 199-201
Beijing, xvii, xxi; commercial real estate development, 202-4; economic and social changes, 64; future urban development, 188-95, 205-12; historical planning and development, 3-15; planning and development since 1949, 16-43; regional integration, 24-8, 208-9; rehabilitation of historic cities, 56-65; residential development, 44-55, 92; urban population growth, 44-6
Beijing-Tianjin-Hebei region, 207-8
Building height control, 34-6

Canadian International Development Agency (CIDA), xiii
Central Axis, 10-12, 35
Central business districts (CBD), xii, 206, 225n.2
Chen, Zhanxiang, 17-21, 28
Chinese dynasties, 213-4
Chinese terms, glossary, 230-1
City walls and gates, 18, 30, 32, 69-73
Colour design and control, 13-14, 37-8

Commercial real estate development, 202-4
Commodity housing, 53-4
Courtyard house conservation areas, 58-9. *See also* Nan Luogu Xiang
Courtyard houses, 78-82; access and circulation routes, 74-7, 111; emergence of new prototype, x, 82-103; and Ju'er Hutong project, 104-62, 163-81; urban development and rehabilitation, xvii, xix-xx, 37, 47, 57-9, 61-3

Decentralized poly-nuclear development, 28-9
Demolition, large-scale, 59-61
Derelict and hazardous housing, 22-3, 44, 47-55, 203

East City Development Company, 192

Floor-area ratio, 120-4
Forbidden City, 12

Gardens, 12, 14-5, 101-2
Green space, 14-5, 29
Gridiron cities, 66-8
Gropius, Walter, 87-9
Guozijian area, 198-9

Historic buildings and sites: conservation of, xvii, 4-5, 56-7
Holistic design thinking, xxii
Hongdeshanlin, 106, 112
Housing: commodity, 53-4; derelict, 22-3, 44, 47-55, 203; development since 1949, 44-5, 51-4, 92; economics of, 52-4, 184-7, 190-1; perimeter block, 91;

prefabricated, 45-6. *See also* Courtyard houses; Ju'er Hutong project; Neighbourhoods
Housing co-operative, 140, 144, 175, 187, 192-3
Housing density, 45-6, 51, 92-4
Housing estate model, 59
Housing policy, in China, 186-7
Housing reform, in China, 189-90, 192
Housing shortage, xviii
Housing standards, 182-3, 193-4
Housing styles, in China, 86
Hutong, 69, 74, 77, 78

Imperial City, 12
Imperial Gardens, 12
Infrastructure and services: in Beijing, 47-9, 50, 54-5, 191, 204-5; in Ju'er Hutong, 117, 118-9, 176, 185
Inner City, 12
Integrated conservation, 32-3

Jacobs, Jane, 64
Jingtian system, 66-9, 230
Ju'er Hutong project, xix-xxii; architectural awards, xviii, 222; building density, 116, 121-4; community facilities, 115, 118, 130, 132; construction, 175; courtyard house system, 119-49, 129-31, 140-51, 163-81; courtyards, 130, 133, 134; development process, 140-51; factory, 144, 150; fire regulations, 174; flooding, 117; floor-area ratio, 120-4; housing cooperative, 140, 144, 175, 187, 192-3; infrastructure, 117, 118-9, 176, 185; land use, 115, 116, 118; living conditions, 108, 109, 112-9, 163-73; location, 104-5, 106; management issues, 173; planning and design, ix-x, xiii, 104-62, 192-3, 215-21; population density, 112, 113, 115, 116; property ownership, 116; resettlement, 170-2, 174, 183-4, 190; roofscape, 135, 136, 137; sunlight penetration, 172-3, 185; traffic, 118, 174; waste disposal, 172

Kleihues, Josef P., 91
Krier, Rob, 91

Land, historical division, 66-9
Lane culture, 74, 77, 78
Liang, Sicheng, 6-7, 10, 17-21, 28
Liang-Chen urban plan, 17-21, 28
Longfusi Market, 42

Management model, Ju'er Hutong project, 192-3
Master Plan of 1951 (Beijing), 23-4
Modern architecture, 87-92

Nan Luogu Xiang, xx, 106, 151, 157-62, 196-8
Natural landscape, in architecture of Beijing, 14-5, 29
Neighbourhoods: courtyard-based, 94-103; history of development, 66-74. *See also* names of neighbourhoods

Open spaces, 14-5, 29
Organic renewal, xix, xx, xxii, 56-65, 196, 201-2
Outer City, 12
Overcrowding, in Ju'er Hutong, 112, 113

Palace City, 12
Perimeter block housing, 91
Planning statistics, Ju'er Hutong project, 215-21
Population densities, 44-6, 49, 112, 113
Prefabricated housing, 45-6
Preservation: of courtyard houses, xvii, 58-9; of historic and cultural monuments, xvii, 4-5, 56-7, 225n.2; integrated urban conservation policy, 32; of Old City, 16-43; recommendations, 209-10; of traditional neighbourhoods, xvii, xx, 106, 151, 157-62, 196-8

Regional integration (Beijing), 24-8, 208-9
Rehabilitation of historic cities, 56-65
Resettlement, 170-2, 174, 183-4, 190
Roads. *See* Street systems
Rossi, Aldo, 91

Second Ring Road, 30
Shichahai area, 39, 40, 105-6
Sitte, Camillo, 90
Skyline, 32-5
Social and economic changes, 49, 64
State funding, for redevelopment projects, 54
Street systems, 12-3, 30, 35-7, 49, 99, 101; Bai-Yi Road, 228n.10; regional road network, 24; Zhaohui-Jinggong Fang, 77-8. *See also* Gridiron cities; Traffic planning
Suburbs, 51-4
Sustainable development, 64-5

Tiananmen Square, 5, 17, 18, 19, 23
Traffic planning, 30, 204-5. *See also* Street systems
Tsinghua University: School of Architecture, 24, 105-6; Urban Planning Group, 23-7, 28-9

United Nations World Cultural Heritage Sites, 225n.2
Urban conservation, 38-9, 43
Urban design, modern, 87-92
Urban planning and development (Beijing): historical, 3-15; post-1949, 16-43; real estate development, 202-4; recommendations, 205-12
Urban spaces, hierarchy of, 74

Walls and gates, 18, 30, 32, 69-73
Well and field system, 66-9, 226n.10
Wu, Liangyong, ix

***X**iao qu*, 59, 231

Yanshi Lei approach, 231

Zhaohui-Jinggong Fang, 77-8, 106

Set in Stone by Artegraphica Design Co.
Printed and bound in Canada by Friesens
Copy editor: Joanne Richardson
Proofreader: Rachelle Kanefsky
Indexer: Elizabeth Bell